RELIGIOUS STUDIES

TABLE OF CONTENTS & ACKNOWLEDGEMENTS

	PAGE

Why This Study is Needed, and Why it is Needed Now   1
     Anderson, P.
     John, Jesus, and History, Volume 1: Critical Appraisals of Critical Views, Anderson, P. et al. (eds.)
     © 2007 Scholars Press
     This material has been copied under licence from Access Copyright.
     Resale or further copying of this material is strictly prohibited.

Excerpt from The Fourth Gospel and the Quest for Jesus: Modern Foundations Reconsidered   19
     Anderson, P. N.
     The Fourth Gospel and the Quest for Jesus: Modern Foundations Reconsidered, Anderson, P. N.
     © 2006 T&T Clark
     This material has been copied under licence from Access Copyright.
     Resale or further copying of this material is strictly prohibited.

Excerpt from The Testimony of the Beloved Disciple: Narrative, History, and Theology in the Gospel of John   29
     Bauckham, R.
     The Testimony of the Beloved Disciple: Narrative, History, and Theology in the Gospel of John, Bauckham, R.
     © 2007 BakerBooks
     This material has been copied under licence from Access Copyright.
     Resale or further copying of this material is strictly prohibited.

Excerpt from Aposynagogos and the Historical Jesus in John: Rethinking the Historicity of the Johannine Expulsion   51
     Bernier, J.
     Aposynagogos and the Historical Jesus in John: Rethinking the Historicity of the Johannine Expulsion, Bernier, J.
     © 2013 Leiden University
     This material has been copied under licence from Access Copyright.
     Resale or further copying of this material is strictly prohibited.

The Gospel of John and the Signs Gospel 65
    Fortna, R. T.
    <u>What We Have Heard From the Beginning: The Past, Present, and the Future of Johnannine Studies</u>, Thatcher, T. (ed.)
    © 2007 Baylor University
    This material has been copied under licence from Access Copyright.
    Resale or further copying of this material is strictly prohibited.

The Prologue of the Gospel of John as the Gateway to Christological Truth 71
    Hengel, M.
    <u>The Gospel of John and Christian Theology</u>, Bauckham, R. and Mosser, C. (eds.)
    © 2008 William B. Eerdmans Publishing Co.
    This material has been copied under licence from Access Copyright.
    Resale or further copying of this material is strictly prohibited.

We Behold His Glory 87
    Keener, C. S.
    <u>John, Jesus, and History: Aspects of Historicity in the Fourth Gospel</u>, Anderson, P. N. et al. (eds.)
    © 2009 Scholars Press
    This material has been copied under licence from Access Copyright.
    Resale or further copying of this material is strictly prohibited.

Early Christian Community: A Study of the Community Construct and its Functional Potential in Early Christianity 93
    Klink, E. W.
    <u>The Sheep of the Fold: The Audience and Origin of the Gospel of John</u>, Klink, E. W.
    © 2007 ** Cambridge University Press - UK
    This material has been copied under licence from Access Copyright.
    Resale or further copying of this material is strictly prohibited.

Anti-Judaism, the Jews, and the Worlds of the Fourth Gospel 105
    Lieu, J.
    <u>The Gospel of John and Christian Theology</u>, Bauckham, R. and Mosser, C. (eds.)
    © 2008 William B. Eerdmans Publishing Co.
    This material has been copied under licence from Access Copyright.
    Resale or further copying of this material is strictly prohibited.

Excerpts from The Word in the World: The Cosmological Tale in the Fourth Gospel   113
    Reinhartz, A.
    <u>The Word in the World: The Cosmological Tale in the Fourth Gospel</u>, Reinhartz, A.
    © 1992 Scholars Press
    This material has been copied under licence from Access Copyright.
    Resale or further copying of this material is strictly prohibited.

Excerpts from The Jewish Targums and John's Logos Theology   121
    Ronning, J.
    <u>The Jewish Targums and John's Logos Theology</u>, Ronning, J.
    © 2010 BakerBooks
    This material has been copied under licence from Access Copyright.
    Resale or further copying of this material is strictly prohibited.

Excerpts from Jesus, Gnosis, and Dogma   133
    Roukema, R.
    <u>Jesus, Gnosis, and Dogma</u>, Roukema, R.
    © 2010 T&T Clark
    This material has been copied under licence from Access Copyright.
    Resale or further copying of this material is strictly prohibited.

Excerpts from John Among the Gospels   147
    Smith, M. D.
    <u>John Among the Gospels (Second Edition)</u>, Smith, M. D.
    © 2001 U of South Carolina Press
    This material has been copied under licence from Access Copyright.
    Resale or further copying of this material is strictly prohibited.

Declaration on the Church's Relation to Non-Christian Religious (Nostra Aetate)   153
    Arnold, L. (trans.)
    <u>Vatican II: The Essential Texts</u>, Tanner, N. (ed.)
    © 2012 Image Books
    This material has been copied under licence from Access Copyright.
    Resale or further copying of this material is strictly prohibited.

Why This Study Is Needed, and Why It Is Needed Now

Paul N. Anderson

Jesus and Gospel studies possess rich histories of analysis, and within those histories new findings and distinctive trends emerge. Few scholarly developments—in any field—have been as interesting, however, as the modernistic dehistoricization of John and the de-Johannification of Jesus.[1] To a certain degree, each of these trends has bolstered the other, and the assertion of many a scholar claiming the authoritative weight of critical and scientific study is that the one thing we know for sure is actually two: the Fourth Gospel is of *no* historical value, and historical Jesus research must be performed *untainted* by any Johannine influence.[2] The question is the degree to which either of these assertions is true, a solid platform upon which to base the frameworks of further studies. Negative claims are even more difficult to substantiate than positive ones, and surprisingly large numbers of scholars speak in terms of certainty along either or both of these propositions. Simply challenging

---

1. These terms were coined by the John, Jesus, and History steering committee, as they seemed to describe pointedly the so-called "critical consensus" on the two primary issues involved. Happy to grant them privileged status as prevalent modernist views, the question is how well they stand up to critical scrutiny as predominant platforms for conducting further critical investigations. This essay was published as part 2 in Paul Anderson, *The Fourth Gospel and the Quest for Jesus* (2006b) as "On Planks and Platforms—A Critical Assessment of Critical Foundations Regarding John, Jesus and History" (pp. 43–97). Permission to republish it within this volume is appreciated.

2. Can it be put any clearer than the introductory statement of Funk, Hoover, and the Jesus Seminar (1997, 10)? "The first step is to understand the diminished role the Gospel of John plays in the search for the Jesus of history. The two pictures painted by John and the synoptics cannot be both historically accurate.... The differences between the two portraits of Jesus show up in a dramatic way in the evaluation, by the Jesus Seminar, of the words attributed to Jesus in the Gospel of John. The Fellows of the Seminar were unable to find a single saying they could with certainty trace back to the historical Jesus." So much for the words of Jesus; the results of the Jesus Seminar's analysis of the actions of Jesus (Robert Funk and the Jesus Seminar 1998) are equally sparse. *None of Jesus' deeds in John are rooted in history, save the death of Jesus* (433, 435), in their analysis.

a traditional view, however, does not confirm an alternative view, and the planks in these platforms should be tested with the same critical scrutiny and rigor as those they endeavor to supplant. This is *why* this study is needed.

Obviously, John's ahistoricity goes against the traditional view that the Fourth Gospel was written by the apostle John, connected inferentially with the redactor's claim that the Johannine Evangelist was an eyewitness who leaned against Jesus' breast at the Last Supper, was present at the crucifixion, and that "his witness is true" (John 13:23; 19:26, 34–35; 21:7, 20, 24). Over half a century ago Pierson Parker declared, "If there was one 'assured result of biblical criticism' for such scholars of the 20's, 30's and 40's, it was that John, the son of Zebedee, had nothing at all to do with the writing of this gospel" (1962, 35). Another scholar more recently has even declared that the burden of proof is now upon any who would challenge the purported scholarly consensus regarding John's patent ahistoricity.[3] This claim reflects an interest in establishing the sort of "critical orthodoxy" Bishop Robinson alluded to half a century ago.[4] Whereas the question in traditionalist circles used to be whether or not one believed in the historicity of John, the litmus test for the modernist biblical scholar has come to be: Do you believe in the *ahistoricity* of John? Because a scholar's livelihood and career may hinge upon distinguishing oneself as a hard-minded scientific scholar rather than a soft-hearted traditionalist, the stakes are indeed high. Further, no scholar wants to come across as embracing a naively traditionalistic view, yet the present critical question remains: Is the ahistoricity of John an open-and-shut case—on *critical grounds*? If so, fine. Scholars may build on a solid platform, conducting further studies upon an established foundation. However, if the modernist platform fails to stand up to critical analyses, or if parts of it are found to be less solid than others, critical scholarship at the dawn of the postmodern era demands an alternative. This is why this study is needed *now*.

Before continuing with analysis, however, two points deserve to be made before acknowledging a scholarly consensus exists at all on the matter. First, many, perhaps even most, of the leading Johannine scholars over the last two centuries would not have agreed to John's patent ahistoricity; so, if any "consensus" exists, it must be regarded as one that is purported among a group that excludes many of the

---

3. Robert Funk (1996, 127) goes on to say: "In the Gospel of John, Jesus is a self-confessing messiah rather than a self-effacing sage. In John, Jesus seems to have little concern for the impoverished, the disabled, and the religious outcasts. Although John preserves the illusion of combining a real Jesus with the mythic Christ, the human side of Jesus is in fact diminished. For all these reasons, the current quest for the historical Jesus makes little use of the heavily interpreted data found in the Gospel of John."

4. While John A. T. Robinson's essay (1959) called for a "New Look at the Fourth Gospel," his monograph on the "priority of John" (1985) claimed too much by equating early tradition with early finalization. A more plausible approach would connect primitivity of tradition with its development and later finalization.

keenest experts in the field. One need only consider the works of Schleiermacher, Lightfoot, Westcott, Sanday, Robinson, Hoskyns, Dodd, Brown, Schnackenburg, Barrett, Lindars, Carson, Beasley-Murray, Morris, Hengel, and many others to realize that many of the great Johannine scholars of the modern era stood or would have stood against the purported consensus. As Raymond Brown says:

> We are not always to assume facilely that the Synoptic Gospels are recording the historical fact and that Jn has theologically reorganized the data. In the cases we have studied, an interesting case can be made out for the basic historicity of the Johannine picture and for theological reorganization on the part of the Synoptic Gospels. We are coming to realize more and more that the critics have played us false in their minimal estimate of the historicity of the Fourth Gospel.[5] (1965, 271)

A second fact, however, is that even some of the most skeptical of scholars have expressed reservations regarding the degree to which certainty about John's ahistoricity can be assumed. A telling example of such a turnaround may be found in David Strauss's introduction to his third edition of his *Life of Christ*. In response to criticisms regarding his earlier marginalizations of John's historicity, he reversed himself as follows:[6]

> The changes offered by this new edition are all more or less related to the fact that a renewed study of the Fourth Gospel, on the basis of de Wette's commentary and Neander's *Leben Jesu Christi*, has made me again *doubtful of my earlier doubt* concerning the authenticity and credibility of this Gospel. It is not that I have become convinced of its authenticity, merely that I am *no longer certain of its inauthenticity*. From among the peculiarly striking and frustrating features of credibility and incredibility, of proximity to and distance from the truth, which exist in this most remarkable Gospel, I had emphasized in the first composition of my work, with one-sided polemical zeal, only what seemed to me the adverse and unfavorable side. In the meanwhile the other side has gradually come into its own for me.

Ironically, many scholars aligning themselves with the revisionist view outlined by Strauss, F. C. Baur, and others have failed to balance their critical views with reflective nuance. Just as a traditionalist arguing for the eyewitness historicity of

---

5. In another essay on John's historicity (1962), Brown argues that the Johannine rendering of the Last Supper on Thursday seems more plausible historically. Arguably, the Synoptics have stylized it as a Passover meal to conform with emerging Christian worship practices, a judgment bolstered by the criterion of dissimilarity. Brown further develops and refines his belief in John's historicity in his revised and expanded introduction to John (2003, 90–114).

6. Here David Friedrich Strauss (1972, lvii) seeks to hold the negative and positive aspects of critical study together in tension, but he reverts to his earlier skepticism in his fourth edition under the influence of Baur.

everything in John based upon shallow assumptions is flawed, so is an unreflective arguing of a critical view. For some reason, while the Gospel of John possesses the most extensive and explicit claims to represent a firsthand narration of Jesus' works and ministry, it has ceded place to the Gospel of Thomas and other second-century apocryphal narratives in some recent Jesus studies. The question is whether those exchanges are warranted and whether a distorted presentation of Jesus is being constructed by those who claim to know. On the other hand, there are good reasons for scholars to question John's historicity and contribution to understanding Jesus and his ministry, so the bases for these platforms deserve fresh critical consideration. Such is the critical interest of the present investigation.

1. Planks in Platform A: The Dehistoricization of John

John's claims to historicity are problematic. In many ways John's presentation differs significantly from those of Matthew, Mark, and Luke, and the Johannine Jesus is clearly crafted in the image of the Evangelist's own convictions. Further, the Fourth Evangelist's presentation of Jesus is a spiritualized one, which raises questions as to the motives for particular aspects in the construction of the Johannine narrative. As the main planks in the platform of John's dehistoricization are analyzed, including an assessment of their strengths and weaknesses, the bases for this judgment will be better ascertained. Fresh considerations of classic problems also may lead to other ways forward not yet considered, but such can only be envisioned at the end of such an analysis.

1.1. John's Differences with the Synoptics

A great and puzzling fact of biblical studies is that John is *very* different from the Synoptics. Rather than a birth narrative, John's story begins with the advent of the eternal Logos. Rather than ministering for only one year, three Passovers are mentioned in John. Rather than cleansing the temple at the end of Jesus' ministry, John's temple incident is at the beginning, and John mentions two miracles that were the first ones performed in Cana of Galilee. Rather than ministering exclusively in Galilee, the Johannine Jesus goes to and from Jerusalem and performs three Judean miracles. Rather than teaching pervasively about the kingdom of God and doing so in parables and in short, pithy sayings, the Johannine Jesus speaks in long I-Am discourses, engaging the kingdom motif in only two passages. In contrast to the Synoptic Jesus, John's Jesus performs no exorcisms but knows what is in the hearts of humans and escapes capture in knowing ways. Finally, rather than celebrating the Last Supper as a Passover meal where the Eucharist is instituted, the Johannine rendering omits the words of institution and presents the event as happening the day before the Passover meal would have taken place. These are just some of the facts that contribute to preferring the Synoptics' presentation historically over the Johannine.

Strengths. John's ahistoricity seems to be confirmed if one assumes a three-against-one majority, with John being the lone Gospel out. This indeed was the argument of Karl Gottlieb Bretschneider, who in 1820 argued that, because of the threefold witness of the Synoptics, they could not possibly have concocted their view, while the same cannot be claimed for John.[7] Rather, he argued that the historical probability of material in John should be considered low, and a generation later Strauss levied this argument against Friedrich Schleiermacher's preference for John's historicity over and against the Synoptics, designating Bretschneider to be *the true man of science* on the matter.[8] Indeed, Jesus could have cleared the temple more than once, but John's presentation, because it is out of step with the majority, calls for explanations on grounds other than historical ones. Likewise, in the presentation of Jesus' teachings, the Synoptic presentation of Jesus' use of parables seems far more reliable as a guide to Jesus' teaching ministry than the more elevated revelatory discourses in the Johannine I-Am sayings. These are some of the good reasons for questioning John's historicity on the basis of major differences with the Synoptics.

Weaknesses. If Luke and Matthew used Mark, however, viewing John's differences with the Synoptics as a three-against-one minority must be reconsidered. Critically, scholars in the nineteenth and early twentieth centuries who took this view did so *before* Markan priority was established, but later scholars failed to make the appropriate self-correction along the way. If Mark got it wrong here and there, so did Matthew and Luke. If John and Mark are worthy of being considered *the Bi-Optic Gospels*, as several recent studies have argued,[9] this means that the door must be held open in ascribing greater or lesser degrees of historicity to the Johannine and Markan traditions. For instance, John may be more realistic in presenting a Jesus who traveled to and from Jerusalem, like most observant Jews would have done during his time. This being the case, John's three-year ministry also seems more realistic than Mark's one-year presentation, perhaps locating all the Jerusalem and judgment material at the end for the purposes of a narrative climax rather than reflecting chronological knowledge. Indeed, Mark's gathering of Jesus material and ordering it into a progressive narrative must have involved some conjecture, and the killing of Jesus due to a temple disturbance is far more

---

[7]. Karl Gottlieb Bretschneider (1820) questions several features of John as being inauthentic: Jesus' speaking with exalted self-references; his knowing the hearts of others; his claim to represent God; and all his miraculous deeds. By hastily excluding all of John's wondrous reports and themes from his perceived categories of naturalism, Bretschneider expels John from the canons of historicity in the name of modest, scientific inquiry.

[8]. Strauss (1977, 41) fails, however, to appreciate much of the critically significant work conducted by Schleiermacher, such as his extensive observations about the fragmented character of the Synoptic narratives in contrast to the more unitive Johannine narrations.

[9]. See part 3 in Anderson 2006b, especially table 3.3, reproduced below as appendix 1.

likely to have been inferred ("concocted," to use Bretschneider's language) than the unlikely-to-have-been imagined "threat of the risen Lazarus" as portrayed in John.

Was this a factor in the second-century opinion of Papias (quoted in Eusebius, *Hist. eccl.* 3.39; few scholars if any have noted that Papias cites *the Johannine Elder* as the source of this opinion!), that while Mark preserved Peter's preaching effectively, he got it down *in the wrong order*? If such were the case, one of the motivations for producing the "second Gospel" (John's first edition was completed around 80–85 C.E., *before* the Gospels of Luke and Matthew) might have been to set the record straight.[10] John should thus be reconceived at least in part as a complementary presentation for readers and hearers of Mark,[11] and some of John's contrasts to Mark may have been intentional. Indeed, Matthew and Luke eventually did the same, as did the editor who added the second ending of Mark. With these issues in mind, the fact of John's differences from the Synoptics does not force a three-against-one overruling of John's account. We have two individuated perspectives between John and Mark, the Bi-Optic Gospels, and any early Christian narrators would have gathered and presented their material must also be subjected to critical scrutiny. The case is thus still open, and exploring these distinctive presentations analytically may yet lead to some new ways of approaching longstanding New Testament riddles.

1.2. SYNOPTIC OMISSIONS IN JOHN

One of the strongest arguments against an apostolic origin of John's material is that leading themes and events reported as being present, are missing. First, the calling of the Twelve is not found in John, nor are more than eight disciples mentioned. Second, the transfiguration is not mentioned in John, nor is it reported that Peter, James, and John had gone with Jesus to the Garden of Gethsemane. Third, if the Beloved Disciple really had been leaning against the breast of Jesus at the Last Supper, how could he have missed the institution of a meal of remembrance? That would certainly have been an unlikely event to have forgotten or omitted. Fourth, Jesus'

---

10. Of all the theories of John's composition, the most compelling is the two-edition theory of Barnabas Lindars (1984), inferring a first edition emerging around 80, to which the editor added supplementary material after the death of the Beloved Disciple around 100 CE. Here I agree with Bultmann, however, that the compiler may likely have been the author of the Johannine Epistles, rather than the evangelist himself (contra Lindars), thus leading one to believe that the Epistles were plausibly written *between* these two editions. I concur with Lindars that material added to the final edition included the Prologue (John 1:1–18), chs. 6, 15–17, and 21, and Beloved Disciple and eyewitness passages. Contra Lindars, evidence for the translocation of the Temple cleansing making space for the Lazarus narrative seems weak.

11. The relation between John and Mark as the two "Bi-Optic Gospels" is developed elsewhere (Anderson 2001a, 2001b, 2002a, and 2006b).

having spoken in parables about the kingdom of God is terribly conspicuous as a pervasive omission in John. Fifth, Jesus' exorcisms are not mentioned at all in John. These facts pose major problems for anyone arguing that the Synoptic and Johannine presentations of Jesus are both historically reliable.

Strengths. Indeed, if the apostle John were in some way connected to the purveying of the Johannine witness, it seems odd that many of the points at which we might expect an event to have been embellished or expanded are characterized by pervasive silence. How could the son of Zebedee, for instance, have omitted the calling of the Twelve, the transfiguration, the words of the institution, and the anguish of Jesus at Gethsemane, if he were indeed both present at those events *and* the traditional source of the Fourth Gospel? These facts pose major problems for the traditional view of John's authorship, and they are one of the key reasons critical scholars reject it. A further problem is that the sons of Zebedee are referred to as βοανηργές (sons of thunder) in Mark 3:17, and elsewhere they are reported as wanting to call down fire from heaven (Luke 9:54). The reflective character of the Fourth Gospel seems to betray a very different personality type, to say the least. Beyond these particulars, the omission of Jesus' parables, major teachings on the kingdom of God, and exorcisms make it very difficult to reconcile an apostolic or eyewitness origin of John's material, even if the author was not the son of Zebedee. For these reasons, one can understand why critical scholars might find the traditional view of John's authorship problematic.

Weaknesses. On the other hand, the Markan presentation of the disciples, including the sons of Zebedee, might not have been completely untainted by subjectivity when considering *its* historicity. The ambivalent presentation of the sons of Zebedee would certainly have furthered the personal interests of someone like Peter, if he or anyone like him were indeed a source of Mark's tradition. For instance, their having been included along with Peter here and there might reflect a Petrine co-opting of *their* authority, whereby the inclusion of Peter within an inner ring (the sons of his employer) would have served his own interests as a narrator, let alone the interests of those wanting to preserve his memory. Note that it was Peter who in Acts 1 is presented as wanting to preserve "the Twelve" and who calls for a successor to Judas. Certainly the presentation of the sons of Zebedee as desiring precedence among the disciples is rejected by the Markan Jesus—just as Peter's failure to comprehend servanthood is presented graphically in John 13 and 21. Note that the martyrdom of the sons of Zebedee is predicted by Jesus in Mark (10:38–39), whereas the martyrdom of Peter is predicted by Jesus in John (21:18–19). Was the labeling of James and John as thunderheads a sober, *historical* judgment in the Markan or pre-Markan tradition, or was it a factor of Petrine projection?[12] The point here is not to argue for particular personalities

---

12. Neither is the point being made here that Peter, or John, or any other *particular* person lay behind these trajectories. Impressive, however, is the fact that from the earliest stages of

underlying Gospel traditions; the point is that making too much about what can and cannot have been true regarding particular disciples, based upon a few terse comments in Mark, overreaches the bounds of historical demonstrability from the Synoptic side. Motive criticism may be the tool more appropriate here than historical criticism. Therefore, the grounds for excluding *anyone* from Johannine authorship based upon Synoptic presentations of Jesus' followers are weak.

Another weakness of making too much out of Johannine omissions of the Synoptic presentations of Jesus' ministry is that it fails to account for more plausible explanations. For instance, if the Fourth Evangelist were familiar with at least parts of Mark, it could be that parts were left out because of a desire to be complementary.[13] A primitive witness poses that John filled out the earlier parts of Jesus' ministry,[14] and this might explain the emphasis upon the wedding miracle and the healing of the official's son as the first two signs performed in Galilee. The point may have been setting the record straight over and against the Markan presentation of the exorcism of the demoniac and the healing of Peter's mother-in-law in Mark 1. Likewise, the other three miracles in the first edition of John[15] are all three *Judean miracles*, perhaps filling out the almost entirely northern ministry of Jesus in the Synoptics. Therefore, if the Fourth Evangelist were intentionally seeking to complement and augment Mark, this would explain why much of Mark's material was left out. Matthew and Luke built *upon* Mark; John built *around* Mark.[16] The likelihood that John 6 was added as part of the final edition of John throws the augmentive function of John's first edition (probably between 80 and 85 C.E.) into sharper relief. If the five signs in John's first edition fill out the earlier and the Judean aspects of Jesus' ministry as a complement to Mark, John's omissions of most of Mark's material are not scandalous but understandable.

A further point deserves to be made here. The omission of the transfiguration scene in John is more likely to have been related to the Johannine distinctive presentation of Moses and Elijah than an oversight. In Mark, the roles of Moses and Elijah are fulfilled in two ways: they appear at the transfiguration (in keeping with the prophecy of Mal 4:4–5); and they are present in the ministry of John the Baptist. In John, however, the Baptist denies that he is either the prophet (Moses) or Elijah (John 1:19–27). Here Johannine augmentation of Mark moves to correction. The Baptist explicitly denies these associations in John, clearing the way for both typologies being fulfilled in Jesus. Not only does Jesus perform the same sort of signs as Elijah had performed (in the Johannine feeding, even the same word is used for the barley loaves that Elijah had reproduced: κρίθινος; see 2 Kgs 4:43 LXX), but he is explicitly hailed as the prophet like Moses predicted in Deut 18:15–22 (John 6:1–15). It is no exaggeration to say that the entirety of the Johannine Jesus' sense of agency is cast in the form of the Mosaic prophet,[17] and this may have played a role in John's omission of the Markan transfiguration scene. Jesus, not the Baptist, fulfills the typologies of Elijah *and* Moses in John.

A strict "omission of Synoptic material" view of John, however, must be tempered by noticing the many nonidentical similarities between the two traditions. Many of John's miracles are similar to Synoptic ones (healing of an official's servant/child, healing of a paralytic, healing of a blind man, raising of someone from the dead, etc.), but other than the feeding and the sea crossing, they do not appear to refer to the same events. Likewise, Synoptic-like sayings have long been noted in John, but they have not been thought of as authentic aphorisms by recent historical Jesus studies. The characteristic agrarian metaphors associated with the Synoptic Jesus—presented in terse, aphoristic form—appear to have been displaced by long revelatory discourses in John. A closer look, however, shows that these sorts of sayings are far from missing in John. Indeed, Jesus' revelatory discourses do develop themes in ways quite distinctive from sayings in the Synoptics, but it cannot be said that agrarian images are missing from John or that short, terse Jesus-sayings are absent from the Johannine text. A factor in their having been missed is their placement within dialogues and within the body of larger discourses. They are not *absent* from John, and one cannot say that their presence in John simply marks Synoptic derivation. Several agrarian wisdom aphorisms are found in distinctively Johannine settings, and these sayings conform very closely to the criteria otherwise used to distinguish historical Jesus sayings. If they were found in Mark or Thomas, rather than John, few scholars would question their authenticity. Consider, for instance, the great number of Synoptic-like aphorisms in John 4 and 12 alone.[18]

---

13. The impressive 1998 Ph.D. thesis of Ian Donald Mackay on John 6 and Mark 6 and 8 changed my mind on this score (published 2004). I now see John's independence from Mark as *nondependence* rather than *isolation*.

14. Note the comment in Eusebius, *Hist. eccl.* 3.24.7–13 to this effect. The connecting of the first two signs in Cana of Galilee with a chronological augmentation interest casts at least part of the Johannine Evangelist's purpose into sharp relief with reference to Mark in particular.

15. A flawed assumption is that because the Johannine Evangelist fills out the Judean ministry of Jesus, he must have been a southerner rather than a Galilean (see, e.g., Parker 1962). None of Parker's twenty-one points is compelling—individually or collectively.

16. See Anderson 2006b, part 3.

17. See the many connections between the septuagintal rendering of Deut 18:15–22 and the Johannine Father-Son relationship (Anderson 1999a).

18. See below the over six dozen aphorisms in John detected by Drummond 1904 and Bridges 1987.

- "I have 'food' to eat you know nothing about." (4:32)
- "My 'food' is that I might do the work of the Having-Sent-Me-One and might accomplish his work." (4:34)
- "Do you not say, 'It will take about four months for the harvest to come?' Look, I say to you, lift up your eyes and see the fields because they are already white with harvest." (4:35)
- "The one reaping receives wages and gathers grain unto eternal life in order that the sower might celebrate together with the reaper. For in this the saying is true, that 'one sows and another reaps,' I sent you to harvest what you have not worked for; others have labored, and you have enjoyed the benefits of their hard work." (4:36–38)
- "Unless a wheat kernel dies by dropping into the ground, it remains alone; but if it dies it bears great quantities of wheat." (12:24)
- "The one loving his life will lose it; but the one hating his life in this world will keep it for eternity." (12:25)
- "If anyone serves me, let him follow me, and where I am there will my servant be. If anyone serves me, my Father will honor him." (12:26)
- "The time for the judgment of this world has now arrived: the ruler of this world shall now be cast out; and I, if I be lifted up from the earth, will draw all to myself." (12:31–32)
- "You only have the light among you for a short time. Walk in the light you have lest darkness overtake you; because the one walking in darkness does not know where he is going. While you have light, believe in the light, that you may become children of light." (12:35–36)

The Johannine omission of kingdom sayings, parables, and exorcisms is more problematic. John does have two "kingdom" passages in John 3 and 18, but both are corrective rather than elucidative. The kingdom is *not* this but that. Then again, while John has no Synoptic-like parables, Jesus' disciples report being troubled by his speaking in riddles (παροιμίας, John 10:6; 16:25–30) and celebrate his speaking plainly. This harkens back to the more primitive Markan presentation of parables as wedges dividing insiders and outsiders rather than being means of clarification (Mark 4:11–12, 33–34). Of course, John's I-Am sayings are highly metaphorical, as are the Synoptic parables, but they are presented in a distinctively Johannine form. Why the exorcisms of Jesus are omitted from John is difficult to explain, other than to point out that *all* the Synoptic miracles were omitted from the first Johannine edition. Then again, an incidental Markan detail is interesting to consider. The particular disciple who was uncomfortable with other exorcists in Mark and who reported to Jesus that they had asked them to desist was none other than John, the son of Zebedee (Mark 9:38).[19] If this disciple,

or others like him, had anything to do with any stage of the Johannine presentation of Jesus' ministry, discomfort with exorcist ministries may have been a factor in John's omission of Jesus' exorcisms. Because of the vulnerability of making too much out of John's omissions of Synoptic material, especially with relation to who could and could not have been connected to the Johannine tradition, the critical scholar should exercise caution before dehistoricizing John too readily.

Unlike Mark, John contains only two sections that develop the kingdom motif, and rather than being illustrative they are antithetical. They suggest what the active reign of God is like *in contrast to* alternative understandings of it. In contrast to Nicodemus's religious understanding of the kingdom of God, Jesus emphasizes the need to be born from above, using the powerful effect of the invisible wind as a metaphor (John 3:1–21). And, with reference to Pilate's political understanding of power, Jesus declares that the kingdom is one of truth (18:33–38), explaining that this is why his disciples do not fight or resort to force. In these two passages one could infer a Johannine contrasting of the reign of God to two primary worldly spheres: the *religious* and the *political*. Does this mean, however, that the teachings of Jesus on the βασιλεία τοῦ θεοῦ (kingdom of God) are pervasively missing in John, or do we have a Johannine representation of the essential kingdom teaching of Jesus, even as represented in the fuller Synoptic accounts? After all, the spiritual workings of God's active and dynamic reign are indeed contrasted with the human scaffoldings of the religious quest in the Synoptics, and the truthful and penetrating activity of God's present-and-ultimate reign is contrasted to all worldly powers—political and otherwise. In that sense, rather than leaving out Jesus' teachings on the kingdom, it could be said that John *summarizes* them. When considering kingdom language in John, however, it is not entirely void. John has a considerable number of kingdom references, but they focus largely on the βασιλεύς, Jesus, rather than on the βασιλεία, the kingdom.[20] On the face of it, one could consider John's dearth of Synoptic-like kingdom parables and teachings as evidence of disconnectedness from a Jesus tradition, but this misreads the evidence. John's presentation of *Jesus as king*

---

[19] While the discovery of a hitherto overlooked first-century clue to Johannine authorship might not make much of a difference to scholars convinced of John's nonapostolic authorship (Anderson 1996, 274–77), it challenges the view that Irenaeus was the first to make such a connection. Peter and John are presented as speaking in Acts 4:19–20 in two characteristic statements: one Petrine and the other Johannine (see Acts 5:29 and 11:17 for the first; 1 John 1:3 and John 3:32 for the second). Luke's even unintended connecting of the apostle John with a characteristically Johannine phrase—a full century before Irenaeus—approximates a fact, calling for critical consideration of the implications.

[20] Consider, for instance, these references to Jesus in Johannine kingdom terms: Jesus is acclaimed as the king of Israel (John 1:49; 12:13), is embraced as a king like Moses (6:15), fulfills the kingly prophecy of Zech 9:9 (John 12:15), is questioned and affirmed as a king (18:37; 19:12), and is presented and disputed as the king of the Jews (18:33, 39; 19:3, 14, 15, 19, 21). John's is a Christocentric basileiology.

is even more pronounced than those of the Synoptics, and the source of those differences more likely resides in an alternative emphasis and the individuated development of the Johannine tradition itself.

While major Synoptic themes and features are omitted from John, the default inference of John's ahistoricity is naïve and simplistic. Other motives and factors are more compelling in explaining these facts. Such interests as "building around" Mark in nonduplicative ways, reserving the Moses and Elijah typologies for Jesus (not John the Baptist), preferences against exorcisms (especially when rendering a narrative in a Gentile setting), and a practice of paraphrasing Jesus' teachings in Johannine forms of delivery cause a rethinking of the larger issues. It is also a fact that much Synoptic-type material is present in a distinctively Johannine form, so "total absence" is often *not* the case; rather, an alternative presentation is. A classic case in point is the way the Lord's Prayer can be said to be found in embellished form in John 17.[21] Finally, since argument from silence is an extremely tenuous basis on which to build, it cannot be said that this is a very sturdy plank, able to support much interpretive weight.

1.3. JOHANNINE OMISSIONS IN THE SYNOPTICS

Considering the material distinctive to John, many of Jesus' sayings and deeds are among the most memorable in the four Gospels. The great I-Am sayings (I am the bread of life, light of the world, resurrection and the life, good shepherd, true vine, and the way, the truth, and the life) in John are certainly rich with content and of great importance christologically. Five of John's miracles (the wedding miracle, the healing of the official's son, the healing of the Jerusalem paralytic, the healing of the blind man, and the raising of Lazarus) are nowhere mentioned in the Synoptics. The oddity here is that *if* these sayings and events really happened, how could they *not* be mentioned or closely replicated in the other three Gospels? Other distinctively Johannine events also stand out, such as Jesus' dramatic dialogues with the likes of Nicodemus, the Samaritan woman, the Jewish leaders, Pilate, and Peter. Finally, Jesus is portrayed in John as having visited Jerusalem at least four times during his ministry, whereas in the Synoptics he visits Jerusalem the *only once*—the time when he was crucified. Given their absence from the Synoptics, the inference is that much of John's material must have originated in some way *other* than historicity, requiring alternative explanations.

Strengths. Obviously, the raising of Lazarus would have been considered one of Jesus' greatest miracles by all who knew about it, and its absence from the Synoptics strongly suggests that it was not known by their writers. Put otherwise, if the raising of Lazarus indeed happened, how could it possibly be confined to a minority report of one Gospel narrative?[22] Because the Johannine signs clearly serve the rhetorical purposes of the Fourth Evangelist, presenting evidence that Jesus was indeed the Jewish Messiah, the distinctive Johannine signs could have had an origin other than public historical events in the presence of Jesus' disciples. The same can be said of the wedding miracle—by no means a private or secluded event. Likewise, the I-Am sayings must be considered the most theologically significant statements uttered by Jesus about himself anywhere in the four canonical Gospels. If Jesus indeed uttered them, how could they not have been included in the Synoptics? Conversely, the language and diction of Jesus in John is nearly identical to that of John the Baptist (see John 3:31–36) and the Fourth Evangelist. In that sense, the Johannine Jesus' discourses probably reflect the Evangelist's paraphrasing of Jesus' teachings rather than a historical rendering of such teachings. Further, they are far more self-referential than the kingdom sayings of the Synoptics and the Markan messianic secret, and one can understand how John's presentation of Jesus would call for explanations *other* than historical ones.

Weaknesses. As with the former issue, one of the primary weaknesses of questioning the origin of the distinctive Johannine material is that it also argues from silence. Such arguments can only be tenuous, and by definition they elude certainty. To argue that *everything significant* said or done by Jesus would be included in the Synoptics, or even in all the Gospel records, is likewise fallacious. The conclusion of John explicitly declares intentional selectivity (21:24–25), and the same was probably true of Mark and the other Gospels. It is also problematic to argue that Mark had access to *all* of Peter's preaching material (or whatever Mark's primary source might have been), let alone other narrative sources that might have been connected to particular geographical regions.[23] Further, if the patterning of the Johannine miracles in chapters 2, 4, 5, 9, and 11 seems to be crafted to augment the Markan narration of Jesus' ministry, the Cana miracles apparently fill out the early part of Jesus' ministry, and the other three contribute Judean miracles to the mix—perhaps reflecting the sentiment that Mark's rendering was incomplete. In that sense, the distinctive Johannine signs appear to have been presented as a means of filling some of the gaps left by the Markan project, and the final words of the first edition of John allude to that possibility. The Evangelist is apparently aware of other signs reported that "are *not in this book*" (in other words, "Yes, I know Mark is out there, and I know I am leaving things out, so stop reminding me"), "but *these* are written that you might believe" (in

---

21. C. F. Evans builds this case in his provocative essay (1977), making one wonder if the Johannine prayer is an expansion or the Q prayer of Jesus an abbreviation.

22. While the so-called Secret Gospel of Mark might betray an independent account of a resurrection narrative very much like the account in John 11, its existence is itself in doubt, thus offering little or no corroboration of the Johannine Lazarus narrative.

23. Angus J. B. Higgins raises significant questions about John's topography in his third chapter: "Is John the Fourth Gospel?" (1960, 63–82).

other words, "but the above material has a purpose *beyond* what Mark sought to accomplish"; John 20:30–31).

While the Johannine Jesus clearly speaks in the language of the Evangelist, this is not to say the Johannine paraphrase has no root in the ministry of the historical Jesus.[24] Indeed, the Markan Jesus also delivers several I-Am sayings, although they are not as fully developed as those in John.[25] What one *cannot* say is that Jesus' I-Am sayings are absent from, or insignificant in, Mark, as the following list of similar ἐγώ εἰμι sayings of Jesus in Mark and John makes clear.

- ἐγώ εἰμι· μὴ φοβεῖσθε. In Mark 6:50, an epiphany (it is not a ghost; "It is I!"); in John 6:20, a theophany ("I Am!") on the lake.
- An I-Am association with the burning bush, Abraham, and Exod 3:14–15 is declared by Jesus before the Jerusalem leaders (εἰμι understood in Mark 12:26), explicitly declared in John 8:58).
- I-Am claims are mentioned regarding alternative Messiah figures: false messiahs will say "I am the Christ" in Mark 13:6; John the Baptist confessed, "I am *not* the Christ!" in John 1:20.
- A christological claim in response to Pilate's question (Mark 14:62: "Are you the Christ, the Son of the Blessed?" "I am!"; John 18:37: "Are you a king, then?" "You say that I am a king.").

One could also argue that the I-Am sayings in John that make use of the predicate nominative are similar in their metaphorical character to the parables of the Synoptics (especially the shepherd/sheepgate imagery, truth and way emphases, the light-of-the-world motif, the vine/vineyard theme, the resurrection and life themes, and the bread and subsistence motif), although they clearly are not couched in the same parabolic form as the Synoptic teachings of Jesus. While it could be argued that Synoptic developments were constructed upon themes present in John, it is more likely to see the Johannine discourses as Christocentric developments of plausible Jesus sayings. What *cannot* be said is that the Johannine I-Am metaphors are at all missing from the Synoptics, as the following list reveals.

- ἄρτος: Jesus is tempted to turn stones into *bread* (Matt 4:1–4; Luke 4:1–4; Mark 14:13–21; 15:32–39; Mark 6:32–44; 8:1–10; Luke 9:10–17).
- φῶς: Jesus' disciples are the *light of the world* (Matt 5:14–16).
- θύρα: The (narrow) *gate* is emphasized (Matt 7:13–14; Luke 13:24) as the way to *life*.
- ποιμήν: The parable of the *shepherd* and the sheep (Matt 18:10–14; Luke 15:3–7) emphasizes the care of Jesus for his fold.
- ἀνάστασις: Debates over the *resurrection* arise between Jesus and Jewish leaders (Matt 22:23–33; Mark 12:18–27; Luke 20:27–40), and the raising of Jairus's daughter (Matt 9:18–26; Mark 5:21–43; Luke 8:40–56) brings life out of death.
- ὁδός: The "*way* of righteousness" (Matt 21:28–32) is advocated over "the *way* that leads to destruction" (Matt 7:13–14).
- ἀλήθεια: The way of God in *truth* is what Jesus teaches (Matt 22:16; Mark 12:14, 32; Luke 20:21).
- ζωή: The narrow way leads to *life* (Matt 7:14), and Jesus discusses what it means to inherit eternal life (Matt 19:16, 23–30; Mark 10:17, 23–31; Luke 18:18, 24–30).

Even some of the associated clusters of I-am metaphors can be found together in Jesus' teaching in the Synoptics. Indeed, while much material thought to be characteristic of Jesus found in the Synoptics is not found in the same way in John, it cannot be said that it is altogether missing. Some of it is situated in different sets of contexts and forms. John's tradition reflects a distinctively Christocentric rendering of Jesus' teachings, but that does not imply a radical disconnection from the Jesus represented by the Synoptics. If these and other Johannine aphoristic sayings in John would have been found in Mark, or even in the second-century Gospel of Thomas, it is doubtful they would have been passed over quite as readily in the selection of Jesus-sayings material.

1.4. The Johannine Jesus Speaks and Acts in the Mode of the Evangelist

One of the great puzzlements of John's witness is that the Johannine Jesus speaks with the voice of the Evangelist. Then again, so does John the Baptist. The ending of John 3 is notoriously difficult when trying to ascertain who is speaking the last six verses. It appears the Baptist is continuing into a monologue, having moved into it from a dialogue with his own followers about Jesus being the Messiah. Then again, it sounds a great deal like the climactic christological declaration of Jesus in John 12:44–50, so one may be tempted to infer a resorting to the words of the Lord in John 3:31–36 without having marked narratologically a change of voice.

Or, is it the Evangelist's way of inserting the core of his own theological beliefs into the narrative, thereby granting the Baptist a pedestal on which to

---

[24] Franz Mussner (1966) shows how the Johannine memory and paraphrastic work may have developed in distinctive, gnoseological terms.

[25] See, for instance, Jesus' response to the high priest in Mark 14:61–64, where, when asked if he were the Christ, the Son of the Blessed, Jesus declared, "I Am! And you shall see the Son of Man seated at the right hand of power and coming with the clouds of heaven." At this, the high priest tore his garments and called for the blasphemy to be penalized. See also the words of Jesus at the sea crossing: ἐγώ εἰμι· μὴ φοβεῖσθε ("It is I; fear not!" Mark 6:50), which are identical to the words of Jesus in John 6:20, despite contextual differences.

declare the Evangelist's own theological convictions? After all, William Loader has shown effectively that these two passages comprise the "central structure" of John's Christology and that they provide a valuable lens for viewing the Son's saving mission from the Father and his ambivalent reception in the world, rife with implications (1984; 1989). However, if indeed it is the case that the Evangelist has imbued the Baptist's climactic witness to Jesus' mission with his own theological framework and terms, why not infer the same for the declaration of Jesus at the climax of his ministry and elsewhere in John? Especially when the language of John's Jesus is so dissimilar to that of the Synoptic Jesus, this makes it extremely difficult to imagine the *ipsissima verba* of the historical Jesus coming to us through the Johannine text. The words (and deeds) of Jesus in John betray such an obvious projection of the Johannine rendering that considerable caution must be exercised before attributing too much of the Johannine Jesus' teaching to the Jesus of history, proper.

Strengths. First, the Johannine witness comes to us explicitly from the perspective of postresurrection consciousness. Several times the point is made that the disciples did not "understand" the action or words of Jesus at the time, but later, after the resurrection, they understood fully what he was getting at (John 2:22; 12:16). Likewise, Jesus himself emphasizes that their comprehension will be fuller in the future, as mediated by the Holy Spirit, and this prediction is borne out in the perceptions of the Johannine narration (7:37–39; 13:7, 19–20; 14:25–31; 15:26–16:4; 16:12–16). From this perspective, the Johannine memory is pervasively influenced by later discovery, and this perspective by its own admission presents the past in the light of future valuations. In that sense, a "what really happened back then" mode of historicity is less important to the evangelist than the connecting of "what happened" to a "what it really meant … *and means now*" form of narration.

A second question relates to the connections between the language and thought forms of the Johannine Jesus and those of the Johannine Evangelist. As mentioned above, the Johannine Jesus speaks in the language of the Evangelist, and impressive similarities can be observed between the corporate Johannine situation reflected by the Prologue, the interpretive work of the Baptist, the witness of the Evangelist, the words of Jesus, and the narration of Jesus' works. In contrast to the gnostic redeemer myth as the central history of religions origin of the mission of Jesus in John, its similarities are much closer to the prophet-like-Moses agency schema of Deut 18:15–22. Indeed, many of these features can be found throughout the Fourth Gospel, and it is indeed the case that the Evangelist's understanding of Jesus' ministry has been subsumed into this agency schema.

Therefore, aspects of historicity must be read through such a missional and theological lens, which includes the following themes: (1) No one has seen God at any time, and only by the saving/revealing initiative of God can humanity be "drawn" to the Father. (2) Jesus came to the world as God's agent, revealing God's love and truth to the world. (3) The world's reception of the Revealer was ambivalent; some believed, but some did not. (4) Those who knew God received the Revealer, but those who challenged the authenticity of Jesus' mission exposed their spiritual condition. (5) Jesus affirmed that he spoke and did only what he had seen and heard from the Father, attested by his words and works. (6) The world is therefore invited to respond believingly to the Father's Agent as responding to the Father (Deut 18:15–22). (7) Those who believe receive life and further light; those who reject the Revealer seek to preserve the "comfort" of their darkness.

Nearly all these seven themes may be found in each of the above five portions of the Johannine Gospel, showing the degree to which the Evangelist's presentation of the ministry of Jesus and the witness of the Baptist had become integrated within his own ministry. This set of connections leads to a third question: To what extent does John's presentation of Jesus' teachings reflect the teaching of the historical Jesus as opposed to the Evangelist's teaching within the evolving history of his situation? Certainly the above outline reflects at least two levels of history (using Martyn's construct): the mission and reception of Jesus and his message, and the mission and reception of the Evangelist and his message. Indeed, nearly everything claimed for Jesus (he came unto his own and his own received him not, but as many as received the Gospel are given the power to become the children of God, John 1:12) can also be claimed for the Evangelist and the Johannine leadership. At least *four* crises within the Johannine situation can be inferred in the narration of the feeding and the sea crossing in John 6, not just the one in John 9.[26] In that sense, because John's narration addresses the evolving needs of the Johannine audience and represents the teaching ministry of the Evangelist, its reliability as a guide to the historical Jesus comes into question.

Weaknesses. The cardinal weakness, of course, of assuming that interpretive relevance completely eclipses originative history is that it simply is not true. True historicity is never limited to the irrelevant, and to assert such misjudges the character of historiography itself. Every historical project distinguishes events of greater significance from their alternatives, and that implies subjectivity of judgment. Mark's narrative also distinguishes important events from others, so the question is better put as to whether the Markan selection of historically significant content is closer to the historical Jesus than that of the Johannine rendering. Further, to assume that an independent Gospel tradition either did not accommodate to Jesus' teachings or that it did not adapt Jesus' teachings to its own content needs is fallacious and unrealistic. Given the fact that the Johannine

---

26. Note that (a) the desire for more loaves corrects Synoptic-type valuations of the feeding (*not a sēmeia* source); (b) the Jewish leaders' request for manna as Moses gave reflects debates over the authority of the Torah (Deut 8:3); (c) the disciples' being scandalized over eating and drinking the flesh and blood of Jesus is aimed at docetizing Gentile believers; and (d) Peter's figurative "returning the keys to Jesus" corrects the proto-Ignatian tendencies of Diotrephes and his kin (these four crises behind John 6 are developed further in Anderson 1997).

ciples identical to those addressed to the multitudes? Probably not. Therefore, to assert that Jesus' teachings are not at all represented in the distinctively Johannine presentation cannot be critically maintained.

A third fallacy is the assertion that a Johannine paraphrase of Jesus' teachings cannot represent the content or character of the teaching of the historical Jesus. Earlier impressions are not necessarily more authentic when not interpreted or paraphrased. Franz Mussner's intriguing monograph on the historical Jesus in the Gospel of John takes for granted a spiritualized reflection underlying the Johannine "memory," but he performs upon that premise a critical analysis of how the Johannine tradition might have developed as *anamnesis*.[30] In his analysis of key Johannine vocabulary terms ("gnoseological terminology"), Mussner applies the terms "to see," "to hear," "to come to know," "to testify," "to remember" (and to have brought to remembrance) to a realistic estimation of how the "historical reason" of the Evangelist might have developed. While Mussner's investigation is motivated by the desire to reconcile historicity with inspiration, he makes a significant set of phenomenological contributions. First, he acknowledges the distinctive features of Johannine spirituality and memory. Second, he describes how such memory from a distance really might have been experienced as a factor of the work of the παράκλητος calling to present earlier content for the needs of the emerging Johannine situation. Third, rather than seeing such developments as a historical disjunction with a more primitive Jesus tradition, he shows how continuity between earlier experiences and later perceptions may have emerged within the Johannine circle of leadership. In that sense, he gives us an alternative cognitive-critical model for historical investigation within a distinctive situation such as the Johannine.

While the Johannine Jesus clearly speaks in the language of the Evangelist, so do John the Baptist and others in the Fourth Gospel. This being the case, however, it cannot be said that aphoristic sayings of Jesus are totally absent. No fewer than seventy to eighty have been identified, and their embeddedness within longer sections may explain why some scholars have missed them. Nor can it be claimed that Jesus' characteristic aphorisms constituted the totality of everything he ever said. While the paraphrases of Jesus' teachings are a given in John, this is not to say, however, that they are completely truncated from the teaching ministry of the historical Jesus. This plank rests upon a significant problem, but it cannot be said to solidly support a total divorce between historical sayings of Jesus and later Johannine renderings. As Mark's source (and thus, Matthew's and Luke's) rendered Jesus' sayings meaningfully for the needs of emerging audiences

---

Jesus' teachings are rendered in the modes of the Evangelist's own teaching ministry, the following features must be taken into consideration.

First, despite distinctively Johannine characteristics, there are dozens of aphorisms in John that sound very much like the sort of thing the historical Jesus would have said. Those mentioned above are only some of the most distinctive ones; others have been identified in analyses not noted by so-called historical Jesus studies. For instance, Wilbert Francis Howard lists no fewer than sixty aphorisms in John,[27] and Linda Bridges isolates twenty-six aphoristic sayings in John.[28] About half of those identified by Bridges are also selected by Drummond and Howard. Given the prolific inclusion of aphoristic sayings in John, it is extremely difficult to imagine *why* these sayings go unnoticed by Jesus scholars preferring instead the mid-second-century Gospel of Thomas with its gnostic proclivities over the Gospel of John in terms of historicity.[29] An explanation of that fact may lie in the tendency to analyze Johannine discourses as longer units, therefore missing aphorisms embedded within the larger contexts. Many of the above sayings, however, are not found in larger discourse sections, so the fact that they are overlooked entirely comes across as a striking oversight among otherwise astute critical scholars.

A second mistake in judgment is to infer that, because the historical Jesus spoke in characteristically terse, pithy aphorisms, he therefore did not deliver *any* longer discourses. Here a meaningful criterion for inclusion becomes used inappropriately as a measure of exclusion, which is faulty logic. Given that set A (aphorisms) overlaps with set B (Jesus' characteristic style of teaching), it does not follow that set C (longer discourses or alternative diction) cannot have had any overlap with set B. Put otherwise, how did Jesus hold the attention of multitudes for more than a few minutes at a time? If he held the attention of crowds for hours on end at times (as the feeding narratives and other sections in all four Gospels suggest), he must have delivered longer discourses as well as short aphorisms. Thus, aphoristic sayings were probably included in these longer discourses, but it is difficult to imagine that they were the *only* content or form delivered. Another variable also presents itself: Were Jesus' teachings delivered to his dis-

---

27. John 1:51; 2:16, 19; 3:3, 6, 8; 4:14, 21, 23, 31, 34, 44, 48; 5:14, 17, 19, 23, 30, 40, 44; 6:27, 33, 35, 44, 63; 7:7, 17, 24, 37; 8:12, 26, 32, 34, 36, 51; 9:4, 39, 41; 11:25; 12:24, 25, 26, 32, 36, 44, 47; 13:15, 20, 34, 35; 14:1, 2, 6, 9, 15, 21, 27; 17:11; 18:36, 37. Howard (1931, 267) cites these verses as examples given by James Drummond (1904, 17–19). He also says, "Many more can be found, particularly in chaps. xiii–xvii. One of the most striking is xx. 29."

28. John 1:51; 2:19; 3:3, 5; 4:14, 35, 38; 5:19; 8:12, 34–35; 9:4–5; 11:25–26; 12:24–25, 35–36; 13:16, 20; 14:6; 15:13, 16, 20; 16:20–21, 23; 20:23, 27b, 29. See appendices A and B in Linda McKinnish Bridges 1987, 253–58.

29. Indeed, the Jesus Seminar's according of authentic Jesus sayings is more prolific in Thomas than all the canonical Gospels put together (see Anderson 2000b)—a surprising judgment for such a clearly gnostic second-century collection!

30. Mussner's question, "Who is really speaking here?" is a good one (1966). Throughout the course of his analysis, he is able to show how both the historical Jesus *and* the paraphrastic Evangelist might have been implicated together.

in the church, so did the Johannine narrator, and in some ways the Johannine paraphrase may have been closer to original teachings of Jesus than scholars have thought.

1.5. The Johannine Material Is Rendered in Response to the History of the Johannine Situation

Because much of John's material shows evidence of development within the history of the Johannine situation, at least two levels of history must be considered in assessing the historical character of the Johannine material. In reality, *all* Gospel narrative is historical; the only question is, What *aspect* of history is represented regarding a particular passage or detail? As well as historical origins in the ministry of Jesus and within the influence of history of religions background, at least six or seven crises can be inferred within the Johannine situation. In the earlier period, the Palestinian period (30–70 C.E.), the first two crises appear. The first betrays tensions between northern Galileans or Samaritans and their southern neighbors, the Judeans, with the issue here apparently related to centralizing pressures and the rejection of northern perspectives by the Jerusalem-centered authorities. The second crisis betrays an interest in emphasizing that John the Baptist was not the Messiah, and it probably reflects dialogues seeking to convince Baptist adherents that Jesus was. In the middle period, the Asia Minor I period (70–85 C.E.), the Johannine Christians faced two more crises. The third crisis involved tensions with the local Jewish synagogue over the orthodoxy of the Jesus movement and their attempts to convince Jewish family and friends that Jesus was the Jewish Messiah. The fourth involved hardship experienced at the hand of the local Roman presence under the reign of Domitian (81–96 C.E.), as residents of the empire were forced to offer emperor laud or suffer the consequences. The later period, the Asia Minor II period (85–100 C.E.), saw the emergence of multiple communities in the Johannine situation. The fifth crisis stemmed directly from the attempts of Gentile Christians to diminish the effects of required emperor laud. They taught a message of assimilation, legitimated by a nonsuffering and docetic Jesus. The sixth crisis reflects intramural tensions with rising institutionalism within the Christian movement, as the Johannine tradition calls for more egalitarian and familial approaches to church governance. The first edition of John was probably finalized around 80–85 C.E., and the Johannine Epistles were probably written in the interim between that time and the Gospel's finalization around 100 C.E. (see the table below). A seventh set of dialogues that spanned all six of the above crises involved dialectical interaction with other Gospel traditions. Within these evolving issues—largely sequential but also somewhat overlapping—the Johannine presentation of Jesus was formed in response to the needs of the churches, as were the Markan and other Gospel traditions.

An Outline of the Johannine Situation in Longitudinal Perspective

Period 1: The Palestinian period, developing tradition (ca. 30–70 C.E.)
- Crisis A — Dealing with north/south tensions (Galileans/Judeans)
- Crisis B — Reaching followers of John the Baptist

The oral Johannine tradition develops.

Period 2: The Asia Minor period I, the forging of community (ca. 70–85 C.E.)
- Crisis A — Engaging local Jewish family and friends
- Crisis B — Dealing with the local Roman presence

The first edition of the Johannine Gospel is prepared.

Period 3: The Asia Minor period II, dialogues between communities (ca. 85–100 C.E.)
- Crisis A — Engaging docetizing Gentile Christians and their teachings
- Crisis B — Engaging Christian institutionalizing tendencies (Diotrephes and his kin)
- Crisis C — Engaging dialectically Christians presentations of Jesus and his ministry (actually reflecting a running dialogue over all three periods)

The Epistles are written by the Johannine Elder, who then finalizes and circulates the testimony of the Beloved Disciple after his death.

Strengths. Strict objectivity in historiography, as such, is of little value to interpreters. For instance, weeks and months of flat-line seismograph readings are objectively historical, but they are far less significant than the punctuating measures of seismic activity, even if they last for only moments. The relevant recording of the past always hinges upon inferred meanings for later generations, and in that sense the subjective inference of original significance is always determined in the light of an account's eventual impact and relevance. That being the case, many aspects of the Johannine memory appear to have been formed on at least two levels of history. What happened "even back then" (John 9:22; 12:42; 16:2) is brought to bear on "what's happening now."

Regarding crisis one, a crisis involving hegemonic actions and attitudes of Jerusalem-centered Judaism would have affected the preservation of material within the northern situation of the Evangelist. Whether he lived in Samaria, Galilee, or the Transjordan (Galilee seems the most plausible), the presentation of the *Ioudaioi* and leaders of Jerusalem, who reject the northern prophet and are scandalized by Jesus' healing on the Sabbath and claim of divine agency, would have borne resonance with the experience of northern Jewish populations traveling to Jerusalem for festivals and worship several times a year. In that sense, the relevance of the northern prophet being rejected by the Judean authorities (John 4:4–5; 7–8) would have matched the experience of Galilean and Samaritan populations seeking to worship authentically as children of Israel. With relation to the second crisis—still in the first period—the Evangelist takes great pains to connect the Baptist's testimony with the authenticity of Jesus as a means either of reaching Baptist adherents or of cashing in on his authority in respect to his apologetic interests (20:30–31). The Johannine tradition is distinctive in this matter, and it is possible that some of the Johannine leadership originally were followers of the Baptist but left him and followed Jesus. Indeed, John 1 portrays Jesus' first disciples as such. Therefore, the Evangelist's vested interest should be kept in mind regarding the Baptistic material in John.

The middle period of the Johannine situation appears to have involved the movement of the Evangelist to one of the mission churches, probably in Asia Minor; several details bear witness to such a possibility. First, the explanation of Jewish customs interprets the story of Jesus for a Gentile audience. Second, the translation of Aramaic words into Greek connects the original language of the Lord with later Hellenistic audiences. Third, tensions with Jewish and Roman leaders in the earlier period of the Christian movement find resonance with what is happening in the fifth and sixth decades of the Johannine situation. With the destruction of the temple in 70 C.E., religious authority in Judaism shifted from the cultic religion of Jerusalem to scriptural religion practiced more broadly. As the emphasis upon Jewish biblical faith continued to collide with Jesus adherents claiming his divine agency and status rooted in Deut 18:15–22 and Christian worship (John 1:1–18), local religious authorities understandably sought to retard the Jesus movement. The Birkat Haminim of the Jamnia Council codified some of the threats of expulsion that were already at work in Asia Minor and elsewhere, and the Johannine historical project connected religious hostility in the past with the impending crisis in the present. "Even back then" believers were put out of the synagogue for confessing Jesus openly (9:22; 12:42; 16:2), and this historical marker connects earlier memories with present experience. In that sense, it reflects the emerging process of self-identification, as Johannine Christianity individuates away from its Jewish origins. This was the first crisis within this period. The second crisis within this period involved the hardship received at the hand of the local Roman presence, intensifying the requirement to express loyalty to the empire by requiring public emperor laud. Domitian (81–96 C.E.) even required his Roman subjects to refer him as "Lord and God," thus providing a backdrop to the confession of Thomas and the presentation of Pilate in John 18–20. Against these likely Jewish and Roman historical backgrounds, the Johannine narration must be read as reflecting a contextual history of delivery rather than an originative history alone. It was probably at the end of this phase in the history of the Johannine situation that the first edition of John was written.

The later period of the Johannine situation brought with it two more crises (85–100 C.E.): the crisis of having to confront docetic tendencies among Gentile Christian teachers advocating a doctrine of assimilation with Rome, and the resultant remedy to Docetism: the emergence of proto-Ignatian hierarchies within the Christian movement. As a result, the emphasis on water and blood flowing from the side of Jesus (John 19:34–35) emphasizes the physicality of his having suffered, and this antidocetic emphasis is the acute occasion for asserting the eyewitness origin of the Johannine tradition. Indeed, nearly all the incarnational and antidocetic material in John can be found in the supplementary material added to the first edition (including 1:1–18; 6; 15–17; 21; and eyewitness and Beloved Disciple passages).[31] Likewise, the juxtaposition of Peter and the Beloved Disciple speaks with relevance to issues surrounding emerging institutionalization in the late first-century church. Here investigations of the "historical Peter" and the "historical Beloved Disciple," seeking to prove or disprove John's historicity, miss the point entirely. The seventh set of dialogues was less of a crisis and more of a running dialogue with alternative Synoptic traditions. This being the case, at least some of John's presentation of Jesus history emerges in dialogue with alternative perspectives. Historiography is itself a rhetorical venture, and the primary historical interest involves unpacking the meaning of these figures' authority being yoked to the addressing of needs within the historical Johannine situation.[32]

In these and other ways, the Johannine memory is thoroughly engaged in history, but the question is: *Which* history? All of John relates to history; the question is whether particular material reflects originative history in the ministry of Jesus, the religious history of the Johannine tradition itself, or an echo of the historical Johannine situation evolving from one period to another. The fact that audiences in the history of the Johannine situation were being addressed by the Johannine narration raises serious questions about the degree to which the Jesus of history is being presented here, as opposed to John's Jesus simply being a projection of the emerging needs of the Johannine historical situation.

Weaknesses. Again, like many of the previous issues, some merit is granted the concern, but the fallacy comes when an overly reductionistic approach to the Johannine tradition displaces other plausible aspects of Johannine historicity. Two points deserve to be made here. First, the Johannine tradition is not the only Gospel tradition crafting the words and deeds of Jesus to address the later needs of the Johannine audience. Mark too, according to Papias, preserved the preaching of Peter, which itself was reportedly crafted to meet the needs of the church. One might infer several "craftings" of Mark's Jesus tradition to address

---

31. For a two-edition outline of Johannine composition, see Anderson 2006b, 193–95.
32. Kevin Quast develops this view (1989), as structure and charisma complement each other within the Johannine narrative and situation.

the needs of the early church: the way of the cross and costly discipleship; anticipations of the return of Christ; the messianic secret as an antidote to messianic embellishments; and exhortations to be faithful in following Jesus regardless of apparent outcomes. Likewise, Matthew's tradition crafted a Jesus relevant to the teaching needs of Matthean sectors of Christianity, demonstrating Jesus as the authentically Jewish Messiah, and Luke constructed a portrayal of Jesus presenting him as a just and righteous man as a way of minimizing Roman criticisms or concerns about the Jesus movement. In these ways the Synoptic traditions also applied originative histories of Jesus to emerging histories of their respective situations, so John is not alone in such a venture.

A second point is to emphasize the fallacy of assuming that, because John's narration shows signs of later developments, it cannot have represented anything historical about the events in Jesus' ministry. The inference of a history of tradition development does not demonstrate the absence of originative history. Put otherwise, eventual relevance in itself does not negate historical origination. Indeed, the emerging Johannine narrative certainly evolved into its eventual form, but arguing that its originative history was *not* rooted in events or reflections upon them is impossible to demonstrate or maintain. This is especially the case when several aspects of John's presentation of Jesus square very closely with the basic historic elements of the Synoptic tradition, despite not having been dependent upon them.

First, Jesus' cleansing of the temple is included in John as well as the other Gospels, and while John's rendering is at the beginning rather than the end of Jesus' ministry, this independent narration arguably goes back to an originative incident. Second, Jesus' teaching on the love of God in John is parallel with, though not dependent on, the presentation of the same theme in the Synoptics. While the *Abba*-Father language of Mark is probably closer to the language of the historical Jesus than the Johannine Father-Son relationship, the two are nonetheless close and can be said to reflect consonance with each other as windows into the sort of relationship Jesus plausibly described. Third, Jesus' healing on the Sabbath and challenge of religious authority is presented as clearly in John as it is in the Synoptics, despite its many distinctive features. Fourth, the passion narrative in John is very similar to those of the other Gospels, yet John's rendering is also different enough to evince Synoptic derivation. Just because the sequence is the same between the entry, the supper, the garden scene, the arrest, two trials (one Jewish and one Roman), the crucifixion and death of Jesus, and his resurrection and appearances, this does *not* imply common source dependence. Rearranging the order of *any* of these elements in the stories does not work. The trial cannot come after the death, nor can the garden scene come after the arrest, nor can the supper come after trials. A more plausible explanation is that the Johannine and Synoptic traditions represent parallel narrations of a common set of events impressed upon the memories of different traditions, and this is why even Bultmann had to infer a passion source underlying John.[33] The Johannine narration cannot be explained adequately on any other basis. For these and other reasons, while the historical development of the Johannine situation must be considered when analyzing John's historicity, it cannot in and of itself negate any theory of Johannine origins, whether it be rooted in a reflection upon the ministry of Jesus or in an imaginary novelization of later Christian beliefs.

1.6. The Johannine Evangelist Spiritualizes and Theologizes According to His Purposes

The distinction made by Clement, that while the Synoptics wrote about the bodily aspects of Jesus' ministry, John wrote a "spiritual Gospel," has provided a heuristic key for dehistoricizing the Johannine witness. Based upon this inference, differences between John and the Synoptics have been largely ascribed to Synoptic factuality versus Johannine theologization. With regard to the message of Jesus, the Johannine paraphrase of Jesus' teachings and the spiritualization of how he was received (both positively and negatively) bolster this move. With respect to Jesus' ministry, his signs are clearly discussed symbolically and theologically, and the revelatory function of the signs—including their pointing to the mission of Jesus—becomes their primary interpretive value in John. And, with regard to distinctive aspects of chronology or narration in John, such as the timing of the temple cleansing and the Last Supper, "the theologizing work of the Evangelist" receives attribution as the basis for Johannine peculiarities. Scholars explain that John does not present a historical challenge to the Synoptic tradition; John's presentation reflects *theological* interests rather than *historical* ones. The question is the degree to which this thesis holds.

Strengths. Indeed, the Fourth Evangelist is the most spiritualizing and theologizing among the four canonical Gospel writers, and since the second century C.E. he has simply been called "the theologian." In John, the theological import of Jesus' teachings—highlighted by the I-Am sayings and the Son's relation to the Father—form the basis for most of the christological debates within the history of Christian theology. As mentioned above, the origin of that work must be credited as including centrally the theologizing work of the Evangelist. Likewise, the presentation of the theological significance of Jesus' miracles is also rooted in the reflective process of the Evangelist's thinking. Even the existential value of Jesus' signs betrays the theological engagement of the Evangelist's thinking, operating on a stage 5 level of faith (Conjunctive Faith, according to James Fowler's approach), contrasted to less dialectical and more conventional

---

33. For further details, see Anderson 1996, 33–36.

ones.[34] On theologizing explanations of John's distinctive chronology, the "paschal theology of the Evangelist" gets credited with the placement of the temple cleansing early and the location of the Last Supper on Thursday, the day the paschal lambs were slain. These moves preserve the three-against-one approach to the Johannine/Synoptic problem, alleviating historical embarrassment from the Johannine distinctives. If John's differences of presentation were rooted in theological interests rather than historical differences, the four canonical Gospels can more easily be harmonized. The theological valuation of John's witness thus displaces apparent historical incongruities, and Clement's dictum finds its destined modernistic application.

Weaknesses. While Jesus' teachings and deeds are indeed spiritualized and theologized in John, Clement was not declaring John to be historically inferior. The word translated "facts" (as in, the Synoptics preserved the "facts" in contrast to John) is actually σωματικά, referring to the bodily aspects of Jesus' ministry as contrasted to the spiritual perspective of John. In that sense, it is a mistake to interpret Clement as making a historical judgment about John or the Synoptics. Clement was not a modern positivist. He was simply declaring, nearly a century after the four Gospels' completion, his inference of their tone and approach, not respective degrees of historical reliability. Therefore, to employ Clement's dictum as a license for dehistoricizing the Johannine witness falls flat from a critical standpoint. It was nothing of the sort originally, but it came to be used in the modern era as a means of bolstering a three-against-one marginalization of John before Markan priority was established. In the light of a bi-optic approach to the Johannine/Markan analysis, the spiritualistic discounting of John's distinctive presentation no longer holds.

A second problem emerges when seeking to explain John's chronological differences on the basis that the Evangelist's "paschal theology" caused the moving of the temple cleansing early and the location of the Last Supper on a Thursday rather than on a Friday. The first fact to consider is that the Evangelist cannot really be said to have much of a paschal theology to begin with. Indeed, John the Baptist declares at the beginning, "Behold the Lamb of God, who takes away the sin of the world!" (John 1:29, 36), but the Lamb of God theme occurs nowhere else in the rest of the Gospel. The Johannine Apocalypse culminates with Christ as the victorious Lamb, but it is a mistake to connect the Johannine Apocalypse and Gospel too closely together, as though one can be read through the other. John has no explicit paschal theology other than the witness of the Baptist in the first chapter, so this cannot be said to have been a pervasive interest or investment of the Evangelist. It could be argued that the interpretation of Caiaphas's willingness to "sacrifice" Jesus instead of risking a Roman onslaught as an economy of violence

---

34. See cognitive-critical approaches to biblical analysis in Anderson 2004a; 1996, 136–65, as well as in Anderson, Ellens, and Fowler 2004.

---

reflects a Johannine atonement theology (11:45-57), but the thrust of the larger passage is more political than theological. Of the paschal imagery present in John, Jesus is more clearly portrayed as the Good Shepherd, the True Shepherd, who lays down his life for the sheep. The pastoral image of Christ as Shepherd in John is far stronger than the presentation of Jesus as the Lamb, so it thus is not a strong basis upon which to build any sort of a heuristic platform. Further, as the outline of John's central christological structure above shows, it centers not around atonement theology (that is more properly Pauline) but around revelation. Imputing Pauline or Synoptic atonement theology onto that of the Fourth Evangelist is itself an unfounded move.

A third weakness with this particular approach is that it assumes an absence of otherwise historical factors in the location of the Johannine temple cleansing and Last Supper. Indeed, rhetorical interests are present in the construction of all narratives, historical and otherwise, but to assert that no historical-type awareness or motivation is evident in the Johannine ordering and presentation of these events simply is not true. Regarding the temple cleansing, the following apparently historical associations are present. First, the unit (John 2:12–25) is hemmed by chronotopic markers. The beginning of the passage bears three chronological details: μετὰ τοῦτο ("after this") is a general reference, not necessarily a chronological one, as is καὶ ἐκεῖ ἔμειναν οὐ πολλὰς ἡμέρας ("and there [in Capernaum] they remained a just few days," 2:12). The next statement, however, is more particular: καὶ ἐγγὺς ἦν τὸ πάσχα τῶν Ἰουδαίων ("And the Passover of the Jews was near") locates the event at a particular festival time, although which Passover season is meant may be debated.[35] The end of the passage also bears with it chronological references, again mentioning the Passover feast and the σημεῖα ("signs") he had been doing (2:23). Whether the Evangelist used these references with particularly chronological meanings in mind, and even if they were wrong, it cannot be said that historical-type details are entirely missing. They are present at least in general ways.

A second fact is that it cannot be claimed that the temple cleansing unit has no references to the narration of events before and after. First, the way to Jerusalem (via Capernaum, 2:12) again draws in the mother of Jesus, who had just been mentioned in 2:1-5. While she is not mentioned as being present in Jerusalem, Jesus' disciples are. At the beginning of John 3, however, Nicodemus

---

35. The question of which Passover festival this may have been is relevant here; if indeed the reference were to the same Passover mentioned in John 11:55, a theory of transposition would be required. Such is the view of Barnabas Lindars, for instance. In addition to these references, a third mention of the proximity of the Passover is found in John 6:4, but in none of them is an explicit connection made with the paschal atonement theology. The unwitting prolepsis of Caiaphas in 11:50 is a response to a reference to Roman violence and destruction, and this theme of impending political violence is more closely associated with ἐγγὺς τὸ πάσχα in John than an inferred Pauline atonement motif (see Anderson 1996, 172–73).

makes reference to Jesus' "signs," and this statement (in addition to 2:23) appears to include the temple cleansing as a σημεῖον. These references, of course, are not necessarily made with the temple cleansing in mind, but in John 4 Jesus appears to be traveling from the south to the north (thus having to pass through Samaria), and the events in John 5 are inexplicable without Jesus having been to Jerusalem before. Already in John 5:18 the Jerusalem-based leaders are presented as wanting to kill Jesus, and if the only thing he had done in Jerusalem up until that time was the healing of the paralytic, this extremely hostile reaction is hard to explain. The desire to put Jesus to death is again mentioned in John 7, and without an early temple cleansing in the mind of the narrator it is difficult to imagine why these references would have been mentioned during the *early* ministry of Jesus. Again, the point is not to argue John's chronological veracity; it is to challenge the often-made assertion that the early placement of John's temple cleansing bore no chronological/sequential associations with it.

A third difficulty with the current "consensus" is that several aspects of the Markan locating of the temple incident at the end of Jesus' ministry do not appear to be ordered by "factual" knowledge or information. For one thing, Mark locates all the Jerusalem events at the end of Jesus' ministry, as though he only visited the city once during his entire ministry. John's presentation of several visits to Jerusalem indeed seems more plausible than the Markan singular visit. Mark also locates nearly all the judgment and apocalyptic teachings of Jesus as happening on that eventful visit to Jerusalem, but such could simply be a factor of conjecture or climactic narration, clumping material together at the end, rather than motivated by factual information. Further, Mark mentions only one Passover, the one at which Jesus was killed, implying that Jesus' ministry and opposition were all mounted within a relatively short period of time rather than over a period of several years. This could have been the case, but John's rendering here seems more plausible. Another oddity is that Mark's presentation of the events narrated in the Johannine rendering of the temple cleansing are more fragmented than they are in John. For instance, the mention of the event itself is in Mark 11:15–17 (cf. John 2:14–17), while the challenging of Jesus' authority comes in a return visit in Mark 11:27–33 (cf. John 2:18–22). Still less integrated are two references to Jesus' declaration that he would raise up "this temple" in three days: that made by those who stood before the chief priests and the Jewish council (Mark 14:58); and that made by those who observed him hanging on the cross (Mark 15:30). Interestingly, while both of these statements assert that Jesus had made this declaration, he is only *portrayed* as having done so in John 2:19. Because the material in John 2:13–25 is more integrated, and the parallel material in Mark is more disintegrated and diffuse, it cannot be said that the best explanation for the differences is Mark's "factuality" at the expense of John's.

A fourth problem with the "scholarly consensus" that Mark's rendering is rooted in objective fact and John's is rooted in spiritualizing fancy is that John's presentation correlates impressively with several aspects of historicity. First, the reference to the forty-six years it had taken to reconstruct the temple locates the event around the year 27 C.E., toward the beginning of Jesus' ministry, as Herod had begun the construction of the temple around 19 B.C.E.[36] Further, this particular detail in John 2:20, declared on behalf of the Jewish leaders, is not explicable on the basis of numerology or semeiology; it is mentioned simply as an "innocent" objection to the three-day reconstruction reference. Second, the mention of the disciples' later remembering his word, after the resurrection (2:21–22), appears to require a considerable passing of time rather than just a few days. Again, John's presentation could have been wrong, but it cannot be said that the Synoptic/Johannine differences are simply due to factuality versus spirituality. A third fact is also interesting here: Papias's opinion that Mark preserved Peter's teaching favorably—but in the *wrong order*—is attributed to "the Elder" (*Hist. eccl.* 3.39.15). Was this the Johannine Elder, reflecting a second-century opinion that Mark's conjectural ordering of events deserved to be set straight? If so, John's presentation may have been a corrective in the name of a *historical* opinion in opposition to the Markan rendering. For these reasons at least, the temple-cleansing differences between John and Mark cannot be said to confirm a "factual" Mark in opposition to a "spiritual" John. After all, John too is *somatic*, as Origen declares (*Commentary on John* 1.9).

But what about the dating of the Last Supper? Is not Mark's presentation of the event as a Passover meal a more likely timing than John's rendering of the event on Thursday night? After all, Mark 14:12–16 records that the Last Supper was being prepared on the day the paschal lambs were killed, the Day of Preparation, making it a more formal Passover meal. Supposedly, John's location of the event on the eve of the Day of Preparation (John 19:14, 31, 42) would have been motivated by the paschal theologizing interests of the Evangelist over and against the superior chronology of Mark. Two major problems accompany this view. First, if the Passover were observed on the Sabbath, it seems highly unlikely that Jesus' crucifixion would have happened on the Sabbath, and if Mark's rendering in chapter 14 is correct, this would have been the case. John's report of the sense of urgency that the bodies needed to be removed from the crosses *before* the Sabbath seems far more likely. Another problem with the Markan rendering is that Mark presents the appearance narratives as happening on the "first day," the day after the Sabbath (as does John), which would mean that Jesus was only in the tomb overnight (Mark 16:1–2, 9). Given Mark 14 on its own, to allow three days in the tomb, the Johannine rendering is required. Yet Mark 15:42 claims that Jesus was actually crucified on the Day of Preparation, thus contradicting the earlier Markan passage that the meal was on the same day. Like Jesus' words about the three-day raising up of the temple, this is not just a matter of John

---

36. See Higgins 1960, 44–46, and Josephus, *A.J.* 15.11.1.

against Mark; it also is a matter of Mark against Mark. Then again, if the Passover was held the day before the Sabbath that year, the above could be more easily harmonized. Another fact is that "eating the Passover" would not necessarily have been confined to one day; it could have involved a week-long set of celebrations. The problem for such a move is that John 19:31 declares that the Sabbath was a "high day" that year, implying that the Passover and Sabbath were on the same day.

A second problem with preferring a Passover meal setting over a less formalistic meal in John is that the former too easily can be explained as an adapted meal conforming to evolving Christian cultic practice. John's assertion that Jesus did not baptize (4:2) and the omission of the words of the institution of the Eucharist in John 13 cannot be explained on the basis of "spiritualization" or the representation of evolving cultic practice. Indeed, John goes *against* those cultic developments within the broader Christian movement, but the Markan renderings advances them. For these and other reasons, the primary examples used to explain Synoptic/Johannine differences on the basis of factuality versus spiritualization fall far short of a compelling critical argument.

The "theological interests of the Evangelist" is one of the most inexact and carelessly used explanations given among scholars who do not otherwise know what to do with a particular Johannine feature (see Anderson 2006c). Rarely is its use subjected to critical assessment, and seldom are the bases for its use laid out clearly. The dehistoricizing treatment of the above issue is a telling example. First, despite John making no mention of the paschal lambs being killed, this exclusively Markan theme (Mark 14:12) is carelessly imputed into the Fourth Evangelist's motives despite the relative dearth of paschal theology in John.[37] Second, the issue is set up as John versus Mark, when Mark also disagrees with Mark. Third, the more cultic Passover meal and institutionalizing rendering in Mark gets precedence over John's more innocent presentation, against the criterion of dissimilarity. Fourth, these specious moves are amassed as critical evidence illustrating a prime case of Johannine ahistoricity, functioning to deconstruct other apparently historical Johannine material. If these same sorts of moves were made *in favor of* John's historicity or apostolic authorship, critical scholars would certainly raise objections—yet, as challenges to its historicity, it appears they are given a critical pass.

A final fallacy also accompanies this discussion: the assumption that theologization and spiritualization necessarily imply ahistoricity. Indeed, the spiritualization of earlier events calls into question the memory of purported events, and evolving narrations may have supplanted earlier renderings, but to say that symbolization, spiritualization, or theologization displaces originative history is terribly flawed as a historiographic procedure. Apply the premise to any subject, and the extent of its fallacious character becomes evident. Does the phenomenon of "war-story embellishment" prove that a war never happened or that there was no connection between originative events and later reflections? Do symbolized expansions upon traumatic experiences prove that they never happened? The embellishment of events does not negate their ontology. Indeed, the case can be made that dialectical processes of thought and reflection betray a first-order level of encounter rather than second-order reasoning (Anderson 2004a). For these and other reasons, equating John's spiritualization of events in the ministry of Jesus cannot be considered a solid proof of its ahistoricity.

In summary, of the various planks in the platform contributing to the dehistoricization of John, *none* of the strengths of these positions are decidedly compelling. Problems indeed are inferred, and ones that need to be addressed critically, but John's aspects of historicity are as disruptive for the purported consensus as obstacles to John's ahistoricity were to the traditionalist view. Therefore, a blunt appraisal of John's ahistoricity is devoid of nuance and fails to account for dozens of exceptions to its claims. For this reason the genuinely critical scholar cannot be satisfied with the purported critical consensus.

Planks in Platform B: The De-Johannification of Jesus

Attempting to employ the Gospel of John for Jesus studies is indeed problematic. A Jesus who possesses sole control over his future and who "knows" what is in the hearts of humans is hard to equate with the incarnation. Likewise, it is difficult to know how to square the Logos, who was with God in the beginning and through whom all was created, with the historical Jesus who suffered and died under Pontius Pilate. John's historicity seems to have been subsumed into John's Christology, and thus John is thought to provide very little insight into what the historical Jesus may have been like. After John is removed from the database used to reconstruct the "historical" Jesus, criteria are established that function to separate John further from historical Jesus quests. The problem, however, is that this move is circular in its conception and its exercise. This being the case, the planks in the platform of the de-Johannification of Jesus must also be assessed critically to determine whether John's marginalization from Jesus studies is warranted or not.

2.1. John's Similarities with the Synoptics—Especially Mark

An obverse problem of John's differences from the Synoptics is the fact that John is also very similar to them. Many similarities between John and Mark can be

---

37. The witness of the Baptist, "Behold the Lamb of God, who takes away the sin of the world!" (John 1:29, 36), is more fittingly a reference to Isa 53:7, where it is the suffering and faithfulness of Israel as the Suffering Servant of Yahweh through which the world is redeemed, than a paschal atonement theme.

found, and despite the sustained objections of P. Gardner-Smith, Raymond E. Brown, and D. Moody Smith, such scholars as C. K. Barrett, Franz Neirynck, and Thomas Brodie have inferred John's spiritualized use of Mark.[38] The significance of this inference as it relates to Jesus, John, and history is that, if John is a spiritualization of Mark, this would account for a major factor in the origin of John's tradition. On one hand, seeing John as an expansion upon Mark would bolster interests in securing a historical basis for John. On the other hand, dependence upon Mark casts John in a derivative relation to Mark rather than having an original claim to its own tradition. Whatever the case, John's many differences from Mark continue to pose difficulties for a Markan dependence view and is, in fact, one of its major vulnerabilities.

Strengths. The hypothesis that John is derivative from Mark has several strengths, although it is by no means embraced by the majority of Johannine scholars. The first strength involves the similar beginnings and endings of Mark and John. Both begin (after the Johannine Prologue) with the beginning of the "Gospel" and the ministry of John the Baptist, and both end with the passion, death, resurrection, and appearances narratives. Second, similarities in the passion accounts are impressive. Both begin with an acclaimed entry to Jerusalem, a Last Supper, prayer and arrest in the garden, two trials (a Jewish and a Roman trial), the crucifixion and death, the resurrection, and, finally, appearance to women. Third, both have an impressive number of general similarities around the feeding of the multitude, the sea crossing, further discussions of the feeding, and the confession of Peter. Fourth, multiple particular similarities (distinctive to Mark and John) exist regarding graphic detail (the mention of two hundred and three hundred δηνάριοι; the grass upon which the people sat; "Holy One of God" as a christological title; and the use of Isa 6:9–10 to explain the Galileans' unbelief). These similarities imply some form of contact between these traditions. Fifth, some aspects of John's witness show signs of being crafted for readers and hearers of Mark. The references to the adverse reception in Nazareth and the timing of the Baptist's imprisonment point to familiarity with the Markan witness,[39] as do the clarification of the first two signs were performed in Galilee (John 2:11; 4:54) and the acknowledgement that other signs were performed by Jesus not reported in "this book" (20:30). For these and other reasons, some scholars have inferred a derivative relationship between the Johannine and Markan traditions.

Weaknesses. The problem with such a view, however, is that despite all these similarities, none of them is identical. Mark has "green" grass; John has "much" grass. While "Holy One of God" is used as a title for Jesus in both Gospels, in Mark it is uttered by the demoniac (Mark 1:24), in John by Peter (John 6:69). In fact, of the forty-five similarities between John 6 and Mark 6 and 8, *none* of them is identical.[40] Further, the placement of the temple cleansing at the beginning of Jesus' ministry argues strongly against John's dependence upon Mark. After an extensive analysis of John's relation to the Synoptics, in particular Mark, Moody Smith resolutely affirms the same conclusion that Perceval Gardner-Smith came up with in 1938: if the Fourth Evangelist was aware of Mark or the other Synoptics extensively, he disagreed with them at almost every turn.[41] Certainly if there were some contact or familiarity, the relation of John to Mark was nowhere near the much closer connections evidenced between Mark and the other two Gospels. A further problem is that much of the Johannine archaeological and geographical detail is found only in John, so the Markan tradition cannot have been a source of the majority of the Johannine material most likely to be considered historical. For these reasons, Johannine familiarity with Mark cannot be ruled out, but dependence upon Mark can. Therefore, John's independence from Mark should be regarded as nondependence, or autonomy, rather than isolation.

2.2. John's Composition: Diachronic or Synchronic?

John's composition has been a considerable interest of Johannine scholars due to its many perplexities (*aporias*). First, formal and vocabulary differences exist between the Prologue (1:1–18) and the rest of John's narrative. The Prologue is poetic and stanza-based in its form (suggesting a worship setting in its origin), whereas the rest of John is prose. A second perplexity is that several odd progressions require attention: chapters 5 and 7 are in Jerusalem, while chapters 4 and 6 are in Galilee; after Jesus says "let us leave" in 14:31, it takes three chapters for them to arrive at the garden (18:1); John 20:31 seems to have been an original first ending, with chapter 21 added at a later time; Mary is mentioned in chapter 11 as the one who anointed the feet of Jesus, but she does not actually do so until chapter 12; Jesus says "none of you asks where I am going" in 16:5, yet Thomas had just asked him about where he was going and how to know the way in 14:5; finally, neither 5:4 nor 7:53–8:11 is found in the earliest Greek manuscripts of John, suggesting at least some later textual additions. These perplexities

---

38. When comparing the theories of Gardner-Smith 1938, Brown 2003, and Smith 2001 with Barrett 1978, Neirynck 1977, and Brodie 1993, the weaknesses of Markan-dependence theories appear greater than those of independence theories.

39. Richard Bauckham's essay "John for Readers of Mark" (1997, 147–72) raises the sort of possibility that Ian Mackay (2004) argues in greater detail. Johannine-Markan traditional contact, however, need not imply derivation.

40. For the particulars, see tables 10–15 in Anderson 1996, 187–90. See also appendix 1 below.

41. After a thorough review of the literature, D. Moody Smith (2001) sides with Gardner-Smith, although with the move of Raymond Brown (2003) toward considering "cross-influence" between John and other traditions, a theory of "interfluence" deserves development.

raise more than a few questions about John's order and composition, and some scholars have advocated a diachronic history of John's composition. The relevant question here involves the degree to which John's narration represents a coherent presentation of Jesus or whether it represents a fragmented one, composed of alien material and disparate sources possessing varying degrees of historicity.

Strengths. The greatest of Johannine diachronic composition schemes is the theory devised by Rudolf Bultmann. He argued for three primary sources from which the Evangelist derived his Gospel material, for the constructive work of the Evangelist that then fell into a disordered state, and for the reconstructive (and reordering) work of the redactor who prepared the Fourth Gospel into the perplexing state in which we find it today.[42] This being the case, a σημεῖα source provided the distinctive signs found in John, a gnostic revelation-sayings source availed the Evangelist's distinctive I-Am sayings explaining their origin, and an individuated passion narrative made it possible for John's distinctive material to be gathered without the Evangelist's having been an eyewitness. A redactor then added his own material, rearranging the text that had fallen into disorder and reconciling the Johannine Gospel with Synoptic renderings and ecclesial interests. Bultmann's source-critical inferences were based on stylistic, contextual, and theological bases, and they accounted for several perplexing Johannine features: (1) the rough transitions in John, and even some smooth ones; (2) the origins of John's christological tensions, as these were due to dialogues between sources and Evangelist and redactor; and (3) the inferred historical origins of John's material, which was derivative from other sources and from mythological origins, from which a distinctive narrative was constructed. Thus John's distinctive presentation of Jesus was accounted for, and John's theological-rather-than-historical character was explained. Other diachronic schemes have abounded, but Bultmann's represents the zenith of modern Johannine diachronic reconstruction.

Weaknesses. Despite the brilliance of Bultmann's approach, it falls flat when tested on the basis of its own evidence. Regarding the differences between "Hellenised Aramaic" and "Semitising Greek," when *all* of Bultmann's stylistic evidence is gathered and applied to John 6 as a case study (the very place where four of his five sources should be discernibly present), its distribution is not only nonconvincing, but it is nonindicative. Other than the fact of a narrator's stylistic work being obvious (which does not imply the use of alien material), the rest of the features are evenly distributed throughout John 6.[43] Likewise, contextual reasons for inferring a disordering and a reordering of John's text are terribly weak. Bultmann misses the irony of Jesus' knowing response to the crowd's question about his arrival in John 6:26 ("When did you get here?" as in "When's lunch?") and infers instead a displacement of material. His inference of a disordered John 4; 6; 5; 7 makes better sense if it is seen as the insertion of John 6 into an earlier version of the Gospel.[44] Theologically, John's christological tensions should be viewed not as dialogues between sources and editors but as a function of the dialectical thinking of the Evangelist. In that sense, these tensions are *internal* to the thinking of the Evangelist rather than external. While Bultmann is happy to describe modern theologians as dialectical thinkers, he ironically fails to allow a first-century theologian the same privilege. With relation to the Evangelist's subject, Jesus, this dialectical level of engagement may reflect proximity to Jesus rather than distance.

As mentioned above, the most plausible and least speculative of Johannine composition theories involves a two-edition theory of composition, inferring that a first edition of John was finalized around 80–85 C.E. and a final edition compiled around 100 C.E. by the redactor after the death of the Beloved Disciple (implied in John 21:18–24). Material added to the final edition would have included the Prologue, chapters 6, 15–17, and 21, and Beloved Disciple and eyewitness passages. *With Bultmann here, the editor appears to have added several sections that are quite similar to 1 John, so it is plausible to identify the author of the Johannine Epistles as the final compiler of the Johannine Gospel.* This would explain the third-person references to the purported author and appeals to authority otherwise (1 John 1:1–3, etc.). If something like this two-edition process took place, the Johannine Gospel was written *before and after* the Epistles (which were probably written between 85 and 95 C.E.). What can be inferred in the first-edition material, then, is the concern to present Jesus apologetically as the Jewish Messiah in response to engagement with the local synagogue presence, while the supplementary material shows signs of antidocetic emphases on the suffering and humanity of Jesus, the incarnated Word.

---

42. See especially the analysis of Bultmann's program (1971) by Moody Smith 1965.

43. See an analysis of the viability of Bultmann's evidence on its own terms in Anderson 1996, 70–136.

44. This is the view of Barnabas Lindars 1972, 46–54; independently of one another, John Ashton and I came to the same favorable impressions of its prime viability (see Ashton 1991, 124–204), although he embraces a final editor along the lines of Brown, as do I. See appendix 1 below.

PART I
MODERN FOUNDATIONS
FOR THE CRITICAL INVESTIGATION OF JOHN,
JESUS AND HISTORY

'But, last of all, John, perceiving that the *somatic material* had been made plain in the Gospel [of Mark?], being urged by his friends and inspired by the Spirit, composed a *pneumatic gospel*. This is the account of Clement'.

Eusebius, *Hist. Eccles.* 6.14

The rise of the Modern era produced many intellectual advances, especially in the Western world. With the emergence of the scientific era in the seventeenth century, technological advances paved the way for empirical methods of hypothesis verification. Following the Thirty Years War in Europe and the Civil War in England, rationalism replaced religious authority as the primary coin of intellectual exchange. With the rise of philosophic naturalism in the eighteenth century and the emergence of historical-critical methodology in the nineteenth, much of biblical content and perspective was expelled from canons of historicity – evoking defences of traditionalism on one hand, and requiring alternative critical approaches on the other. As a result, scientific and modernistic authorities came to be pitted against religious and traditionalistic authorities, and nowhere has this adversarial embattlement been more intense than within discussions of John, Jesus and history.

Within these discussions, particular sources of authority have been yoked to one agenda or another, bringing to bear the weightiest of authority claims of the times. 'Scientific investigation' was often pitted against 'authoritative tradition', and vice versa, at times obscuring the issues and deflecting the discussion away from a focused weighing of the evidence. Likewise, bolstering one theological view or another on the basis of John's historicity or apostolic authority has understandably evoked critical reactions. On the traditionalistic side, misappropriating the perspective of the Johannine Prologue, for instance, imposing it upon the more mundane Johannine narrative, has claimed too much out of too little. On the critical side, arguments constructed upon the silence or upon Johannine-Synoptic differences have also overreached the evidence. As new theories have been posed as a means of addressing the Johannine riddles, each new set of theories comes with its own set of new problems. Any approach taken by scholars thus needs to be mindful of its particular strengths and weaknesses, seeking always to improve one's tools and approaches to these important issues. Therefore, the developing story of the investigations of John, Jesus and history deserves consideration at the outset.

A. *The Story of John's Historical Marginalization and its Implications*

The story of John's historical marginalization begins with questions of authorship and the distinctive origin and character of the Johannine tradition. As the purported source of an eyewitness tradition, John's historicity received few serious challenges for 17 centuries. Things changed in the Modern era with the analysis shifting to comparisons and contrasts between John and the Synoptics, leading to inferences as to which tradition bore greater historical veracity. During the nineteenth and twentieth centuries, John became largely marginalized as a historical document, and critical scholars were forced to explain the origin of John's content otherwise. Historical investigations thus shifted to the history of comparative religions, tradition development and source analysis. Studies arguing in favour of John's historical origin abounded, but

rather than being engaged and improved upon by critical scholarship, they were largely sidestepped. The same might also be said of some traditionalist approaches to historical-critical methods. A final development has been the circumventing of the modernist historical-critical project altogether, with the posing of fresh literary-critical theory to the Johannine riddles, as a means of contributing to meaningful interpretation. While these approaches overlap, their progression and relatedness deserve consideration.

1) *The Traditional View and its Development – From Papias (or Luke?) to Schleiermacher*

For the first 17 centuries of the Christian movement, neither the authorship nor the historicity of John was questioned seriously by interpreters. Some exceptions were taken to particular aspects of earlier theories, but by and large, John's composition by 'the eyewitness' and 'the theologian' carried the day within most analyses. They simply assumed that John's differences were either a factor of theological interest or particular traditional material. Some interpreters actually preferred John's historical presentation to the other gospels, although most interpreters sought to work out some sort of harmonization between them.[1] Discussions of historicity tended to hinge upon questions of John's authorship and apostolic character. As a review of the literature suggests, little improvement was made over the basic treatments of second-century witnesses and the impressions of Eusebius.[2]

The early second-century associations of the Apostle John with the Johannine writings were indirect. Echoes from the Gospel of John are apparent in the writings of 1 Clement, Ignatius of Antioch, Polycarp of Smyrna, Justin Martyr, the Gospel of Philip and certainly Tatian's 'Diatessaron'.[3] The sorts of contacts between John and these writings include their use of Johannine concepts and language, but most of the references are not direct ones. Due to this fact, critical scholars have tended to argue that the lack of explicit mention of the Apostle John suggests a lack of awareness that the Johannine tradition had anything to do with him. Their silence is taken as an argument against

---

1. See, for instance, Augustine's *Harmony of the Evangelists* and Johannes Albrecht Bengel's *Gnomon Novi Testamenti* (Tübingen, 1745) as examples of classic attempts to harmonize the gospels.
2. In reviewing Sean Kealy's analysis (2002, pp. 1–366) of 19 centuries of Johannine interpretation, it is clear that it is really not until the turn of the eighteenth century that the traditional view of Johannine authorship became questioned by serious scholars.
3. See Charles Hill's analysis of the near-unanimous second-century opinion regarding the apostolic origin of John (2004, pp. 294–446, 75–171). In this exhaustive treatment of the primary literature, Hill concludes that John was *not* the exclusively favoured gospel of heretics, and that John was *not* pervasively ignored by second-century Christian leadership. Rather, Hill shows that John was known and used by *no fewer than 43 different second-century sources* (p. 450), with some of these even involving multiple references (see, for example, the letters of Ignatius). Hill also demonstrates that orthodox writings referenced the Johannine writings far more than the Gnostic and heterodox writings did, thus challenging inferences of orthodox 'Johannophobia' in the early church.

the apostolicity, and thus veracity, of the Johannine tradition, but this assumption is hyperextended critically. Familiarity could just as easily have been a factor in leaving out particular statements of attribution. What is impressive is the fact that the Johannine writings are actually extensively discussed and referenced in the second century, and that there are more papyri and manuscript fragments from John than there are from any other ancient Christian text.[12]

A more striking discovery, however, pushing the connection even earlier into the late first century, is the fact that Luke attributes a Johannine phrase to the Apostle John in Acts 4.19-20. The reason this connection has been overlooked by all sides of the debate is likely the fact that it is 'Peter and John' who are credited with speaking, rather than John alone. Whereas scholars might have overlooked this passage as a joint statement, it is actually two separate statements, and a closer analysis of the first statement illuminates the second. In verse 19, the statement is very similar to ones made by Peter in Acts 5.29 and 11.17. In all three of these statements Peter is credited with saying something like, 'We must *obey God rather than man*'. This being the case, the association of the second statement, 'We cannot help but speak about *what we have seen and heard*', bears an unmistakably Johannine ring. Its closest parallel is 1 Jn 1.3, and in Jn 3.32 Jesus is the one who declares what he has 'seen and heard' from the Father. Add to this connection the facts that Luke departs from Mark no fewer than three dozen times in which he sides with John, that he includes Johannine theological content in his Gospel and Acts, and that he expresses appreciation in his first prologue to 'eyewitnesses and servants of the *Logos*', and this first-century connecting of the Apostle John with the Johannine tradition approximates a fact.[13]

Beyond Luke's unwitting connecting of John the apostle with the Johannine tradition, other references are more direct. The testimony of Papias, Bishop of Hieropolis, certainly makes a contribution here, although scholars are divided as to his diction, meaning and value. This may be because some of his connections appear to be incidental rather than emphatic, but the converse is also true. Papias identifies at least three Johannine leaders: John the disciple of the Lord, John the presbyter and Aristion. He connects all three of these with being actual followers of Jesus, even if not members of the Twelve, and this is another reason for some of the confusion. In particular, his emphasis is upon John the presbyter, of whom he claimed to be a hearer, and his preference for the living voice of the oral tradition over the written text suggests the primitivity of his opinion. A further problem with the Papias tradition is that we do not have access to any of his five books containing expositions on the Lord's sayings (arguably the first full history of the early church after the Acts of the Apostles), so we are left with interpreting a dozen or more fragments of his writings and references by later historians.[14]

Beyond the puzzling details of the presentation of Papias' fragments, scholars tend to make several sorts of mistakes regarding what Papias does and does not say. Errors by traditional scholars tend to include the following: a) inferring his references to 'John', 'the elder', or 'disciples of the Lord' imply a reference to John the apostle (this error appears to have been made by Irenaeus, who mistakes his being a follower of John the elder with John the apostle); b) inferring that he connected John the apostle with the authorship of the Fourth Gospel explicitly (again, Irenaeus makes this connection, although direct evidence from Papias is lacking); and c) assuming that he was a follower and disciple of John the apostle rather than John the presbyter. Papias distinguishes John the apostle from John the elder, although he lists them both (along with Aristion) among the disciples of the Lord. Eusebius distinguishes the two 'Johns' buried at Ephesus by referring to one as the apostle and the other as the presbyter.

Errors by critical scholars tend to include the following: a) assuming that a preference for the living Word rather than the written word implies a disparaging of the Johannine written Gospel; b) assuming that a failure to mention a connection with the Apostle John implies a disregard for his contribution, thereby discounting the possibility of his witness being historic or

---

12. According to Victor Salmon (1976), there are over 300 biblical papyri in the Chester Beatty manuscript collection, and many of these are from John. Likewise, the earliness of the Bodmer Papyrus (Birdsall 1960; Roberts 1935) and other second-century fragments from the Gospel of John push the dating of the Fourth Gospel toward the turn of the first Christian century rather than the middle second century.

13. This discovery is laid out in the last appendix at the end of *The Christology of the Fourth Gospel* (Anderson, 1996, pp. 274–7), and it will be developed briefly in Part III. Even if Luke was misguided or wrong, or even if he was imitating reality mimetically, this first-century clue to Johannine authorship deserves critical consideration. It connects the Johannine Gospel with John the apostle a *full century before* Irenaeus.

14. Other questions also persist with the Papias tradition: a) He does not always distinguish between 'disciples' and 'elders'. Therefore, whether John the 'presbyter' is distinguished from the disciple John becomes a factor of debate. b) His disparagement of Matthew (or at least portions of it), claiming it had first been written in Hebrew and had then been translated with difficulty by others, has raised questions as to his knowledge. c) His description of Mark as Peter's companion and as having gotten down his teachings in the wrong order has seemed problematic to some. d) His attributing of embellished teachings found in apocryphal writings (2 Bar. 29.5) to the Apostle John's teachings of Jesus is problematic from a historicity standpoint. e) Eusebius refers to him as a man of limited intelligence (with reference to his millenarian perspective – counter to that of Eusebius), although his works are also referenced extensively by the same. f) Papias is credited *wrongly* with references to the early martyrdom of the Apostle John by Philip of Side and George the Sinner; they included John's martyrdom as fulfilled with that of James (Mk 10.38-9), although *neither* suggests they were killed at the same time or early. The point of the latter is that after his martyrological exile on Patmos, John returned to a martyr's death as predicted by the Lord. g) While Papias does not claim to have met any of the Apostles of the Lord (presumably including John), he is associated with the tradition that John the apostle and John the elder were both buried at Ephesus, and some later interpreters confused his speaking of the Presbyter as references to the Apostle.

Haer. 3.11). Irenaeus then asserted their apostolic authorship, either on a first- or a second-generation basis. Matthew and John were thus accorded to apostles and eyewitnesses of the Lord, and Luke and Mark were accorded to followers of Paul, with Mark having been an interpreter and recorder of Peter's preaching to the churches.

While Irenaeus appears to be constructing his argument on solid traditional bases, three primary questions have been raised by critical scholars. First, the fact of his anti-Marcionite agenda raises a question as to whether his work should be considered historical or rhetorical. Second, the appeal to four winds and creatures of the apocalypse – and thus a perfect number of 'four Gospels' – is not exactly the stuff of historical 'proof' when it comes to determining the authentic number of canonical gospels. Third, the interest in connecting these four Gospels with apostolic or sub-apostolic personalities – given his apparent distortion of the Papias testimony on his having been a disciple of John the apostle – raises a question as to whether he may have committed an error here and elsewhere. Nonetheless, Irenaeus carried the day within the church, and by the fourth and fifth centuries Church Fathers commonly came to refer to Papias as a disciple of John the apostle, thus embellishing the connections between Papias and the first-generation apostles. Nonetheless, Papias' connection with John the presbyter remains unchallenged,[18] and despite his not having been one of the Twelve, but the author of the Johannine Epistles, Papias still regards him as a disciple of the Lord, which coheres with the eyewitness appeals of 1 Jn 1.1-3.

Aside from mistaken inferences that John the son of Zebedee died an early death along with James, therefore excluding him from authorship consideration, the majority opinion embraced a selection of the following tenets found in Eusebius:

Table 1.1

Eusebius on John

- Citing Clement, after the ascension of Jesus, Peter, James and John did not claim preeminence in church leadership, but they chose James the brother of Jesus to be the head of the Jerusalem church (*Hist. Eccles.* 2.1).

18. Martin Hengel argues convincingly for the connecting of the Johannine Elder with the final authorship of John (1989), and according to Papias, he may also have been an eyewitness. This would account for the 'we' language in 1 Jn. 1, where eyewitness authority is claimed by the Johannine community. Nonetheless, the view of B.H. Streeter (1929) is not altogether unlikely that '…John the Elder was "ordained" by John the Apostle' (p. 97), accounting for the two Christian leaders named 'John' at Ephesus.

significant; c) interpreting the references to the martyrdom of John along with James by Philip of Sides and George the Sinner implied an early death of John the apostle (the emphasis is made here that John's martyrdom was *after* the reign of Domitian as the last of the surviving Apostles);[15] and d) inferring that because Eusebius questions his intelligence, this proves what he had to say was of no historical worth.[16] These are some of the reasons why even competent scholars have differed in their assessments of Papias' testimony on matters Johannine.

While the authority of the Fourth Gospel gets significant treatment by such figures as Montanus, Heracleon and the author of the Apocryphon of John, one of the first orthodox direct references to John's being the author of the Fourth Gospel comes from Theophilus, Bishop of Antioch, whose apology was directed against Marcion.[17] Explicit connections between John the apostle and the Fourth Gospel include the Muratorian Canon, where a tradition surfaces declaring that the fourth of the Gospels was written by John, one of the disciples, who was encouraged to write down his own impression of what was revealed to his fellow disciples and bishops about the ministry of the Lord. This tradition accounts for the differences between John and the Synoptics as a factor of inspiration. In addition, Polycrates, who was engaged with second-century debates over the celebration of Easter, is cited by Eusebius as referring to the disciple who leaned against the breast of the Lord explicitly as 'John' (*Hist. Eccles.* 5.24).

By far the most explicit and controversial second-century witness to the connection between the Fourth Gospel and the Apostle John is Irenaeus, Bishop of Lyons. Irenaeus also sought to challenge the work of Marcion. A particular concern was to challenge Marcion's disparagement of Matthew, Mark and John, due to his preference for Luke. As a countering of this move, Irenaeus advocated the four-fold Gospel. There were four winds, four corners of the earth, four creatures of the Apocalypse and therefore four Gospels (*Adv.*

15. A closer look at the Papias Fragments along these lines will make it clear that neither Philip nor George (in the fourth and seventh centuries, respectively) imply anything about an early martyrdom of John, and George even emphasizes John's having returned from Patmos after the death of Domitian. It could be that John died in 44 CE, but it *cannot* be said that there is any evidence for it, or even any substantive suggestion of it, in early church history. It is not until the Modern era that such shaky inferences became foundational for 'critical' studies – but inadequately so.

16. When Eusebius' comment about Papias' intelligence is considered in its context, it becomes apparent that he is expressing frustration with his millenarian approaches to the end of the world – views that Eusebius strongly opposed. It is wrong to infer a negative judgement regarding Papias' historical sensibilities otherwise. Again, they may have been wrong, but Eusebius' pejorative statement cannot be used for such an inference, and it should be noted that Eusebius cites Papias more frequently than any other second-century historiographer – always with deference to his authority.

17. Alan Culpepper credits him with being the first orthodox writer to identify John as the author of the Fourth Gospel (2000, p. 122).

- After the destruction of Jerusalem and Palestine by the Romans (66–70 CE), apostles and disciples of Jesus were assigned to different sectors of the Christian movement, and John was assigned to Asia, where he remained until his death at Ephesus (*Hist. Eccles.* 3.1).
- During the reign of Domitian (81–96 CE), John the apostle and evangelist was sentenced to confinement on the island of Patmos, where he wrote the Apocalypse (according to Irenaeus, *Hist. Eccles.* 3.18, 21), and he returned to Ephesus after the death of Domitian.
- John remained at Ephesus until Trajan's time as a true witness of what the apostles taught; and stories developed about his pastoral care, loving concern for the flock, the challenging of heretics such as Cerinthus, and his raising of a dead man at Ephesus (*Hist. Eccles.* 3.23, 29; 4.14; 5.18).
- As the Gospels of Matthew and John were alone considered memoirs of the ministry of Jesus, John's Gospel had the benefit of the other three, complementing the others by including reports of the *early ministry of Jesus* (the events *before* John had been thrown into prison – baptizing near Aenon near Salim – Jn 3.23-24), by providing an alternative to the single-year-of-ministry presentation of the Synoptics, and by converting oral tradition into a written one. Whereas Matthew and Luke had produced human genealogies of Jesus, John produced the spiritual (pre-existent) genealogy of Jesus as the greatest of the four Gospels (*Hist. Eccles.* 3.24).
- From Polycrates, Bishop of Ephesus, John is said to be the one who leaned against the Lord's breast. He also argues that John became a sacrificing priest, a witness and a teacher, and he also refers to him as sleeping (buried) in Ephesus (*Hist. Eccles.* 3.31; 5.24).
- From Papias' five volumes (*The Sayings of the Lord Explained*), he claims to have listened to John and to have been a companion of Polycarp. Papias lists John the apostle and John the presbyter as disciples of the Lord (*Hist. Eccles.* 3.39), explaining also that this testimony addressed the fact that the two tombs in Ephesus bearing the same name belonged to different persons: John (the evangelist) and John the presbyter – the latter of which is claimed to have been his personal tutor. Papias also claims to have reproduced the teachings of both in his writings (*Hist. Eccles.* 3.39).
- According to the presbyter John, Mark, who had never heard or met Jesus, served as Peter's interpreter, writing down Peter's stories, but not in the correct order. Peter had adapted his teaching according to the needs of the church without making a systematic (or chronological?) ordering of them, so Mark was justified in preserving everything he had heard and representing it faithfully as he had received it, taking care to not leave anything out (*Hist. Eccles.* 3.39).
- Irenaeus claims personal contact with Polycarp, who claims to have had personal contact with the Apostle John and others who had seen the Lord, and Polycarp is reported to have recited their words about the Lord: his teachings and miracles, and things that had been heard from the 'eyewitnesses of the Word of Life' (*Hist. Eccles.* 5.20). Irenaeus also declares that the Johannine teachings of Polycarp were 'in complete harmony with Scripture'.
- The authority of John who leaned against the breast of the Lord is garnered by one of the leading bishops of Asia (according to Polycrates' letter to Victor and the Roman church) with reference to keeping the 14th of Nissan as the beginning of the Paschal festival (the churches of Asia Minor had begun to celebrate Easter on the 14th of Nissan regardless of the day of the week; see Jn 12.1, 12). Upon citing the Petrine logion of Acts 4.19 and 5.29, however ('We must obey God rather than men'), Victor of Rome responded by attempting to cut off all the bishops of Asia Minor (*Hist. Eccles.* 5.24).
- Origen's commentary on John is also mentioned, including his belief that John was the Beloved Disciple (*Hist. Eccles.* 6.25).

In addition to perspectives on John contributed by Eusebius, other Patristic testimony continued to play a role in later discussions. Especially Origen's commentary on John and his trip to Palestine – tracing out the steps of Jesus' ministry and identifying 'Bethabara' as the place of John's baptism (Jn 1.28) – caught on and found its way into later discussions. Augustine's treatments, of course, moved toward a spiritualization of John's content, and later discussions of John's presentation of Jesus were primarily theological, even through the Reformation. The emphases of Zwingli, Luther, Calvin and Wesley all primarily had to do with theological interpretations of John, and it was not until the rise of Jesus studies and the emergence of historical- and literary-critical methodologies that the basic historicity of John came to be questioned.

At this point, the impressive contribution of Friedrich Schleiermacher is difficult to categorize. On one hand, his contribution makes him the father of modern theology; intellectual rigour of theological analysis characterizes his work, and the Christian faith has never been the same since. Regarding his approach to Jesus, however, he believed that the Johannine perspective on the Jesus of history was superior to that of the Synoptics based upon literary analysis. He believed that the Johannine Gospel was not only written by John the apostle, but that it also conveyed a profound and intimate sentiment regarding the spiritual life of faith. In that sense, Schleiermacher casts the Jesus of history in enlightenment terms as one who came to bring revelation and God's saving love to humanity as its central hope for life. It was that sentiment that also provoked the disdainful reaction of Strauss and others, marking the turn of an era in Johannine and Jesus scholarship.

2) *Modern Challenges and Advances – From Bretschneider to Bultmann*

The historical study of Jesus did not really get going until the late eighteenth and early nineteenth centuries, but when it did, things changed on many levels.

With the rise of historical Jesus studies, precipitated by the unpublished work of Hermann Samuel Reimarus in 1778, the Gospel of John came under critical scrutiny on matters of historicity.[19] Reimarus made several compelling observations that moved the discussions further after his death. He noticed that the Gospels spiritualized the presentation of Jesus and asked whether the actual goal of Jesus may have been more akin to the first-century messianic prophets, who sought to deliver Israel from the occupation of Rome. Given this likelihood, the theological presentation of Jesus in the Gospels came into question as to whether their origins were religious or historical. Especially the miracles of Jesus and his resurrection were suspect among naturalistic approaches to historiography, and such concerns are understandable.

During the ensuing discussions, Karl Gottlieb Bretschneider[20] surmised that John's Gospel could not possibly be authentic because it appears 'concocted' in contrast to the threefold witness of the Synoptics. Citing a number of difficulties with the Johannine text and rendering of the Jesus story, Bretschneider's work was written in Latin so as to engage the academic world primarily, but it still evoked considerable reactions. One of these was that of Friedrich Schleiermacher,[21] who constructed a life of Jesus rooted primarily in his analysis of the Gospel of John. Schleiermacher observed correctly that much of the Synoptic tradition appeared to be composed of disparate units of tradition that had been brought together by editorial and compilation processes. John's pervasive unity of style and form, though, presented evidence of the integrity of the Johannine tradition, bolstering the view that John provides a superior window into understanding the purposes and activities of Jesus.

With the opposition of Schleiermacher by David Strauss, however (1835–6), the place of John within the historical-Jesus investigations was eroded considerably, and as a rationalist challenge to supernaturalistic presentations in the Gospels, the origin of John's material was ascribed to mythological origins rather than historical ones. Strauss, however, continued to assume a 3-against-1 approach to the Synoptic/John question (versus Schleiermacher's 1-against-1 approach, assuming wrongly, however, Matthean priority), and the central obsession of his later book (1865) was largely consumed with proving Schleiermacher's analysis inadequate.[22] F.C. Baur bolstered the work of Strauss (his former student) with his own contributions, and by the middle of the nineteenth century, John's ahistoricity was well on the way to being established as the 'revisionist' view among many critical biblical scholars. This view asserts that because John is different from the Synoptics, and because John is distinctively theological and spiritualized, John must be regarded as ahistorical, rendering its material irrelevant – and even misleading – for the critical investigation of the historical Jesus.

Despite many problems with the revisionist view, it continues to be assumed by many scholars despite considerable evidence to the contrary. For instance, with the eventual emergence of Markan priority, the 3-against-1 denigration of John falls flat. If Mark rendered things one way, and if Matthew and Luke followed its lead, this would confirm the basic approach of Schleiermacher over and against that of Bretschneider. Strauss also began to reverse several of his anti-Johannine judgements in the preface to his third edition, not so much as an indicator of renewed confidence in John, but as a reflection of growing doubts regarding the certainty of his earlier negative conclusions.[23] In order to account for the origin of John's material, Strauss argued that contemporary mythological parallels formed the moulds within which Johannine renderings of Jesus' teachings and ministry were cast.

The work of F.C. Baur (1847) located John in the late middle second century (around 170 CE), and this required a fuller development of a History-of-Religions approach to explaining the origins of gospel material if it were not connected to an eyewitness or an independent tradition. In addition, the projection of the Prologue's Logos theology over the rest of the Johannine

---

19. Extended discussions of the history of historical Jesus quests may be found elsewhere (Borg, 1994; Powell, 1998; Anderson, 2000a).

20. In this book, Bretschneider (1820) questions several features of John as being inauthentic: namely, the three Synoptics against the singular John, John's elevated and theological presentation of Jesus, the non-Jewish character of John's Christology, purported errors in the Johannine text, and challenges to the traditional view.

21. According to Jack C. Verheyden (Schleiermacher, 1975), 'In a way, Schleiermacher agreed with Bretschneider's point that the critic must choose between the Synoptics and John, but Schleiermacher chose the latter rather than the former' (p. xxxii).

22. In this book-length critique of Schleiermacher, Strauss puts the matter polemically: 'But in criticism of the Fourth Gospel, Bretschneider is the strong man of science, and Schleiermacher the man of frail religious-aesthetic partiality.' (1977, p. 41) As evidence, Strauss cites Schleiermacher's tendencies to speak of John's representing first-hand information in contrast to the Synoptics' representing second-hand and disparate material as superficial and uncritical. In several ways, however, Strauss does not appear to have understood Schleiermacher's treatment of John fully; he is unable to separate the faith claims of the Fourth Evangelist and Schleiermacher's theological interests from John's text-critical realities and Schleiermacher's exegetical observations. On that matter in particular, especially given the dialectical character of the Fourth Evangelist's thought, Schleiermacher's observation is *closer* to the 'science' of epistemological inquiry and literary criticism than Strauss recognizes.

23. Interestingly, in the preface to the third edition of his *Life of Jesus* (1972, p. lvii), Strauss confesses that he has become more doubtful of his doubts regarding John's historicity, and in that sense, his change of thought tracks entirely with the critical thrust of the present study (see below, Part II). It is precisely the critical evaluation of the doubts themselves that raises doubts about the de-historicization of John as a direct factor of critical inquiry. Strauss goes on to credit his earlier polemical zeal (and blindness) as a factor in his earlier countering of John's 'adverse and unfavorable side', while the other side of John has had a chance to grow on him. He later went back to some of his more critical views regarding John, however, due in part to the influence of his former teacher, F.C. Baur.

I. Modern Foundations

narrative evoked the extensive inference of mythological origins of John's distinctive material rather than having an origin in anything historical. Further elaborations upon the Hellenistic origins of Johannine theology, combined with naturalistic aversions to the wondrous, played major roles in removing John from the canons of historical narrative. Wellhausen, Schwarz and others,[24] however, attempted to locate the origins of the Johannine tradition as rooting either in earlier sources or more primitive layers, allowing a later finalization to have been built upon earlier material. It is these works, as well as those of Spitta and Wendt,[25] that Bultmann later employed in constructing his monumental source-critical synthesis. With the epoch-changing effect of Albert Schweitzer's *Quest for the Historical Jesus*, however, a new set of issues emerged.[26]

Schweitzer's application of critical analysis to critical investigations of Jesus' life exposed the subjectivity of so-called 'objective' historical studies. His work demonstrated, as none had hitherto done, how closely scholars' outcomes were to their personal investments. This caused a great deal of questioning as to whether we could *ever* know what the historical Jesus might actually have said or done. This being the case, the forward strides made during the first half of the twentieth century explored the history of traditional material, and headway was made in two particular directions as far as Johannine studies are concerned.

The watershed event in post-Schweitzer Johannine research involved the commentary of Rudolf Bultmann (1971). Published in German in 1941, this impressive work promised to explain the historical origin of the Johannine Gospel's material, while at the same time explaining the epistemological origins of its theological tensions.[27] Building on the works of scholars who had preceded him, and engaging the spectrum of available primary extra-canonical literature (especially emerging Gnostic literature), Bultmann's genius lay in his remarkable ability to combine theological perceptivity with linguistic deftness. Not only did he infer at least four other major sources underlying and overlaying the contribution of the Fourth Evangelist, he also inferred distinctive history-of-religions origins of each and claimed to be able to distinguish them on the basis of stylistic, contextual and theological evidence. As well as

---

24. Julius Wellhausen not only championed a documentary approach to the Pentateuch; he also laid out a documentary approach to the Gospel of John (1907). Eduard Schwartz also developed an intricate approach to John's *aporias*' (perplexities), laying out his analyses in four major critical essays published from 1907-08.

25. Friedrich Spitta actually believed that the identification of sources underlying John could provide historical information about Jesus (1910), as did Hans Heinrich Wendt (1902). It was their contributions among others upon which Bultmann constructed his impressive source-critical synthesis.

26. See now John Bowden's new complete translation, published in 2001.

27. An extensive treatment of the literary, historical and theological aspects of Bultmann's approach to John is developed elsewhere (Anderson 1996, pp. 33-169).

---

accounting for the origins of John's material as rooted in Hellenistic and Jewish mythic narratives and discourses, Bultmann also showed how John's major Christological and theological tensions originated from a set of literary dialogues between three sources, the evangelist and the redactor.

With the adumbration of Bultmann's approach for English-speaking audiences by D. Moody Smith in 1965 and its translation into English by George R. Beasley-Murray and others in 1971,[28] Bultmann's work began to command an international hold on Johannine scholarship.[29] In essence, most developments in Johannine studies over the second half of the twentieth century were formed in response to (both positively and negatively) his epoch-making commentary. Within that period, source theories came and went, traditionalist advocates targeted Bultmann as the adversary, composition and situation history theories abounded, and new literary studies emerged.

Regarding Jesus studies over this same period of time, Bultmann had also made his mark. Assuming that nothing could be known about the historical Jesus, following Schweitzer, Bultmann developed an extensive analysis of the Synoptic tradition (1963a) in which he outlined a history-of-religions and a form-critical analysis of the Synoptics. Of course, Bultmann argued that because history-as-such had little bearing on saving faith, the only hope for humanity was to respond in faith to the proclaimed Word. Therefore, he was willing to ascribe the bulk of gospel narrative to contemporary mythological origins, seeking instead to preserve the existential core of Jesus' teachings and the theological commitments of the evangelists. A reaction against Bultmann's de-historicizing platform, however, was championed by his former student, Ernst Käsemann. In his 1953 lecture, calling for a fresh investigation into the life and teachings of Jesus, Käsemann argued that something of the ministry of Jesus could be distinguished from gospel traditions, especially if it sounded significantly different. Another Bultmannian scholar, Günther Bornkamm (1960), argued that even if the Gospels gave us something like a religious understanding of the historical Jesus, this was still worthy material on which to build a historical appraisal of Jesus of Nazareth. With the reporting of these fresh calls for a renewed historical investigation into the life and ministry of

---

28. An excellent service provided by Smith (1965) was to outline the sorts of materials comprising each of Bultmann's five different sources, explaining also the reasons Bultmann made the sorts of source-, rearrangement- and redaction-critical moves that he did. Smith's work deserves credit for Bultmann's work becoming accessible to English-speaking scholarship, even before it was translated into English.

29. See Bultmann 1971. Says Ernst Haenchen (Vol. 1, 1984, p. 34):

...like a mighty tree, it appeared not to permit anything strong and important to prosper in its shadow. This effect did not set in immediately, but once it began, it became clear that Bultmann's commentary on the Gospel of John decisively dominated an entire generation.

With the evidentiary failure of Bultmann's platform, though (Anderson, 1996, pp. 33-169), bringing back into play some of the leading critical works Bultmann's monograph displaced seems an important venture to consider.

Jesus, James Robinson inaugurated officially 'the New Quest' for the historical Jesus (1959).

While the renewed quest for the historical Jesus did not set out to marginalize the Gospel of John, it did result as a factor of the desire to begin with that which was most certain and proceed to that which was less, the Synoptics. In addition to Markan studies, Q studies also emerged as an academic discipline, and this led to the yoking of the Gospel of Thomas with Jesus sayings. Building upon the view that a hypothetical Q source may have been gathered as early as two decades after the ministry of Jesus, some scholars came to view Thomas as a later form of the material underlying primitive Q, thereby suggesting at least its partial primitivity. This claim for Thomas has especially been argued by the Claremont School, and the voting of participants in the Jesus Seminar has shown a pattern that endorses a higher valuing of the Gospel of Thomas than the canonical Gospel of John. What this has meant is that the Gospel of John, for all practical purposes, has been considered off-limits for any who are doing serious Jesus studies, and the impasse has been nearly a complete one.

The pinnacle expression of this modernistic tendency is displayed in the two volumes on the words and works of Jesus resulting from the investigations of the Jesus Seminar.[30] Between these two volumes, the only saying attributed plausibly to Jesus in John is the reference to the prophet not receiving honour in his homeland (Jn 4.44), and the only actions receiving the status of plausible or probable confidence are the inferences that Jesus was a follower of John the Baptist (and that his disciples had also been John's followers, Jn 1.35-42), that Jewish leaders accused Jesus of being uneducated (Jn 7.15), that Annas was the father-in-law of Caiaphas (Jn 18.13), from whose home Jesus was taken to the Governor's residence (Jn 18.28), and that Jesus was beaten and turned over by Pilate to be crucified (Jn 19.1, 16, 18).[31] It must be acknowledged, however, that archaeological research has not been noted as a primary factor in such studies, and one wonders what a more comprehensive historical investigation of John might produce. Given the empirical proclivity of the modern mind, this is an astonishing feature of this particular venture, claiming to use the tools of modern historians in arriving at its judgements. It seems as though the fact of Jesus' elevated presentation in John has displaced the scholarly regard for any of John's other historical material (such as archaeological and topographical detail), even when it might be superior to the presentations of Jesus in the Synoptics. As a culminating expression of the New Quest, it should be questioned whether the results of the Jesus Seminar give us a portraiture of the 'historical' Jesus or the '*modernistic*' Jesus. At the dawn of the post-Modern era, the two may be considered very different realities.[32]

Over the last three decades or so, interdisciplinary studies – especially from the social sciences – have also been applied to Jesus quests, and Tom Wright has appropriately called this trend 'the third quest' for the historical Jesus. Within this venture, modernistic categories of thought are supplanted by the endeavour to appreciate how people would have perceived things in the first-century Mediterranean world. Sociology, religious anthropology, psychology and newer literary-critical methodologies have been applied to the classic issues seeking to understand what sort of narratives the Gospel traditions represent and how they might be read more profitably in the interest of casting fresh light on Jesus and his ministry. Seeing Jesus as a transformer of Judaism (*not* advocating a radical break with it), challenging purity laws in the name of divine love, considering the political and economic aspects of Jesus' prophetic work, and fitting Jesus with emerging constructs of first-century charismatic leaders are all examples of the benefits of these sorts of studies.[33] For Johannine studies, a new wave of incisive literary-critical approaches to the text has given new life to many aspects of reading the Fourth Gospel, and in combination with emerging theories of the Johannine situation, rhetorical devices in John are sometimes effectively combined with inferences as to the intended audiences. While some details in the Johannine narrative indeed served the rhetorical interests of the evangelist, ascribing *all* of them to that origin – including all of John's archaeological content – moves beyond the evidence. Therefore, even within the third quest for the historical Jesus, as with the earlier ones, John's historical-type material remains a problem deserving to be addressed.

3) *Critiques of Modern Hypotheses – From Neander to Blomberg*

While Schleiermacher mounted a rigorous opposition to Bretschneider, his work was not published until 1864, after his death. Other critiques of Bretschneider, however, caused him to soften his critical claims against John,

---

30. See the works edited by Funk and others (1993, 1998), as well as his own monograph (1996) on the subject, for an excellent overview of their findings. See also Marcus Borg's survey of leading models for interpreting the historical Jesus (1994).

31. An excellent clarification is made by Marcus Borg in his *QRT* response to the question of whether 18% of Jesus' sayings within the Gospels does justice to their historicity. According to Borg, at least 18% of them being authentic is very different from 'only' 18% being authentic, and he affirms the former is the way he and most members of the Jesus Seminar understand their work (2002, pp. 23-4).

32. This question emerges helpfully from the dialogue with Marcus Borg in the 2002 issue of *QRT* (Borg, 2002; Anderson, 2002b). If the criteria for determining historicity are particularly modernistic, and if the work is constructed on the modernistic platforms of Strauss, Baur, Bultmann and Perrin (rather than employing, say, first-century Mediterranean criteria for determining historicity, or other methodologies, including Cognitive-Critical methodologies and socio-religious analyses), the 'historicity' analyses must be contextualized rather than absolutized. The quest for the 'historical Jesus' may indeed differ from the quest for the 'modern Jesus'.

33. See especially the 1980 monograph by John Riches on the ways Jesus sought to transform Judaism toward its better expressions, rather than supplant it.

presented in John. Not only did Dodd identify many non-identical parallels between John's and the Synoptics' renderings of events, but he argued for an inference of independence as an individuated perspective on the ministry of Jesus. The work of John A.T. Robinson (1985) argued for the priority of John (rather than its posteriority), and the works of Morris (1969, 1995), Carson (1991) and Blomberg (2002) pose vigorous defences of John's historicity and apostolic authority. As with the other categories, these studies are only suggestive of a much larger current of investigative inquiry.

4) *The Autonomy and Development of the Johannine Tradition – From Gardner-Smith to Smith*

As a factor of seeking to infer the character, origin and development of the Johannine tradition with less of an apologetic interest for or against modernist or traditionalist perspectives, a significant thrust of twentieth century Johannine studies has explored the Johannine tradition as an autonomous development whether or not anything can be known in particular about its authorship. Within this venue, the highly significant work by P. Gardner-Smith (1938) demonstrates John's pervasive independence from the Synoptic gospels. This short book demonstrates with impressive clarity that at every turn, where John overlaps with the Synoptics, John also departs from the Synoptics. Unless one is prepared to adopt a view of pervasive contrariness, John must be considered largely independent from the Synoptic traditions.[34] Upon this approach many other analyses of John's tradition were developed, although the works of a significant number of scholars (notably Barrett, Neirynck, Brodie and others) argued for some form of Johannine dependence upon Mark.

During the second half of the twentieth century, however, major commentaries and studies affirmed the autonomy of the Johannine tradition. Typical of the tendency to forfeit the discussion on authorship for the sake of establishing positive headway on the question of the character of the Johannine tradition, Raymond Brown declared his move away from an earlier assertion of the Fourth Evangelist being the son of Zebedee in favour of his being an anonymous eyewitness, who was a Christian leader, but not a member of the Twelve (1979, 2003). Brown thus inferred the Johannine tradition as having had an apostolic source, but not necessarily one that would have come from the inner ring of the apostles. This would have thus allowed for the independent character of John's tradition, as it developed within its own Palestinian and Asia Minor trajectories. Robert Kysar crowned this inference with the lucid description: *John, the Maverick Gospel* (1993).

C.K. Barrett (1978) and Barnabas Lindars (1972) had also speculated that the Johannine evangelist could indeed have been an independent eyewitness

---

34. This is also D. Moody Smith's conclusion after examining the issue critically for a period spanning four decades, articulated clearly in the addendum to the second edition of his *John Among the Gospels* (2001): 'John, an Independent Gospel', pp. 195–241.

---

although the impact of Strauss, Baur and others became something of the established critical view. Nevertheless, a multiplicity of attacks was raised against the critical view of John's historicity, only allowing the briefest of mention here. In 1837, Johann August Wilhelm Neander challenged Strauss, armed with de Wette's contribution and much of Schleiermacher's work (Kealy 2002, pp. 399–400). His arguments favoured the historicity of John's accounts of the life of Christ, including an early Temple cleansing and a pre-Passover last supper. He argued that John's presentation of Jesus as the Christ casts light upon his ministry from the perspective of eternity. Assaults upon and defences of the critical approach to John continued for the remainder of the nineteenth century.

Several decades later, in Britain a set of vigorous counter-assaults upon the modernist attacks on John's authorship and historicity was launched by three scholars of note: Westcott, Lightfoot and Hort. Their work largely carried the day among many British scholars for the first half of the twentieth century, and they argued for the historicity of John on the basis of textual characteristics and apostolic authorship. In particular, Westcott (1908) worked his way toward Johannine authorship concentrically, from the least unlikely toward the centre of his thesis. By his mounting of internal and external evidence, the Johannine evangelist deserves to be regarded as: a) a Jew, b) of Palestine, c) who was an eyewitness and member of the Twelve, and finally, d) John the apostle. Preceding the commentary of R.H. Lightfoot (1956), a collection of essays by Joseph Barber Lightfoot (1893, pp. 1–198) posed a considerable challenge to the de-historicization of John in arguing for the 'authenticity and genuineness of John's Gospel' on the basis of internal and external evidence. His authority as a Patristic scholar carried over into his investigation of New-Testament historicity, and this work became formative for other treatments of the subject, as well.

During the early twentieth century, several defences of John's apostolic authorship and historicity were produced (Askwith 1910, Headlam 1948, Higgins 1960, Mussner 1966, J.A. Robinson 1908, P.V. Smith 1926), to the extent that Archbishop William Temple was able to declare at the beginning of his commentary on John that any scholar whose work on John did not begin with an apostolic premise stood 'self-condemned' from the start (1939). Other challenges to the Modern critical view of John performed analyses of critical scholarship (especially in Europe), and the literature reviews of Sanday (1872) and Howard (1931) fulfil this role. From the critical side, the literature review of Bacon (1918) takes its place with an apologetic thrust of its own.

Within this set of discussions, internal and external bases of evidence were amassed, and the most extensive of these was C. H. Dodd's 1963 monograph: *Historical Tradition in the Fourth Gospel*. In its own epoch-making way, Dodd's two-volume contribution to Johannine studies (1953, 1963) first assessed the sociological and religious background of John, and then analysed the character historical tradition in the Fourth Gospel by focusing first on the Passion narrative, and moving from there to the works and words of Jesus as without having been John the son of Zebedee, and Rudolf Schnackenburg moved to an agnostic stance on the question of authorship between his earlier and later work, as well.[35] What can be seen in the major critical commentaries of the second half of the twentieth century is a move toward affirming the historicity of the Johannine tradition as a factor of its own developmental history. Characteristic of these approaches is the inference of early oral tradition, produced in written forms, crafted into an earlier edition, followed by further preaching and the finalization of the Johannine Gospel. Building also on the insights of J. Louis Martyn (2003), that history and theology deserve to be considered in evaluating the Johannine narrative, greater emphasis has been placed on the history of traditional development than on the historical character of that tradition, itself. The problem is that not all of John's narrative can be explained as a factor of developing context, so at least some affirmation of traditional historicity is made along the way. For this reason, the authoritative work of D. Moody Smith (2001) on John's independent relation to the Synoptics still carries the day. John's tradition is autonomous, representing an individuated perspective on the ministry of Jesus – *whoever* the author might have been.

Given the explosive character of historical-critical impasses, some scholars have employed new literary-critical methodologies while leaving open the historical-critical issues – moving more toward narrative criticism and reader-response analysis. Having investigated the Johannine 'school' in his earlier work, Alan Culpepper wrote an epoch-changing book considering the Gospel of John simply as a literary work with a plot, characters, dialogues and other features designed to engage the reader with the subject and progression of the text. *The Anatomy of the Fourth Gospel* applied the latest literary tools of analysis to the Johannine text, allowing the reader to derive excellent inferences as to the meaning of the text regardless of the historical character of the material – or the lack thereof. Jeff Staley pioneered work on John from the perspective of reader-response analysis, and he fully engaged the reader as a direct partner in the making of meaning. In addition to these studies, the last decade of the twentieth century and beyond has seen an avalanche of studies exploring such subjects as characterization, new historicism, irony and rhetorical analysis.

The great advantage of the new literary paradigms for interpreting John is that serious and profitable critical analysis of the text can be conducted regardless of one's levels of certainty regarding authorship, differences with the Synoptics, composition and historicity. Of course, the Jesus of history plays no direct role in such analyses, as the narrative is treated as would be any fictive

---

35. Brown calls attention to his having moved to this position independently-yet-concurrently with Schnackenburg in his introduction to *The Community of the Beloved Disciple* (1979), and yet he seems to overstate Schackenburg's movement. Less than certain, however, is different from being of the opinion that such an identification was mistaken or disproven.

literary composition. The problem is that the Johannine narrative has many literary features (let alone, its own direct claims) that call for some sort of historical analysis. Whether challenging the traditional view with the marshalled weight of scientific authority, or sidestepping historicity issues altogether, this is at least some of the story of the de-historicization of John, resulting in the de-Johannification of Jesus.

---

36. See the engagement by five scholars in the inaugural issue of *Review of Biblical Literature* 1, 1999, pp. 39–72); see also Anderson, Ellens and Fowler (2004).
37. Fuller treatments can be found regarding a) the history of the Johannine situation (1991, 1996, 1997), b) the agency schema (1999a), c) cognitive-critical analyses (2004b), d) rhetorical analysis (2000b) and e) Johannine-Markan relations (2001).

2

Papias and Polycrates on the Origin of the Gospel of John

Hypotheses of Authorship

The external evidence for the origin of the Fourth Gospel has been reviewed so often[1] that it might be thought there could be no new conclusions to be drawn from it. In recent Johannine studies it has tended to be treated as irrelevant. But Martin Hengel's book, *The Johannine Question*,[2] uses a fairly traditional assessment of the external evidence to support a relatively novel solution to "the

---

Originally published in a slightly different form in *Journal of Theological Studies* 44 (1993): 24-69. Reprinted by permission of the publisher.

1. E.g., J. B. Lightfoot, *Biblical Essays* (London: Macmillan, 1983), 47–122; V. H. Stanton, *The Gospels as Historical Documents*, part 1 (Cambridge: Cambridge University Press, 1903); B. W. Bacon, *The Fourth Gospel in Research and Debate* (London/Leipzig: T. Fisher Unwin, 1910), 73–154; A. E. Garvie, *The Beloved Disciple* (London: Hodder & Stoughton, 1922), 204–21; C. F. Nolloth, *The Fourth Evangelist* (London: J. Murray, 1925), 37–71; J. E. Carpenter, *The Johannine Writings* (London: Constable, 1927), 208–17; H. P. V. Nunn, *The Authorship of the Fourth Gospel* (Eton: Alden and Blackwell, 1952); F-M. Braun, *Jean le Théologien et son évangile dans l'église ancienne* (Paris: Gabalda, 1959), 299–392; R. E. Brown, *The Gospel according to John (I–XII)*, AB 29 (Garden City, NY: Doubleday, 1966), lxxxviii–xcii; R. Schnackenburg, *The Gospel according to St. John*, trans. K. Smith (London: Burns & Oates/New York: Herder and Herder, 1968), 1:77–91.

2. M. Hengel, *The Johannine Question*, trans. J. Bowden (London: SCM, 1989).

"Johannine question." It is the argument of this chapter that a fresh look at the most important external evidence can show that it supports Hengel's case much more strongly than he realizes.

In essence, Hengel's solution to "the Johannine question" is that John the Elder, to whom Papias refers in the famous fragment of his prologue (ap. Eusebius, *Hist. eccl.* 3.39.4), was both the beloved disciple and the author of the Fourth Gospel (as well as of the Johannine letters).[3] This simple statement of Hengel's position requires two qualifications. First, with regard to the authorship of the Gospel, he regards it as substantially the work of John the Elder, but allows that the form of the Gospel that we have (the only form that was ever "published") is the result of a redaction by members of the Johannine school after John the Elder's death. The editors added at least the closing verses; Hengel leaves open the extent to which their editorial activity may have affected the rest of the Gospel.[4] Second, with regard to the identification of the beloved disciple, Hengel thinks that the portrayal of the disciple in the Gospel is to some extent deliberately enigmatic and may be intended to hint at two possible identifications: John the Elder and John the son of Zebedee.[5] I have argued elsewhere[6] that in this respect Hengel has unnecessarily complicated and compromised his proposal by retaining a relic of the traditional identification of the beloved disciple with John the son of Zebedee. The alleged hints of this identification within the Gospel are illusory. In the present chapter we shall proceed on the basis of the view that the Gospel portrays the beloved disciple not as one of the Twelve, but as a Jerusalem disciple of Jesus. This view is accepted by many of those recent scholars who hold that the beloved disciple is portrayed in the Gospel as a historical individual, not as a purely ideal figure.

The threefold identification of the beloved disciple, the author of the Gospel, and John the Elder, has several major advantages: (1) It accepts the only plausible meaning of John 21:24: that it designates the beloved disciple as the author of the Gospel.[7] An author may, of course, employ a secretary, and an author's work may be edited by others, but he is substantially responsible for the content of the work. This verse designates the beloved disciple the author of the Gospel, not merely the source or guarantor of the tradition behind it. I have argued elsewhere that the references to the beloved disciple within the Gospel also portray him precisely as the author.[8] (2) This proposal accepts that the Gospel itself does not support the identification of the beloved disciple with John the son of Zebedee. (3) It avoids the supposition that the name of one of the greatest teachers of the early church, author of one of its finest literary products, has inexplicably disappeared without any trace in the historical evidence. (4) It takes account of the fact that there is no evidence that the Gospel was ever regarded as anonymous (unlike the case of Hebrews), and that all the evidence for its attribution ascribes it to "John" (though not always unambiguously to John the son of Zebedee).[9] (5) It can explain the attribution to John the son of Zebedee, which eventually prevailed in the early church, as the result of an assimilation of John the Elder, a disciple of Jesus who was not one of the Twelve, to the better known and more prestigious Apostle John the son of Zebedee.

It is surprising to find that, although John the Elder has in the past enjoyed a certain popularity in Johannine scholarship as a candidate for the authorship of the Gospel, the threefold identification of John the Elder with the author of the Gospel *and* with the beloved disciple has only rarely been proposed before Hengel. Hengel himself refers to no precedents for it,[10] and I know of only three: the arguments of H. Delff[11] (though he distinguished the beloved disciple's work from extensive later interpolations), C. F. Burney[12] (whose case was only very briefly argued), and J. Colson.[13] In the period when authorship of the Gospel by John the Elder was quite often canvassed, the possibility that he could also be the beloved disciple was rarely raised even though it was usually rightly recognized that, according to Papias, he had been a personal disciple of Jesus. This seems to have been because of the continuing strength of the view that the evidence of the Gospel itself indicates the identification of the beloved disciple with John the son of Zebedee. In English scholarship at least, this view was very widely accepted well into this century as a result of Westcott's famous case for it.[14] B. H. Streeter, who in England especially espoused the cause of John the Elder's authorship of the Gospel, also regarded the identification of the beloved disciple with John the

---

3. The common authorship of the Gospel and the letters is important to Hengel's overall case, but in this chapter we shall focus almost exclusively on the Gospel.
4. Hengel, *Johannine Question*, 84, 94–96, 99–100, and esp. 105–8.
5. Ibid, 127–32.
6. R. Bauckham, "The Beloved Disciple as Ideal Author," *JSNT* 49 (1993): 21–44, reprinted as chapter 3 of the present volume.
7. The meaning of γράψας, though it can easily accommodate an author's use of a secretary, cannot be so extended as to make the beloved disciple less than the author. G. Schrenk, "γράφω," *TDNT* 1:743, offers no evidence at all for such a usage, while F. R. M. Hitchcock, "The Use of γράφειν," *JTS* 31 (1930): 271–75, shows that the kind of evidence that is sometimes alleged does not meet the need.
8. Bauckham, "Beloved Disciple."
9. The only exception is Gaius's polemical attribution of the Gospel to John's traditional enemy Cerinthus, an attribution obviously parasitic on the attribution to John.
10. Hengel, *Johannine Question*, 200 n. 45, refers to Delff's work, but not as a precedent for the threefold identification.
11. H. K. H. Delff, *Die Geschichte des Rabbi Jesus von Nazareth* (Leipzig: W. Friedrich, 1889); idem, *Das vierte Evangelium: Ein authentischer Bericht über Jesus von Nazareth* (Husum: C. F. Delff, 1890). Delff was followed rather tentatively by W. Sanday, *The Criticism of the Fourth Gospel* (Oxford: Clarendon, 1905), 17–18, 98–99; F. C. Burkitt, *The Gospel History and Its Transmission* (Edinburgh: T. & T. Clark, 1911), 247–55.
12. C. F. Burney, *The Aramaic Origin of the Fourth Gospel* (Oxford: Clarendon, 1922), 133–49.
13. J. Colson, *L'énigme du disciple que Jésus aimait*, Théologie Historique 10 (Paris: Beauchesne, 1969). Cf. now also M.-L. Rigato, "L' apostolo ed evangelista Giovanni,' sacerdoto' levitico," *Rivista Biblica* 38 (1990): 451–83.
14. B. F. Westcott, *The Gospel according to St. John* (London: J. Murray, 1881), v–xxiv; cf. J. B. Lightfoot, *Biblical Essays* (London: Macmillan, 1893), 41–42.

son of Zebedee as virtually self-evident, and so was obliged to postulate some historical connection between the two Johns and to resort to supposing that in 21:20–23 the author of the Gospel, John the Elder, refers both to himself and to the son of Zebedee.[15] But the real strength of the case for attributing the Gospel to John the Elder could not be appreciated when the beloved disciple was still supposed to be John the son of Zebedee.

More recently, a number of scholars have recognized that the Gospel does not portray the beloved disciple as one of the Twelve, who accompanied Jesus throughout the ministry, but as a Jerusalem disciple.[16] In the meantime, however, the idea of associating the Gospel with John the Elder had fallen out of favor. Whoever the beloved disciple might have been and whoever might have written the Gospel, there seemed no good reason for identifying either or both with the shadowy figure of John the Elder,[17] known only from one reference to him by Papias.[18] Moreover, since the external evidence has usually been thought to offer no identification of the beloved disciple or of the author of the Gospel other than John the son of Zebedee, recent scholars who correctly think the internal evidence tells decisively against his being either have tended to treat the external evidence as wholly unreliable and therefore irrelevant.[19] There have been some challenges to the view that the external evidence points unanimously to John the son of Zebedee as the beloved disciple and the author,[20] but these have not succeeded in disturbing the generally accepted account of the external evidence, which almost all recent Johannine scholarship has presupposed. It is time that the external evidence was reexamined, to see whether after all it may not so completely contradict the internal evidence. In this chapter, we shall argue that the best external evidence in fact supports the internal evidence in seeing the beloved disciple, the author of the Gospel, as a disciple of Jesus who was not one of the Twelve. This coincidence with the best reading of the internal evidence strongly suggests that the external evidence is also reliable when it calls this disciple John, indicating a John of Ephesus who must be not the son of Zebedee, but Papias's John the Elder.

The only church, so far as we know, that ever claimed to be the place of origin of the Fourth Gospel was Ephesus. This means that if the external evidence is of any value, the most reliable is likely to be that of writers who can witness to the local tradition of Ephesus and its neighborhood in the second century. Such writers are Papias of Hierapolis and Polycrates of Ephesus. We shall begin with Polycrates, since what he said on this subject is extant, whereas whether Papias said anything on the subject is disputed and what he said will have to be reconstructed from other authors who used his work. In the light of a fresh interpretation of Polycrates and Papias, the rest of the external evidence will fall into a different pattern from the way it has usually been represented.

The Letter of Polycrates

The tradition of the church of Ephesus as to the authorship of the Gospel is preserved for us by Polycrates, bishop of Ephesus, in a letter written in the last decade of the second century to Victor of Rome during the paschal controversy. The purpose of the letter is to defend the quartodeciman observance of Asia as supported by the highest authority in local tradition:

As for us, then, we keep the day without tampering with it, neither adding, nor subtracting. For indeed in Asia great luminaries have fallen asleep, such as shall rise again on the day of the Lord's appearing, when he comes with glory from heaven to seek out all his saints: to wit, Philip, one of the twelve apostles, who has fallen asleep in Hierapolis, [as have] also his two daughters who grew old in virginity, and his other daughter who lived in the Holy Spirit and rests at Ephesus; and, moreover, [there is] John too, he who leant back on the Lord's breast, who was a priest, wearing the sacerdotal plate (τὸ πέταλον πεφορεκώς), both martyr (μάρτυς) and teacher. He has fallen asleep at Ephesus. Moreover, Polycarp too, at Smyrna, both bishop and martyr; and Thraseas, both bishop and martyr, of Eumenia, who has fallen asleep at Smyrna. And why need I mention Sagaris, both bishop and martyr, who has fallen asleep at Laodicea? or the blessed Papirius, or Melito the eunuch who in all things lived in the Holy Spirit, who lies at Sardis, awaiting the visitation from heaven when he shall rise from the dead? These all observed the fourteenth day for the Pascha according to the Gospel, in no way deviating therefrom, but following the rule of faith. And moreover I also, Polycrates, the least of you all, [do] according to the tradition of my kinsmen, some of whom also I have followed closely (παρηκολούθησα). Seven of my kinsmen were bishops, and I am the eighth. And my kinsmen always kept the day when the people put away the leaven. Therefore I

---

15. B. H. Streeter, *The Four Gospels* (London: Macmillan, 1924), 430–81; cf. idem, *The Primitive Church* (London: Macmillan, 1929), 89–97. A similar position was taken by A. Harnack, *Die Chronologie der altchristlichen Litteratur bis Eusebius* (Leipzig: J. C. Hinrichs, 1897), 1:659–80.

16. J. N. Sanders, *The Fourth Gospel in the Early Church* (Cambridge: Cambridge University Press, 1943), 43–45; O. Cullmann, *The Johannine Circle*, trans. J. Bowden (London: SCM, 1976), 63–85; R. E. Brown, *The Community of the Beloved Disciple* (London: G. Chapman, 1979), 31–34 (a change of view from that in idem, *Gospel according to John*, XCII–XCVII); G. R. Beasley-Murray, *John*, Word Biblical Commentary 36 (Waco: Word Books, 1987), lxx–lxxv. These hold that the beloved disciple must remain anonymous. For older arguments to this effect, see Burkitt, *Gospel History*, 247–50; Garvie, *The Beloved Disciple*, 202–4. Others who see the beloved disciple as a Jerusalem disciple have identified him with Lazarus or John Mark: see the references and discussion in Cullmann, *Johannine Circle*, 76–77; S. S. Smalley, *John: Evangelist and Interpreter* (Exeter: Paternoster, 1978), 77–78.

17. Of course, the view that in Papias's prologue John the Elder is a distinct person from John the son of Zebedee has been challenged, notably by J. Chapman, *John the Presbyter and the Fourth Gospel* (Oxford: Clarendon, 1911); G. M. Lee, "The Presbyter John: A Reconsideration," in *Studia Evangelica*, ed. E. A. Livingstone, TU 112 (Berlin: Akademie-Verlag, 1973), 311–20. But it remains the most plausible interpretation of Papias and is accepted by the vast majority of scholars.

18. Cf. Cullmann, *Johannine Circle*, 70.

19. E.g., Brown, *Community*, 33–34, abandoning the view that the beloved disciple is John the son of Zebedee, says, "I now recognize that the external and internal evidence are probably not to be 'harmonized.'"

20. E.g., Burney, *Aramaic Origin*, 134–40.

for my part, brethren, who number sixty-five years in the Lord and have conversed with the brethren from all parts of the world and traversed the entire range of holy Scripture, am not affrighted by threats. (ap. Eusebius, *Hist. eccl.* 5.24.2–7)[21]

Discussions of this passage have usually failed to appreciate its careful artistry. Polycrates adduces *seven* great luminaries of Asia who practiced the quartodeciman observance. As the number of completeness, seven indicates the sufficiency of their evidence.[22] When Polycrates subsequently refers to his seven relatives, who were bishops and to some of whom he had been a disciple (παρηκολούθησα), he is not adducing a second, unnecessary set of witnesses, but claiming the seven great luminaries themselves as his relatives. In the interests of modesty, he does not claim them as his relatives until he has first named them all and then introduced himself, "the least of you all,"[23] as a supernumerary eighth, whose witness is therefore strictly superfluous. In this way he is able to add his own testimony to that of his illustrious relatives in a suitably modest way. Clearly he regards all seven luminaries as bishops, but uses the word in the list only of those to whom he can attach the phrase ἐπίσκοπος καὶ μάρτυς (Polycarp, Thraseas, Sagaris).

Polycrates' claim to some kind of family relationship with all seven luminaries is not in the least improbable. It is surely significant that, whereas the two daughters of Philip who died at Hierapolis are said to have grown old as virgins, this is not said of the third daughter who died at Ephesus and whom we should presume was therefore an ancestor of Polycrates. It may well be that Polycrates' catalog of his illustrious episcopal relatives was not compiled especially for this occasion, but was one he had proudly rehearsed before. The deliberate limitation of the list to his own relatives, as well as to the number seven, explains the omission of other Asian notables who could presumably have been cited in support of the quartodeciman observance, such as Aristion the disciple of the Lord or Onesimus of Ephesus or Papias of Hierapolis.

Polycrates' reference to Philip is of interest before we turn to John. The Philip in question is certainly Philip the evangelist, whose four virgin daughters prophesied, according to Acts 21:8–9.[24] At least two of the daughters had been known to Papias of Hierapolis (Eusebius, *Hist. eccl.* 3.39.9). Polycrates is clearly dependent on local tradition about the daughters rather than on Acts 21:8–9, in contrast with the Montanist writer Proclus who knew the tradition associating Philip and his daughters with Hierapolis (and therefore no doubt cited them as part of a Phrygian succession of prophets preceding the Montanist prophets) but refers to four daughters, all prophets, as in Acts 21:8–9 (ap. Eusebius, *Hist. eccl.* 3.31.4). But by calling Philip one of the twelve apostles, Polycrates appears to have confused the two Philips, the apostle and the evangelist. Probably it would be more accurate to say that he identified Philip the apostle and Philip the evangelist as the same person.[25] Early Christian exegetes of New Testament writings, following the similar practice in Jewish exegesis of the Old Testament, frequently assumed that scriptural characters bearing the same names were the same person. The identification of the two Philips by Polycrates, no doubt following an exegetical tradition of the church of Ephesus, is very similar to the way Mary Magdalene and Mary of Bethany were treated as the same person by most Christian writers later than the canonical Gospels. Thus, in his reference to Philip, Polycrates follows a tradition that draws both on local memory of the evangelist and his daughters at Hierapolis and Ephesus and also on an exegetical identification of this Philip with the Philip who was one of the Twelve. We shall see that his reference to John displays the same combination of local historical tradition and local exegetical tradition.

The reference to John is as follows: ἔτι δὲ καὶ Ἰωάννης, ὁ ἐπὶ τὸ στῆθος τοῦ κυρίου ἀναπεσών, ὃς ἐγενήθη ἱερεὺς τὸ πέταλον πεφορεκὼς καὶ μάρτυς καὶ διδάσκαλος, οὗτος ἐν Ἐφέσῳ κεκοίμηται. Of the elements of this description, the most puzzling and debated is the reference to John as a priest who wore the πέταλον. This will therefore be left until last in our discussion. The clause ὁ ἐπὶ τὸ στῆθος τοῦ κυρίου ἀναπεσών is drawn virtually verbatim from the Fourth Gospel (13:25: ἀναπεσὼν ... ἐπὶ τὸ στῆθος τοῦ Ἰησοῦ; 21:20: ὃς καὶ ἀνέπεσεν ... ἐπὶ τὸ στῆθος αὐτοῦ). The allusion is most likely to 21:20, because here the beloved disciple is introduced for the last time in the Gospel before being identified as the Gospel's author in 21:24. The phrase indicates the special intimacy with Jesus that qualified the beloved disciple to be the author of the Fourth Gospel. By means of it Polycrates not only identifies John as the author of the Fourth Gospel, but also suggests the special value of the fourth Gospel as deriving from a disciple who was especially close to the Lord. That Irenaeus uses precisely the same words (*Haer.* 3.1.1 = Eusebius, *Hist. eccl.* 5.8.4: ὁ καὶ ἐπὶ τὸ στῆθος αὐτοῦ ἀναπεσών) to indicate John as the author of

---

21. Translation from H. J. Lawlor and J. E. L. Oulton, *Eusebius Bishop of Caesarea: The Ecclesiastical History and the Martyrs of Palestine* (London: SPCK, 1927), 1:169.

22. Cf. the way the *Muratorian Canon* understands the seven churches to which Paul wrote and the seven churches to which John wrote in Revelation as representative of the whole church.

23. All Greek manuscripts have ὑμῶν, but it is tempting to follow the Syriac version of Eusebius in omitting it.

24. The attempt by Chapman, *John the Presbyter*, 64–71, to argue that Polycrates was correct in identifying the Philip who died at Hierapolis with Philip the apostle, rather than Philip the evangelist, fails because he misunderstands the statement of Polycrates that one of Philip's daughters "lived in the Holy Spirit" (ἐν ἁγίῳ πνεύματι πολιτευσαμένη). This phrase, which Polycrates also uses of Melito, means not just that she was "a holy and venerable person" but that she was a prophetess. Consequently the parallel between the Philip of Polycrates and Philip the evangelist (Acts 21:8–9) is not just that they had daughters (three or, as Chapman thinks, two according to Polycrates, four according to Acts), but also that at least one daughter of the former was a prophetess, as all four daughters of the latter were.

25. When J. J. Gunther, "Early Identifications of Authorship of the Johannine Writings," *JEH* 31 (1980): 417, says, "A learned ecclesiastic would be able to recognize that Philip the Evangelist was not one of the Twelve," he mistakes the character of learned exegesis in this period. Eusebius fully accepts the identification of the two Philips (*Hist. eccl.* 3.31.2–5).

the Gospel probably reflects a traditional Asian way of referring to the author of the Gospel, rather than Polycrates' dependence on Irenaeus.[26]

Reference to John as the author of the Gospel probably continues with the word μάρτυς. It is not κεκοίμηται that prevents μάρτυς from referring to death as a martyr;[27] for κεκοίμηται is also used of Thraseas and Sagaris who, like Polycarp, are designated martyrs. But whereas Thraseas, Sagaris, and Polycarp are all called ἐπίσκοπος καὶ μάρτυς, with μάρτυς appropriately placed second in the pair, John is called ἱερεύς ... καὶ μάρτυς καὶ διδάσκαλος, where μάρτυς, if it referred to his death, would be oddly sandwiched between ἱερεύς and διδάσκαλος. It has often been taken to allude to Revelation 1:2, 9, identifying the author of the Fourth Gospel with the author of Revelation, and referring to his sufferings as a witness to the Gospel in exile on Patmos.[28] But it is more likely to allude to his authorship of the Gospel, which in John 21:24 (cf. 19:35) is treated as equivalent to the beloved disciple's witness.[29] The pair of terms μάρτυς καὶ διδάσκαλος may well designate John as respectively the author of the Gospel and the author of the Johannine letters.[30] We do not need to suppose that Ephesian church tradition had yet identified John the seer of Patmos with John the beloved disciple, the author of the Gospel.

Polycrates' stress on John's authorship of the Gospel may well be connected with the importance of the authority of the Fourth Gospel for defense of the quartodeciman observance. Claudius Apollinaris, bishop of Hierapolis, writing a little earlier or contemporaneously, strongly associates the quartodeciman observance with the Johannine chronology of the passion and refers to opponents of it who appealed to the Matthaean chronology (ap. *Chron. pasch.* praef.). He evidently thought that the Gospels do not disagree, but that the proper way to harmonize them was to take the Johannine chronology as authoritative for correctly interpreting the Matthaean.[31] That Polycrates shared this view is suggested by the way he refers to the 14 Nisan, as "the day when the people put away the leaven." This means that for him the date was identified not as the day on which the Jews ate the Passover meal (since, according to the Jewish reckoning of the day from sunset to sunset, this took place at the beginning of the 15 Nisan), but as the day of preparation for the Passover (cf. John 19:14), when leaven had to be removed from houses before sunset. In that case, the significance for Polycrates of observing 14 Nisan can only be that, according to the Johannine chronology, it was the day Christ was crucified. Thus his reference to observing the fourteenth day "according to the Gospel" must be to John's Gospel as authoritative on this point.

Polycrates' final statement about John—that he died at Ephesus—is an obvious claim to local tradition. It means that the tomb of this author of the Gospel was known at Ephesus. It corresponds to Irenaeus's statement, doubtless also based on local Asian tradition, that John wrote the Gospel while living at Ephesus (*Haer.* 3.1.1 = Eusebius, *Hist. eccl.* 5.8.4).

On the basis of the information so far discussed, it has occasionally been argued that Polycrates was clearly not thinking of John the son of Zebedee.[32] The arguments used are suggestive, but not fully conclusive. It is pointed out that whereas Philip is explicitly called one of the twelve apostles, this is not said of John. But it could be replied that, if it were generally believed that the John who wrote the Gospel was one of the twelve apostles, Polycrates could take this for granted, while using instead a description (ὁ ἐπὶ τὸ στῆθος τοῦ κυρίου ἀναπεσών) that gave him even greater authority: not just one of the Twelve, but that member of the Twelve who was most intimate with the Lord. However, this reply begs the question whether it was generally accepted that the author of the Gospel was one of the Twelve. It is also pointed out that Philip, first in the list, is given precedence over John, but the order could merely reflect the belief that Philip had died before John, who according to Irenaeus survived until the reign of Trajan.[33] It is possible, though we cannot be sure, that the rest of the list continues in chronological order of death. A decisive argument for the view that Polycrates refers to a John other than the son of Zebedee will emerge only when we establish the correct interpretation of the remaining item in Polycrates' description of him: his priesthood.

Wearing the *Petalon*

To the puzzle of Polycrates' words ὃς ἐγενήθη ἱερεὺς τὸ πέταλον πεφορεκώς a satisfactory solution has not yet been proposed, but one is available. Before proposing this solution, we need to examine the use of the word πέταλον with reference to the vestments of the Jewish priesthood. The word undoubtedly refers to part of the headdress of the high priest, but it is a matter of some confusion precisely which part is indicated.

---

26. J. N. Sanders's treatment of the Johannine question is seriously marred by the way he dismisses Polycrates' evidence, without discussion, as merely dependent on Irenaeus and lacking any independent authority (*Fourth Gospel*, 7). He requires us to believe that no one in Asia thought of considering John of Ephesus the author of the Fourth Gospel until Polycrates read Irenaeus, and that this aged bishop of Ephesus then accepted this entirely novel idea purely on Irenaeus's authority. Local church tradition counted for more than this in the late second century. In fact, the association of the author of the Fourth Gospel with Ephesus is attested quite independently of Irenaeus by the *Acts of John*. For the superiority of Polycrates' evidence to that of Irenaeus, cf. Colson, *L'énigme*, 35.
27. As Gunther, "Early Identifications," 420, and others think.
28. E.g., Braun, *Jean le Théologien*, 339.
29. J. H. Bernard, *A Critical and Exegetical Commentary on the Gospel according to St. John*, ed. A. H. McNeile, ICC (Edinburgh: T. & T. Clark, 1928), 1:li.
30. The fact that John is called ὁ διδάσκαλος in *Acts of John* 37 is probably coincidental.
31. R. M. Grant, *The Earliest Lives of Jesus* (New York: Harper, 1961), 30.
32. E.g., Delff, *Geschichte*, 69–72; idem, *Das vierte Evangelium*, 2–11; Burney, *Aramaic Origin*, 134; Colson, *L'énigme*, 35–42; Gunther, "Early Identifications," 420–21; cf. Hengel, *Johannine Question*, 7.
33. Cf. Stanton, *Gospels*, 229.

There need be no doubt at all about what the high priests of the late Second Temple period actually wore on their heads. The problem is rather one of terminology. Josephus, who does not use the word πέταλον at all in this connection, provides a detailed description of the high priest's headdress, with which all other briefer descriptions and allusions are entirely consistent. According to Josephus, the high priest wore the ordinary linen turban (πῖλος) of the priests (*Ant.* 3.172; cf. 157–58) and over it another turban embroidered in blue. This was encircled by a golden crown (στέφανος) (κάλυξ) resembling the calyx of a flower (*Ant.* 3.172–78). The part of the crown that covered the forehead was a band (τελαμών) of gold, on which was inscribed the tetragrammaton. This detailed account is not inconsistent with the briefer description in *Jewish War* 5.235, where the high priest's linen turban (τιάρα), wreathed (κατέστεπτο) with blue, is said to be encircled by a golden crown (στέφανος),[34] on which the tetragrammaton is engraved. The major difference is that here Josephus does not specify on which part of the crown the letters of the divine name appear.[35]

The confusion arises as to how the terms in the Pentateuch's account of the vestments of Aaron should be understood to correspond with this high priestly headdress, in particular the crown. In addition to Aaron's linen turban (מצנפת), Exodus and Leviticus refer both to a holy crown (נזר: Exod. 29:6; 39:30; Lev. 8:9) and to a golden object fastened on the front of the turban (Exod. 28:37), which bears the inscription "Holy to YHWH." The latter is the ציץ (Exod. 28:36; 39:30; Lev. 8:9), a word that normally means "flower." It might be understood to be a flower-shaped ornament (cf. NRSV: "rosette") strapped to the forehead and distinct from the crown, but Exodus 39:30 and Leviticus 8:9 appear to identify the two, using the two words ציץ and נזר in apposition. In the Second Temple period, there seem to have been two traditions of interpretation. In the Hebrew text of Sirach 45:12, the ציץ, with the sacred inscription, is mentioned after and in addition to the golden crown (עטרה) (cf. also 40:4,[36] where the ציץ is mentioned along with the turban: צניף). But Josephus, with his elaborate explanation of how the crown has the shape of a flower, seems dependent on a tradition that understood the ציץ ("flower") to be the whole crown.

In both traditions of interpretation, πέταλον could be used to translate ציץ. Thus *Aristeas* 98, distinguishing the ציץ from the נזר as Ben Sira does, refers to "the hallowed diadem (βασίλειον) having in relief on the front in the middle in holy letters on a golden leaf (πετάλῳ) the name of God, ineffable in glory." Similarly, the list of the high priestly garments in *Testament of Levi* distinguishes the crown (στέφανος) from the πέταλον (8:2, cf. vv. 9–10, where the διάδημα seems to be the same as the πέταλον of v. 2). But the Septuagint translators of Exodus and Leviticus seem to agree with the tradition of interpretation reflected in Josephus. They clearly took the ציץ to be the whole crown. They translate ציץ as πέταλον (Exod. 28:30 [= Heb. 36]; 36:38 [= Heb. 39:30]; Lev. 8:9), and where the Hebrew refers to the נזר along with the ציץ, they take ציץ הנזר to describe the ציץ as a sanctified object (Exod. 36:38: ἀφόρισμα τοῦ ἁγίου, Lev. 8:9: τὸ καθηγιασμένον ἅγιον). But where ציץ הנזר occurs alone (Exod. 29:6), it is translated as τὸ πέταλον τὸ ἁγίασμα. The same tradition of interpretation is found in Philo, who speaks of a gold πέταλον in the form of a crown (χρυσοῦν δὲ πέταλον ὡσανεί στέφανος), on which the tetragrammaton was engraved (*Mos.* 2.114, cf. 116, 132), and probably in Clement of Alexandria who, evidently dependent on Jewish information (cf. *b. Yoma* 31b–32a), says that the high priest on the Day of Atonement removes the πέταλον before entering the holy of holies (*Exc. ex Theod.* 27.1,[37] cf. *Strom.* 5.6.38.6). This most likely means that he removes the whole crown, since according to Josephus's description, it is unlikely that the gold band on the forehead could have been worn separated from the crown of which it was part. We should also note that, although the word πέταλον is not used, in the Greek translation of Sirach both occurrences of ציץ are suppressed (Sir. 40:4; 45:12), presumably because the Hebrew word was understood to mean nothing other than the golden crown (στέφανος) itself, which had already been mentioned.

We cannot tell, therefore, whether the πέταλον is understood by Polycrates to be the whole of the high priest's golden crown or only the part of it that formed a band across the forehead and on which the tetragrammaton was engraved. What is important is that, in either case, the reference is to a distinctively high-priestly item of headdress. Of the various golden garments distinctive to the high priest, the golden crown bearing on its front the sacred letters is always treated as the most significant. It appears as the climax of the description of the awe-inspiring garments of Eleazar the high priest in *Aristeas* 96–99, and similarly climaxes Sirach's description of the vestments of Aaron (Sir. 45:8–12). He claims that the crown with its engraved frontlet was a spectacular sight (45:12). Josephus similarly ends his descriptions of the high-priestly vestments with the crown and its sacred inscription (*BJ* 5.231–35; *Ant.* 3.159–78). It was the unique privilege of the high priest to bear the divine name, graven in gold, on his forehead. Josephus also indicates that, whereas there could be any number of sets of the other high-priestly vestments (Solomon, he says, made thousands), "the crown on which Moses had inscribed God's name was unique

---

34. Cf. also the reference to the crown in *Ant.* 20.12.

35. Josephus's statement that what was engraved on the front of the crown was the four letters of the divine name (*Ant.* 3.178; *BJ* 5.235) is supported by Philo, *Mos.* 2.114–15, 132; *Aristeas* 98; Clement of Alexandria, *Strom.* 5.6.38.6. However, Exod. 28:36; 39:30 appear to give the inscription as "Holiness to YHWH" (קדש ליהוה). J. E. Hogg, "A Note on Two Points in Aaron's Headdress," *JTS* 26 (1925): 74–75, argues that the texts in Exodus should be interpreted in line with the later evidence.

36. The reference in 40:4a is certainly to the high priest, corresponding to the reference to the king in 40:3a.

37. On the Jewish background to this passage, see the note by H. A. Wolfson in R. P. Casey, *The Excerpta ex Theodoto of Clement of Alexandria*, Studies and Documents 1 (London: Christophers, 1934), 122–24.

(e.g., 1 Kings 1:8; Bar. 1:7; 1 Macc. 15:1; *Gos. Heb.* 7). Since the πέταλον was the most distinctively high-priestly accoutrement, the phrase τὸ πέταλον τοῦ ἱερέως is wholly unambiguous and would probably be preferred to the virtually tautologous τὸ πέταλον τοῦ ἀρχιερέως. This is also why Polycrates does not say that John ἐγενήθη ἀρχιερεὺς τὸ πέταλον πεφορεκώς. The sense of the prefix ἀρχ- is actually conveyed more accurately by the phrase τὸ πέταλον πεφορεκώς, since the latter means precisely that he officiated as high priest in the temple.

Among other Christian references to the πέταλον, the most important as a parallel to Polycrates is Epiphanius's claim that James the Lord's brother wore the πέταλον. He makes this statement in two passages:

> For he [James] was Joseph's eldest born and consecrated. Moreover, we have found that he exercised a priestly office (ἱερατεύσαντα) according to the old priesthood. Wherefore it was permitted to him to enter once a year into the holy of holies, as the law enjoined the high priests in accordance with the Scriptures. For so it is recorded concerning him by many before us, Eusebius and Clement and others. Nay, he was allowed to wear the πέταλον on his head (τὸ πέταλον ἐπὶ τῆς κεφαλῆς ἐξῆν αὐτῷ φορεῖν), as the aforementioned trustworthy persons testified in the same memoirs (ὑπομνηματισμοῖς). (*Pan.* 29.4)[41]

> Only to this James was it permitted (μόνον τούτῳ τῷ Ἰακώβῳ ἐξῆν) to enter (εἰσιέναι) once a year into the holy of holies (εἰς τὰ ἅγια τῶν ἁγίων), because he was a Nazirite (Ναζωραῖον), and took part in the office of priesthood (μέμικται τῇ ἱερωσύνῃ)... This James also wore the πέταλον on his head (πέταλον ἐπὶ τῆς κεφαλῆς ἐφόρεσε) (*Pan.* 78.13–14).[42]

Since the first passage is clearly connected with Hegesippus's statements that James was holy from his mother's womb and that James alone was allowed to enter the sanctuary (ap. Eusebius, *Hist. eccl.* 2.23.6), and since the second passage occurs in a context in which Epiphanius plainly reproduces what Hegesippus said about James's asceticism and his prayer for the people, as well as his death (*Pan.* 78.13–14; cf. Eusebius, *Hist. eccl.* 2.23.5–7, 11–12, 17), Lawlor argued that the information about James in these two passages must also have come from Hegesippus.[43] It is much more likely that they represent an elaboration of what Hegesippus had said, though one that Epiphanius already found in a source. The relevant words of Hegesippus, reported by Eusebius, are:

> To him alone it was permitted to enter the holy place (τούτῳ μόνῳ ἐξῆν εἰς τὰ ἅγια τῶν ἁγίων εἰσιέναι); for he wore nothing woollen, but linen garments. And

---

41. Translation from H. J. Lawlor, *Eusebiana: Essays on the Ecclesiastical History of Eusebius Pamphili* (1917; repr. Amsterdam: Philo, 1973), 10.
42. Translation partly from Lawlor, *Eusebiana*, 13.
43. Ibid., 9–15. The word ὑπομνηματισμοῖς in *Pan.* 29.4 probably does allude to the ὑπομνήματα of Hegesippus, but this need not mean that Epiphanius knew Hegesippus's work other than as quoted by Eusebius.

---

and has remained to this day" (*Ant.* 8.93).[38] There was only one πέταλον, believed to be the original one made for Aaron. To wear the πέταλον, then, was to officiate as high priest. According to a rabbinic tradition in *b. Qidd.* 66a, when King Jannai (John Hyrcanus?) wished to provoke the Pharisees, who objected to his claiming the high priesthood, he made that claim clear to them by wearing the ץיצ. Thus, when Polycrates claims that John ἐγενήθη ἱερεὺς τὸ πέταλον πεφορεκώς, the words mean, as precisely and unambiguously as it was possible to do, that he officiated as high priest in the temple. They cannot even make him one of the ἀρχιερεῖς in the broader sense of that term, as used in the New Testament and Josephus, whether it means members of the high priestly families or the holders of a number of higher offices in the temple. Polycrates' words must mean that John held the office of high priest in succession to Aaron.

They are an accurately Jewish way of expressing this. We may compare Polycrates' description of 14 Nisan as the day "when the people remove the leaven" (ὅταν ὁ λαὸς ἤρνυε τὴν ζύμην). This cannot be simply derived from Exodus 15:12, but reflects both the contemporary Jewish practice (of removing leaven from houses before the beginning of the first day of unleavened bread) and the technical language for it (cf. *m. Pesaḥ.* 1–2). The use of the simple ὁ λαός to mean the Jews is diaspora Jewish practice, known from inscriptions in Asia Minor.[39] Living close to the large Jewish community of Ephesus and in a church with a strongly Jewish-Christian background, it is not surprising that Polycrates can speak of things Jewish in an accurately Jewish way. His doing so may even reflect pride in his own at least partly Jewish descent if, as we have suggested, he claimed descent from one of the daughters of Philip.

In any case, there is no evidence that Christian writers of this period ever imagined that the πέταλον was worn by anyone except the Jewish high priest himself when officiating in the temple. A passage that might be thought to mean that ordinary priests wore the πέταλον is *Protevangelium of James* 5:1, in which Joachim goes to offer sacrifice in the temple and is somehow able to tell from the πέταλον of the priest that God has forgiven his sins. Certainly this writer is not too well informed about what went on in the temple (cf. 8:2–3), but it is not necessary to suppose, as has been argued,[40] that he here confuses the πέταλον with the high priest's breastpiece that contained the Urim and Thummim (Exod. 28:30). Rather, he is interpreting Exodus 28:38 (LXX 34), which connects the πέταλον of the high priest with the removal of the guilt of those who offer sacrifice. Nor does the phrase τὸ πέταλον τοῦ ἱερέως indicate that he thinks the πέταλον was worn by a priest other than the high priest. The simple term "the priest" was not infrequently used when the context made clear reference to the high priest

---

38. Presumably Josephus thinks it was taken with other temple treasures (cf. *BJ* 6.387–91) to Rome after the fall of Jerusalem.
39. H. Strathmann, "λαός," *TDNT* 4:39.
40. Bernard, *John*, 2:595 n. 1; A. de Santos Otero, *Los Euangelios Apócrifos*, 6th ed. (Madrid: Biblioteca de Autores Cristianos, 1988), 138.

alone he entered into the sanctuary, and was found on his knees asking forgiveness on behalf of the people, so that his knees became hard like a camel's, for he was continually bending the knee in worship to God, and asking forgiveness for the people. (Eusebius, *Hist. eccl.* 2.23.6)[44]

Hegesippus probably meant that James, because of his ascetic sanctity and because he dressed like the priests in linen, was the only man other than the priests who was allowed to enter the holy place. But a reader of Hegesippus has thought the reference must be to the privilege of the high priest to be the only man to enter the holy of holies, once a year on the day of atonement. This interpretation was encouraged by Hegesippus's statements that what James did in the holy place was to pray for the people's forgiveness. So the opening statement of the passage quoted above from Epiphanius, *Pan.* 78.13 is clearly an interpretative rewriting of the first nine words of the passage just quoted from Hegesippus. The passage in Epiphanius then proceeds to interpret the reasons Hegesippus gave for James's privilege of being allowed to enter the holy place. It understands James's ascetic practices and holiness from his mother's womb (Eusebius, *Hist. eccl.* 2.23.4–5) to mean that he was a Nazirite, and it takes his wearing only linen to mean that he actually was a priest.

This secondary interpretation of Hegesippus therefore supposes that James was permitted to officiate on the day of atonement as only the high priest may, entering the holy of holies as if he were high priest. This claim that James officiated as high priest is then expressed by the statement that he wore the πέταλον.

It is clear that this statement about James, despite its extremely improbable nature, is meant literally. It offers no support to the view that what Polycrates said of John was meant metaphorically, with reference to his exercise of authority within the Christian church. Nor does it offer any possibility that wearing the πέταλον could mean anything other than officiating as high priest in the temple. It is not clear whether Epiphanius means that James actually held office as high priest. He seems to mean rather that, although not officially appointed high priest, James was allowed to perform the function reserved exclusively for the high priest. The whole point of his reference to the πέταλον is that it was worn only by the high priest. Moreover, comparison between the way Epiphanius speaks of James (τὸ πέταλον ἐπὶ τῆς κεφαλῆς ἐξῆν αὐτῷ φορεῖν) and the way Polycrates speaks of John (ἐγενήθη ἱερεὺς τὸ πέταλον πεφορεκώς) indicates that, whereas Epiphanius's language suggests that James, though not appointed high priest, was permitted to officiate as high priest, Polycrates' language suggests that John was actually appointed high priest.

These claims about James and John probably originated quite independently, and we should resist attempts, such as Bernard's,[45] to find a common explanation for both. We have seen how the tradition about James derived from a misunderstanding of Hegesippus. It is unnecessary to suppose that Epiphanius or his source was influenced by what Polycrates said about John.[46] This is also unlikely, because Epiphanius states so emphatically the unique privilege of James in this respect.[47] It is also unlikely that the tradition about James influenced the claim that John was high priest, even supposing it antedated Polycrates, which is entirely uncertain. There would be no reason for transferring, without further explanation, this very remarkable claim about James to John. The two traditions are independent, but share the same—evidently stereotyped—way of referring to the exercise of the high priest's office in the temple: wearing the πέταλον.

Attempts to explain Polycrates' words have hitherto fallen into two categories: metaphorical[48] and historical. The idea that Jewish high priesthood is used as a metaphorical way of referring to John's position of authority in the church can claim support from just two allegedly parallel usages. In *Didache* 13:3, Christians are instructed to give the first fruits of their produce to the prophets, "for they are your high priests" (ἀρχιερεῖς ὑμῶν). Hippolytus (*Ref.* 1.prooem.6) claims that the successors of the apostles participate with them in the same grace of high priesthood (τῆς τε αὐτῆς χάριτος μετέχοντες ἀρχιερατείας). This latter passage may actually be based on a misunderstanding of Polycrates' words about John,[49] but in any case neither of these passages really parallels the latter. The general idea of high priesthood might occasionally be used metaphorically of Christian prophets or bishops, whose position in some respects resembled that of Jewish high priests. But in such a usage it would be odd to use the precise expression τὸ πέταλον πεφορεκώς. Polycrates' words are a straightforward statement that John officiated as high priest in the temple. Their context offers no indication that they are meant other than literally, while their place in the sequence of statements about John naturally associates them with his early life in Jerusalem, where he had been a disciple of Jesus and could have been a high priest.

The other form of interpretation takes seriously the apparently intended literal meaning and explains the words as a historical reminiscence of the beloved disciple or the author of the Fourth Gospel who, it is suggested, belonged to a priestly family in Jerusalem and perhaps officiated in the temple in some capacity. The difficulty in interpretations along these lines is that the historical basis they postulate for Polycrates' words is only historically plausible when it is something

---

[44]. Translation from Lawlor and Oulton, *Eusebius*, 57.

[45]. Bernard, *John*, 2:594–97. Bernard connects these two traditions about James and John with a similar statement about Mark, but the late Latin source of the latter seems to be no longer known. It is probably ultimately dependent on Polycrates' statement about John, used to elaborate the existing tradition that Mark was a Levite.

[46]. Contra Rigato, "Giovanni," 469.

[47]. This in spite of the fact that he also says that the sons of Zebedee practiced the same kind of ascetic lifestyle as James: *Pan.* 78.13.

[48]. E.g., Braun, *Jean le Théologien*, 339–40; F. F. Bruce, "St. John at Ephesus," *BJRL* 60 (1978): 343.

[49]. R. Eisler, *The Enigma of the Fourth Gospel* (London: Methuen, 1938), 55, quotes an apparently unpublished fragment of a lost work of Hippolytus that refers to John as ἀρχιερεὺς Ἐφέσου. Whether genuine or not, this is certainly dependent on Polycrates. If genuine, it would explain *Ref.* 1.prooem.6.

much less than Polycrates states: that John was high priest. Bernard's speculation that the πέταλον might sometimes have been worn by ordinary Jewish priests in New Testament times[50] is contradicted by all the evidence. Internal evidence from the Fourth Gospel (including 18:15) alleged to show that the author—or the source of the author's tradition—belonged to Jerusalem priestly circles has some force,[51] but does not really explain why Polycrates should have thought John actually held the office of high priest.

The boldest historical speculation is that of Eisler.[52] Following Delff,[53] he identifies John, the author of the Fourth Gospel, with the John who appears as a member of the high-priestly family (ἐκ γένους ἀρχιερατικοῦ) in Acts 4:6. Going further than Delff,[54] he claims that this John actually was high priest by identifying him with Theophilus the son of Annas (Josephus, *Ant.* 18.123), who was high priest from 37 to 41 CE. He suggests that Theophilus was used as the Greek name roughly equivalent in meaning to Yohanan. This is possible, but identification of the John of whom Polycrates speaks with the high priest Theophilus is achieved only by a series of unverifiable guesses and requires us to believe that only Polycrates has preserved any reference to the fact that the high priest Theophilus was a disciple of Jesus. In a recent article, Rigato, apparently without knowledge of Eisler's work, has taken Polycrates' statement fully seriously, identified John the author of the Fourth Gospel with the John of Acts 4:6,[55] and supposed that this John must at some time have officiated as high priest.[56] He allows three possibilities:[57] that Josephus's record of the high priests is not complete and does not happen to refer to John (perhaps the name of John, as a Christian, was subject to a kind of *damnatio memoriae*), that John was another name of one of those mentioned by Josephus, or that on one day of atonement John substituted for the reigning high priest (according to the practice of substituting another member of the family if the high priest were ill or ritually impure).[58] Certainly these are possibilities, but it remains surprising that only Polycrates should have preserved any reference to the remarkable fact that a disciple of Jesus, the author of the Fourth Gospel, was or substituted for the high priest.

The improbable and speculative nature of Eisler's proposal has distracted attention from the way in which Acts 4:6 really can explain Polycrates' words about John. The simplest explanation of them is that Polycrates (or the Ephesian church tradition that he followed) identified John the beloved disciple, who had died in Ephesus, with the John of Acts 4:6, not because he had any historical information to this effect, but as a piece of scriptural exegesis.[59] The tradition that John the beloved disciple was a high priest is neither metaphorical nor historical, but exegetical. As we already noted in connection with Polycrates' identification of the two Philips, it was common practice for early Christian exegetes of the New Testament writings to identify characters who bore the same name. Other examples are the identification, in the second-century *Acts of Paul* (written in Asia in Polycrates' time), of the Judas who was Paul's host in Damascus (Acts 9:17) with Judas the Lord's brother (Mark 6:3),[60] or the identification that the *Protevangelium of James* (23–24) makes between Zechariah the father of John the Baptist and the Zechariah who was murdered in the temple (Matt. 23:35). We may also recall how prominent figures of the early postapostolic church—comparable with John of Ephesus—were assumed to be the same as persons of the same name who appear in New Testament writings: Clement of Rome was identified as the Clement of Philippians 4:3 (Eusebius, *Hist. eccl.* 3.4.9); Linus of Rome was identified as the Linus of 2 Timothy 4:21 (Irenaeus, *Haer.* 3.3.3; Eusebius, *Hist. eccl.* 3.4.8). Hermas the prophet, author of the *Shepherd*, was identified as the Hermas of Romans 16:14 (Origen, ad. loc.). These last two instances may have some historical plausibility, but these identifications were made in the same way as the others, as an exegetical procedure.

It is quite likely that the identification of the beloved disciple with the John of Acts 4:6 was facilitated by John 18:15, which, if it is understood to refer to the beloved disciple, depicts him as intimately acquainted (γνωστός) with the high priest. In Acts 4:6, John is listed third after Annas the high priest and Caiaphas. Someone who knew that in the New Testament period the Jewish high priests mostly held office for short periods only, or who was misled by John 18:13 into thinking the office was filled annually, would easily suppose that such a senior member of the high-priestly family as the John of Acts 4:6 appears to be must have himself held the office of high priest at some time. The motive for identifying John the beloved disciple with this John will have been—in addition to the general exegetical tendency already mentioned—the natural desire of the Ephesian church to find their own John, the author of the Gospel they prized, mentioned somewhere else in the writings of the emergent New Testament canon. But the identification also served well Polycrates' particular purpose in his letter to Pope Victor: the justification of the quartodeciman observance in line with the

---

50. Bernard, *John*, 2:596; cf. Colson, *L'énigme*, 37, who defies all the evidence in stating: "il n'est pas prouvé que l'usage, au temps de Jésus, n'était pas étendu."
51. E.g., Burney, *Aramaic Origin*, 133–34; Colson, *L'énigme*, 18–27, 94–97; Hengel, *Johannine Question*, 109–11, 125–26; Rigato, "Giovanni," 469–81.
52. Eisler, *Enigma*, 36–45.
53. Delff, *Geschichte*, 95.
54. Delff, *Das vierte Evangelium*, 9–10, supposed that John stood in for the high priest on one occasion. This possibility is also suggested by Rigato, "Giovanni," 464 n. 33 (see below).
55. Rigato, "Giovanni," 465–66.
56. Ibid., 463–65.
57. Ibid., 464–65 n. 33.
58. J. Jeremias, *Jerusalem in the Time of Jesus*, trans. F. H. and C. H. Cave (London: SCM, 1969), 157.

59. That Polycrates was well acquainted with the early chapters of Acts is shown by his quotation of Acts 5:9 later in his letter.
60. Coptic text of a section of the *Acts of Paul*, in *New Testament Apocrypha*, ed. E. Hennecke, W. Schneemelcher, and R. McL. Wilson (London: Lutterworth, 1965), 2:388.

Johannine chronology of the passion. An eyewitness of the passion who actually himself served as high priest could be expected to remember correctly its precise chronological relation to the Jewish festival.

It is quite likely that Polycrates, who in his letter prides himself on his considerable knowledge of the scriptures, himself made this identification of his own illustrious relative with the John of Acts 4:6. But whether Polycrates made or inherited it, it is of considerable importance. For it is now clear that when the Ephesian church looked for its own John, the beloved disciple, in New Testament writings other than the Fourth Gospel, they did not identify him with John the son of Zebedee. The identification of him with the John of Acts 4:6 makes it impossible to identify him also with John the son of Zebedee, who appears in the same narrative, along with Peter, as one of the two disciples who are there interrogated before Annas, Caiaphas, John, and Alexander. The Ephesian church's own tradition about their own John evidently made them quite sure that he could not be John the son of Zebedee and obliged them, even at the end of the second century, to resist this identification, which was already proving irresistible elsewhere and seems to have become universal in the next century.

The John to whom Polycrates ascribed the Fourth Gospel was a very definite person. His tomb was at Ephesus. Polycrates could have explained how he was related to him. He was not the son of Zebedee, one of the Twelve, but he was a personal disciple of Jesus. He must be John the Elder, a disciple of the Lord, to whom Papias referred in the famous passage of his prologue (ap. Eusebius, *Hist. eccl.* 3.39.4). This John the Elder, who was still teaching when the young Papias was gathering his traditions, lived near enough to Hierapolis for Papias to have heard him in person on occasion (Eusebius, *Hist. eccl.* 3.39.7;[61] cf. Irenaeus, *Haer.* 5.33.4). His association with Ephesus is confirmed by the *Apostolic Constitutions* (7.46), which lists "John," appointed by the apostle John the son of Zebedee, as second bishop of Ephesus after Timothy. At this point in his lists of early bishops, the author of the *Apostolic Constitutions* was probably not dependent on Eusebius, since he would certainly have thought the John of Polycrates' letter was the son of Zebedee and since Eusebius's own association of Papias's John the Elder with Ephesus is tied up with his attribution of the Apocalypse to him (*Hist. eccl.* 3.39.6). He follows, no doubt, the same source of local Asian tradition that led him to associate Ariston (Papias's Aristion) with Smyrna, an association which Streeter showed is probably correct.[62]

The discovery that local Ephesian church tradition attributed the Fourth Gospel to Papias's John the Elder requires us to raise again the question of what Papias himself may have said about the Fourth Gospel. In this case too new light can be shed by a fresh reading of the evidence.

Papias on the Gospels

There should be no doubt that Papias knew the Fourth Gospel.[63] There is his list of seven disciples (ap. Eusebius, *Hist. eccl.* 3.39.4), the first six of whom (Andrew, Peter, Philip, Thomas, James, John) are in a distinctively Johannine order,[64] the order they appear in the Fourth Gospel, with James and John in fifth and sixth place (cf. John 21:2), and Matthew, a non-Johannine disciple important for Papias as a disciple who wrote a Gospel, added in seventh place.[65] There is the quotation from John 14:2 in a passage Irenaeus ascribes to the elders and very probably borrowed from Papias (*Haer.* 5.36.1–2).[66] The Armenian reference to Papias seems to depend on a comment he made on John 19:39.[67] But it does not follow necessarily that Papias said anything about the authorship and origin of the Fourth Gospel.[68] If he merely quoted from and alluded to it occasionally, Eusebius's silence on the matter would be not at all surprising. Eusebius does not say that Papias quoted the Apocalypse, which he certainly did.[69] Eusebius does not say that he quoted Luke's Gospel, as he does in the fragment of Papias in the Armenian version of Andrew of Caesarea[70] (unless we suppose that he knew the saying in Luke 10:18 from oral tradition). But Eusebius's silence will need some explanation if Papias dealt with the origin of the Fourth Gospel in the context of his well-known comments on the origins of the Gospels of Mark and Matthew. A preliminary indication that he did so can be found from a consideration of these comments on Mark and Matthew:

---

61. On this passage, see Chapman, *John the Presbyter* 28–32; Hengel, *Johannine Question*, 22.
62. Streeter, *Primitive Church*, 92–97.
63. Contra, e.g., U. H. J. Körtner, *Papias von Hierapolis* (Göttingen: Vandenhoeck & Ruprecht, 1983), 197.
64. On this list, see Hengel, *Johannine Question*, 17–21.
65. Cf. Grant, *Earliest Lives*, 16.
66. Lightfoot, *Biblical Essays*, 67–68; idem, *Essays on the Work Entitled Supernatural Religion* (London: Macmillan, 1889), 194–202.
67. Fragment 24 in J. Kürzinger, *Papias von Hierapolis und die Evangelien des Neuen Testaments*, Eichstätter Materialien 4 (Regensburg: F. Pustet, 1983), 132–35; = fragment 25 in *The Apostolic Fathers in English*, 3rd ed., trans. and ed. M. W. Holmes after the earlier version of J. B. Lightfoot and J. R. Harmer (Grand Rapids: Baker Academic, 2006), 319.
68. No weight can be given to the so-called Anti-Marcionite Prologue to John (fragment 21 in Körtner, *Papias*, 124–25; = fragment 19 in Holmes, *Apostolic Fathers*, 316–17; cf. also fragment 20 in Kürzinger, *Papias*, 122–23; = fragment 20 in Holmes, *Apostolic Fathers*, 317), which claims to report from Papias that John wrote the Gospel and says that Papias was a hearer (ἀκουστής) of John (*Haer.* 5.33.4). On this Prologue, see Lightfoot, *Supernatural Religion*, 210–14 (who makes the best of the evidence, but admits that it can be allowed no weight); Braun, *Jean le Théologien*, 345–49.
69. Fragments 12, 13, 23 in Kürzinger, *Papias*, 110–23, 128–33; = fragments 10, 11, 24, in Holmes, *Apostolic Fathers*, 313–14, 318–19.
70. Fragment 23 in Kürzinger, *Papias*, 128–33; = fragment 24 in Holmes, *Apostolic Fathers*, 318–19. It is striking that Lightfoot, *Supernatural Religion*, 186, 200–201, already concluded that Papias must have referred to Luke 10:18.

And the Elder[71] used to say this: Mark, having become Peter's interpreter (ἑρμηνευτής), wrote down accurately everything he remembered, though not in order (οὐ μέντοι τάξει), of the things either said or done by the Lord. For he neither heard the Lord nor followed him, but afterwards, as I said, followed Peter, who adapted his teachings as needed (πρός τὰς χρείας) but not giving, as it were, an ordered account (σύνταξιν) of the oracles[72] of the Lord. Consequently Mark did nothing wrong in writing down single points (ἕνια) as he remembered them, for he made it his own concern not to omit anything which he had heard or to make any false statement in them. (ap. Eusebius, *Hist. eccl.* 3.39.15)

So (οὖν) Matthew composed (συνετάξατο) the oracles in the Hebrew language, but each person interpreted (ἡρμήνευσεν) them as best he could. (ap. Eusebius, *Hist. eccl.* 3.39.16)

It is worth noticing immediately that Eusebius has clearly not given us everything that Papias said about Matthew and Mark. In the case of Matthew, the οὖν shows that the quoted sentence was preceded by something else, probably to the effect that Matthew (unlike Mark) had been a personal disciple of the Lord. In the case of Mark, we can infer from Eusebius that Papias also quoted 1 Peter 5:13 to substantiate his claim that Mark was a disciple of Peter. This is clear from the comment Eusebius makes after the quotation of Papias on Matthew (3.39.17: "The same writer utilized testimonies from the first letter of John and, likewise, from that of Peter"), taken together with the conclusion to Eusebius's own account of the origin of the Gospel of Mark and Clement of Alexandria. Eusebius concludes:

> Clement has given the story in the sixth book of the *Hypotyposeis*; and the bishop of Hierapolis also, Papias by name, corroborates his testimony (συνεπιμαρτυρεῖ), [saying] that Peter mentions Mark in his first letter; which also it is said (φασίν) he composed at Rome itself, and indicates the fact when he calls the city, somewhat metaphorically, "Babylon," in these words: "She who is at Babylon, who is likewise chosen, sends you greetings; and so does my son Mark." (*Hist. eccl.* 2.15.2; cf. 1 Pet. 5:13)

Although the report "that Peter mentions Mark in his first letter" (τοῦ δὲ Μάρκου μνημονεύειν τὸν Πέτρον ...) is not quite unequivocally said to be that of Papias, it is most naturally connected with συνεπιμαρτυρεῖ, while the further implications of 1 Peter 5:13 are unattributed (φασίν). This interpretation is the more probable because it explains Eusebius's reference to Papias's use of 1 Peter in 3.39.17. It was as a "testimony" (μαρτυρία) to the value of Mark's Gospel, as dependent on Peter's preaching, that Papias used a quotation from 1 Peter. This raises the possibility, to which we shall return, that Papias similarly quoted 1 John in order to validate the Fourth Gospel as based on eyewitness testimony. For the moment we conclude that Eusebius, guided by his own interests, has evidently lifted Papias's remarks about Mark and Matthew out of a context in which he said more about both.

Much discussion of Papias's comments about Mark and Matthew, preoccupied either with showing their reliability as evidence for the origins of these Gospels or with emphasizing their apologetic character in order to discredit their reliability, has failed to understand why Papias made these comments. The quoted comments on the two Gospels have two interests in common. First, they are both concerned with the way these Gospels are based on eyewitness authority (Peter's and Matthew's). A concern with reliable access to eyewitness reports of the Lord's deeds and sayings is prominent in the passage Eusebius quotes from Papias's prologue (*Hist. eccl.* 3.39.3–4), and so it is likely to have been a major concern in his discussion of the Gospels. Second, both comments are concerned with "order." Although the use of συνετάξατο of Matthew need not, by itself, be very significant, in the context of the two comments on Mark and Matthew it demands to be connected with the statements that Mark wrote the deeds and sayings of the Lord accurately but not in order (οὐ μέντοι τάξει), and that Peter did not give an ordered account (σύνταξιν) of the oracles of the Lord.

A common mistake has been to suppose that Papias is contrasting the lack of order in Mark's Gospel with the presence of order in Matthew, whether "order" is understood as a matter of chronological sequence or of literary arrangement. But this ignores the fact that Papias's comment on Matthew is by no means wholly positive. He appears to be acknowledging the fact that the Greek Gospel of Matthew known to him and his readers had suffered something in the translation from Matthew's original Hebrew.[73] If we allow the μὲν ... δὲ structure of the statement about Matthew its contrastive sense, then Papias is saying that, although Matthew himself arranged the oracles of the Lord in order when he wrote his Gospel in Hebrew, those who translated his work as best they could (ὡς ἦν δυνατός) cannot be relied on to have preserved this σύνταξις. Quite probably Papias went on to make this more explicit in a further comment, which Eusebius omitted because he did not like the notion that the Greek Gospel of Matthew used by the church diverged rather considerably from Matthew's original Hebrew Gospel. From what we know Papias to have said about Matthew, it is clear that he thought there had been more than one translation of the original Hebrew Gospel into Greek. Probably he knew something about Greek Gospels, under the name of Matthew and related to our Matthew, which were used by Jewish-Christians in Palestine and

---

71. "The Elder" is presumably John the Elder, but we cannot be quite certain of this, since the fact that the quotation in Eusebius follows a mention of John the Elder by Irenaeus (*Haer.* 3.39.14) may be misleading in this respect and the context from which Eusebius has taken the quotation might have made it clear that another elder is the one referred to. It is not certain how much of the comment on Mark's Gospel Papias attributed to the Elder. Whether the comment on Matthew came from John the Elder there is no way of knowing.

72. Papias's use of λόγια here evidently covers "the things either said or done by the Lord," already mentioned (so Lightfoot, *Supernatural Religion*, 175–76). This is the best guide to the meaning of λόγια both in Papias's comment on Matthew and in the title of his own work.

73. Cf. Lightfoot, *Supernatural Religion*, 208.

Syria.[74] He knew they exhibited major divergences from the Gospel of Matthew used in Hierapolis and neighboring churches. He referred to these various Greek Matthews to show that none of them could be presumed to preserve accurately the σύνταξις of the original Hebrew Matthew.

This probably explains Eusebius's final remark about Papias's work. Following the statement already quoted that Papias used testimonies from 1 John and 1 Peter, he says, "he also related another story about a woman accused of many sins before the Lord, which the Gospel according to the Hebrews contains" (*Hist. eccl.* 3.39.17). The "Gospel according to the Hebrews" is no doubt what Eusebius has called Papias's source. It is the Jewish-Christian gospel in Greek to which he elsewhere refers (*Hist. eccl.* 3.25.5; 3.27.4; 4.22.8), distinguishing it from a Jewish-Christian Gospel in Aramaic of which he also knew (*Hist. eccl.* 4.22.8; cf. *Theoph.* 4.12). There is no evidence in his writings that Eusebius knew the Greek Gospel he calls the Gospel according to the Hebrews other than by report. So he did not have knowledge independent of Papias that it contained Papias's story of the accused woman. Probably Papias said it occurred in a Greek Gospel used by Jewish-Christians[75] and so Eusebius assumed that this Gospel must be the only such Greek Gospel of which he knew: the Gospel according to the Hebrews. But for Papias himself, we may assume that the significance of this Gospel was that he regarded it (probably not without reason) as a version of Matthew. He cited the story of the accused woman, which occurred in this Gospel but not in the Gospel of Matthew generally used in the churches of his area, to show how far the various Greek versions of the Hebrew Matthew differed. It is not surprising that Eusebius does not make this clear, but this explanation of the reason Papias quoted the story of the accused woman has the advantage of allowing us to suppose that all three of the quotations made by Papias to which Eusebius refers immediately after giving Papias's comments on Mark and Matthew (*Hist. eccl.* 3.39.17) he found in Papias in the same context as those comments.

If this explanation of Papias's use of the story of the woman is correct, it would mean that Papias attributed to the translators of the various versions of Matthew not minor differences of translation, but major variations in content. This may be confirmed by the implied contrast between Mark, as Peter's interpreter (ἑρμηνευτής), and those who interpreted (ἡρμήνευσεν) Matthew's Hebrew Gospel. Whereas Mark's accuracy and scrupulosity in recording everything he had heard from Peter, leaving nothing out and falsifying nothing, is stressed, those who interpreted Matthew as best they could were evidently much less careful and competent.

---

74. For the "Gospel of the Ebionites," see now G. Howard, "The Gospel according to Matthew," see Epiphanius, *Pan.* 30.13.2.

75. It may be significant that Papias's version of the story seems closest to that in the Syriac *Didascalia* (7.2.24); see B. D. Ehrman, "Jesus and the Adulteress," *NTS* 34 (1988): 24–44; Holmes, *Apostolic Fathers*, 303–5, 311. The *Didascalia* certainly used *Gospel of Peter*, and could have had access to a Jewish-Christian Gospel used in Syria.

We can now see that the purpose of Papias in his comments on both Mark and Matthew is to explain why it is that, although both Gospels are based on eyewitness testimony, neither arranges the λόγια of the Lord "in order." This view of his purpose has the great advantage of doing justice to both of the concerns that we noted are common to the comments on both Gospels—the concerns with eyewitness authority and with "order"—and also of accounting for everything Papias says in both comments, which is not often done by other explanations of his purpose. In the case of Mark, the Gospel is a most valuable record of eyewitness testimony, because Mark carefully and accurately recorded everything he remembered of Peter's preaching, but since Peter in his preaching naturally did not put the λόγια in order, neither does the Gospel of Mark. In the case of Matthew, however, Papias believes that Matthew himself, a disciple and eyewitness, wrote the λόγια and so it must be presumed that he would have arranged them in the correct order. The fact that (as Papias supposes) they are not in order in the Gospel of Matthew known to Papias and his readers is not therefore due to Matthew himself. It results from the fact that Matthew wrote in Hebrew and various different versions of his work were made in Greek. So in the case of Mark, the lack of order is the fault neither of the eyewitness (Peter) nor of the interpreter (Mark), but is due to the oral nature of the eyewitness's testimony, whereas in the case of Matthew, the lack of order is not the fault of the eyewitness (Matthew), although he himself wrote the λόγια, but is due to his translators.

It follows that the "order" with which Papias is concerned must be chronological sequence, not literary arrangement.[76] The latter need not be expected of eyewitnesses, but the former could reasonably be expected of eyewitness testimony, and so Papias is at pains to explain why two Gospels that certainly derive from eyewitness testimony do not exhibit it. The only reason Papias could have had for arguing this point is that he knew another Gospel, also recording eyewitness testimony, which in his view did arrange the λόγια of the Lord in the correct order. This must be John.[77] Leaving aside gospels such as Thomas, which do not offer a sequential account of Jesus' ministry, John's is the extant Gospel that differs most markedly in this respect from Matthew and Mark. From later patristic discussions of the differences between the Gospels, we know that the differences of order between the Synoptics did not greatly matter to ancient readers by comparison with the differences between John and the Synoptics.

Thus the context of Papias's comments on Mark and Matthew was not an account of the origins of the Gospels per se, nor an apologetic defense of these two Gospels against attacks, but a discussion of the most obvious difference between those Gospels that were generally accepted—in the churches around

---

76. The case for the latter is most fully argued by Kürzinger, *Papias*, chaps. 1–3. The critique of Kürzinger by M. Black, "The Use of Rhetorical Terminology in Papias on Mark and Matthew," *JSNT* 37 (1989): 31–41, only deals in passing with τάξις.

77. So also Lightfoot, *Supernatural Religion*, 165; A. Wright, "τάξει in Papias," *JTS* 14 (1913): 300; Hengel, *Johannine Question*, 157 n. 118.

Hierapolis—as embodying eyewitness testimony. Probably Papias cited the authority of the elders for his view that Matthew, Mark, and John were all, in some sense, eyewitness records, but this was not the point of discussion. If this was accepted, the question of the differences between John on the one hand and Matthew and Mark on the other could not be avoided, and there is no reason why it should not already have become a topic of discussion in the circles Papias knew, where all three of these Gospels were in use. Our best evidence for such discussion comes from perhaps a century later, in the attacks made by Gaius and the Alogi (if the latter are not simply Gaius himself) on the Fourth Gospel,[78] which they attributed to John's heretical adversary Cerinthus.[79] In pointing out the disagreements between John and the Synoptics, they evidently focused especially on John 1:29–2:1, where John's carefully stated sequence of days from the baptism (if 1:32–33 is read as a narrative of it) through the call of the disciples to the miracle at Cana (1:29, 35, 39, 43; 2:1) allows no room for the forty days in the wilderness, which Matthew and Mark place between the baptism and the return to Galilee, where Jesus then calls the disciples.[80] For Gaius and the Alogi, this was evidence against the authenticity of John's Gospel, which they wished to discredit because of its use by the Montanists. But in pointing out this obvious incompatibility in chronological sequence in the early sections of the Gospels, they would no doubt be taking up a question that already had been raised before the Montanist controversy. We may find some evidence of this in the *Epistle of the Apostles*, which should probably not be dated later than circa 150.[81] Though dependent on all four Gospels, it gives precedence to John's by placing John, detached from his brother James, first in the list of the twelve apostles who purport to be the authors (2: John, Thomas, Peter, Andrew, James, Philip . . .). Its extensive catalog of the miracles of Jesus, which fills chapter 5, consists mostly of Synoptic Gospel miracles and follows the order of no particular Gospel, but it emphatically begins with the Johannine miracle at Cana, evidently taking seriously the Fourth Gospel's claim to provide the chronological order (John 2:11: "the first of his signs"). Tatian's *Diatessaron* was also no doubt motivated more by the discrepancies in order between the Gospels than by differences between them in parallel pericopes. Tatian did not consistently prefer the Johannine order, but he tended to accept John's authority where his Gospel made explicit chronological statements.[82]

If the question of order focused especially on the events around the beginning of the ministry, it may be that Papias's prologue already indicates which order he

preferred. We have noticed that his list of seven disciples (Andrew, Peter, Philip, Thomas, James, John, Matthew) is (up to Matthew) a Johannine list and contrasts with the synoptic lists of the Twelve, but it also begins by following the Johannine order in which the disciples were called (Andrew, Peter, Philip . . .), in contrast to the Matthaean and Marcan order (Peter, Andrew, James, John, Matthew/Levi).

If Papias mentioned Luke in his discussion of the differences of order between the Gospels, he need only have pointed out that Luke's Gospel does not rest as immediately on eyewitness testimony as the others were thought to do. If he mentioned Luke, Eusebius did not report the fact, either because what Papias said about Luke was not significant enough to be worth quoting or because it distanced Luke further from eyewitness testimony than Eusebius would have liked (cf. his own view of the matter in *Hist. eccl.* 3.24.15). But our argument requires that Papias must have said something quite significant about the Fourth Gospel to justify his own preference for its order. There may be two reasons why Eusebius did not report this.[83] In the first place, if (as we shall argue later) Papias ascribed the Fourth Gospel to John the Elder, Eusebius, who emphatically draws attention to Papias's distinction between John the son of Zebedee and John the Elder, in order to suggest that the latter may be the author of the Apocalypse, could not have missed or disguised the fact that, according to Papias, the author of the Fourth Gospel was not the son of Zebedee.

But second, Eusebius would not have liked Papias's solution to the problem of the differences of order between the Gospels: that John's is correct and the others unreliable in this respect. His own understanding of the way the sequences of events in the four Gospels relate (expounded in 3.24.5–16) is that the three synoptic evangelists only record the ministry of Jesus after the imprisonment of John the Baptist. John wrote his Gospel precisely to fill in the gap they had left: he records the ministry before the imprisonment of John the Baptist. This seems to settle the matter. Eusebius apparently sees no need to admit that the order in any Gospel ever needs to be preferred to the order in another. It is significant that, despite his interest in recording what early authors said about the Gospels,[84] and despite the fact that the chronological differences between the Gospels were certainly discussed in some of his sources, he never quotes or refers to such discussions. He does not quote Claudius Apollinaris on the chronology of the passion in relation to the quartodeciman question, and his account of the paschal controversy gives no hint that it bore any relation to differences between the Gospels. But his sensitivity on this issue appears especially in his treatment of Gaius. Of the fact that Gaius rejected the Fourth Gospel on the grounds of its discrepancies with the Synoptics and ascribed it to Cerinthus,[85] he gives no hint. In

---

78. On the Alogi, see Gunther, "Early Identifications," 413–17 (but most of his paragraph on pp. 416–17 is unfounded speculation); Grant, *Earliest Lives*, 28–29.

79. See fragments 10, 12, and 16 in the collection of fragments in R. M. Grant, *Second-Century Christianity: A Collection of Fragments* (London: SPCK, 1946), 106–8.

80. See fragments 11, 13, 15, and 16 in Grant, *Second-Century Christianity*, 105–8.

81. On the indication of date in chap. 17, see the list of interpretations in J. Hills, *Tradition and Composition in the Epistula Apostolorum*, HDR 24 (Minneapolis: Fortress, 1990), 166 n. 73.

82. Grant, *Earliest Lives*, 23–26.

83. See also Lightfoot's discussion of Eusebius's "silence": *Supernatural Religion*, 36–52.

84. Cf. *Hist. eccl.* 3.3.3; 3.24.16.

85. See fragments 10 and 11 (from Dionysius Bar Salibi) in Grant, *Second-Century Christianity*, 106. In both of these, Gaius is named. On the reliability of this ascription to Gaius, see J. R. Harris, *Hermas in Arcadia and Other Essays* (Cambridge: Cambridge University Press, 1896), 43–57.

his account of Cerinthus, he quotes Gaius's attribution of the Apocalypse to him, but not the similar attribution of the Fourth Gospel (3.28.2). More significantly, when giving his account of Gaius's work (6.20.3), he refers to the questions of the authenticity of the thirteen Pauline epistles and the authorship of Hebrews, but makes no reference to the Gospels. Clearly Eusebius did not record everything his sources said about the origins of the Gospels, but only those comments with which he agreed.

Papias's comment on Mark is the only admission of a lack of correct order in any of the Gospels that Eusebius has allowed into his work. It has slipped through his net not because what Papias said about Mark's accuracy in recording Peter's preaching was too valuable to omit. But he has obscured the importance of the question of order in Papias's quoted comments on Mark and Matthew by drastically censoring the context from which he selects these quotations. We can well imagine that he would not quote a statement about John's Gospel that was inextricable from Papias's assertion of its superiority to Matthew and Mark in the question of order.

Papias and the *Muratorian Canon*

If Papias wrote something about the origin of the Fourth Gospel that Eusebius did not record, we might expect it to have left some trace in other writers who knew Papias's work. In search of such a trace we may turn first to the *Muratorian Canon*,[86] whose relation to Papias has been occasionally noticed[87] but insufficiently examined. The section dealing with the Gospels unfortunately preserves only the last six words of the comment on Mark, followed by the comments on Luke and John:

... at which he was present, and thus he wrote them down.

The third book of the gospel is according to Luke. Luke the physician, when Paul had taken him with him after the ascension of Christ, as one skilled in writing, wrote from report in his own name, though he did not himself see the Lord in the flesh; and on that account, as he was able to ascertain [events], so [he set them down]. So he began his story from the birth of John.

The fourth of the gospels is of John, one of the disciples. To his fellow-disciples and bishops, who were encouraging him, he said, "Fast with me today for three days, and whatever will be revealed to each of us, let us tell to one another." The same night it was revealed to Andrew, one of the apostles, that all should certify what John wrote in his own name.

Therefore, while various elements may be taught in the several books of gospels, it makes no difference to the faith of believers, for by the one chief Spirit all things have been declared in all: concerning the nativity, the passion, the resurrection, the life with his disciples, and his double advent, first in lowliness and contempt (which has taken place), second in glorious royal power (which is to be).

Why, then, is it remarkable that John so constantly brings forth single points even in his epistles, saying of himself, "What we have seen with our eyes and heard with our ears and our hands have handled, these we write to you"?[88] Thus he professes himself not only an eyewitness and hearer but also a writer of all the miracles of the Lord in order.[89]

The words with which the fragment begins (*quibus tamen interfuit et ita posuit*) are most easily intelligible as dependent on what Papias said about Mark. They cannot mean that Mark was present at the events he recorded, not only because no early tradition suggests this, but also because the subsequent statement about Luke, that "he did not himself see the Lord in the flesh" (*dominum tamen nec ipse vidit in carne*), should probably be translated: "he also did not see. ..." In other words, Luke, like Mark, was not an eyewitness of the ministry of Jesus.[90] Therefore the comment on Mark was probably to the effect that (as Papias said) he had not been a disciple of Jesus, but he had been present at Peter's preaching and set down in writing what he heard from Peter. If the surviving words mean that Mark set down what Peter said just as he heard it, this reflects Papias's own account, not the accounts of Irenaeus and Clement of Alexandria dependent on Papias. The whole *Muratorian Canon* is, in fact, notable for the lack of any sign of Irenaeus's influence.[91]

The last sentence of the quoted section should also be compared with Papias on Mark. That John was not only an eye and ear witness but also wrote all the miracles of the Lord in order (*non solum uisurem sed et auditorem sed et scriptorem omnium mirabilium domini per ordinem*) corresponds to Papias's assertion that Mark "neither heard the Lord nor followed him" and did not write "in order" what was said and done by the Lord. Because John, unlike Mark, was an eyewitness he was able to write "in order" (*per ordinem*, surely corresponding to τάξει in Papias). Moreover, the order thus validated is that of the Lord's miracles, referring to the

---

86. The usual dating of the *Muratorian Canon* in the late second century was challenged by A. C. Sundberg, "Canon Muratori: A Fourth-Century List," *HTR* 66 (1973): 1–41, but his challenge has not been regarded as successful: see E. Ferguson, "Canon Muratori: Date and Provenance," *Studia Patristica* 18 (1982): 677–83; F. F. Bruce, "Some Thoughts on the Beginning of the New Testament Canon," *BJRL* 65 (1983): 56–57; B. M. Metzger, *The Canon of the New Testament: Its Origin, Development, and Significance* (Oxford: Clarendon, 1987), 193–94.
87. Lightfoot, *Biblical Essays*, 100; idem, *Supernatural Religion*, 205–7; Braun, *Jean le Théologien*, 355; A. Ehrhardt, "The Gospels in the Muratorian Fragment," in *The Framework of the New Testament Stories*, ed. A. Ehrhardt (Manchester: Manchester University Press, 1964), 12–13.
88. Cf. 1 John 1:1, 4.
89. Translation from Grant, *Second-Century Christianity*, 118 (slightly adapted).
90. Lightfoot, *Supernatural Religion*, 206; Ehrhardt, "Gospels," 13.
91. Ehrhardt rather oddly comments: "Irenaeus's influence upon the *Muratorian Canon* scarcely extended beyond a commendation of Papias" ("Gospels," 14). There is no reason why the author should not have known Papias's work without Irenaeus's commendation.

The Testimony of the Beloved Disciple

most obvious way in which the Fourth Gospel appears to insist on chronological order: in specifying the first two signs as the first and the second of a sequence (2:11; 4:54). Though we do not know what the *Muratorian Canon* said about Matthew, this concluding statement clearly makes John superior to Mark and Luke when it comes to order.

Such a statement is the kind of claim we have already concluded that Papias probably made about the Fourth Gospel. The suspicion that the *Muratorian Canon* is here borrowing from Papias is confirmed by the quotation from 1 John, which is used to substantiate the claim that John wrote as an eyewitness and therefore "in order."[92] This can be related to Eusebius's statement that Papias cited testimonies from 1 John and 1 Peter (*Hist. eccl.* 3.39.17).[93] If, as we have argued, the testimony from 1 Peter was a quotation of 1 Peter 5:13, adduced in support of what Papias said about Mark's Gospel, a quotation of 1 John 1:1–4, in support of what he said about John's Gospel, would be an appropriate parallel.

Thus it is likely that the last paragraph in our quoted section of the *Muratorian Canon* is closely dependent on Papias. The preceding paragraph reflects the author's own apologetic concern about the differences between the Gospels.[94] It is not out of place in the middle of the comments on John, because no doubt the author was particularly conscious of the differences between John and the Synoptics. He makes the observation immediately after the story he has told about the origin of John's Gospel, because the story tells how John's fellow disciples certified John's own account. He takes this to mean that John's Gospel cannot really be in disagreement with others, as the Alogi, for example, alleged. But it is notable that his own concern (which he shares with Tertullian, *Marc.* 4.2) seems to be to stress that on the essential points in the story of Jesus (including presumably their sequence) the four Gospels agree. This is rather different from the point his subsequent statement about John's Gospel seems to make: that, as far as order is concerned, John is superior. This confirms that the latter point comes from his source.

Echoes of Papias in Irenaeus and Clement

If the *Muratorian Canon*'s quotation from 1 John and the conclusions drawn from it about the Fourth Gospel very probably follow Papias quite closely, the

Muratorian Canon's story about the origin of the Gospel is more problematic.[95] Papias is likely to have had some account of the origin of the Gospel. Just as his quotation of 1 Peter 5:13 was most likely used to substantiate the account he had given of the origin of Mark's Gospel, so we should expect that the quotation from 1 John would have been used to substantiate something he had already said about the origin of the Fourth Gospel. But we should also be alert to the possibility that the *Muratorian Canon*'s story may be a considerably embroidered version of what Papias said, if the fortunes of his account of the origin of Mark are anything to go by. This was elaborated by Clement of Alexandria and then further by Eusebius (*Hist. eccl.* 2.15.1–2), even while the latter claimed only to be repeating Papias's and Clement's account. The elaborations served the apologetic purpose of enhancing the apostolic authority of the Gospel. The same could be true of the *Muratorian Canon*'s story of the origin of the Fourth Gospel.

We should notice, in the first place, that there is good reason for supposing that this story bears some relation to Papias, and that it treats not John the son of Zebedee, but Papias's John the Elder, as the author of the Gospel.[96] This is shown by the terminology. John himself is "one of the disciples" (*ex decipulis*). He is encouraged to write by his "fellow-disciples and bishops" (*condescipulis et episcopis*), one of whom is Andrew, "one of the apostles" (*ex apostolis*). The contract between John, one of the disciples, and Andrew, one of the apostles, is striking. We recall that in the passage from his prologue that Eusebius quotes (*Hist. eccl.* 3.39.4), Papias uses the term "disciples of the Lord" for all who had been personal disciples of the Lord, whether members of the Twelve (such as the seven he lists) or others (such as Aristion and John the Elder). He uses the term "apostle" for those who were members of the Twelve, in preference to the term "apostle," no doubt because it is the fact that they had been personal disciples of Jesus that matters to him. The term "apostle" as such did not necessarily convey this meaning, especially as in Asia, even for Papias, Paul was "the Apostle."[97] But in the passage from the prologue Papias uses no term that distinguishes members of the Twelve from other disciples of the Lord. The author of the *Muratorian Canon* makes this distinction by calling John "one of the disciples" and Andrew "one of the apostles." He did not need to call Andrew this to distinguish him from some other Andrew, but evidently did so to distinguish a member of the Twelve from John, who was not a member of the Twelve. This is the distinction Papias

---

92. In his discussion of this section of the *Muratorian Canon*, Ehrhardt, "Gospels," 26–36, is led astray by connecting the quotation from 1 John with 1 Cor. 2:9 and regarding the latter as a Pauline slogan. The quotation in 1 Cor. 2:9 was much too widely used to have been considered a Pauline slogan: see M. E. Stone and J. Strugnell, *The Books of Elijah: Parts 1–2* (Missoula, MT: Scholars Press, 1979), 42–73.

93. Already suggested by Lightfoot, *Supernatural Religion*, 206.

94. Ehrhardt, "Gospels," 26, is mistaken in seeing the influence of Papias on this passage.

95. There is no evidence to support the suggestion (cf. B. W. Bacon, *The Gospel of the Hellenists* [New York: H. Holt, 1933], 37) that the story comes from the *Acts of John*. In that case we should expect it to be more widely known, whereas in fact it is extant only in the *Muratorian Canon*.

96. That Streeter, *Four Gospels*, 439–40, was able to quote the *Muratorian Canon* without noticing its support for his own view that the author of the Fourth Gospel was John the Elder is remarkable, and illustrates how far study of the external evidence has been dominated by an uncritical assumption that second-century references to "John" as the author of the Fourth Gospel must be to the son of Zebedee.

97. Papias refers to Paul as "the Apostle" in fragment 23 in Kürzinger, *Papias*, 128–29, = fragment 24 in Holmes, *Apostolic Fathers*, 318–19 (fragment 24.7).

in fact makes, in the prologue, between Andrew and John the Elder—although he does not there need to use the word "apostle" to do so. That the author of the *Muratorian Canon* is deliberately working with the categories of disciples Papias distinguishes in the prologue is further suggested by the fact that the apostle he singles out is Andrew, who heads Papias's list of seven disciples.

Thus the author of the *Muratorian Canon* evidently means that John, who was a disciple but not a member of the Twelve, met with his fellow disciples of the Twelve and other personal disciples of Jesus, and it was to Andrew, the foremost member of the Twelve who was present, that the revelation came. The greatest obstacle to supposing that this account as such derives from Papias is that it presupposes that when the Fourth Gospel was written not only Andrew but also a number of other disciples of Jesus were still alive. Papias in his prologue clearly implies that at the time when he was collecting oral traditions not only Andrew but also all other disciples of the Lord whose teaching could have been accessible to him, with the exception of Aristion and John the Elder, were already dead. It is possible that he dated the writing of the Fourth Gospel considerably earlier than this, but unlikely, in view of the fact that Irenaeus and Clement of Alexandria, who both knew Papias's work, both thought John's the last Gospel to be written.

In order to discern just what the *Muratorian Canon* owes to Papias, it will be useful to notice that, whereas its story of the origin of the Fourth Gospel does not occur in any other extant source, two elements of the story are found elsewhere. These are the two aspects of the part that the other disciples play in the origin of the Gospel: they encourage (*cohortantibus*) John to write and they certify (*recognoscentibus*) what John writes as true. The second aspect is most likely, as has long been recognized, an interpretation of John 21:24.[98]

This second aspect can also be found in Irenaeus, whose evidence is important because he undoubtedly knew Papias's work very well. In *Haer.* 2.22, Irenaeus is arguing against the Valentinians who laid great stress on the symbolism of the number "30." On the basis of Luke 3:23 and the supposition, which could be made on the basis of the Synoptics, that Jesus' ministry lasted only one year, they thought that Jesus was no more than thirty years old when he died. Irenaeus appeals to the Johannine chronology to support a ministry of several years, and argues that in fact Jesus was between forty and fifty when he died. The point has theological importance for him, because it enables him to claim that Jesus entered the last of the periods of human life, and so passed through all the stages of human life (2.22.4). But he also has evidence that Jesus lived beyond forty:

For everyone will admit that the age of thirty is that of someone still young and this period of youth extends to the fortieth year.[99] It is only from the fortieth and fiftieth year that a person begins to decline towards old age. This is the age which our Lord possessed while he was still teaching, as the Gospel testifies and all the elders who associated (συμβεβληκότες) with John the disciple of the Lord in Asia testify (μαρτυροῦσιν), [saying that] John transmitted [to them the same tradition]. For he remained with them until the time of Trajan. Some of them saw not only John but also other apostles, and heard the same things from them, and testify to the truth of this report (*testantur de huiusmodi relatione*). Whom then should we rather believe? Such men as these, or Ptolemaeus, who never saw the apostles and even in his dreams never followed even the footprint of an apostle? (*Haer.* 2.22.5; Greek text partly in Eusebius, *Hist. eccl.* 3.23.3)

Irenaeus goes on (in 2.22.6) to expound John 8:57 ("You are not yet fifty years old") as implying that Jesus had passed forty (otherwise the Jews would have said, "You are not yet forty years old"). Clearly it is to this text that he refers in the passage just quoted ("as the Gospel testifies"). His further reference to the elders has commonly been taken to mean that he knew a tradition from the elders that *also* affirmed that Jesus lived beyond forty years.[100] Irenaeus, of course, several times quotes traditions of the elders, and sometimes, if not always,[101] derives them from Papias. But in this case the more probable explanation, though it seems to have gone unnoticed, is that Irenaeus is referring to John 21:24 ("we know that his testimony is true"). He takes the "we" of that verse to be the elders who knew John in Asia, and by that statement testified to the truth of all he had written in the Gospel. Thus they testified to the truth of John 8:57 along with every other part of the Gospel record of Jesus. They were able to certify the truth of all that John had written, both by testifying that it was John the disciple of the Lord who transmitted these traditions and because some of them had in the past also known other apostles and were able to testify that John's record agreed with what they had heard from other apostles. Irenaeus gives this explanation of John 21:24 here because it is at this point very important to him to maintain the eyewitness authority of a statement peculiar to the Fourth Gospel.

So far as it goes, this report that the elders certified the truth of John's Gospel coincides with the story in the *Muratorian Canon*. What they have in common may well go back to Papias. But there are two important differences. First, Irenaeus, by placing John the disciple of the Lord alongside "the other apostles" (*alios apostolos*) seems to include John among the apostles in a way that he does very occasionally elsewhere. We shall return later to Irenaeus's identification of John. But his language thus differs from that of the *Muratorian Canon*, in which John and Andrew are contrasted as "one of the disciples" and "one of the apostles." The latter must preserve Papias's attribution of the gospel to John the Elder. Second,

---

98. Bacon, *Gospel of the Hellenists*, 36–37.
99. The Latin text of this sentence is corrupt: see the note in A. Rousseau and L. Doutreleau, *Irénée de Lyon: Contre les hérésies, Livre II*, vol. 1, Sources chrétiennes 293 (Paris: Cerf, 1982), 288.
100. Lightfoot, *Biblical Essays*, 56–58; idem, *Supernatural Religion*, 245–47; J. Chapman, "Papias on the Age of Our Lord," *JTS* 9 (1908): 53–61 (who thinks Irenaeus misunderstood a statement of Papias); Gunther, "Early Identifications," 408.
101. Cf. Chapman, *John the Presbyter*, 16, for the view that he always derives them from Papias.

those who certify the Gospel are, in Irenaeus, the elders who knew John, but in the *Muratorian Canon* they are John's "fellow-disciples and bishops." An explanation of this difference will confirm that both writers are indebted to Papias.

In Irenaeus "the elders" are usually the generation of Christian teachers in Asia who had known the apostles but outlived them.[102] There is good reason to think that this is also how Papias used the term. The elders were those who were teaching in the churches of Asia in the late first century and whose traditions, which they had received from those who had been personal disciples of the Lord, Papias recorded in his work. At the time when he was collecting his oral traditions, the only personal disciples of Jesus still alive were Aristion and John the Elder.[103] These were elders in the sense that at that time they belonged to the same circle of senior teachers as the rest of the elders, but unlike the rest they had themselves been disciples of Jesus. Thus John the Elder was so called to distinguish him from the other disciple of Jesus called John, who was one of the Twelve. Papias collected both the traditions of the elders who had known disciples of the Lord no longer alive and the traditions of Aristion and John the Elder who were at that time still alive. But Papias's use of the term "elders" in the famous sentence of his prologue about the disciples of the Lord is notoriously ambiguous: εἰ δέ που καὶ παρηκολουθηκώς τις τοῖς πρεσβυτέροις ἔλθοι, τοὺς τῶν πρεσβυτέρων ἀνέκρινον λόγους, τί Ἀνδρέας ἢ Πέτρος εἶπεν . . . (Eusebius, *Hist. eccl.* 3.39.4). The most probably meaning, which makes Papias's use of the term "elders" here consistent with that of Irenaeus who knew his work well, is that the elders are not the same people as Peter and Andrew and the other disciples listed.[104] The elders are the senior Christian teachers in various cities of Asia at the time when Papias was collecting traditions. Papias, living at Hierapolis, did not normally have the opportunity to hear them himself, but when any of their followers visited Hierapolis "he inquired about the words of the elders, [that is] what [according to the elders] Andrew and Peter had said." This interpretation is much more obviously consistent with the statement Papias had made just before, that he himself had learned from the elders (παρὰ τῶν πρεσβυτέρων . . . ἔμαθον), than is the interpretation that equates the elders with Andrew and Peter and the rest of the disciples of the Lord. Papias's words are ambiguous only because he takes it for granted that the words of the elders in which he would be interested are those that transmit traditions from Andrew and Peter and the other disciples of the Lord.

However, it is possible to read Papias's words as equating the elders with Andrew and Peter and the rest. This seems to have been how Eusebius read them (*Hist. eccl.* 3.39.7).[105] If we suppose that this is also how the author of the *Muratorian Canon* read them, we can see why his identification of those who certified John's Gospel differs from Irenaeus's. Papias, we may suppose, said that John's Gospel was certified by the elders. Perhaps he even called them John's fellow elders (συνπρεσβύτεροι). The author of the *Muratorian Canon*, guided by a misunderstanding of Papias's words in the prologue, assumed that these elders were the other disciples of the Lord whom Papias there names. He therefore calls them John's "fellow-disciples." Asking himself why they were called elders and perhaps remembering 1 Peter 5:1–2, he assumes this must be because they were also bishops.[106] So he calls them John's "fellow-disciples and bishops," and when he wishes to name one of them, he naturally selects the first name in Papias's list of these supposed elders: Andrew.

Irenaeus, on the other hand, correctly understood Papias. The elders could vouch for the truth of John's Gospel, not because they themselves had been disciples of the Lord, but because some of them had known other disciples of the Lord besides John. When Irenaeus adds that John survived to the reign of Trajan (also in *Haer.* 3.3.4),[107] it is possible he drew this from Papias's account of the origin of the Fourth Gospel, but chronological indications of this kind do not seem to be characteristic of Papias. So it is also quite possible that Irenaeus calculated this one himself, knowing that John's was the last of the four Gospels to be written (*Haer.* 3.1.1) and believing that the same John wrote the Apocalypse in the reign of Domitian (*Haer.* 5.30.3). Such a deduction would be comparable with the way he adds greater chronological precision to Papias's accounts of the origins of the Gospels of Matthew and Mark, doubtless by intelligent deduction rather than because he had additional information (*Haer.* 3.1.1).[108] Thus John the Elder need not have been quite so young at the time of Jesus' ministry or quite as old at the end of his life when he wrote the Gospel as Irenaeus's calculation would require.

The other aspect of the role of John's fellow disciples in the story in the *Muratorian Canon* is that they urged (*cohortantibus*) him to write. This has a kind of parallel in Clement of Alexandria, another writer who seems to have known Papias's work, since his account of the origin of Mark's Gospel (ap. Eusebius, *Hist. eccl.* 6.14.6) is dependent on Papias. Of the Fourth Gospel he said:

---

102. See the references and discussion in ibid, 13–16.

103. Carpenter, *Johannine Writings*, 214; and Schnackenburg, *John*, 1.89–90, deny that Aristion and John the Elder had been personal disciples of Jesus, apparently because they think Papias means that they were still alive when he wrote his book. The date of Papias's work is very uncertain, but his statement in the prologue need mean only that they were still alive when he was collecting oral traditions. This could have been as early as the 80s.

104. The interpretation of Papias's statement by Chapman, *John the Presbyter*, 9–27, is in this respect convincing. Cf. also Körtner, *Papias*, 114–22, who agrees, but also, more questionably, sees the elders as itinerant teachers.

105. But cf. Chapman, *John the Presbyter*, 17–19.

106. That the elders are bishops is also the interpretation of Irenaeus, *Haer.* 2.22.5, in the passages of Victorinus, Jerome, and the *Monarchian Prologue* quoted in "Some False Leads," below.

107. The recurrence of the same phraseology in 2.22.5 and 3.3.4 could indicate a common literary source (Papias: so Chapman, "Papias," 57 n. 1) or a traditional Asian way of speaking of John of Ephesus, but could merely mean that Irenaeus repeats himself.

108. Cf. R. Bauckham, "The Martyrdom of Peter in the New Testament and Early Christian Literature," *ANRW* 2.26.1:539–95. J. Chapman, "St. Irenaeus and the Dates of the Gospels," *JTS* 6 (1905): 563–69, agrees that Irenaeus had only Papias's information, but denies that he intends to give greater chronological precision than Papias.

that John, conscious that the outward facts (τὰ σωματικά) had been set forth in the [other] Gospels, was urged on by his disciples[109] (προτραπέντα ὑπὸ τῶν γνωρίμων), and, divinely moved by the Spirit, composed a spiritual (πνευματικόν) Gospel. (*Hypotyposeis*, ap. Eusebius, *Hist. eccl.* 6.14.7)

The contrast here between the Synoptics, as recording τὰ σωματικά, and the Fourth Gospel, as a spiritual Gospel, is certainly Clement's own. This leaves, as the only detail that could be derived from Papias, the comment that John was urged to write by his disciples. However, we should note that in his account of the origin of Mark's Gospel, Clement (ap. Eusebius, *Hist. eccl.* 6.14.6) added to what he knew from Papias the information that those who had heard Peter's preaching exhorted (παρακαλέσαι) Mark to write a record of what he had said (cf. the further elaboration of this point by Eusebius, *Hist. eccl.* 2.15.1). So although the coincidence between Clement and the *Muratorian Canon* is notable and may well indicate that Papias said the elders urged John to write his Gospel, as well as certifying it when it was written, it is possible that this is a conventional topos to explain why an author put pen to paper and that the agreement between Clement and the *Muratorian Canon* is just a coincidence. If Clement read in Papias that the elders certified John's Gospel, it is not surprising that he did not reproduce this. He would not have seen why John should need to have the truth of his Gospel authenticated by mere elders.[110] But Clement's account of the origin of the Gospel confirms that Papias provided no more interesting detail about this matter than we have so far reconstructed.

We conclude that what Papias said about the origin of the Fourth Gospel was that John the Elder, the disciple of the Lord, wrote it.[111] He may have said he was urged to do so by the elders of Asia. He certainly said that the elders vouched for the truth of the Gospel (referring to John 21:24). (Papias's readers knew from his prologue, if not from elsewhere in his work, that these elders were able to do so because they had known other very prominent disciples of the Lord and themselves passed on traditions from them.) He then quoted part of 1 John 1:1–4 to show that John the Elder was both an eyewitness of the events of the Gospel history and wrote them in his Gospel. Therefore he (alone of the evangelists) wrote the λόγια of the Lord in order.

109. The translation given by Ehrhardt ("Gospels," 20) has "urged on by the 'Elders.'" This must be a mistake, but it is a serious one because it makes Clement's statement look closer to the elders of Papias and Irenaeus than it is. John's disciples no doubt are the elders, but Clement does not here call them so.
110. This is also why in the passages from Victorinus, Jerome, and the *Monarchian Prologue*, quoted in "Some False Leads" below, there is no reference to certification by the bishops, even though these passages are dependent on Irenaeus, *Haer.* 2.22.5. They have followed Clement in substituting encouragement to John to write for certification of what John had written.
111. There is no need in this context to adjudicate the vexed question of whether Papias referred to the martyrdom of John the son of Zebedee (and so is not likely to have ascribed the Fourth Gospel to him). For recent arguments in favor of the authenticity of such a reference, see Colson, *L'énigme*, 65–84; Hengel, *Johannine Question*, 158–59.

It might be objected that surely Papias, who was in a good position to know about the origin of the Fourth Gospel, could have given more information than this. In reply, we recall that it was not Papias's purpose to state all he may have known about the origins of the Gospels. What we have reconstructed serves precisely his purpose in proving the superiority of the Fourth Gospel, as far as order is concerned, over the other two Gospels believed to derive from eyewitness testimony.

Some False Leads

It remains to consider three related passages in later writers, which at first sight look as though they may be dependent on Papias but will turn out not to be:

For when Valentinus, Cerinthus and Ebion and the others of the school of Satan were spread over the world, all the bishops came together to him (*conuenerunt ad illum*) from the most distant provinces and compelled (*compulerunt*) him to write a testimony. (Victorinus of Pettau, *In apoc.* 11.1)[112]

John, the apostle whom Jesus most loved, the son of Zebedee and brother of James the apostle, whom Herod, after the Lord's passion, beheaded, was the last one to write a Gospel, at the request (*rogatus*) of the bishops of Asia, against Cerinthus and other heretics and especially against the then growing doctrine of the Ebionites, who asserted that Christ did not exist before Mary. For this reason he was compelled (*compulsus est*) also to announce his divine nativity. (Jerome, *Vir. ill.* 9)[113]

When, however, after the death of Domitian, [John] was set free and returned from exile to Ephesus, and the seeds of the heretics—of Cerinthus, Ebion, and others who deny that Christ existed before Mary—already budded forth at that time, he was compelled (*compulsus est*) by almost all the bishops at that time in Asia and embassies from many churches to write about the divinity of Christ in a more profound way. (*Monarchian Prologue to John*)[114]

These passages, like many later patristic statements about the origins of the Gospels, result from bringing together the bits of information that could be gathered from early sources. In this case, information is drawn from three sources: (1) a statement by Irenaeus that John wrote his Gospel against Cerinthus (*Haer.* 3.11.1); (2) the passage in Irenaeus, *Haer.* 2.22.5, which we have already discussed (and which it is interesting to find was understood correctly as a reference to the origin of the Fourth Gospel): this supplied the information about the bishops;

112. Translation adapted from A. F. J. Klijn and G. J. Reinink, *Patristic Evidence for Jewish-Christian Sects*, Supplements to *Novum Testamentum* 36 (Leiden: Brill, 1973), 137.
113. Translation adapted from ibid., 211.
114. Ibid., 235.

and (3) Clement of Alexandria's statement that John was urged to write by his disciples (ap. Eusebius, *Hist. eccl.* 6.14.7). In the case of Victorinus,[115] it can be demonstrated that any debt to Papias is only indirect, via Irenaeus (*Haer.* 2.22.5). In that passage, the Greek text that Eusebius preserves says that the elders οἱ κατὰ τὴν Ἀσίαν Ἰωάννῃ τῷ τοῦ Κυρίου μαθητῇ συμβεβληκότες (*Hist. eccl.* 3.23.3), but the Latin translator of Irenaeus evidently read συμβεβηκότες for συμβεβληκότες and so translated: *qui in Asia apud Johannem discipulum domini conuenerunt.* That Eusebius has the correct text can be seen from the parallel statement about Clement of Rome that Irenaeus makes in *Adversus haereses* 3.3.3 (συμβεβληκὼς αὐτοῖς, i.e., the apostles).[116] Victorinus evidently understood the Latin version of Irenaeus to mean that bishops from outside Asia came together to John in Asia. Jerome's statement, because it does not make the same mistake about the identity of the bishops but speaks of "the bishops of Asia," must be based not on Victorinus but on a common source used by both Victorinus and Jerome. They cannot be independently based on Irenaeus, because both take the elders in Irenaeus to be bishops, and both combine information from this passage of Irenaeus with information from *Adversus haereses* 3.11.1, adding Ebion or the Ebionites to Irenaeus's mention of Cerinthus,[117] and with information from Jerome. Clement of Alexandria. The *Monarchian Prologue* is probably directly dependent on Jerome.

John the Elder Conflated with John the Son of Zebedee

The Fourth Gospel was never anonymous. As Hengel has shown,[118] as soon as Gospels circulated in the churches, they must have been known with authors' names attached to them. The Fourth Gospel was known as John's. In Asia, the tradition from Papias early in the second century to Polycrates at its end was that this John, the beloved disciple and the author of the Gospel, was John the Elder, a disciple of the Lord but not one of the Twelve, who had died in Ephesus.

115. Chapman ("Papias," 47–53) argues that Victorinus was dependent on Papias. Not all of his evidence is convincing, but some of it is, especially Victorinus's account of Mark's authorship of his Gospel. However, it is not certain that Victorinus knew Papias's work directly. If he did, he need not be dependent on Papias in the quoted passage.
116. See the discussion in Rousseau and Doutreleau, *Irénée de Lyon*, 1:288.
117. That John wrote his Gospel against the Cerinthians and the Ebionites is also found in Epiphanius, *Pan.* 51.2; 69.23; cf. 51.12. In 51.12 it is not clear whether Epiphanius means that John was compelled (ἀναγκάζεται) to write the Gospel by the Holy Spirit (already mentioned) or the bishops (not mentioned).
118. Hengel, *Johannine Question*, 74–76; cf. also, in more detail, Hengel, *Studies in the Gospel of Mark and Their History and Development* (London: SCM, 1985), 64–84, and the criticism of his view by H. Koester, *Ancient Christian Gospels: Their History and Development* (London: SCM, 1990), 26–27. But it is noteworthy that Koester's objection is to the view that the Gospels originally bore titles of the form, "The Gospel according to . . ." (τὸ εὐαγγέλιον κατά . . .). He allows that Hengel may be correct in arguing that the Gospels must have circulated under the names of specific authors from the beginning.

We know of no dissent from this tradition in Asia before the third century. It is not certain when the identification of this John of Ephesus with John the son of Zebedee was first accepted in Asia,[119] but it does not appear to have happened for more than a century after the writing of the Gospel.

The identification of John of Ephesus, the beloved disciple and the author of the Fourth Gospel, with John the son of Zebedee seems to have been first made in Egypt. The only unambiguous identifications of the author of the Fourth Gospel with John the son of Zebedee in second-century literature are in the *Epistle of the Apostles* and the *Acts of John*, which both appear to be Egyptian works[120] from around the middle of the second century.[121] In addition, Valentinian teachers of the second half of the second century—Ptolemy[122] and Theodotus[123]—call the author of the Fourth Gospel an apostle. Probably the Valentinian school derived from Egyptian Christian tradition the view that the author of the Fourth Gospel was the apostle John the son of Zebedee. Admittedly, the term "apostle" was sufficiently flexible to leave this in some doubt, as is also the case when Clement of Alexandria refers to John of Ephesus, author of the Apocalypse and presumably also of the Fourth Gospel (cf. Eusebius, *Hist. eccl.* 6.14.7) as "John the apostle" (*Quis div.* 42 = Eusebius, *Hist. eccl.* 3.23.6). After all, Clement of Alexandria can refer to Clement of Rome as "the apostle Clement" (*Strom.* 4.17.105.1). But probably these references to John as the apostle belong to an originally Egyptian tradition of identifying the author of the Fourth Gospel with John the son of Zebedee. This tradition will have originated quite naturally from an attempt to relate the Fourth Gospel to other traditions about the disciples of Jesus, among whom only one, the son of Zebedee, was known by the name of John. It was not that in Egypt nothing was known of the author of the Fourth Gospel except his name John. The *Acts of John* show that he was known to have lived and died at Ephesus, and Clement of Alexandria knew traditions about the John of Ephesus

119. Eusebius, *Hist. eccl.* 5.18.14, reports that Apollonius, the anti-Montanist writer, who was probably writing at Ephesus at the beginning of the third century, quoted the Apocalypse and told a story about a resurrection performed by John of Ephesus, but Eusebius is suspiciously silent about his views on the Fourth Gospel. It is possible that the Montanist writer Proclus thought that John the son of Zebedee wrote the Fourth Gospel and the Apocalypse, since his opponent Gaius seems to be rejecting the authorship of both by an apostle (fragments 2, 10, in Grant, *Second-Century Christianity*, 105–6), but is not certain that Proclus came from Asia.
120. For the Egyptian origin of the *Epistle of the Apostles*, see M. Hornschuh, *Studien zur Epistula Apostolorum* (Berlin: de Gruyter, 1965). For the Egyptian origin of the *Acts of John*, see E. Junod and J.-D. Kaestli, *Acta Johannis*, Corpus Christianorum Series Apocryphorum 2 (Turnhout: Brepols, 1983), 692–94; they consider Syria also possible (691–92), but Asia Minor impossible (691).
121. For the date of the *Acts of John*, see Junod and Kaestli, *Acta Johannis* 694–700. Colson, who attributes the confusion of the author of the Fourth Gospel with John the son of Zebedee to Irenaeus's confusion of them in his memory of what in his youth he had heard Polycarp say (*L'énigme*, 32–34, 55–56, 113), ignores the *Epistle of the Apostles* and the *Acts of John*.
122. *Letter to Flora*, ap. Epiphanius, *Pan.* 33.3.6. He also called the author of the Fourth Gospel, as Irenaeus did, "John the Lord's disciple" (ap. Irenaeus, *Haer.* 1.8.5).
123. Clement of Alexandria, *Exc.* 7.3; 35.1.1; 41.3.

whom he took to be the author of the Gospel (*Quis div.* 42 = Eusebius, *Hist. eccl.* 3.23.5–19).[124] The Gospel must have come to Egypt, as we should expect, along with some oral information about its author, though not enough to prevent his identification with the son of Zebedee. The ascription of the Gospel to John the son of Zebedee probably spread through the churches from the late second century through the influence of the *Acts of John*, Clement of Alexandria, and other representatives of the Egyptian tradition.[125]

The writings of Irenaeus help to show us why this ascription would prove acceptable. It has been commonly assumed and sometimes argued[126] that Irenaeus identified the author of the Fourth Gospel with John the son of Zebedee, but this has also been vigorously contested.[127] Decisive evidence is surprisingly and significantly elusive, despite Irenaeus's frequent references to the Fourth Gospel and its author. Irenaeus knew of John of Ephesus both from Papias and independently from the Asian traditions he learned in Smyrna as a young man (ap. Eusebius, *Hist. eccl.* 5.20.6; *Haer.* 3.3.4).[128] He refers to John (regarding him as the author of all the Johannine writings, including the Apocalypse)[129] twenty-two times as "the disciple of the Lord" (and thirty-four times as just "John"), never as "John the apostle," by contrast with his references to Paul, who is quite frequently "Paul the apostle" (and much more frequently just "the Apostle"), Matthew (once "Matthew the apostle," usually just "Matthew"), and Peter (three times "Peter the apostle," usually just "Peter").[130] No doubt "John the disciple of the Lord" is traditional Asian usage,[131] firmly fixed in Irenaeus's terminology from his early days in Smyrna. The term itself merely indicates a personal disciple of Jesus and could apply, as in Papias, to members of the Twelve as well as to others. In the Asian tradition of emphasizing tradition from the eyewitnesses of the ministry of Jesus, which Irenaeus's references to John continue (cf. especially Eusebius, *Hist. eccl.* 5.20.6), the term "disciple of the Lord" was preferable to "apostle," which, as in the case of "*the Apostle*" (Paul), need not imply this. But it is significant that Irenaeus applies this term to no individual except John (while in *Haer.* 3.12.5 the plural seems to refer to disciples who were explicitly not apostles).

However, Irenaeus twice calls the author of the Fourth Gospel "the apostle" (*Haer.* 1.9.2–3), twice puts John alongside "the other apostles" (*Haer.* 2.22.5; *Letter to Victor*, ap. Eusebius, *Hist. eccl.* 5.24.16), and in one other passage clearly includes John in the category of the apostles (*Haer.* 3.3.4). We can see why he does so.[132] In *Haer.* 1.9.2–3 he is arguing with the Valentinian Ptolemy (who himself calls the author of the Fourth Gospel "the apostle")[133] and from whom Irenaeus may in this context have borrowed the usage). In *Haer.* 2.22.5, he is concerned with the elders' certification of the eyewitness authority of John's Gospel. In the other two passages he is concerned with Polycarp's role as the next link after the apostles in a chain of apostolic tradition. All these passages reflect Irenaeus's concern with apostolicity as the criterion of truth against the Gnostics, including both the apostolicity of the reliable scriptures of the New Testament and the succession of public teaching from the apostles through the bishops of the apostolic sees. In these contexts, the term "apostle" indicates reliable authority, authorized by Christ, publicly recognized, by contrast with the chains of secret tradition from disciples of Jesus that the Gnostics claimed.[134] It is understandable that Irenaeus should assimilate to this concept of apostolicity his own favorite evangelist and the most important source of eyewitness tradition from the ministry of Jesus in his native Asia. But since Irenaeus can treat the seventy as "other apostles" in addition to the Twelve (*Haer.* 2.21.1), there is no need to suppose he included the fourth evangelist among the Twelve. He himself valued the Asian tradition too highly to identify John of Ephesus with John the son of Zebedee, but it is understandable that others, influenced by the same concept of apostolicity, should have welcomed the opportunity to do so. Increasing (and related) use of the terms, found in the *Muratorian Canon*, "the prophets" and "the apostles" to refer respectively to the Old and New Testament scriptures would have the same effect. Mark and Luke qualified as New Testament authors by being considered disciples of the apostles, but the notion of a writer of scripture who was a disciple of Jesus but not an apostle

---

124. Identification of the author of the Fourth Gospel with the author of the Apocalypse would not necessarily lead to any special relationship with Ephesus, which is only one of the seven churches of Asia addressed in Revelation.

125. In North Africa, Tertullian, ca. 200, considered the author of the Fourth Gospel and the Apocalypse to be John the son of Zebedee: *Praescr.* 22, 36. But from Theophilus, *Autol.* 2.22, it is impossible to tell whether the identification of the author of the Fourth Gospel with the son of Zebedee was yet current in Syria.

126. E.g., Chapman, *John the Presbyter*, 42–43.

127. E.g., Burney, *Aramaic Origin*, 138–42; Gunther, "Early Identifications," 418–19; cf. Colson, *L'énigme*, 29–34.

128. For Irenaeus's age when he knew Polycarp, see Chapman, *John the Presbyter*, 44; Colson, *L'énigme*, 32–33.

129. The development of views on the authorship of the Apocalypse is even more difficult to trace than that of views on the authorship of the Fourth Gospel. From Irenaeus onward, common authorship of all the Johannine writings seems to have been widely accepted, but there is no evidence for this before Irenaeus. Justin, *Dial.* 81.4, ascribes the Apocalypse to the apostle John, but his view of the authorship of the Fourth Gospel is unknown. I am inclined to think that the two tombs of two Johns at Ephesus, of which Dionysius of Alexandria had heard and which he thought were those of John the son of Zebedee (author of the Gospel) and John the Elder (author of the Apocalypse), were actually those of John the Elder (author of the Gospel) and John the prophet (author of the Apocalypse). But it is possible that the association of the author of the Apocalypse with Ephesus in particular is a mistake resulting from the late second-century identification of him with the author of the Gospel.

130. The calculations are my own.

131. It is also found, outside Asia, in Ptolemy (ap. Irenaeus, *Haer.* 1.8.5), and Heracleon (ap. Origen, *Comm. Jo.* 6.3); cf. the apocryphal letter of John quoted by Pseudo-Cyprian, *De Montibus Sina et Sion* 13; also *Apocryphon of John* 1.4.

132. Cf. Carpenter, *Johannine Writings*, 208.

133. *Letter to Flora*, ap. Epiphanius, *Pan.* 33.3.6.

134. Cf. also Tertullian, *Marc.* 4.5.

must have been too anomalous to persist. Once he was considered an apostle, John of Ephesus easily became indistinguishable from the son of Zebedee.

Martin Hengel writes, "In Asia Minor there was a special interest in the 'promotion' of the 'elder John' and 'disciple of the Lord' to an 'apostle and member of the Twelve.' Like Rome and Antioch, their great competitors, they now possessed two apostles as founders."135 The more plausible this seems, the more remarkable it is that this "promotion" did not in fact take place in Asia before the third century. This gives the Asian tradition that the beloved disciple who wrote the Fourth Gospel was John the Elder a right to be taken very seriously.136

---

135. Hengel, *Johannine Question*, 31–32; cf. Sanders, *Fourth Gospel*, 38–39.

136. In *Jesus and the Eyewitnesses: The Gospels as Eyewitness Testimony* (Grand Rapids: Eerdmans, 2006), chapter 16 ("Papias on John") and chapter 17 ("Polycrates and Irenaeus on John"), I have summarized the main arguments of the present chapter and added some additional discussion of John the Elder as author of the Gospel of John. In the appendix to chapter 16, I have discussed Charles Hill's argument (Charles E. Hill, "What Papias Said about John [and Luke]: A 'New' Papias Fragment," *JTS* 49 [1998], 582–629) that Papias's views on John's Gospel are preserved in Eusebius, *Hist. eccl.* 3.14.5–13. In *Jesus and the Eyewitnesses*, chapter 17, I have provided a more extensive and detailed discussion of Irenaeus, strengthening the case for thinking he did not identify John, the author of the Gospel, with John the son of Zebedee. Hill may be correct in locating the *Epistle of the Apostles* in Asia Minor (Charles E. Hill, "The *Epistula Apostolorum*: An Asian Tract from the Time of Polycarp," *JECS* 7 [1999], 1–53), in which case my view that the identification of John the author of the Gospel with John the son of Zebedee originated in Egypt would need some qualification. The identification could well have originated independently in more than one context. On the very debatable issue of Gaius and the Alogi, reference should now be made to Charles E. Hill, *The Johannine Corpus in the Early Church* (Oxford: Oxford University Press, 2004), chapter 4.

CHAPTER ONE

INTRODUCTION

1.1 An Initial Orientation

In a 2011 article on what this study will designate collectively the Johannine *aposynagōgos* passages (John 9:22, 12:42, 16:2), John Kloppenborg offers several "grounds for supposing that a time later than the early 1st century CE is reflected by John 9:22."[1] The first of these grounds, Kloppenborg suggests, is that "it is quite unthinkable that in Jesus' day such a decision had already been taken."[2] Kloppenborg refers here to the report, in 9:22, that συνετέθειντο οἱ Ἰουδαῖοι ἵνα ἐάν τις αὐτὸν ὁμολογήσῃ Χριστόν, ἀποσυνάγωγος γένηται ("the [Judeans] had already agreed that if anyone confessed Jesus to be the Christ, he would be put out of the synagogue").[3] Surprisingly, given that this is his initial ground for supposing that a later date is reflected by 9:22, Kloppenborg makes no effort to substantiate the claim.[4]

---

[1] John S. Kloppenborg, "Disaffiliation in Associations and the ἀποσυναγωγός of John," *HTS Teologiese Studies/Theological Studies* 61/1, article 962 (2011), p. 1.

[2] Kloppenborg, "Disaffiliation," 1.

[3] Translations here and elsewhere in the study following the New Revised Standard Version, with modification. Note that the *aposynagōgos* verses proper (9:22, 12:42, and 16:2) are in italics. *Ioudaioi* is here modified from the more typical translation, "Jew," to "Judean," following Steve Mason, "Jews, Judaeans, Judaizing, Judaism: Problems of Categorization in Ancient History," *Journal for the Study of Judaism in the Persian, Hellenistic and Roman Period* 38 (2007): 457–512.

[4] Kloppenborg, "Disaffiliation," 1, offers three further "grounds for supposing that a time later than the early 1st century CE is reflected by John 9:22." None fare any better than the first. The second, that "the Pharisees, who are depicted as the interrogators in vv. 13, 15, 16, and 40, were scarcely in a position to police membership in the synagogues," would be relevant only if οἱ Ἰουδαῖοι mentioned in 9:22 are in fact the Pharisees mentioned elsewhere. As will be argued more fully in this study, it is not self-evident that the individuals who carry out the interrogation in vv. 13, 15, 16, and 40, are the same as those who made the decision referenced in 9:22. Kloppenborg's third ground is two-fold: first, that 9:22 focuses upon a Christological confession never made by the blind man whose healing triggered the interrogation; second, that this confession is inconceivable during Jesus' lifetime. The first part of this ground is irrelevant, as the matter under discussion in 9:22 is the blind man's parents' fear that they might be thought to confess Jesus. The blind man's confession is thus not an issue at all. The second part of this third ground is, as with the first ground, stated without support. As for the fourth ground, "the alleged decision concerns expulsion from a *synagogue* but the story itself is set in the shadow of the Temple," it is not at all

CHAPTER ONE

Kloppenborg might be a particularly recent voice stating without argument that the decision attested in 9:22 cannot refer to events of Jesus' life, but he is hardly the first. Raymond Brown assures us that "the description of Jesus' followers in v. 22 as those who acknowledged that he was the Messiah is too formal for the ministry of Jesus."5 C.K. Barrett writes "[t]hat the synagogue had already at that time applied a test of Christian heresy is unthinkable."6 Andrew Lincoln writes that "[a]ll the elements of this assertion [in 9:22] are anachronistic."7 Yet, how do these scholars know their statements to be true?

When few if any of a discipline's finest practitioners consider it necessary to support a particular historical claim with adequate argumentation, then the time has come to re-evaluate that claim. That is the purpose of this study. All its questions are subordinated to, and aimed at facilitating, an answer to but one larger question, namely "Could the *aposynagōgos* passages describe events that happened during Jesus' lifetime?" In the face of numerous scholars who say that they cannot possibly do so, it would be an advance in our knowledge to demonstrate even that such events are plausible. The present author aims to go further, however, and demonstrate that a judgment of probability on the matter of these passages' historicity is the best-warranted by conscientious investigation of the data.

John's *aposynagōgos* passages contain the earliest extant uses of the word ἀποσυνάγωγος, an adjective that might be most woodenly translated as "from-synagogue." Within the extant literature from antiquity, the word subsequently appears only in texts referring to these passages. 9:22 and 12:42 report that during Jesus' lifetime some of those who confessed him as messiah were afraid of being put out of the synagogue, and 16:2 reports that Jesus anticipated that such expulsions would occur after his death. Including also a broader literary context, these passages read as follows.

INTRODUCTION

9:13 "Ἄγουσιν αὐτὸν πρὸς τοὺς Φαρισαίους τόν ποτε τυφλόν. 14 ἦν δὲ σάββατον ἐν ᾗ ἡμέρᾳ τὸν πηλὸν ἐποίησεν ὁ Ἰησοῦς καὶ ἀνέῳξεν αὐτοῦ τοὺς ὀφθαλμούς. 15 πάλιν οὖν ἠρώτων αὐτὸν καὶ οἱ Φαρισαῖοι πῶς ἀνέβλεψεν. ὁ δὲ εἶπεν αὐτοῖς· πηλὸν ἐπέθηκέν μου ἐπὶ τοὺς ὀφθαλμοὺς καὶ ἐνιψάμην καὶ βλέπω. 16 ἔλεγον οὖν ἐκ τῶν Φαρισαίων τινές· οὐκ ἔστιν οὗτος παρὰ θεοῦ ὁ ἄνθρωπος, ὅτι τὸ σάββατον οὐ τηρεῖ. ἄλλοι [δὲ] ἔλεγον· πῶς δύναται ἄνθρωπος ἁμαρτωλὸς τοιαῦτα σημεῖα ποιεῖν; καὶ σχίσμα ἦν ἐν αὐτοῖς. 17 λέγουσιν οὖν τῷ τυφλῷ πάλιν· τί σὺ λέγεις περὶ αὐτοῦ, ὅτι ἠνέῳξέν σου τοὺς ὀφθαλμούς; ὁ δὲ εἶπεν ὅτι προφήτης ἐστίν. 18 Οὐκ ἐπίστευσαν οὖν οἱ Ἰουδαῖοι περὶ αὐτοῦ ὅτι ἦν τυφλὸς καὶ ἀνέβλεψεν ἕως ὅτου ἐφώνησαν τοὺς γονεῖς αὐτοῦ τοῦ ἀναβλέψαντος 19 καὶ ἠρώτησαν αὐτοὺς λέγοντες· οὗτός ἐστιν ὁ υἱὸς ὑμῶν, ὃν ὑμεῖς λέγετε ὅτι τυφλὸς ἐγεννήθη; πῶς οὖν βλέπει ἄρτι; 20 ἀπεκρίθησαν οὖν οἱ γονεῖς αὐτοῦ καὶ εἶπαν· οἴδαμεν ὅτι οὗτός ἐστιν ὁ υἱὸς ἡμῶν καὶ ὅτι τυφλὸς ἐγεννήθη· 21 πῶς δὲ νῦν βλέπει οὐκ οἴδαμεν, ἢ τίς ἤνοιξεν αὐτοῦ τοὺς ὀφθαλμοὺς ἡμεῖς οὐκ οἴδαμεν· αὐτὸν ἐρωτήσατε, ἡλικίαν ἔχει, αὐτὸς περὶ ἑαυτοῦ λαλήσει. 22 ταῦτα εἶπαν οἱ γονεῖς αὐτοῦ ὅτι ἐφοβοῦντο τοὺς Ἰουδαίους· ἤδη γὰρ συνετέθειντο οἱ Ἰουδαῖοι ἵνα ἐάν τις αὐτὸν ὁμολογήσῃ Χριστόν, ἀποσυνάγωγος γένηται.	9:13 They brought to the Pharisees the man who had formerly been blind. 14 Now it was a sabbath day when Jesus made the mud and opened his eyes. 15 Then the Pharisees also began to ask him how he had received his sight. He said to them, "He put mud on my eyes. Then I washed, and now I see." 16 Some of the Pharisees said, "This man is not from God, for he does not observe the sabbath." But others said, "How can a man who is a sinner perform such signs?" And they were divided. 17 So they said again to the blind man, "What do you say about him? It was your eyes he opened." He said, "He is a prophet." 18 The Judeans did not believe that he had been blind and had received his sight until they called the parents of the man who had received his sight 19 and asked them, "Is this your son, who you say was born blind? How then does he now see?" 20 His parents answered, "We know that this is our son, and that he was born blind; 21 but we do not know how it is that now he sees, nor do we know who opened his eyes. Ask him; he is of age. He will speak for himself." 22 *His parents said this because they were afraid of the Judeans; for the Judeans had already agreed that anyone who confessed Jesus to be the Messiah would be put out of the synagogue.*
12:37 Τοσαῦτα δὲ αὐτοῦ σημεῖα πεποιηκότος ἔμπροσθεν αὐτῶν οὐκ ἐπίστευον εἰς αὐτόν, 38 ἵνα ὁ λόγος Ἠσαΐου τοῦ προφήτου πληρωθῇ ὃν εἶπεν· κύριε, τίς ἐπίστευσεν τῇ ἀκοῇ ἡμῶν; καὶ ὁ βραχίων κυρίου τίνι ἀπεκαλύφθη; 39 διὰ τοῦτο οὐκ ἠδύναντο πιστεύειν, ὅτι πάλιν εἶπεν Ἠσαΐας· 40 τετύφλωκεν αὐτῶν τοὺς ὀφθαλμοὺς καὶ ἐπώρωσεν αὐτῶν τὴν καρδίαν, ἵνα μὴ ἴδωσιν τοῖς ὀφθαλμοῖς καὶ νοήσωσιν τῇ καρδίᾳ καὶ στραφῶσιν, καὶ ἰάσομαι αὐτούς. 41 ταῦτα εἶπεν Ἠσαΐας ὅτι εἶδεν τὴν δόξαν αὐτοῦ, καὶ ἐλάλησεν περὶ αὐτοῦ. 42 ὅμως μέντοι καὶ ἐκ τῶν ἀρχόντων πολλοὶ ἐπίστευσαν εἰς αὐτόν, ἀλλὰ διὰ τοὺς Φαρισαίους οὐχ ὡμολόγουν ἵνα μὴ ἀποσυνάγωγοι γένωνται· 43 ἠγάπησαν γὰρ τὴν δόξαν τῶν ἀνθρώπων μᾶλλον ἤπερ τὴν δόξαν τοῦ θεοῦ.	12:37 Although he had performed so many signs in their presence, they did not believe in him. 38 This was to fulfill the word spoken by the prophet Isaiah: "Lord, who has believed our message, and to whom has the arm of the Lord been revealed?" 39 And so they could not believe, because Isaiah also said, 40 "He has blinded their eyes and hardened their heart, so that

---

clear why this would stand against thinking that John intends to report events of the early first-century, and, indeed, if anything, the significance of the temple should incline us towards the idea that John intends to refer to events prior to its destruction in 70 CE.

5 Raymond E. Brown, *The Gospel According to John* (2 vols.; New York: Doubleday, 1966), 1:380.

6 C.K. Barrett, *The Gospel According to St. John* (2nd ed.; Philadelphia: The Westminster Press, 1978), 361.

7 Andrew T. Lincoln, *The Gospel According to Saint John* (London: Continuum, 2005), 284.

they might not look with their eyes, and understand with their heart and turn—and I would heal them." 41 Isaiah said this because he saw his glory and spoke about him. 42 Nevertheless many, even of the authorities, believed in him. But because of the Pharisees they did not confess it, for fear that they would be put out of the synagogue; 43 for they loved human glory more than the glory that comes from God.

16:1 Ταῦτα λελάληκα ὑμῖν ἵνα μὴ σκανδαλισθῆτε. 2 ἀποσυναγώγους ποιήσουσιν ὑμᾶς· ἀλλ' ἔρχεται ὥρα ἵνα πᾶς ὁ ἀποκτείνας ὑμᾶς δόξῃ λατρείαν προσφέρειν τῷ θεῷ. 3 καὶ ταῦτα ποιήσουσιν ὅτι οὐκ ἔγνωσαν τὸν πατέρα οὐδὲ ἐμέ.

16:1 I have said these things to you to keep you from stumbling. 2 They will put you out of the synagogues. Indeed, an hour is coming when those who kill you will think that by doing so they are offering worship to God. 3 And they will do this because they have not known the Father or me.

It seems little, if any, exaggeration to state that cumulatively these three passages, or more precisely a particular way of reading them, have exerted more influence upon Johannine scholarship over the last four decades than any other passages in John's Gospel. J. Louis Martyn, in his *History and Theology in the Fourth Gospel*, first published in 1968 and now in its third (2003) edition,[8] argued that the *aposynagōgos* passages describe not events that took place during Jesus' life, but rather events experienced decades later by the so-called Johannine community. As such, argued Martyn, they tell a story on two levels, *viz.* that of Jesus' life as well as that of the Johannine community. Adele Reinhartz later described Martyn's two levels as the "historical" and the "ecclesiological" tales: the former, a tale about the historical Jesus c. 30 CE; the latter, a tale set in the life of the Johannine community c. 70–100.[9]

Martyn proceeded to generalize this two-level reading strategy to the entirety of John's Gospel. His work pioneered within Johannine studies what might be called "community criticism,"[10] i.e. criticism that supposes

programmatically that proper interpretation of any given Gospel entails reconstruction of the communities from which they were written.[11] Through the 1970s to the late 1990s, community criticism reigned as the default hermeneutical framework by which scholars read John's Gospel. Although more recent New Testament scholarship has challenged community criticism's hermeneutical validity, beginning with Richard Bauckham's 1998 edited volume, *The Gospel for All Christians*,[12] section 1.2.

---

[8] J. Louis Martyn, *History and Theology in the Fourth Gospel* (3rd ed.; Louisville, Ky.: Westminster John Knox, 2003).

[9] Cf. Adele Reinhartz, *Word in the World: The Cosmological Tale in the Fourth Gospel* (Atlanta, Ga.: Scholars Press, 1992), 1–3.

[10] On Martyn's influence in this regard, cf. Adele Reinhartz, "The Johannine Community and its Jewish Neighbors: A Reappraisal," in "*What is John?" Volume II: Literary and Social Readings of the Fourth Gospel* (ed. Fernando Segovia; Atlanta, Ga.: Scholars Press, 1998), 111–138; Adele Reinhartz, "Reading History in the Fourth Gospel," in *What We Have Heard from the Beginning: The Past, Present, and Future of Johannine Studies* (ed. Tom Thatcher; Waco, Tex.: Baylor University Press, 2007), 190–194; D. Moody Smith, "The Contribution of J. Louis Martyn to the Understanding of the Fourth Gospel," in Martyn, *History and Theology*, 1–23.

[11] For Matthean community criticism, cf. J. Andrew Overman, *Matthew's Gospel and Formative Judaism: The Social World of the Matthean Community* (Minneapolis: Fortress, 1990); Anthony Saldarini, *Matthew's Christian-Jewish Community* (Chicago: Chicago, 1994); David C. Sim, *The Gospel of Matthew and Christian Judaism: The History and Social Setting of the Matthean Community* (Edinburgh: T&T Clark, 1998); Graham Stanton, *A Gospel for a New People: Studies in Matthew* (Edinburgh: T&T Clark, 1992). For Markan, cf. Howard Clark Kee, *Community of the New Age: Studies in Mark's Gospel* (Philadelphia: Westminster Press, 1977); Willi Marxsen, *Mark The Evangelist: Studies on the Redaction History of the Gospel* (trans. by J. Boyce, D. Juel, W. Poehlmann and R.A. Harrisville; Nashville: Abingdon Press, 1969); Ched Myers, *Binding the Strong Man: A Political Reading of Mark's Story of Jesus* (Maryknoll, NY: Orbis Books, 1994); Theodore J. Weeden, Sr., *Mark: Traditions in Conflict* (Philadelphia: Fortress Press, 1971). For Lukan, cf. Philip Francis Esler, *Community and Gospel in Luke-Acts: The Social and Political Motivations of Lucan Theology* (Cambridge: Cambridge, 1987). For examples of Johannine community criticism in addition to Martyn, cf. Raymond E. Brown, *The Community of the Beloved Disciple: The Life, Loves, and Hates of an Individual Church in New Testament Times* (New York: Paulist Press, 1979); Oscar Cullmann, *The Johannine Circle* (trans. John Bowden; Philadelphia: Westminster Press, 1976); R. Alan Culpepper, *The Johannine School: An Evaluation of the Johannine-School Hypothesis Based on a Investigation of the Nature of Ancient Schools* (Missoula, Mont.: Scholars Press, 1975); Wes Howard-Brook, *Becoming Children of God: John's Gospel and Radical Discipleship* (Maryknoll: Orbis Books, 1994); David Rensberger, *Johannine Faith and Liberating Community* (Philadelphia: The Westminster Press, 1988); Lance Byron Richey, *Roman Imperial Ideology and the Gospel of John* (Washington, DC: The Catholic Biblical Association of America, 2007).

[12] Richard Bauckham, ed., *The Gospels for All Christians: Rethinking the Gospel Audiences* (ed. Richard Bauckham; Grand Rapids, Mich.: Eerdmans, 1998). Cf. also the critiques of Bauckham in Philip F. Esler, "A Response to Richard Bauckham's *Gospels for All Christians*," *Scottish Journal of Theology* 51 (1998): 235–248; Thomas Kazen, "Sectarian Gospels for Some Christians? Intention and Mirror Reading in the Light of Extra-Canonical Texts," *New Testament Studies* 51 (2005): 561–578; Margaret M. Mitchell, "Patristic Counter-Evidence to the Claim that the 'Gospels Were Written for All Christians'," *New Testament Studies* 51 (2005): 36–79; David C. Sim, "The Gospels for All Christians? A Response to Richard Bauckham," *Journal for the Study of the New Testament* 84 (2001): 3–27. Each of these critiques focuses primarily upon the question of whether the Gospels were written for a general Christian audience, as per Bauckham, or a more circumscribed community, as per community criticism. Whilst an interesting question, they tend to neglect what seems to be Bauckham's more significant contribution to Gospel scholarship, namely his wholesale rejection of the

of the present study will demonstrate that community criticism remains the regnant framework through which John's Gospel and more specifically the *aposynagōgos* passages are read.

1.2 HISTORY OF SCHOLARSHIP

This section begins with a general overview of how modern scholarship has construed the relationship between John's Gospel and the historical Jesus, then develops a scheme for describing scholarship on the *aposynagōgos* passages published subsequent to Martyn's *History and Theology*. This scheme will identify within contemporary Johannine scholarship what will be called the "classic Martynian" and "neo-Martynian" traditions. The aim overall is to provide the reader with an understanding not only of what has been and what is still being argued about these passages, but also where these arguments fit into broader scholarly discussions.

1.2.1 *The De-Historicization of John and the De-Johannification of Jesus*

The title for this section comes from the Society of Biblical Literature's "John, Jesus, and History Group," which has already produced two volumes and plans at least one more.[13] Most immediately relevant to the current discussion is the first of these volumes, in which various contributors discuss how, throughout the course of the nineteenth and twentieth centuries, John's Gospel was increasingly judged to be irrelevant to historical Jesus studies.[14] The last two decades has witnessed a significant reevaluation of this older judgment.[15] The discussion has ranged widely, focusing upon such disparate, albeit related, issues as follows: the hermeneutical and historiographical suppositions that are typically shared by those who consider John's Gospel less relevant to historical Jesus studies than the Synoptic Gospels and perhaps other texts; the intellectual genealogy of such suppositions; the authorship of John's Gospel; and the relationship between John's theology and his historiography. Less attention has been directed towards the historical reliability of individual events reported in John's Gospel, and those contributions[16] that do focus upon individual events tend to be articles or book chapters, rather than monograph-length studies. The present study aims to help fill this lacuna.

The Martynian traditions, to be discussed more fully below, and particularly their readings of the *aposynagōgos* passages, should be understood within these broader processes of dehistoricization and de-Johannification, by which these passages were removed from the early first-century historical context in which John's Gospel sets them explicitly, and then re-contextualized in novel, late first-century contexts crafted by contemporary exegetes. The post-Martynian alternative advanced in this study should in its turn be understood as an exercise in both re-historicizing John and re-Johannifying Jesus.

Albert Schweitzer described the decision to favour "*either* [the] Synoptic *or* [the] Johannine" traditions as the second "great alternative which the study of the life of Jesus had to meet," the first being "*either* purely historical *or* purely supernatural," and the third "*either* eschatological *or*

---

hermeneutical supposition that, if one is to properly construe the canonical and potentially also certain extra-canonical Gospels (cf. Kazen, "Sectarian Gospels"), then one must reconstruct a hypothetical local community situation.

[13] Paul N. Anderson, Felix Just, and Tom Thatcher, eds., *John, Jesus, and History: Volume 1: Critical Appraisals of Critical Views* (Atlanta, Ga.: Society of Biblical Literature, 2007); Anderson, Paul N, Felix Just, and Tom Thatcher, eds., *John, Jesus, and History, Volume 2: Aspects of Historicity in the Fourth Gospel* (Atlanta, Ga.: Society of Biblical Literature, 2009).

[14] Cf. esp. Robert Kysar, "The Dehistoricizing of the Gospel of John," in Anderson, Just, and Thatcher, *John, Jesus, and History, Volume 1*, 75–101; Mark Allen Powell, "The De-Johannification of Jesus: The Twentieth Century and Beyond," in Anderson, Just, and Thatcher, *John, Jesus, and History, Volume 1*, 121–132; Jack Verheyden, "The De-Johannification of Jesus: The Revisionist Contribution of Some Nineteenth century German Scholarship," in Anderson, Just and Thatcher, *John, Jesus, and History, Volume 1*, 109–120.

[15] In addition to the volumes published by the John, Jesus, and History Group, other contributions to this reassessment include Paul N. Anderson, "Aspects of Historicity in the Gospel of John: Implications for Investigations of Jesus and Archaeology," in *Jesus and Archaeology* (ed. James H. Charlesworth; Grand Rapids, Mich.: Eerdmans, 2006), 587–618; Paul N. Anderson, *The Fourth Gospel and the Quest for Jesus: Modern Foundations Reconsidered* (London: T&T Clark, 2006); Richard Bauckham, *The Testimony of the Beloved Disciple: Narrative, History, and Theology in the Gospel of John* (Grand Rapids, Mich.: Baker Academic, 2007), 93–112, 173–189; Craig L. Blomberg, *The Historical Reliability of John's Gospel: Issues and Commentary* (Downers Grove, Ill.: InterVarsity Press, 2001); Urban C. von Wahlde, "Archaeology and John's Gospel," in Charlesworth, *Jesus and Archaeology*, 523–586; Cf. also C.H. Dodd, *Historical Tradition in the Fourth Gospel* (Cambridge: Cambridge, 1963), which predates the recent spate of scholarship on John and history, but remains nonetheless a classic on the matter.

[16] Examples include Bauckham, *Testimony*, 173–189, reprinted as Richard Bauckham, "The Bethany Family in John 11–12: History or Fiction?", in Anderson, Just and Thatcher, *John, Jesus, and History, Volume 2*, 185–201; Paula Fredriksen, "The Historical Jesus, the Scene in the Temple, and the Gospel of John," in Anderson, Just and Thatcher, *John, Jesus, and History, Volume 1*; 249–276; Edward W. Klink III, "Expulsion from the Synagogue? Rethinking a Johannine Anachronism," *Tyndale Bulletin* 59/1 (2008): 99–118; Edward W. Klink III, "The Overrealized Expulsion in the Gospel of John," in Anderson, Just and Thatcher, *John, Jesus, and History, Volume 2*, 175–184; Mark A. Matson, "The Historical Plausibility of John's Passion Dating," in Anderson, Just and Thatcher, *John, Jesus, and History, Volume 2*, 291–312.

non-eschatological."[17] The first two of these great alternatives are of most immediate relevance to the present discussion, with both deriving to a large extent from the work of David Friedrich Strauss. Schweitzer argued explicitly that Strauss had laid down the first alternative, that between purely historical or purely supernatural.[18] Opting for the purely historical, Strauss considered all the "supernatural" aspects of the four gospels to be instances of myth.[19]

Although Schweitzer suggests that the second alternative—that between a Synoptic or a Johannine Jesus—was "worked out by the Tübingen school and Holtzmann,"[20] Strauss had already argued vigourously that one cannot reasonably reconcile the Synoptic portrayals with the Johannine. This argument was in part a consequence of Strauss's judgment that, with its incarnate God-man, John's Gospel is the most supernatural and thus the most myth-laden of the gospels. Since Strauss defined myth as a fundamentally ahistorical mode of thought that can develop only in the absence of eyewitnesses,[21] by hermeneutical necessity he had to conclude that John was the latest of the canonical gospels written, and consequently the most removed temporally and theologically from actual eyewitnesses to Jesus' life.[22]

F.C. Baur, doyen of the Tübingen school, argued likewise that John's Gospel must be set to one side in favour of the Synoptics, at least for those interested in the historical Jesus, for in John's Gospel "[t]he history is so determined and absorbed by the element of miracle [*viz.* the Incarnation], as nowhere to afford any firm footing for the scientific inquirer."[23] For both Strauss and Baur, as well as those influenced by them, John's Gospel contained what we might call the most "derived" Christology, which is to say the least primitive and thus least genuinely historical, among the canonical gospels.[24] Given Schweitzer's own influence, it is likely that he contributed as much as Strauss, Baur, and Holtzmann to solidify the bias towards the Synoptic Gospels and against John's in historical Jesus studies. This bias was followed by the majority of subsequent historical Jesus scholars, resulting in a Johannine Gospel that was thought to bear little upon the various quests for the historical Jesus, and a Jesus who was thought to bear little resemblance to his Johannine representation.

In his study of the historical Jesus, Bultmann dismissed John's Gospel in a single sentence, *viz.* "The Gospel of John cannot be taken into account at all as a source for the teaching of Jesus."[25] When dealing with the alternative between a Synoptic and a Johannine Jesus, Bultmann opted unconditionally for the Synoptic. Yet even *vis-à-vis* the Synoptic Gospels, he argues that "[w]hat the sources [i.e. the Synoptic Gospels] offer us is first of all the message of the early Christian community, which for the most part the church freely attributed to Jesus."[26] This view, elaborated more fully in Bultmann's form critical classic, *The History of the Synoptic Tradition*,[27] became the hermeneutical basis for community criticism in general, and the Martynian tradition in particular.

1.2.2   Aposynagōgos *and the Martynian Tradition*

In what amounts to a synopsis of his exegetical technique, Martyn argues that "in the two-level drama of John 9, the man born blind plays not only the part of a Jew in Jerusalem healed by Jesus of Nazareth, but also the part of Jews known to John who have become members of the separated

---

[17] Albert Schweitzer, *The Quest of the Historical Jesus: A Critical Study of its Progress from Reimarus to Wrede* (trans. unknown; New York: Macmillan, 1968), 238.

[18] Schweitzer, *Quest*, 238. For Schweitzer's discussion of Strauss, cf. the same volume, pp. 68–120.

[19] Cf. David Friedrich Strauss, *The Life of Jesus Critical Examined* (trans. George Eliot; London: SCM Press, 1973), 47–92. Mention here should be made of the recent, magisterial work on miracles, by Craig S. Keener, *Miracles: The Credibility of the New Testament Accounts* (2 vols.; Grand Rapids, Mich.: Eerdmans, 2011). For a recent argument in favour of anti-supernaturalism, cf. Zeba Crook, "On the Treatment of Miracles in New Testament Scholarship," *Studies in Religion* 40/4 (2011): 461–478.

[20] Schweitzer, *Quest*, 238. Schweitzer refers here to Heinrich Holtzmann, *Lehrbuch der Historisch-Kritischen Einleitung in das Neue Testament* (Freiburg: Mohr Siebeck, 1892).

[21] Cf. Strauss, *Life of Jesus*, 47–92.

[22] Cf. Strauss, *Life of Jesus*, 52–92; David Friedrich Strauss, *The Christ of Faith and the Jesus of History: A Critique of Schleiermacher's Life of Jesus* (trans. Leander E. Keck; Philadelphia: Fortress, 1977), 41–47.

[23] Ferdinand Christian Baur, *The Church History of the First Three Centuries* (3rd ed.; 2 vols.; trans. Allan Menzies; London: Williams and Norgate, 1878), 1.25.

[24] Cf. Strauss, *Life of Jesus*, 52–92. One of the strongest champions for conceiving John's theology as "primitive", rather than derived, is John A.T. Robinson, *The Priority of John* (ed. J.F. Coakley; London: SCM Press, 1985).

[25] Rudolf Bultmann, *Jesus and the Word* (trans. Louise Pettibone Smith and Erminie Huntress Lantero; New York: Charles Scribner's Sons, 1958), 12.

[26] Bultmann, *Jesus and the Word*, 12.

[27] Rudolf Bultmann, *The History of the Synoptic Tradition* (2nd ed.; trans. John Marsh; New York: Harper and Row, 1968).

church because of their messianic faith."²⁸ In this reading, Jesus is allegorically identified, or "doubled," with a late first century, anonymous, Johannine preacher.²⁹ In constructing his two-level reading strategy, Martyn argued the following key propositions.

1. The *aposynagōgos* passages narrate formal expulsions of Christians from the synagogue.³⁰
2. Prior to 70 CE, there were no mechanisms for formally expelling anyone from the synagogue.³¹
3. Such mechanisms did exist in the immediate post-70 era, namely the Rabbinic prayer known as the *Birkat ha-Minim*.³²
4. In the post-70 era, the Rabbis used the *Birkat ha-Minim* to expel at least some members of the Johannine community from at least one synagogue.³³
5. The *aposynagōgos* passages narrate such expulsions allegorically.³⁴
6. Consequently, John's Gospel is a two-level drama, which upon one level narrates the life of Jesus, and upon the other the life of the Johannine community.³⁵

Chapter Two will consider in greater detail the above claims about the synagogue and the *Birkat ha-Minim*. Here it is sufficient for us to recognize that most Rabbinic scholars, including Ruth Langer, in her 2012 monograph on the *Birkat ha-Minim*, maintain that Martyn's construal of

the *Birkat ha-Minim* is insupportable for various reasons.³⁶ Yet, the two-level strategy remains for many if not most Johannine scholars a hermeneutical fundament. Thus we can speak of a broadly Martynian tradition that has dominated Johannine studies since at least the mid-1970s.

Recently, however, this broader tradition has splintered into two distinct but closely related interpretative traditions, what one might call the classic Martynian³⁷ and the neo-Martynian.³⁸ Both traditions agree that the *aposynagōgos* passages cannot plausibly refer to events that happened during Jesus' life and that, consequently, we should read this passage as a two-level drama. Where they differ is that, whilst classic Martynian scholars hold that the *aposynagōgos* passages plausibly describe first-century expulsions from the synagogue, neo-Martynian scholars hold that the *aposynagōgos* passages cannot plausibly describe any historical events, either c. 30 CE or in the late first-century milieu.

---

²⁸ Martyn, *History and Theology*, 66.

²⁹ Cf. Martyn, *History and Theology*, 38–45. Cf. Francis Watson, "Towards a Literal Reading of the Gospels," in Bauckham, *Gospels for All Christians*, 195–217, and subsequent discussion throughout this study, for a critique of the allegorical hermeneutics frequently employed by those interested in reconstructing the communities that supposedly either wrote or received the gospels. Cf. also Tobias Hägerland, "John's Gospel: A Two-Level Drama?," *Journal for the Study of the New Testament* 25/3 (2003): 309–322, who argues that, if John is to be read as Martyn suggests, it would be entirely without precedent in the ancient world; and William M. Wright, IV, *Rhetoric and Theology: Figural Reading of John 9* (Berlin: Walter de Gruyter, 2009), who argues that whilst pre-modern exegetes engaged in figural readings of John 9, it was not in the service of historical reconstruction. Wright's own solution, that John 9 ought to be read as a form of *chreia* about Jesus is a salutary move, as it directs attention away from a putative Johannine community to the actual object of John's narrative, namely Jesus.

³⁰ Cf. Martyn, *History and Theology*, 46–66.
³¹ Cf. Martyn, *History and Theology*, 46–56.
³² Cf. Martyn, *History and Theology*, 56–66.
³³ Cf. Martyn, *History and Theology*, 65–66.
³⁴ Cf. Martyn, *History and Theology*, 65–66.
³⁵ Cf. Martyn, *History and Theology*, 38–40.

³⁶ Ruth Langer, *Cursing the Christians? A History of the Birkat Haminim* (Oxford: Oxford University Press, 2012), 26–33. Cf. also Stephen Asher Finkel, "Yavneh's Liturgy and Early Christianity," *Journal of Ecumenical Studies* 18/2 (1981): 231–250; Stephen T. Katz, "Issues in the Separation of Judaism and Christianity after 70 CE: A Reconsideration," *Journal of Biblical Literature* 103/1 (1984): 43–76, esp. 64ff.; Reuven Kimelman, "Birkat Ha-Minim and the Lack of Evidence for an Anti-Christian Jewish Prayer in Late Antiquity," in *Jewish and Christian Self-Definition, Volume II: Aspects of Judaism in the Graeco-Roman Period* (ed. E.P. Sanders, A.I. Baumgarten, and Alan Mendelssohn; London: SCM Press, 1981), 226–244; Ephraim E. Urbach, "Self-Isolation or Self-Affirmation in Judaism in the First Three Centuries: Theory and Practice," in Sanders, Baumgarten, and Mendelson, eds., *Jewish and Christian Self-Definition II*, 269–298; Burton Visotzky, "Methodological Considerations in the Study of John's Interaction with First-Century Judaism," in *Life in Abundance: Studies of John's Gospel in Tribute to Raymond E. Brown* (ed. John R. Donahue; Collegeville, Minn.: Liturgical Press, 2005), 91–107.

³⁷ Representatives of which include Anderson, *Fourth Gospel and the Quest for Jesus*; John Ashton, *Understanding the Fourth Gospel* (2nd ed; Oxford: Oxford, 2007); Brown, *Community of the Beloved Disciple*; Marius Heemstra, *The Fiscus Judaicus and the Parting of the Ways* (Tübingen: Mohr Siebeck, 2010); Joel Marcus, "Birkat ha-Minim Revisited," *New Testament Studies* 55 (2009): 523–551; Kloppenborg, "Disaffiliation"; Rensberger, *Johannine Faith*; Richey, *Roman Imperial Ideology*. One could argue that Yaakov Y. Teppler, *Birkat haMinim: Jews and Christians in Conflict in the Ancient World* (trans. Susan Weingarten; Tübingen: Mohr Siebeck, 2007), 353–355, should also be included in the classic Martynian tradition. The present author has opted not to do so, as, even though Teppler remains open to the possibility that John knew the *Birkat ha-Minim*, he remains undecided on the matter.

³⁸ Representatives of which include Warren Carter, *John and Empire: Initial Explorations* (New York: T&T Clark, 2008); Raimo Hakola, *Identity Matters: John, The Jews, and Jewishness* (Leiden: Brill, 2005); Raimo Hakola and Adele Reinhartz, "John's Pharisees," in *In Quest of the Historical Pharisees* (ed. Jacob Neusner and Bruce D. Chilton; Waco, Tex.: Baylor University Press, 2007), 131–147; Reinhartz, "Reading History"; Tom Thatcher, *Greater Than Caesar: Christology and Empire in the Fourth Gospel* (Minneapolis: Fortress Press, 2009); Tom Thatcher, *Why John Wrote a Gospel: Jesus, Memory, History* (Louisville, Ky.: Westminster John Knox Press, 2006).

Thus, if the classic Martynian tradition maintains the six propositions argued by Martyn and articulated above, then the neo-Martynian tradition would reformulate these as follows.

1. The *aposynagōgos* passages narrate formal expulsions of Christians from the synagogue.
2. Prior to 70 CE, there were no mechanisms for formally expelling anyone from the synagogue.
3. Such mechanisms did not exist either in the immediate post-70 era.
4. Thus, no members of the Johannine community were expelled from the synagogue.
5. The *aposynagōgos* passages consequently do not refer to these expulsions that never happened.
6. Nonetheless, John's Gospel is a two-level drama, which upon one level narrates the life of Jesus, and upon the other narrates how the community either perceives itself or how the authors believe the community should perceive itself.

Against both traditions this study will argue in favour of an interpretation that reads John's narrative on just one level, namely that of Jesus' life. This is not to deny that John's initial and subsequent readers could both interpret John's Gospel through their own experiences, and their own experiences through John's Gospel. It is to argue that John wrote the *aposynagōgos* passages in order to describe actions taken against Christians c. 30 CE.

For schematic purposes, the present author has divided contributions to the discussion as follows. It must be noted that there is considerable diversity within each of the traditions enumerated below. For instance, Paul N. Anderson, whose work most properly falls into the "Classic Martynian Tradition," insofar as it supposes that the Johannine community experienced expulsion in the late first-century and that the *Birkat ha-Minim* was instrumental in said expulsion, advocates what might be described as a "dialectical Martynian" position. Building upon source- and redaction- critical work on John's Gospel, and integrating this with James Fowler's developmental theory of faith,[39] Anderson argues that the Johannine Gospel represents in part the experiences of a community and an author that have gone through a succession of crises; the *Birkat ha-Minim*, argues Anderson, was instrumental in the third of these crises.[40] This creates a significantly more nuanced reading of the Johannine text, but nonetheless one that remains susceptible to the same basic hermeneutical critique of any Martynian reading, namely that the second-level reading is exegetically superfluous and thus unnecessary.

The Classic Martynian Tradition
(Two-Level with Expulsion)
J. Louis Martyn
Raymond E. Brown
David Rensberger
John Ashton
Lance Byron Richey
Joel Marcus
Paul N. Anderson
Marius Heemstra
John Kloppenborg

The Neo-Martynian Tradition
(Two-Level without Expulsion)
Adele Reinhartz
Raimo Hakola
Warren Carter
Tom Thatcher

The Post-Martynian Alternative[41]
(One-Level)
Edward W. Klink[42]
This Study

Let us now consider more closely these traditions and alternative.

---

[39] James Fowler, *Stages of Faith* (San Francisco: Harper and Row, 1981); James Fowler, *Becoming Adult, Becoming Christian* (San Francisco: Harper and Row, 1984).

[40] Cf. the discussions in Anderson, *Christology of the Fourth Gospel*, 218; Anderson, *Fourth Gospel and the Quest for Jesus*, 65.

[41] Although certainly far more exegetes throughout the history of Johannine interpretation have supposed that the *aposynagōgos* passages tell us first and foremost about events of Jesus' life, it would be anachronistic to refer to these as "one-level" readings. Only with the development of a tradition of reading allegorically a community history in John's Gospel can it become meaningful to argue against such a reading. For an extended effort to develop what might be characterized as a one-level approach to John's Gospel, although not to the *aposynagōgos* passages specifically, cf. Klink III, *Sheep of the Fold*, esp. pp. 185–246.

[42] Edward Klink, in Klink, "Expulsion from the Synagogue," and Klink, "Overrealized Expulsion," focuses his attention upon a critique of what this study calls the classic Martynian tradition and its effects upon the study of John's Gospel, with relatively little effort devoted to building an alternative, post-Martynian historical reconstruction. Nonetheless, his general approach, both in this article and in Klink, *Sheep of the Fold*, certainly anticipates much of the argumentation in this study, and thus this work warrants inclusion within the category of "post-Martynian."

1.2.2.1 *Two-Level Reading, with Expulsion: The Classic Martynian Tradition*

The classic Martynian tradition builds upon the work of J. Louis Martyn, and can also be described as the "two level with expulsion" reading of the *aposynagōgos* passages. The classic Martynian tradition argues that the *aposynagōgos* passages allegorically describe the late first-century expulsion of at least part of the Johannine community, in most (although not all) articulations due to implementation of the *Birkat ha-Minim* (or "Benediction of the Heretics," an alternate name for the Twelfth of the Eighteen Benedictions).

Raymond E. Brown, writing in the 1970s, David Rensberger in the 1980s, and John Ashton in the 1990s, and John Kloppenborg in the 2010s, registered some doubt regarding whether or not the *Birkat ha-Minim* was the efficient cause of the Johannine community's expulsion, primarily due to certain objections that rabbinic scholars had raised against Martyn's scenario.[43] Nonetheless, their respective interpretations of the *aposynagōgos* passages are in most other respects classic Martynian. In particular, they each suppose that the experience of expulsion reported by the *aposynagōgos* passages happened decades after Jesus' life and was integral to the formation of the Johannine community, such that proper understanding of the Johannine community is a hermeneutical necessity for reading 9:22, 12:42, and 16:2. These scholars all hold to a two-level with expulsion reading of these passages. Indeed, Brown so fully adopted and popularized the classic Martynian scenario that it is sometimes referred to as the "Martyn-Brown hypothesis."[44] Moreover, their doubts about the *Birkat ha-Minim* have been eschewed in the more recent classic Martynian scholarship, represented by Paul N. Anderson, Lance Byron Richey, Joel Marcus, and Marius Heemstra.[45]

Although Anderson leaves open the possibility that these passages might refer at least in part to events of Jesus' life, nonetheless he maintains the two-level reading, continuing to read the *aposynagōgos* passages as evidence for expulsions experienced by the Johannine community in the last third of the first-century, and moreover explicitly linking the expulsion with the *Birkat ha-Minim*.[46] Lance Byron Richey supposes the classic Martynian scenario, and argues for a link between the *Birkat ha-Minim*, the *aposynagōgos* passages, and conflict between the Johannine community and the Roman imperial authorities.[47] As suggested by the title of his 2009 article, "*Birkat Ha-Minim* Revisited," Joel Marcus revisits Martyn's interpretation of the Twelfth Benediction, and offers essentially a recapitulation of the classic Martynian tradition, along with a doctrinaire response to that tradition's critics. Although Marius Heemstra's study *The Fiscus Judaicus and the Parting of the Ways*[48] is concerned primarily with the Jewish tax, the penultimate chapter is devoted to "The issue of Jewish identity: *fiscus Judaicus*, *birkat ha-minim* and the Gospel of John."[49] According to Heemstra, "the expulsion from the synagogue' was felt to be the first and necessary step to a setting in which Jewish Christians could be executed for their beliefs."[50] The recent scholarship of Anderson, Richey, Marcus, and Heemstra demonstrate that Martyn's basic suppositions remain current in certain sectors of Johannine scholarship.

Until recently the classic Martynian tradition was the entirety of the Martynian tradition. As noted above, however, this broader tradition has recently splintered, thus producing a neo-Martynian tradition alongside the classic Martynian. Whilst classic Martynian scholars continue to hold that the *aposynagōgos* passages plausibly describe late first-century expulsions from the synagogue, neo-Martynian scholars hold that the *aposynagōgos* passages cannot plausibly describe any historical events.

1.2.2.2 *Two-Level Reading, without Expulsion: The Neo-Martynian Tradition*

Although not concerned primarily with the interpretation of John's Gospel, Reuven Kimelman's 1981 article on "*Birkat Ha-Minim* and the Lack of Evidence for an Anti-Christian Jewish Prayer in Late Antiquity"[51] can nonetheless be said to at least anticipate if not inaugurate the neo-Martynian tradition. In addition to his critique of Martyn's use of the *Birkat ha-Minim*, Kimelman represents an early instance of the "turn to

---

[43] Cf. Ashton, *Understanding the Fourth Gospel*, 22–33, 100–135; Brown, *Community*, 22; Kloppenborg, "Disaffiliation," 1; Rensberger, *Johannine Faith*, 25–26. These objections will be considered at greater length in Chapter Two.
[44] Cf. Warren Carter, review of Lance Byron Richey, *Roman Imperial Ideology and the Gospel of John*, *Review of Biblical Literature* (2008).
[45] Cf. bibliographic information already provided.

[46] Anderson, *The Fourth Gospel*, 34, 65, 197.
[47] Richey, *Roman Imperial Ideology*, 51–64.
[48] Heemstra, *Fiscus Judaicus*.
[49] Heemstra, *Fiscus Judaicus*, 159–189.
[50] Heemstra, *Fiscus Judaicus*, 187.
[51] Reuven Kimelman, "*Birkat Ha-Minim*," 226–244.

identity" that would come to characterize the neo-Martynian tradition proper. Kimelman argues that the *aposynagōgos* passages do not recall hostile acts carried out by any sort of Jewish group against the Johannine community, but rather represent efforts by the Johannine community to articulate their own identity and negotiate their relationship with Judaism more broadly.

The neo-Martynian tradition's turn to identify is exemplified by Raimo Hakola and Adele Reinhartz, who, in their 2007 article on "John's Pharisees,"[52] argue that we should "see in John's portrayal of the Jews and Jewishness a more prolonged and gradual process of separation from what was regarded as distinctive to Jewishness than a traumatic expulsion from the synagogue."[53] Like the classic Martynian tradition, such a statement necessarily presupposes that the Gospel of John tells at least two stories simultaneously, *viz.* that of Jesus' life, and that of the Johannine community. *Contra* the classic Martynian tradition, however, Hakola and Reinhartz hold that the community story does not include any actual expulsion of Johannine Christians from the late first-century synagogue.[54]

In his monograph, *John and Empire*, Warran Carter states that he "significantly modifies aspects of conventional explanations for the development of Johannine traditions between the time of Jesus and the writing of the Gospel," and that he has "also identified a tendency in Johannine studies to jump from the time of Jesus to the post-70 world and to synagogal separation, ignoring pre-70 and imperial events such as Gaius's action in 40."[55] On closer examination, however, Carter's modifications to the conventional narrative do not in fact appear that significant. As with other Martynian scholarship, Carter's study focuses upon the period "[b]etween the time of Jesus and the writing of the Gospel," the life of Jesus not included therein. Against the idea that John's Gospel, including the *aposynagōgos* passages, retrojects on to Jesus' life events from the 70s or 80s, Carter argues that it retrojects events from the 40s. He never considers the possibility that there is no retrojection at all.

Similar to Hakola and Reinhartz, in his monograph on *John and Empire*, Carter argues that the *aposynagōgos* passages "do not reflect a separation that has already occurred."[56] Instead, "since there is no historically convincing and sustainable scenario for a separation of the Jesus-believers from the rest of the synagogue having already taken place, these three references to synagogue expulsion exist in the narrative as texts consequential rather than descriptive, as performative rather than reflective."[57] According to Carter, the *aposynagōgos* passages were intended as cause rather than effect of a separation from the synagogue; moreover, the impetus for this separation came from John and like-minded Christians.

Tom Thatcher has not analyzed the *aposynagōgos* passages at length. Nonetheless, he has considered "why John wrote a gospel," this phrase being the title of his recent monograph on (to quote also the sub-title) "Jesus—Memory—History."[58] Thatcher argues that John wrote his Gospel not as an archive of Jesus tradition but rather to "freeze" a more fluid, oral, Johannine tradition within the relative stability of text.[59] This was done in order to counter both an "AntiChristian countermemory" and an "AntiChristian mystical memory," which had each developed within John's community.[60] Insofar as Johannine memories of Jesus were inextricably linked with Johannine identity, argues Thatcher, these struggles over memory, and particularly the writing of the Gospel itself, were by necessity also a struggle to define the community.[61]

The neo-Martynian tradition is characterized primarily by a denial that the *aposynagōgos* passages refer to any sort of actual expulsion, and a commitment to read these passages primarily if not exclusively as efforts to construct Johannine identity. It thus engages in an example of what David Hackett Fischer has described as "the fallacy of counterquestions," which "is an attempt at a revision which becomes merely a[n]...inversion of an earlier interpretation and a reiteration of its fundamental assumptions."[62] It maintains the supposition that John is most interested

---

52 Hakola and Reinhartz, "John's Pharisees," 131–147.
53 Hakola and Reinhartz, "John's Pharisees," 143.
54 As noted above, Reinhartz, *Word in the World*, expands upon Martyn's notion of a two-level drama to incorporate the historical and ecclesiological tales—terms which she herself coined to describe Martyn's two levels—into a third tale, that of the cosmos. The monograph's title is a quite precise description of Reinhartz's understanding of the *narratives* contained within John's Gospel: the Word is depicted historically as present in the world c. 30 CE in Palestine, whilst the Word as the risen Christ is depicted as ecclesiastically present in the world c. 80 CE within the Johannine community.
55 Carter, *John and Empire*, 38l.
56 Carter, *John and Empire*, 26.
57 Carter, *John and Empire*, 26.
58 Thatcher, *Why John Wrote*.
59 Thatcher, *Why John Wrote*, 155.
60 Thatcher, *Why John Wrote*, 69–81, 93–102.
61 Thatcher, *Why John Wrote*, 105–124.
62 David Hackett Fischer, *Historians' Fallacies: Toward a Logic of Historical Thought* (New York Perennial, 1970), 28.

CHAPTER ONE

in his community's experience, with that experience defined so as to exclude any substantive interest in the actual events of Jesus' life. Yet, says Fischer, "[a] fight between wild-eyed exponents of *X* and *Y* will help not at all if *Z* was in fact the case."[63] The post-Martynian alternative developed in this study aims to promote *Z* over and against the classic Martynian's *X* and the neo-Martynian's *Y*.

1.3 Toward a Post-Martynian Alternative: Reading John's Gospel on One Level

This section begins by discussing briefly the fundamental problems with the two-level reading strategy which both the classic and neo-Martynian traditions utilize. Problems with more specific aspects particular to either of the two traditions will be discussed in Chapters Two through Five. At least three fundamental problems with the two-level strategy can be discerned. Adele Reinhartz identifies and discusses these fundamental problems quite adroitly.[64] The first is that "there is no indication within the gospel itself that it is meant to be read as anything but a story of Jesus, set within the context of the story of the cosmos."[65] Second, "the two-level strategy is circular, for it reads the text as a reflection of the history of the community and then uses that history as a way of accounting for the features of the text itself."[66] Third, reflecting upon the previously cited articles on "The Johannine Community and Its Jewish Neighbors" and "Women in the Johannine Community," Reinhartz writes, "the [two-level reading] method should be applicable to the entire Gospel, but my own experiments with a more comprehensive application have led to an incoherent, even contradictory, set of results, with limited usefulness for historical reconstruction."[67]

---

[63] Fischer, *Historians' Fallacies*, 29.
[64] Reinhartz, "Women." Cf. her earlier discussion in Reinhartz, "Johannine Community."
[65] Reinhartz, "Women," 16.
[66] Reinhartz, "Women," 17.
[67] Reinhartz, "Reading History," 193. That the two-level reading strategy should be applicable to the entirety of the Gospel is a necessary corollary of the claim, advanced in Martyn, *History and Theology*, 143, that from John's perspective, "[t]he two-level drama makes clear that the Word's dwelling among us and our beholding his glory are not events which transpired only in the past.... These events to which John bears witness transpire on both the *einmalig* and the contemporary levels of the drama, or they do not happen at all." Throughout his Gospel, says Martyn, John witnesses to both the events of Jesus' life, and those of the Johannine community's history. If this is the case, then it should indeed be consistently the case, and the more instances in which one must grant that any given

INTRODUCTION

Yet, says Reinhartz, with regards specifically to the first two of these difficulties, Reinhartz arguments that they "do not militate against the use of the two-level reading."[68] Reinhartz supports this surprising assertion by arguing that

> [r]ather, they emphasize the need for both caution and humility. They remind us that as we engage in the historical enterprise of constructing the Johannine community... we must not lose sight of the hypothetical nature of our results. The very existence of a Johannine community, while it is obvious to Johannine scholars and has taken on a solid reality, is itself hypothetical. The letters of John seem to demand the existence of such a community, as does our understanding of the Fourth Gospel as being addressed to a specific audience.[69]

Reinhartz here advances two arguments in support of a Johannine community: first, that the letters attest to such a community; second, that since John's Gospel was written to a specific audience, there must have been a community. We can reject the latter of these arguments as a tautology, for it simply says that, granted that John's Gospel was written to a tightly circumscribed audience, we can conclude that there was a tightly circumscribed audience to which John's Gospel was written. Yet, it is precisely whether the Gospels were written to such an audience that Bauckham has challenged, and thus the notion that it was written to such an audience cannot be taken for granted.

The first argument, however, merits more attention. It is not self-evident that the letters demand the existence of a Johannine community, at least not in the sense of a community that can be reconstructed from community critical readings of the Gospel. Trebilco argues that "2 and 3 Jn were written to outlying house churches (or groups of house churches) some distance from the elder (who we think is in Ephesus)," and that as such they "testify to events in the wider movement of which the center is (we believe) the Ephesian Johannine community";[70] yet, he also insists that when he speaks of the Johannine community, he means "the house churches addressed in 1–3 Jn, not a community read from the Gospel."[71]

---

passage lacks an *einmalig* level, the more one must concede that the two-level reading fails to make consistent and coherent sense of the Gospel.
[68] Reinhartz, "Women," 17.
[69] Reinhartz, "Women," 17.
[70] Paul Trebilco, *The Early Christians in Ephesus from Paul to Ignatius* (Tübingen: Mohr Siebeck, 2004), 270.
[71] Trebilco, *Early Christians*, 271.

that these believers are engaged in some sort of missionary journey,[73] and probably should lead us to think less in terms of an isolated community and more in terms of a group of churches participating in the larger missionary expansion of the early Jesus movement. Such an understanding of the Johannine community could well begin to look remarkably like what we see developing in the Pauline letters, wherein we have churches scattered throughout a wide region, all with some sort of association with Paul; should we then speak of all the churches founded by Paul as a singular "Pauline community"?

Reinhartz's reasons for considering detrimental to the two-level reading strategy neither an absence of evidence for the existence of a second level nor a circularity of argumentation must be rejected on the bases of inadequate evidence and tautologous argument. This leads us to the third difficulty with the two-level reading that Reinhartz identifies. The two-level reading strategy was developed to provide a coherent reconstruction of the Johannine community. If it cannot do so, then its utility and ultimately its hermeneutical and historiographical validity must be called into question. If Reinhartz's application of Martyn's method to 2:1–11, 4:1–42, 11:1–44, 12:1–8 and 20:1–18 results in a reconstruction of the Johannine community that contradicts Martyn's reconstruction of the Johannine community based upon the *aposynagōgos* and other passages, then whose reconstruction do we prefer? Unless we detect substantive procedural differences in how Martyn and Reinhartz respectively employ the two-level reading strategy (and none seem to be present), then it seems necessary to conclude that, insofar as the second, community, level is an intrinsic part of the Johannine narrative, the narrative is fundamentally incoherent.

This study will argue that whilst the neo-Martynian tradition rightly rejects the classic Martynian interpretation of the *aposynagōgos* passages, the failure to reject also the hermeneutical suppositions upon which that interpretation is predicated leaves the neo-Martynian tradition unable to

[73] That these are missionaries appears a virtual consensus in scholarship on 3 John; Rudolf Bultmann, *The Johannine Epistles: A Commentary on the Johannine Epistles* (trans. R. Philip O'Hara, Lane C. McGaughey, and Robert W. Funk; Philadelphia: Fortress Press, 1973); cf. Rudolf Schnackenburg, *The Johannine Epistles: Introduction and Commentary* (trans. Reginald and Ilse Fuller; New York: Crossroad, 1992), 293–296; Georg Strecker, *The Johannine Epistles: A Commentary on 1, 2, and 3 John* (trans. Linda M. Maloney; Minneapolis, Minn.: Fortress Press, 1996), 258–260; Robert W. Yarbrough, *1–3 John* (Grand Rapids, Mich.: Eerdmans, 2008), 370–376.

Trebilco's recognition that we are dealing with groups at some geographical remove from one another (which the very genre of letter writing would tend to suggest) is a salutary move, and forces us to remember that whatever the Johannine community might have been, it was almost certainly not limited to a single location. Yet, even here, it is questionable to what extent we need suppose that an Ephesus-based Elder could only have written to churches in the Ephesian region. If Paul could write a letter from Corinth to believers in Rome, then it is unclear why the Elder could not similarly write letters destined to travel such distance.

Moreover, the Epistles themselves furnish good reason to think this "Ephesian Johannine community," if we might call it such, was not as isolated as the Martynian tradition has tended to suppose.[72] Of particular interest is 3 John 5–8, wherein the Elder states that he has received word of how Gaius supports believers who sojourn with him. Notably, the Elder states that such support makes people such as Gaius and himself συνεργοί...τῇ ἀληθείᾳ ("co-workers...of the truth"). This would suggest

[72] Among contemporary scholarship, perhaps the best known articulation of this isolation is Brown, *Community of the Beloved Disciple*, 81–88, who insisted that the Johannine Christians were distinct from what he termed the "Apostolic" churches, i.e. those associated with the Twelve; but cf. earlier articulations in Barrett, *St. John*, 13, who argues that the Gospel's "early disuse by orthodox writers and use by gnostics show that it originated in circles that were either gnostic or obscure, or perhaps more probably, both"; and J.N. Sanders, *The Fourth Gospel in the Early Church: Its Origin and Influence on Christian Theology up to Irenaeus* (Cambridge: Cambridge University Press, 1943), whom Charles E. Hill, *The Johannine Corpus in the Early Church*, (Oxford: Oxford University Press, 2004), 15 describes as the "chief architect of the current paradigm on orthodox Johannophobia," by which Hill means the widespread supposition that John's Gospel was favoured by Gnostic Christians and thus studiously avoided by orthodox Christians throughout much of the second-century. Tuomas Rasimus, "Introduction," in *The Legacy of John: Second-Century Reception of the Fourth Gospel* (ed. Tuomas Rasimus; Leiden: Brill, 2010), 1–16, p. 9, sums up well the problems with this "the old paradigm," as he calls it, when he suggests that "[f]irst, it relies on the division between orthodoxy and heresy that did not yet clearly exist in the second century.... Second, there are signs that the 'catholic' authors also knew and used the Fourth Gospel in the first half of the second century." If one accepts the arguments of scholars such as Mark Edwards, *Catholicity and Heresy in the Early Church* (Surrey, UK: Ashgate, 2009), and Thomas A. Robinson, *Ignatius of Antioch and the Parting of the Ways: Early Jewish-Christian Relations* (Peabody, Mass.: Hendrickson Publishers, 2009), that the various early second-century Christians known as docetists and Gnostics were in fact active members of the same Christian communities as were such scions of orthodoxy as Ignatius of Antioch and Justin Martyr, then the argument that John's Gospel or Epistles came from groups outside the ecclesiastical mainstream becomes, if not impossible, certainly less likely. The more that one emphasizes the connections that seem to have existed between churches throughout the Mediterranean, and the earlier that one dates the reception of John's Gospel and Epistles by Christians—Gnostic or otherwise—who gathered in these churches, the less persuasive will be any theory of an isolated Johannine community.

recognize John's Gospel fully for what it is, namely, as Reinhartz aptly says, "a story of Jesus, set within the context of the story of the cosmos."[74] Against Reinhartz, who has argued for up to three levels in John's Gospel—the historical, the ecclesiological, and the cosmological[75]—the post-Martynian alternative advances the hypothesis that there is just one level, that of "The Word in the World."[76] The Word creates the world, as Jesus of Nazareth becomes flesh in the world, following the crucifixion departs from the world, and after his departure sends the Paraclete into the world. The cosmos serves as the frame for Jesus' story, but this frame does not constitute another level, in the sense of a distinct tale encoded within another. The frame that is the cosmos is right there, on the surface. Any hypothetical second or third level, allegorically embedded within the level that is Jesus' story told within the frame of the cosmos, is superfluous.

Rather, the historian should focus attention first and foremost on that level which is often called the literal,[77] which, according to the famous distich commonly attributed to Nicholas of Lyra, is the sense of scripture that teaches events.[78] Although the critical historian is well aware that there is hardly a direct relationship between the letter of the text and the events about which the letter teaches, and that consequently judgments regarding the literal sense are not *ipso facto* judgments regarding what we might call the historical referent, interpretation of the literal sense is nonetheless necessary for proper construal of the historical referent. Not a necessary is interpretation of an allegorical sense whose very presence in the text is far from certain.

Reviewers of this work in its original form as a dissertation suggested that it remains possible to read the Johannine Gospel on two levels. This response was repeated frequently enough that the present author feels constrained to address the matter directly. Yes, I acknowledge, it is possible to do so. One can indeed use a late first-century expulsion from the synagogue, instrumentalized by the *Birkat ha-Mirum*, as the hermeneutical key for an allegorical re-writing of the *aposynagōgos* passages. The question, however, is not whether one can, but rather whether one should. The contention of the present author is such a re-writing is simply unnecessary. The text as it stands is entirely coherent without employing such drastic exegetical procedure. I am employing, quite rigourously, Ockham's Razor, parsing out that which is superfluous from our exegesis so as to produce a clearer vision of both the Johannine literature and the historical Jesus. I recognize of course that among my fellow exegetes there will be those who will not consider the second level unnecessary, and object that my razor is removing the wheat with the chaff; with such exegetes, I must simply agree to disagree.

Fundamental to the present study are the hermeneutical and historiographic contributions of Ben F. Meyer, as well as, less directly, those of Bernard Lonergan, whose critical realist philosophy greatly influenced Meyer's thinking.[79] Of particular significance are what Meyer calls the oblique and direct patterns of inference. These are deliberately adopted over that philosophical morass of procedures known cumulatively as the "criteria of authenticity." Chris Keith has recently suggested that the contemporary study of the historical Jesus needs to be divided between what he designates "The Criteria Approach," and "The Jesus-Memory Approach."[80] With regards to the notion of criteria, the present author is in general agreement with Meyer's suggestion that

"[c]riterion," as the term has been used in discussion of this topic [i.e. the study of the historical Jesus], specifies what is universally requisite that a gospel tradition be acknowledged as historical. But, in fact, no factor proposed by the critics as a "criterion" is invariably requisite to the inference of historicity…. Since what is really at stake in the so-called criterion is not what is uniquely sufficient and so invariably *necessary* to establish historicity but rather what tends to make historicity more likely than non-historicity,

---

[74] Reinhartz, "Women," 16.
[75] Reinhartz, *Word in the World*, passim.
[76] A term borrowed from the title of Reinhartz, *Word in the World*.
[77] On reading the canonical Gospels, including John's, in terms of the literal sense, cf. Watson, "A Literal Reading of the Gospels."
[78] Cf. the discussion of the distich, and of its compositional history, in Henri de Lubac, *Medieval Exegesis, Volume 1* (trans. Mark Sebanc; Grand Rapids, Mich.: Eerdmans, 1998), 1–4.
[79] On the significance of Lonergan for Meyer's thinking, cf. especially the chapters on "Locating Lonerganian Hermeneutics" and "Lonergan's Breakthrough and the Aims of Jesus," in Ben F. Meyer, *Critical Realism and the New Testament* (Eugene, Or.: Pickwick Publications, 1989), 1–16, 147–156. For Lonergan's thought on horizons, cf. Bernard J.F. Lonergan, *Method in Theology* (2nd ed.; Toronto: University of Toronto Press, 1990), 235–237, and his article on "The Subject," in Bernard J.F. Lonergan, *A Second Collection* (Toronto: University of Toronto Press, 1996), 69–86.
[80] Chris Keith, *Jesus' Literacy: Scribal Culture and the Teacher from Galilee* (London: T&T Clark, 2011), 29–70. Cf. the overviews of the so-called criteria of authenticity in Chris Keith and Anthony Le Donne, eds.,*Jesus, Criteria, and the Demise of Authenticity* (London: T&T Clark, 2012); John P. Meier, *A Marginal Jew: Rethinking the Historical Jesus* (4 vols.; New York: Doubleday, 1991–2009), 1:167–195; Stanley E. Porter, *The Criteria of Authenticity in Historical-Jesus Research: Previous Discussion and New Proposals* (Sheffield Academic Press, 2000). Cf. Chapter Five of the present study for further discussion of the "Jesus-memory approach."

I would prefer to drop the term "criterion" altogether in favour of the more modest term "index."[81]

Indices, as Meyer further elaborates, differ from criteria, in that "their presence favours historicity but their absence does not of itself imply a verdict of non-historicity."[82]

Meyer describes such indices as oblique patterns of inference,[83] and contrasts these to the direct pattern of inference, which is that "[i]f the intention of the writer can be defined to include factuality and if the writer is plausibly knowledgeable on the matter and free of the suspicion of fraud, historicity can be inferred."[84] Contrary to the direct pattern of inference, oblique patterns "are oblique inasmuch as they approach the narrative indirectly, neither ambitioning nor depending on definition of its intention."[85] Chapters Two through Four will utilize such oblique patterns, considering, respectively, the ancient synagogue, Christology, and the imperial context, with specific respect to the *aposynagōgos* passages. The purpose of these chapters is to demonstrate, via oblique patterns of inference, that the *aposynagōgos* passages could plausibly refer to events that happened during Jesus' lifetime.

Meyer correctly states that "[t]he usefulness of the direct pattern of inference, however, is limited in biblical criticism because of the frequent indefinability of the factor of intention."[86] Yet, the intended sense is markedly explicit in John's Gospel. That intention will be discussed at greatest length in Chapter Five, wherein, via the direct pattern of inference, we will consider whether John intended factuality, and whether he was plausibly knowledgeable on the events reported in the *aposynagōgos* passages. If it can be shown that these are the cases, and if it has already been shown by oblique inference that the narratives are historically plausible, then we have sufficient warrant to render a judgment of probability with regard to the historicity of the *aposynagōgos* passages.

A word must be given regarding what is meant in this study by an author's intention, lest the reader think that the present author has fallen prey to what is sometimes called the "intentional fallacy," a term coined by literary critics W.K. Wimsatt Jr. and M.C. Beardsley.[87] The intentional fallacy is the belief that the author's intent, as something extrinsic to the text and existing only in the mind of the author, is determinative for construing the meaning of the text. Wimsatt and Beardsley are indeed correct to label this a fallacy. Yet, Meyer correctly observes that "the definers of the so-called intentional fallacy overlooked the far more basic issue of intention precisely as *intrinsic to the text*."[88] If intention is something intrinsic to the text, then the text, not the author's mind, provides the primary data to be interpreted.[89] Thus does Meyer argue that the author's intention, or, as he also calls it, the "intended meaning," is "intrinsic to the text insofar as the text objectifies or incorporates or encodes or expresses the writer's message."[90]

Of course, through interpreting the text, we might learn a great deal about the author and the author's mind, but we do so through a procedure precisely opposite to that of the intentional fallacy, for whereas the intentional fallacy tries to understand the author in order to understand the text, intentionality analysis as advocated by Meyer tries to understand the text in order to understand the author. That such analysis can be done is demonstrated by the fact that Meyer can, along with any other competent reader of Wimsatt and Beardsley's article on the intentional fallacy, judge that they intend in that article to critique something that they call the intentional fallacy.

Cumulatively, the present study aims to demonstrate that, *contra* Martyn,[91] the *aposynagōgos* passages describe events that historically are at least plausible if not probable. Further, it aims to demonstrate that,

---

[81] Ben F. Meyer, *The Aims of Jesus* (Eugene, Or.: Pickwick Publications, 2002), 86.
[82] Meyer, *Aims of Jesus*, 87.
[83] Meyer, *Aims of Jesus*, 85ff.
[84] Meyer, *Aims of Jesus*, 85.
[85] Meyer, *Aims of Jesus*, 85.
[86] Meyer, *Aims of Jesus*, 85.
[87] W.K. Wimsatt, Jr., and M.C. Beardsley, "The Intentional Fallacy," *The Sewanee Review* 54/3 (1946): 468–488.
[88] Ben F. Meyer, *Reality and Illusion in New Testament Scholarship: A Primer in Critical Realist Hermeneutics* (Collegeville, Minn.: The Liturgical Press, 1994), 97.
[89] Such a definition also allows the exegete to sidestep, at least initially, interminable debates regarding who is best defined as the author or writer of John's Gospel. Is it the person who wrote the hypothetical "first edition" of John's Gospel, which is thought to have existed without chapter 21 and perhaps also the Prologue? Is it the hypothetical "final redactor," who added such passages? For a brief overview of the critical issues with regards to "author" as a category, see Raymond E. Brown, *An Introduction to the Gospel of John* (ed. Francis J. Moloney; New York: Doubleday, 2003), 42–62; Craig S. Keener, *The Gospel of John: A Commentary* (2 vols; Peabody, Mass.: Hendrickson Books, 2003), 1:100–114. For the purpose of the present discussion, it is sufficient to recognize that "the author" is whoever has encoded their intentions into the text. Chapter Five will consider more closely who, exactly, this author might have been.
[90] Meyer, *Critical Realism*, 19.
[91] Cf. Martyn, *History and Theology*, 46–66.

in dispensing with the two-level reading strategy, one does not thereby dispense with historical questions about the Johannine *Sitz im Leben*. It will be argued that early Christ-believing communities did indeed have a collective interest in their communal history. Yet, they understood that history to have begun with Jesus. Early Christ-believing communities understood themselves as standing in some sort of continuity with the history of Israel, as this was remembered in the Jewish scriptures, yet also understood that their own chapter in this history began with Jesus, whose life, death, and after-death, had inalterably renovated the cosmos. Necessarily, the acts of remembering and telling that collective history were social acts, certain products of which—notably but not exclusively the canonical gospels—remain available for the historian to consult.

Each of chapters Two through Five will consider an issue of relevance to the interpretation of the *aposynagōgos* passages, respectively synagogue studies, Christology, empire criticism and memory. Chapters Two through Four will employ primarily oblique patterns of inference, with the aim of demonstrating that what the *aposynagōgos* passages report is plausible. Employing the direct pattern of inference, Chapter Five will aim to convert the plausibility inferred in the previous chapters into probability. Finally, Chapter Six will summarize the study.

Chapter 8

THE GOSPEL OF JOHN AND THE SIGNS GOSPEL

Robert T. Fortna

In the early 1970s—when I was still a raw young scholar and not long after my doctoral dissertation had been published as *The Gospel of Signs*—I went for the first time to an overseas annual meeting of the Society of New Testament Studies (SNTS). I was introduced to two senior Europeans (I would guess recovering Bultmannians), each of whom said upon hearing my name, more or less, "Ah, so you are Fortna; you are quite wrong." My children enjoyed that story. At the time, I concluded it was at least good to know that my book had not been ignored. Since then, to be sure, there have been many more detractors.[1] But not a few supporters (for example, Cope 1987), and from some of them I have learned to

---

[1] Folker Siegert, whose recent work *Der Ertsenwurf des Johannes* (2004) builds heavily on my reconstruction, observes that especially in Germany it brought me "scorn and derision." This was partly, I believe, because I claimed to recover the original Greek text of the source. Siegert believes that the signs source, or what he calls the "pre-Johannine non-synoptic tradition," was not written but oral and used from memory by John the Elder (of 2 and 3 John)—the author, as he holds, of the still Christian–Jewish "first version" of the Johannine Gospel. If so, I would contend that the text of that oral tradition was so fixed that when reused by the first Johannine writer, it created many of the aporias in the Fourth Gospel. Siegert is about to publish a commentary on his reconstruction.

adapt my reconstruction (I prefer of course to think of it as a recovery) of the "Signs Gospel," the source from which, I believe, the Fourth Evangelist derived stories about Jesus' miracles and death. Further, I would claim that my early work, and the subsequent work of others, has revealed the extent to which the Signs Gospel hypothesis is more than a study in source criticism. Any answer to the question of possible documentary sources for the Fourth Gospel reflects also on one's beliefs about: (1) the circumstances in which the text of the Fourth Gospel was produced, (2) its literary unity, (3) its relationship to the Synoptics, and (4) the question of historicity. My subsequent work has led me into all these questions. It is now twenty years since the sequel to the 1970 book—and my principal redaction-critical work on John—*The Fourth Gospel and Its Predecessor* (1988) appeared. Despite the fact that in the meantime my attention has turned away from Johannine Studies, how has my mind changed on the existence of the source and these four issues?

I remain fairly sure that a source *once existed*, a relatively brief written (or if still oral, firmly worded) text containing virtually all the narratives in John that happen to be like the Synoptics. In *The Gospel of Signs*, I was rash enough to include a complete, reconstructed Greek text of the source, and I would no longer hold that that reconstruction is legitimate in its detail. Among other revisions, D. Moody Smith (1984, 90–93) convincingly proposed that John 12:37–40 derives from the Signs Gospel, an explanation for the plot against Jesus and a transition into the passion story. But that a document not unlike my somewhat revised version of a signs source in *The Fourth Gospel and Its Predecessor* underlies our Gospel of John does not seem to me any less tenable.

I began my exploration with Bultmann's proposed *Sēmeiaquelle* ("signs source"), attempting to refine his criteria and leaving aside matter not essential to the sign stories themselves. What remains is a barebones account of some of Jesus' notable miracles: water, a lot of it, turned into wine (John 2:1–11); a young man's healing from a distance (4:46–54); an astonishing catch of fish (21:2–11); a shepherd's lunch turned into a meal for thousands (6:1–12); a dead man raised (11:1–45); a man, blind from birth, enabled to see (9:1–7); and a man lame for thirty-eight years healed (5:1–9). In the source, these episodes were called "signs" and were evidently numbered (vestiges remain in 2:11a, 4:54a, and 21:14a). They offered a terse, vivid account of Jesus' ministry first in Galilee and then in Jerusalem—a spellbinding list, in which Jesus acts not out of sympathy for those in need—and scarcely an account of a ministry in any strict sense. Rather it is a collection of stories that demonstrate *who* Jesus was, no less (and no more) than the Messiah of Jewish expectation (20:31a).

As I continued examining the Fourth Gospel's narrative, I also found myself following, in briefest form, Bultmann's outline for a "passion source"—stories about Jesus' death (and its sequel) pulled together and recounted by the same editor as the signs. These two, probably originally distinct sources recounting Jesus' signs and apologizing for his passion and death, had been brought together and made to follow one another so neatly that Jesus' resurrection at the end became the crowning sign of his identity (as indicated by what is now found at John 2:19). In view of this christological emphasis, the Fourth Evangelist's source could scarcely be called anything but a very simple and straightforward *Gospel*, a Gospel of Signs, the story of Jesus' life and death calculated to promote its author's theological vision. The purpose of such a Signs Gospel was solely to show Jews within the synagogue that Jesus had demonstrated his messianic status and that his death was in fulfillment of Scripture. On the basis of these signs, so it argued, Jews ought to join the Christian movement growing within first-century Judaism. This, I believe, rather than any sort of conversion, is the best way to describe what a Signs Gospel intended. It clearly did not promote the incarnational Christology that characterizes the current text of John, found within the first-person discourses, and it was not concerned with a Gentile mission. I therefore date the source somewhere in the 40s or 50s C.E.

Now to the subsequent questions that have arisen. First of all, I will address the circumstances in which the Fourth Gospel was produced. Despite recent attempts to lay it to rest, I cleave to J. Louis Martyn's identification of the crisis confronting the Johannine community in the late first century as both valid and vital (Martyn 2003). Martyn's approach is vital because it almost alone accounts for the creation of our Gospel of John. It seems to me as likely as ever that official post-70 C.E. Judaism disowned the Christian-Jewish movement within the synagogue, a movement that reflected the type of faith in Jesus as the Jewish Messiah advocated by the Signs Gospel. This crisis—the excommunication of the Johannine Christians because of their belief in Jesus (ἀποσυνάγωγος) appearing three times and only in John—led to a revising of the Signs Gospel and, further, to the creation or consolidation of the Johannine discourse material that so differs from the third-person prose narrative. With the official decision late in the century that such believers could no longer think of themselves as Jews, the relatively brief, and by that time perhaps long-standing, Signs Gospel was no longer of much validity and certainly was of little use. It had either to be discarded or, as I believe, revived and greatly expanded—quoted almost verbatim, corrected by brief inserted comments, and expanded and interpreted by the addition of the distinctly Johannine discourses. The uneven, aporia-laden narrative of the Fourth Gospel suggests such a compositional process.

Second, on the question of the literary unity of John: the pronounced contrast between brief narrative and the long discourses of Jesus, the latter unlike anything in the other canonical Gospels (including their various collections of Jesus' sayings), seems to me to be an obvious indication of at least a two-stage development in the text.[2] The canonical book reads in an almost Talmudic fashion—relatively brief stories greatly interspersed with poetic discourses that in some way or other comment on and widely differ from the prose accounts. How would one author have alternately written both?

The signs pericopes have been barely edited internally, but almost entirely rearranged in their order (reflecting the Johannine Jesus' movements to and from Jerusalem), with a few very brief sayings of Jesus inserted (for example, 2:4; 4:48). These changes have produced the numerous aporias, the difficulties within the text (cf. 2:1; 4:54; 6:1) that are virtually absent from the Synoptics. An earlier document (or fixed oral tradition) has been so carefully preserved, with scarcely any rewriting, that we are clearly reading the work of two authors. And, I hold, the Signs Gospel, the earlier, can more or less readily be lifted out of our Gospel of John.

As to literary style, there is simply no way to demonstrate any stylistic unity. One can only disprove the stylistic disunity between hypothetical reconstructions of two or more literary stages. Ruckstuhl and Dschulnigg have attempted the latter (1991), but the former, which they also claim, cannot be done (see below). Of course, many have argued against the existence of such a source on the grounds that it cannot be reconstructed from the current text of the Fourth Gospel. This is the case, my detractors often claim, because the text of John evidences a high level of stylistic unity. But that alleged unity is a chimera. The Gospel of John is, of course, one literary document; the author/redactor intended to create a coherent narrative, and it almost reads as such. But the study of a document's style as a whole can only prove the existence of its sources when they demonstrate a style notably different from that of the document that hypothetically used them. The major twentieth-century studies of John's style could, at best, attempt to falsify particular source theories. Ruckstuhl and Dschulnigg (1991) sought to show that my proposed Signs Gospel does not evidence a style different from that of the Fourth Gospel as a whole. But they used a stylometrically naïve method. More recently, a highly sophisticated stylometric and statistical modeling argues to the contrary, namely that my Signs Gospel does show a distinct style, by a statistically significant margin (Felton and Thatcher 2001). In any case, I believe it is nearly obvious that the reconstructed Signs Gospel does have a distinct style.

As an aside, I want to defend redaction criticism, which has acquired a rather poor press of late, somewhat deservedly. It was the need to provide for the redaction criticism of John that led me in the first place to attempt a reconstruction of sources. A principal achievement of a Signs Gospel theory, as I attempted to demonstrate in a series of articles in the 1970s and in *The Fourth Gospel and Its Predecessor*, is that it makes redaction criticism of John possible. I quite agree that the Gospel of John, or any Gospel, ought to be read as it now stands, not divided for the reader into earlier and later elements. And, further, the text ought not be read with blinders, ignoring the prevailing sociological and political situations (so far as they can be known) of both the author and the intended audience. Thus, I focused on the crisis that evidently required the source, if it was not to be abandoned entirely, to be greatly adapted so as to speak to the Johannine Evangelist's new circumstances. And when I compare the redaction with the source, I seek to show how those very circumstances evoked many of the additions and corrections made by the Johannine author/redactor. Again, yes, of course the modern reader needs to deal with the text lying before her or him. But an auxiliary look over the Fourth Evangelist's shoulder, as the source was presumably adapted, aids considerably in understanding the given text as a response to what author and community had experienced.

On the subject of the Johannine sayings material, I have cast doubt on the likelihood that the composition-history of the discourses can be recovered. My reconstruction of the Signs Gospel includes almost no sayings. In these stories, Jesus merely gives terse directives or asks simple questions relating to his ensuing action—"Fill the jars with water" (2:7) or "Where have you laid him?" (11:34). Even if historically factual, these utterances tell us virtually nothing about the historical Jesus, and it is impossible to say whether they are more than window dressing necessary for the stories. But what about the lengthy Johannine discourses? In *The Gospel of Signs*, I simply left open the question whether the Johannine Evangelist had used traditional sayings material not included in the Signs Gospel. I had not set out to find a purely narrative source, but the more such a source emerged the less I could believe that the discourses stemmed from the same origin. Over time, as evident in *The Fourth Gospel*

---

[2] Siegert's hypothesis (2004) of a relatively early, rudimentary yet Johannine Gospel, later developed into our Gospel of John, needs further study. If valid, it suggests a three-stage development.

and Its Predecessor, I came to recognize a rather fundamental distinction between story and saying in John, with the stories coming from the signs source and the discourses essentially added as theological commentary on the signs and on the controversy with the synagogue. I now see rather clearly that the late-first century crisis I have mentioned may have given rise to the discourses, in at least their final form, out of a more inchoate Johannine tradition; the crisis certainly demanded their addition to the Signs Gospel. And it is even possible that the contentious debate the crisis produced between the evangelist's community and the synagogue accounts for the creative invention of some of the discourse material altogether. In John 5:17–47, for example, the evangelist says that the Jews wanted to kill Jesus because of his self-proclaimed unity with the Father, and he defends his claims on the testimony of a number of "witnesses," including Moses; this appears to reflect the debate with the synagogue as the initiating element. Whether the crisis gave rise to the discourses altogether or in some cases only occasioned their codification, it argues for a later date for John than has sometimes been proposed but not so late a date as others have suggested. The best estimate for the date of the earliest version of a fairly complete version of John's Gospel would be some time after 85 C.E. (or whatever date can be given to the revision of the Twelfth Benediction that required Christian Jews to leave their synagogue and cease thinking of themselves as Jewish).

Third, on the question of John's relationship to the Synoptics: quite obviously, if there was dependence of John upon any of the Synoptics, then no narrative source of the sort I propose would have reason to exist. So what follows is hardly dispassionate. I believe that the Fourth Evangelist did not make use of the Synoptics for three reasons that can be succinctly stated. First, so far as I know, there is in John no evidence of patently redactional matter from the Synoptics, the claims of Frans Neirynck and the Leuven School notwithstanding (Neirynck 1977). If the present Gospel does include material that was clearly created by the Lukan author, for example, the evangelist must have borrowed that from Luke; but I find no material like that in John. This being the case, one cannot hold that information in John was derived from the Synoptics themselves; rather, the Gospel of John depends upon the same general stock of tradition that *underlies* the Synoptics. Second, it requires a very complicated game to explain just how the Fourth Evangelist would have used the Synoptics. There is no way to trace it except by the most ingenious reconstruction. Occam's razor suggests we not try. Third, if the author of John knew and used the Synoptics, this fact would tell us virtually nothing redaction-critically about its meaning. This, of course, is not an argument against dependence as much as it is a reason to look at

a redaction-critical analysis of John to see to what extent it proves useful and self-validating.

There does appear to be at least some connection between John and the Synoptics. John's narratives are not unique in the New Testament the way the discourses are. The narratives are, to be sure, like the Synoptics and in some instances have synoptic parallels, but they are different from their synoptic parallels, sometimes appearing in a more primitive form. Further, the miracle stories in John are more direct, if sometimes even more heightened, than their synoptic counterparts, and the use they are put to is also simpler and, in fact, quite unlike the Synoptics. This situation is readily explained by the Signs Gospel hypothesis. Such a source was dependent upon the same oral tradition that would underlie Mark, Matthew, and Luke. Yet it uses this common tradition differently from the Synoptics in a singular respect, attributing to Jesus' working of miracles the claim that they are fundamental evidence ("signs") of his messiahship. In the Synoptics, of course, Jesus rejects any request for a sign to account for his activity (Mark 8:11–12; Luke 11:29). Further, in the source the signs stem from Jesus, not "from heaven" as Mark's Pharisees demand, and it is the resurrection that satisfies the expectation for signs (2:18–19). Using the kind of oral tradition lying behind the Synoptics, all that was needed was to select a number of Jesus' miracles, arrange them in a logical geographical order, and treat them as demonstrations of his messiahship. The overlap between John and the Synoptics is, once more, best explained by holding that, in a way that reflected its special interests, the Signs Gospel drew from much the same tradition as the Synoptics and that the Fourth Evangelist then absorbed this material into the much fuller Gospel.

Fourth and finally, the tortured question of the Fourth Gospel's value as a source for the historical Jesus. As I have said in the past, there may be details in what I assign to the Signs Gospel that reflect memory from the time of Jesus. This possibility raises several questions about the Johannine claims that the information in the finished Gospel reflects the "witness" of the Beloved Disciple, a close associate of Jesus (John 13:23; 19:25–35; 20:1–10; 21:7, 20–24). I have never been able to fathom with any confidence the provenance of this figure. Yes, possibly there was such a person, whose special relation to Jesus was possibly created within the Johannine tradition. The lack of any such character in the synoptic tradition obviously argues against his full-blown existence from Jesus' time. But it is just as possible, I believe, that the Beloved Disciple is mythic and was created to fill a purpose, very likely no longer discernible, at the time of the completion of the Fourth Gospel (see Thatcher 2001). He first appears in the narrative only at 13:23 (the unnamed disciple of the Baptist in John 1:35–40, like the disciple "known to the high priest" in 18:16, can scarcely be the Beloved Disciple). This argues for his creation, or at least the maturation of his tradition, at the time of the Johannine community's crisis with the synagogue and in connection with the finished form of the story of Jesus' last days. For me then, the question of John's historicity is essentially a question of the historicity of the Signs Gospel, from which virtually all the narrative material derived.

Some stories in the source, as I mentioned, have a simpler form than their synoptic parallels. Does this mean that it can take us back closer to the deeds of the historical Jesus? Probably not to any useful degree. I say this first because I believe that Jesus himself, contrary to the source's presentation, had no Christology. He neither claimed for himself any special status nor viewed himself as Messiah, still less as the Johannine Son of God. This being the case, I cannot accept that Jesus did deeds that he intended to be taken as "signs" of Christology about himself. Second, when this Christological reading is subtracted from the Signs Gospel's stories, one gains very little that can be attributed to Jesus beyond what the Synoptics already offer. The source's presentation evidences a consistent tendency to heighten the miraculous element of Jesus' deeds. At John 2:6, no less than 120 gallons of water are about to be turned to wine; at 4:51–53, the boy is healed at the very moment that Jesus pronounces him alive; at 5:5, the man at Bethesda has been lame for thirty-eight years, and the man in John 9 has been blind from birth; Lazarus was dead in the tomb a full four days before Jesus raised him (11:39); and the miraculous catch of fish is so great that Peter's net was in danger of tearing (21:11). One can easily imagine how the oral tradition came to understand the miracle stories in this enhanced way and especially, how the Signs Gospel would add to them to justify its claims about Jesus' messiahship.

A somewhat different set of problems relates to the Signs Gospel's passion story, which like the pre-Markan (but not the Markan) passion is fundamentally apologetic. The account was no doubt built up from traditional materials and written to counter claims that no one could be Messiah whose life had ended in crucifixion by Rome. Similarly, the source's passion was produced to demonstrate, from the Jewish Scriptures, that the Christ had been destined to die just as Jesus did, according to a series of prophecies. (In Matthew, the same claim is more explicit: what Jesus experienced happened *in order to* fulfill Scripture.) As in the pre-synoptic passion tradition, the Signs Gospel's account was most likely based as much on these OT proof texts as on any historical memory of the events.

But, as I have suggested, the source's passion account has to be earlier than the version we have in Mark. The Markan author has reinterpreted the story so that the death of Jesus is no longer something that needs

to be explained away, but rather the very central focus of that Gospel's message. The Signs Gospel in no way reflects this reinterpretation. Its passion story is so driven by apologetic impulses that its overall accuracy is difficult to determine.

But I do think we can find traces of authentic memory in the Signs Gospel's passion account. On Jesus' action in the temple (John 2:13–20)—which would have appeared in the Signs Gospel as a prelude to the passion, rather than as now in the present Gospel among the signs, following the Cana story—we are told that there were oxen and sheep in the temple, that Jesus used a whip, and that he "poured out" the coins. None of these details appear in the Synoptics. The differences, alongside the many parallels, between the Signs Gospel's version and the Synoptics perhaps make it unlikely that the story was entirely fabricated on the basis of Old Testament texts. More likely, the two versions of the story represent independent attempts to relate the same historical event, and which of the details are historical is probably difficult to determine.

Several features of the anointing at Bethany (John 12:1–8) are possibly factual. I would think that Jesus' premonition that the anointing is a foreshadowing of his burial could be historical, without implying any special self-understanding on his part. Jesus' scriptural quote to Judas, "The poor you always have with you," may be a remembered detail; even his addition, "But you do not always have me." And the opening note that these events took place "six days before Passover" appears gratuitous and, therefore, just possibly factual.

On Jesus' final meal, I believe it is not easy to identify a source behind the present account in John 13. At the same time, John's story, unlike the Synoptics, has no hint of the later Lord's Supper and also shows no evidence of being a Passover meal. The footwashing that replaces the synoptic bread and cup is consistent with the lack of self-aggrandizement found in much of the Jesus tradition, and so perhaps may include authentic memories.

On Jesus' arrest (John 18:1–12), the image of Peter's attack on Malchus, the high-priest's slave, is either a skillful elaboration of the tradition or a gratuitous memory. And it seems highly unlikely to me that stories showing such a prominent leader of the early church having denied Jesus could be fictitious (18:15–27). Jesus' crucifixion, if not the Johannine elaboration of the trial before Pilate, is surely factual, and the memory of the locale (Golgotha), along with Mark and Matthew, appears likely (19:17–19).

Beyond such instances as these, it is now impossible to say whether we are mostly dealing, in Crossan's words, with "history remembered" or "prophecy historicized" (1995, 2–4).

What, finally and parenthetically, of the slight possibility that the Johannine discourses, not in any way deriving from the Signs Gospel, may also take us back toward the historical Jesus? It seems obvious that Jesus' proclamation of the kingdom of God would have been at best overshadowed and all but contradicted, if he taught that he had a very high christological status, the central premise of the Fourth Gospel's lengthy portrayal of his teaching. What is striking about the Synoptics, which are of course decidedly christological, is that this central focus of his public work (the kingdom of God) could still remain intact. In John, it is missing altogether. If Jesus spoke as he does in John, then the voice of the Jewish rabbi, the itinerant teller of subversive parables that we hear in the Synoptics, is simply false.

So we seem to have a certain amount of original, if mainly incidental, information about Jesus' deeds in the Signs Gospel, some of which may reflect authentic memory. John's discourses have been developed, either from previously disconnected traditions or wholesale, as a theological response to the crisis of excommunication. They tell us virtually nothing about the historical Jesus. Emphatic as I am on this last point, and largely convinced on the others, I look forward to the responses and dialogue that may ensue.

The Prologue of the Gospel of John as the Gateway to Christological Truth

Martin Hengel

For James D. G. Dunn on his 65th birthday

The Two "Pillars" — Matthew and John

The portico of Solomon's temple was dominated by two huge brazen pillars, Jachin and Boaz. In the same way, two towering pillars dominate the entrance to the New Testament: the Gospels according to Matthew and according to John. Their manuscript attestation shows how much they shaped Christian teaching in the second and third centuries. Of the around thirty papyri of Gospels dating before Constantine, eleven are of Matthew and fifteen of John; some go right back to the second century. Matthew took the church by storm:

I am grateful to the Rev. Dr. John Bowden for translating this lecture. For abbreviations see S. M. Schwertner, *Internationales Abkürzungsverzeichnis für Theologie und Grenzgebiete*, 2nd ed. (Berlin/New York: Walter de Gruyter, 1993).

The literature to the Prologue of John is boundless. M. Theobald, *Die Fleischwerdung des Logos* (NTA NF 20; Münster: Aschendorf, 1988), gives a survey of research. My exegesis of the text is indebted to Walther Eltester, "Der Logos und sein Prophet. Fragen zur heutigen Erklärung des johanneischen Prologs," in *Apophoreta: Festschrift für Ernst Haenchen zu seinem siebzigsten Geburtstag*, ed. W. Eltester and F. H. Kettler (BZNW 30; Berlin: Töpelmann, 1964), pp. 109-34, and especially to Hartmut Gese, "Der Johannesprolog," in Gese, *Zur biblischen Theologie* (BEvTh 78; München: Kaiser, 1977), pp. 152-201. See there the structure of the Prologue, pp. 172-73, and in my essay below, pp. 293-94. Among the great number of commentaries I only mention two: C. K. Barrett, *The Gospel according to St. John*, 2nd ed. (London: SPCK, 1978), pp. 149-70, and the theologically unsurpassed lectures of Karl Barth, *Erklärung des Johannes-Evangeliums (Kapitel 1-8)*, ed. Walther Fürst (Gesamtausgabe II; Zürich: TVZ, 1976), pp. 12-163, in my opinion theologically the richest exposition of Prologue in the twentieth century.

the Gospel brought what the church needed — a strict ethic on a christological basis.

The Fourth Gospel found it harder to become established: at first it seemed like an alien body alongside the Synoptics. Irenaeus brought the breakthrough. He quotes the Prologue to John around forty times. His Christology is mainly based on it.[1] The Logos is identical with the God *who reveals himself* and takes on personal character by virtue of the fact that this Logos has truly become human in Jesus. In this way Irenaeus, the first theologian of the whole Bible, has recognized the salvation-historical character of the Prologue of John that culminates in incarnation.[2]

Its final victory is marked by the observation of Clement of Alexandria that after the first Evangelists had discussed "the bodily nature" (τὰ σωματικά) of Jesus, John, "inspired by the Spirit, composed a spiritual gospel (εὐαγγέλιον πνευματικόν)."[3] Whereas Matthew remained fundamental to catechetical instruction, John determined the christological thought — not least because the beginning of the Prologue, although not yet stamped by *philosophical* speculation, was open to an interpretation in terms of the dominant Platonism. Augustine reports that a Platonic philosopher had called for the first five verses of the Gospel to be written in golden letters and hung up in the most visible place in all the churches.[4]

This positive verdict of a Neoplatonist has an analogy in German Idealism, for instance in Fichte.[5] However, according to him *only* those first five verses contain what is "absolutely true and valid for all times." What follows holds only for the time of Jesus and has only secondary "temporal" or "historical" significance.[6] Provided that someone is really united with God, it does not matter how he attained this. All that lasts is consciousness of this unity with God that rests in the primal foundation of the love of God.

To oppose this idealistic-mystical reinterpretation of the Prologue that is hostile to history one might cite Anselm of Canterbury's statement *"nondum considerasti quanti ponderis sit peccatum"* ("You have not yet considered the weight of sin").[7] There cannot be either responsibility or human dignity without the reality of guilt that we cannot forgive ourselves. God alone has to do this. The two pillars at the beginning of the New Testament are united on this. In Matthew's prehistory the Hebrew name Jesus/Jeshua is interpreted "and he will *save* his people from their sins,"[8] whereas in the Johannine prehistory John the Baptist describes Jesus: "Behold the lamb of God, who takes away the sin of the world."[9]

On the other hand, the differences between the Christology of the two Gospels could hardly seem greater. Matthew associates Jesus the son of David with the Old Testament history of promise: he begins his Gospel with Abraham (1:1f.) and directs his gaze to the church and the end of the world. So his focal point lies in the concluding words: "All authority in heaven and on earth has been given to me . . . And so, I am with you always, to the end of the world" (28:18-20). By contrast there is no mention of the pre-existence of Christ, and while Christ is also called Son of God, he is never called God.

With unshakeable boldness John looks not to the "end of the world" but to the very beginning of Genesis: *"in the beginning* (ἐν ἀρχῇ) God created heaven and earth." But he reaches out beyond that: *in the beginning* (ἐν ἀρχῇ)

---

1. For the influence of the Gospel of John in the second century before Irenaeus see Titus Nagel, *Die Rezeption des Johannesevangeliums im 2. Jh.* (Leipzig: Evangelische Verlagsanstalt, 2000); M. Hengel, *Die johanneische Frage* (WUNT 67; Tübingen: Mohr-Siebeck, 1993), pp. 9-95. For John and early Christian exegesis see idem, "Die Schriftauslegung des 4. Evangeliums auf dem Hintergrund der urchristlichen Exegese," *JBTh* 4 (1989): 249-88.

2. See now the Heidelberg dissertation of Bernhard Mutschler, *Irenäus als johanneischer Theologe* (STAC 21; Tübingen: Mohr-Siebeck, 2004).

3. According to book VI of the *Hypotyposeis* recorded by Eusebius, *H.E.* 6.14.5-7.

4. *De civ. Dei* 10.29: *aureis litteris conscribendum et per omnes ecclesias in locis eminentissimis proponendum esse.* Presumably he is saying this about Marius Victorinus. Plotinus's pupil Amelius also gives an outline of the Prologue but does not name the author and speaks of him as a representative of "barbarian" philosophy; see Eusebius, *Praep. Ev.* 11.19.4.

5. J. G. Fichte, *Die Anweisung zum seligen Leben*, ed. F. Medicus (PhB 234; Hamburg: Meiner, 1954). See his exposition of the Gospel of John and especially its Prologue (pp. 88-103, 180-86). Only John is the "teacher of true Christianity"; Paul remained half Jewish. Cf. Wilhelm A. Schulze, "Das Johannesevangelium im deutschen Idealismus," *ZPhF* 18 (1964): 85-118 (pp. 87-95); E. Hirsch, *Geschichte der neueren evangelischen Theologie* (Gütersloh: Bertelsmann, 1952), vol. IV, pp. 337-407 (pp. 381-401); W. Janke, "Fichte," *TRE*, vol. 11, pp. 157-71 (pp. 167f.).

6. Fichte, *Die Anweisung*, pp. 89, 93ff.: "Nur das Metaphysische, keineswegs aber das Historische macht selig" (p. 97).

7. *Cur Deus homo* 21, p. 72. Fichte radically denies the Christian conception of sin, guilt, and atonement; cf. Hirsch, *Geschichte*, IV, p. 394; Schulze, "Das Johannesevangelium," pp. 87f., 92f. For the biblical message see M. Hengel, *The Atonement* (London: SCM Press, 1981), pp. 33-75 = *The Cross of the Son of God* (London: SCM Press/Xpress Reprints, 1997), pp. 221-63, and basically H. Gese, "Die Sühne," in *Zur biblischen Theologie*, pp. 85-106: "Der Gekreuzigte repräsentiert den thronenden Gott und verbindet uns mit ihm durch Lebenshingabe des menschlichen Blutes. Gott wird uns zugänglich, erscheint uns im Gekreuzigten. Die Sühne geht nicht mehr vom Menschen . . . aus, sondern von Gott. Gott stellt zu uns die Verbindung her. Die Verbindung mit Gott wird möglich, weil Gott in unserer Not, in unserem Leiden, in unserer Hamartia-Existenz erscheint. Der Vorhang vor dem Allerheiligsten ist zerrissen. Gott ist uns ganz nahe, er ist uns im Tod, im Leiden, im Sterben gegenwärtig" (p. 105, discussing Rom. 3:25).

8. Matt. 1:21; cf. 26:28 (and 27:52).

9. John 1:29, 36; cf. 6:51c; 11:50; 1 John 1:7-2:2; Rev. 5:6-14, etc. On the problem see Th. Knöppler, *Die theologia crucis des Johannesevangeliums* (WMANT 69; Neukirchen-Vluyn: Neukirchen, 1994), and idem, *Sühne im Neuen Testament* (WMANT 88; Neukirchen-Vluyn: Neukirchen, 2001), pp. 220-68.

was the Word, the Word was with God and the Word was God." This God, the divine word, "became flesh" in Jesus Christ.

The Evangelist wants to bring out the true essence of Christ and his task more clearly than the three earlier Gospels by addressing one decisive point: Jesus Christ, in the Prologue God's Word of revelation and Son from eternity, is sent into the world by the Father to free men and women from the power of sin and death and to give them eternal life. Therefore the Johannine Jesus describes his task around fifty times as *being sent by the Father*. The Gospel concentrates on this statement to which in the author's view the Synoptics fail to do justice. Therefore from the beginning an upward gaze, to the association of the Son with the Father and his being sent by him, must stand at the center.

The Prologue and Its Climax in Verse 14

The Prologue is a hymn or psalm to the Logos, composed with great linguistic art and deep reflection. Its original shorter form is disputed. A recent monograph reports forty different attempts at reconstruction. Naivité or hybris on the part of the exegetes — or both?[10] By contrast, I am convinced that this hymn corresponds to the text of the Prologue and that only the two passages about John the Baptist in vv. 6-8 and 15 — written in the same style as the hymn — have been inserted to clamp it to the Gospel. As a whole it relates to the Gospel (and to the beginning of 1 John) and can come from the Evangelist himself, who describes in *stages* the saving revelation of God through his Word.[11]

The climax and goal is the incarnation of the Word in v. 14. It is the key to the twenty-one chapters that follow. Here I disagree with Harnack's opinion that "the prologue of the Gospel is not the key to the understanding of the Gospel but it prepares the Hellenistic reader for this."[12] In that case it would have only a protreptic function. In reality, the one decisive point that is developed in the whole Gospel has already been made in the four words of v. 14, ὁ λόγος σάρξ ἐγένετο. Even more questionable is the attempt to attribute to the Evangelist a "naïve docetism" in which the incarnation and passion are rather unim-

10. Theobald, *Die Fleischwerdung*. See the different models of reconstruction, pp. 7 1 f., 85, 95f. He speaks (p. 134) about "a certain exhaustion" in the production of hypothetical reconstructions of the original form of the "Hymn." At the end he proposes his own hypothetical solution (pp. 468f.).

11. I follow here the convincing argumentation of Gese, "Der Johannesprolog." See his strophic reconstruction on pp. 157f. and 172f. For the stages of revelation see also Eltester, "Der Logos und sein Prophet."

12. A. v. Harnack, "Ueber das Verhältniß des Prologs des vierten Evangeliums zum ganzen Werk," *ZThK* 2 (1892): 189-231 (p. 230).

portant, as happens with Ernst Käsemann, for whom the Johannine Jesus appears as a "God striding over the earth" and the incarnation does not represent "kenosis, a complete entering into our humanity."[13] This is to fail to perceive the sharp paradox of 1:14. For John, σάρξ means man in his creaturely human corporality who has fallen victim to sin, i.e., selfishness, and therefore to death, who stands in opposition to the spirit of God and who cannot know God of himself and therefore cannot attain eternal life.[14] The Old Testament prophets already tell us what σάρξ, *bāśār*, is. As an example I quote the cry of the preacher in the wilderness in Isaiah 40:[15]

All *flesh* is grass
and all the *glory of man*[16]
is like the flower of the field.
The grass is withered . . .
but the *word* of our God abides for ever.

Immediately before this we hear:

And the *glory of the Lord* will be manifested,
and all *flesh* will see God's salvation.

Here we are already in the midst of the vocabulary of our text.[17]

John 1:14 is to be understood against this background, in which we could also include texts from Qumran where *bāśār* takes on an even more strongly

13. Ernst Käsemann, *Jesu letzter Wille nach Johannes 17* (Tübingen: Mohr-Siebeck, ⁴1980 [1966]), pp. 61f. He referred to the idealistic exegesis of F. C. Baur, for whom the conception of the evangelist was "analogous to a gnostic one" (*Kritische Untersuchungen über die kanonischen Evangelien* [Tübingen: Fues, 1847], p. 87, cf. pp. 94-96). For him, like Fichte, the Logos is the expression of the divinity of man(kind).

14. Cf. John 3:6; 6:63 and 8:15 in connection with 1:29; 8:15, 21, 24, 34. John is already in a polemical debate with docetists; see 6:60 in connection with 6:51-56 and 1 John 4:2 and 3 (varia lectio) and 2 John 7 and a little later Ignatius, *Eph.* 7:2; *Magn.* 1:2; *Trall.* 8:1; 9:1f.; *Rom.* 7:3; *Phld* 4:1. In my opinion the letters of John were written before the editing of the Gospel; see M. Hengel, *Johanneische Frage*, pp. 134ff., 161-203; for σάρξ in John see also E. Schweizer, *ThWNT* VII, pp. 138-41.

15. Isa. 40:6-8 LXX; cf. 31:1-3; Jer. 17:5; Gen. 6:3 (Οὐ μὴ καταμείνῃ τὸ πνεῦμά μου ἐν τοῖς ἀνθρώποις τούτοις εἰς τὸν αἰῶνα διὰ τὸ εἶναι αὐτοὺς σάρκας); 2 Chron. 32:8. Texts from Qumran intensify the dualistic meaning of *bāśār*; see J. Frey, "Die paulinische Antithese von 'Fleisch' und 'Geist' und die palästinisch-jüdische Weisheitstradition," *ZNW* 90 (1999): 45-77.

16. LXX: δόξα ἀνθρώπου (cf. 1 Peter 1:24); MT: *ḥasdô*, proposed: *ḥādārô*, others: *ḥemdô*.

17. As a rule I quote the LXX because John is writing for a Greek-speaking community and uses the LXX, but he is also — like the author of Revelation — acquainted with the Hebrew text.

dualistic character. The eternal divine Word enters into a human existence and comes to us human beings, who are subject to the power of the "prince of this world."[18] At the end of the human existence of this word of God "made flesh" stands his rejection and his death on the cross. This casts a shadow on his way from the beginning. The saving significance of the death of Jesus is spoken of more frequently in John than in the Synoptics. He uses the preposition ὑπέρ for the vicarious atoning suffering of Jesus nine times, the first in 6:51: " and the bread that I give is my flesh, for the life of the world." John has a distinctive *theologia crucis*, the foundation for which is laid in 1:14.[19]

Despite all the emphasis on the loftiness of Christ in the Gospel we should not overlook the references to his *human weakness*. Where is there any mention of the physical exhaustion of Jesus in the Gospels outside John 4:6? In 11:35 he weeps over the death of his friend Lazarus. He is angry and deeply troubled; John mentions his being troubled (ταράσσεσθαι) three times. In so doing he contradicts the philosophical ideal of ἀταραξία. Jesus' own disciple betrays him; he is led bound to Annas and Pilate, and put on public display scourged and mocked. His dying cry τετέλεσται, "it is accomplished," represents the goal of the incarnation of the Logos. On the cross the creator of the world completes his work of the "new creation." For observers in antiquity, someone hanging on the cross naked and pitiful does not represent a "God striding over the earth."[20]

Thus John 1:14 forms the starting point of the history of a human being. Of course he is not simply a human being like you or me, but the Synoptic Gospels do not describe such a human being either. Rather, this is what Karl Barth called "the one man corresponding to God," whom the church confesses on the basis of the testimony of Paul[21] and John as *vere homo et vere Deus* and whose

---

18. John 12:31; 14:30; 16:11 cf. 8:44; 13:2, 27; and 1 John 3:12 the mention of Cain. See below n. 58.

19. See the investigation of Knöppler, *Die theologia crucis*.

20. M. Hengel, *Johanneische Frage*, pp. 193-201; idem, *Crucifixion* (London: SCM Press, 1977) = *The Cross of the Son of God* (London: SCM Press/Xpress Reprints, 1997), pp. 93-182. See, e.g., Celsus 2.35: "Why, if not before, does he not at any rate now [like Bacchus against Pentheus, c. 34] show forth something divine, and deliver himself from this shame, and take his revenge in those who insult him and his Father?" 36: "What does he say while his body is being crucified?" John 19:28 proves "that he rushed greedily to drink and did not bear his thirst patiently as even an ordinary man often does it" (2.37; translation by H. Chadwick, *Origen: Contra Celsum* [Cambridge: Cambridge University Press, 1953], pp. 95f.). John 19:28 is the paradoxical counterpart to 4:9-14.

21. Cf. Phil. 2:6ff.; 1 Cor. 8:6; and perhaps Rom. 9:5. See also M. Hengel, "Präexistenz bei Paulus," in *Paulus und Jakobus, Kleine Schriften III* (WUNT 141; Tübingen: Mohr-Siebeck, 2002), pp. 262-301. Already in Paul we find the unity of activity (*Handlungseinheit*) between the Father and the Son.

---

story John *relates as gospel*. However, in his story, testimony to Christ has largely absorbed history and transformed it.

It is precisely this that gives John the freedom to reach out far beyond Mark's ἀρχὴ τοῦ εὐαγγελίου and in the first thirteen verses of the Prologue to narrate an unprecedented "prehistory" that begins with the monumental ἐν ἀρχῇ of Genesis 1. It is the "history" of that creative Word, through which God himself reveals himself to the world as loving Father. From v. 14 the Logos has to retreat because he is now identified with an *historical person*, a man through whom his mystery is disclosed: "grace and truth came through *Jesus Christ*" (v. 17). Thus this concrete man takes the place of the Logos. In him the Logos has "become flesh" in a Galilean Jew. Andrew tells his brother Simon, "We have found the Messiah"; Philip gives his name, "We have found him of whom Moses in the Law and also the Prophets wrote, Jesus from Nazareth, the son of Joseph"; and Nathanael confesses, "Rabbi, you are the Son of God. You are the king of Israel."[22] No Evangelist in the passion narrative emphasizes the need for the Scriptures to be fulfilled and the kingship of Jesus as much as John does.[23] As *narrated Christology* the Fourth Gospel is grounded throughout in the Old Testament. One could point out that no New Testament writing has such a wealth of titles and designations provided from there and Judaism: the Anointed, Messiah, King, Rabbi, Rabbouni, Son of God and Son of Man, the Lord, the Holy One of God, the Elect, the Only-Begotten, the Prophet, the Lamb of God, the Light of the World, the True Vine, the Good Shepherd, and — not least — the absolute ἐγώ εἰμι[24] or even θεός himself.[25] Beyond question "salvation comes from the Jews."[26]

---

22. John 1:41-49; we have here and in 4:25 the only text in early Christian literature that gives the Greek transcription of the Aramaic m^ešîḥā = Μεσσίας.

23. Fulfillment of Scripture: 13:18; 17:12; 19:24, 28, 36f.; cf. 12:16, 38. See M. Hengel, "Die Schriftauslegung des 4. Evangeliums," pp. 249-88. Jesus as king: 12:13, 15; 18:33, 37, 39; 19:3, 12, 14f., 19, 21.

24. See C. H. Williams, *I Am He* (WUNT II/113; Tübingen: Mohr-Siebeck, 2000): John 8:24, 28; cf. v. 58; 13:19; Exod. 3:14; Isa. 43:10; 44:6.

25. John 1:1, 18; 20:28; cf. 1 John 5:20.

26. John 4:22; cf. 1:50. Jesus' answer to the Samaritan woman is surely not a later addition of an impudent "ecclesiastical redactor" — contra R. Bultmann and E. Haenchen in their commentaries *ad loc*. See also J. Becker, *Das Evangelium des Johannes* (ÖTK 4/1; Gütersloh: Mohn 1979), pp. 175f., with typical false alternatives: "Sicher ist Jesus Jude — das leugnet auch Johannes nicht —, aber Jesu Heilsangebot ist 'von oben', 'vom Vater', 'nicht aber von Israel her zu erklären. Eine im qualifizierten Sinne heilsgeschichtliche Vorrangigkeit Israels ist im Joh von Anfang an ausgeschlossen (1, 11-13)." "The Father always revealed himself through the Logos to Israel "from above," as to Abraham, Moses, and Isaiah — but his Word was rejected there as Jesus was himself. Some exegetes in Germany today still like to read the NT with Marcionite spectacles.

The "Prehistory" (Verses 1-13): The Logos ἄσαρκος

All this sheds some light on the "prehistory." The content of the hymn is matched by its artistic form, based on Semitic poetry in the style of the psalms, parallelisms written in a chiastic-chain structure. The author is a gifted poet. He writes a hymn or psalm in the praise of God the Father and the Logos and not a theological treatise in prose. The individual lines are often connected by keywords like links on a chain. These keywords govern the progress of the thought. They give the six strophes their themes.[27]

A. But why is the Logos so emphatically put at the beginning in the *first strophe* (vv. 1-3)? Why is it not only closely associated with God but himself called θεός and has God's own distinctive work, creation, attributed to it? Does that not show that the Evangelist is dependent on Alexandrian philosophy in the style of Philo who uses the term *Logos* 1,300 times and can call the λόγος θεοῦ the second (δεύτερος) after God himself?[28] That is only superficially the case. The author reaches out further. The Word in John 1:1 is not a philosophical first principle; rather, the ἐν ἀρχῇ ἦν ὁ λόγος expresses *the eternal being of the Word right from eternity* in inseparable communion with God: καὶ ὁ λόγος ἦν πρός τὸν θεόν, he was associated with God from eternity, before all time. In the high-priestly prayer Jesus says that the Father loved him "*before the foundation of the world*" (πρὸ καταβολῆς κόσμου).[29] So with complete consistency it is said καὶ θεός ἦν ὁ λόγος — the eternal Word is of one being with God. The concluding v. 2, οὗτος ἦν ἐν ἀρχῇ πρὸς τὸν θεόν, confirms this tremendous statement that transcends all the parallels behind it, for example the preparatory wisdom myth of Proverbs 8, Sirach 24, Wisdom, and even Philo.[30]

John 1:1 corresponds to the key statement in the Gospel, "I and the Father are one," 10:30. Thus the Evangelist is on the way toward the Nicene Creed: Θεὸν ἀληθινὸν ἐκ Θεοῦ ἀληθινοῦ, γεννηθέντα οὐ ποιηθέντα, ὁμοούσιον τῷ πατρί.[31] At the same time God's Word is given *an inalienable personality*: it is with the Father, one with him in will and being, but not simply identical with him. The Logos Christology that starts from the Prologue goes its way to Nicaea between an unreflective Monarchianism and a Neoplatonic-oriented Arianism that wanted to make the Logos the first creature.

Basically the Logos is the Greek equivalent of the Old Testament *dābār*, or the Targumic *memrā*[32] as the proclamation of the creating power and loving will of God in conjunction with the divine name, the *shem*, which denotes God as "person."[33] Psalm 147 says that God "sends his word," which acts as a power of creation and proclaims God's will.[34] Therefore his mediation at creation follows consistently in John 1:3: πάντα δι᾽ αὐτοῦ ἐγένετο.[35] The aorist ἐγένετο, which appears again in 1:14, marks a change from the imperfect ἦν, which denotes the eternity of the Logos with God: As the first act of God's revelation the creation is "event" and with it the world and its history begins. We could also speak of a "word of God history" or a "revelation history." That is what our hymn sets out to describe.

The next clause, "and without the Word nothing came into being," excludes *any* kind of dualism *in principle* — as, for example, found in Zoroastrianism or the widespread Greek idea of the chaos of uncreated matter.[36] This prepares the way for the doctrine of "creation from nothing."

---

27. See the analysis of the text by Gese, "Der Johannesprolog," pp. 154-73, and below, pp. 293-94.

28. *Leg. All.* 2.86; see H. Kleinknecht, *ThWNT* IV, pp. 86ff.

29. 17:24, cf. Rev. 13:8; 1 Peter 1:20.

30. For the Jewish wisdom tradition and the Logos see Gese, "Der Johannesprolog," pp. 173-90. These preparatory parallels of the "wisdom-myth" were already seen by the church fathers after Irenaeus, *Adv. haer.* 2.30.9: *verbum* and *sapientia* can become synonyms: cf. 3.24.1; but see also 4.7.3: *verbum = filius, spiritus sanctus = sapientia* and 4.20.1, 3f.: both together created the world. Irenaeus, on the basis of the Prologue, is already a trinitarian theologian.

31. I quote the text according to the reconstruction of E. Schwartz, "Das Nicaenum und das Constantinopolitanum auf der Synode von Chalkedon," *ZNW* 25 (1926): 51 = J. N. D. Kelly, *Altchristliche Glaubensbekenntnisse* (Göttingen: Vandenhoeck, 1972), p. 215 (translation of the 3d ed. of *Early Christian Creeds* [London: Longman, 1972]). See now U. Schnelle, "Trinitarisches Denken im Johannesevangelium," in *Israel und seine Heilstraditionen im Johannesevangelium*, ed. M. Labahn, K. Scholtissek, and A. Strotmann (Paderborn: Schöningh, 2003), pp. 367-86: "Das johanneische Denken ist trinitarisches Denken!" (p. 386).

32. See now D. Boyarin, "The Gospel and the *Memra*: Jewish Binitarianism and the Prologue of John," *HThR* 94 (2001): 243-84.

33. See G. Gerlemann, in Jenni-Westermann, *THAT* I, pp. 44if., according to O. Grether, "Name und Wort Gottes im AT," *BZAW* 64 (1934): 169; cf. p. 179: "Der schem vermittelt Gottes Gegenwart in der Welt, der dabar seine Wirksamkeit in ihr."

34. Ps. 147:4 LXX (MT v. 15): ὁ ἀποστέλλων τὸ λόγιον αὐτοῦ τῇ γῇ, ἕως τάχους δραμεῖται ὁ λόγος αὐτοῦ, v. 7 (MT v. 18): ἀποστελεῖ τὸν λόγον αὐτοῦ ... πνεύσει τὸ πνεῦμα αὐτοῦ. V. 8 (MT v. 19): ἀπαγγέλλων τὸν λόγον αὐτοῦ τῷ Ἰακώβ. Cf. Ps. 107:20; Isa. 55:11; Wis. 18:14f.; Rev. 19:13. Philo identifies word and work of God: *Sacr. AC* 65; *Somn.* I, 182; *Decal.* 47: ὅσα ἂν λέγῃ ὁ θεός, οὐ ῥήματά ἐστιν ἀλλ᾽ ἔργα.

35. Cf. the Nicene Creed: δι᾽ οὗ τὰ πάντα ἐγένετο, τὰ ἐν τῷ οὐρανῷ καὶ τὰ ἐν τῇ γῇ and already Paul (1 Cor. 8:6d and Col. 1:16f.).

36. See G. May, *Schöpfung aus dem Nichts. Die Entstehung der Lehre von der creatio ex nihilo* (AKG 48; Berlin/New York: Walter de Gruyter, 1978), p. 153: "Tatian ist der erste uns bekannte christliche Theologe, der ... den Satz aufstellt, daß die Materie von Gott hervorgebracht sei." He quotes the Prologue three times: John 1:1 = *Or. ad Gr.* 5.1; 1:3 = 19.4; 1:5 = 13.1; cf. his cosmology in chap. 5. In his *Diatessaron* he puts the Prologue at the beginning. His exclusion of uncreated matter is probably founded on his exegesis of John 1:1ff.

Goethe criticized the translation "In the beginning was the Word" in his *Faust*:

It is written: "In the beginning was the *word*."
I can't concede that words have such high worth
and must . . . translate the term some other way.[37]

He is not content with the translations "meaning" (*Sinn*) and "power" (*Kraft*) either. But then comes illumination:

Now I see a solution
and boldly write: "In the beginning was the *act* (*Tat*)!"

Faust with his false alternatives does not understand that word and act become one in the divine word of creation and revelation, as influenced by Genesis 1:1ff. in Psalm 33:

By the *word of YHWH*[38] were the heavens made
and all their host by the breath of his mouth

. . .

For *he spoke and it came into being*,
he commanded and it was done.[39]

In Wisdom 9:1f, a prayer of Solomon, the creative word of God and the personified Sophia appear in a *parallelismus membrorum*:

O God of my fathers Lord of mercy
who hast made all things by thy *word*
and by thy *wisdom* hast formed man.[40]

Word and wisdom of God are here nearly identified. Like the word of God, wisdom and the Spirit can also be sent by God and word-wisdom can appear not only as mediator of creation and revealer, but also as savior. Especially in Sirach 24 wisdom, the word of creation, and Torah are becoming a unified exponent of God's activity and revelation.[41]

B. The *second strophe* (vv. 3–5) moves from creation to *history*. With the oldest textual witnesses the last part of v. 3, ὃ γέγονεν, is to be taken with v. 4:

What had come into being, in it *he was life,
and the life was the light of men.*

The Logos is contained as subject in the imperfect ἦν, and this ἦν expresses an ongoing event.[42] The Word of God creates *life*. In the account of creation in Genesis 1 the divine "Let there be" brings forth manifold forms of *nepheš ḥayyā*, ψυχὴ ζῶσα, life,[43] and as the climax human beings, into whom God breathes the "breath of life"[44] and who consequently come to be in the image of God, i.e., the creature which as *God's unique partner*[45] is to recognize God and give him glory. Thus in Psalm 36:

For with you is the source of life
and in your light we see light.[46]

---

37. I follow the translation by Stuart Atkins, *Goethe Collected Works*, vol. 2, *Faust I and II*, ed. Stuart Atkins (Princeton: Princeton University Press, 1994), p. 33, vv. 1224–37. See the commentary of A. Schöne, *Johann Wolfgang Goethe, Faust, Kommentare* (Frankfurt: Deutscher Klassiker Verlag, 1999), pp. 246f. Goethe here is dependent on Herder, who gives several different possible paraphrases for the "Urbegriff" λόγος ("Gedanke! Wort! Wort! Will! Tat! Liebe!"); these are all insufficient, but Goethe transforms them into alternative translations and thus misinterprets the text of John.

38. LXX 32:6: τῷ λόγῳ τοῦ κυρίου.

39. LXX 32:9: ὅτι αὐτὸς εἶπεν, καὶ ἐγενήθησαν; cf. Gen. 1:3, 6, 9: καὶ εἶπεν ὁ θεός· Γενηθήτω . . . καὶ ἐγένετο. See also Ps. 148:5b; Isa. 48:13b; Sir. 42:15b; Judith 16:14; and n. 34, above, about Philo.

40. Ὁ ποιήσας τὰ πάντα ἐν λόγῳ σου καὶ τῇ σοφίᾳ σου κατασκευάσας ἄνθρωπον. For the relation of word, wisdom, and spirit in Irenaeus see n. 30, above.

41. Wisdom 9:9ff, 17f.; cf. Ps. 104:30; see M. Hengel, *Studies in Early Christology* (Edinburgh: T & T Clark, 1995), pp. 101f.; Gese, "Der Johannesprolog," pp. 178ff. on Sir. 243–6: "Die Rede der Weisheit beginnt damit, daß sie sich als Schöpfungslogos vorstellt" (243:3a). "Ohne Zweifel liegt in dieser Überlieferung vom Preis der Weisheit der traditionsgeschichtliche Ursprung für den Preis des Logos im Johannesprolog . . . Der Schritt zur θεός-Aussage selbst ist nur noch klein, und wenn sich die Weisheit nach Sir 24,1f. vor allen Gott umgebenden Engelwesen rühmen kann, liegt der Ansatz dazu schon vor" (p. 179).

42. The ἦν already contains the Logos as subject in vv. 9a and 10a. For the period after οὐδὲ ἕν see already the oldest textual witnesses and the early Church Fathers: K. Aland, "Eine Untersuchung zu Joh 1,3.4. Über die Bedeutung eines Punktes," *ZNW* 59 (1968): 174–209 = *Neutestamentliche Entwürfe* (ThB 63; Munich: Chr. Kaiser, 1979), pp. 351–91; Theobald, *Die Fleischwerdung*, pp. 186ff. with a differing translation: "was mit ihm kam, war Leben" (p. 185). For further literature on this much-discussed problem see Theobald, *Die Fleischwerdung*, p. 511.

43. Gen. 1:20, 24, 30. Cf. also Rom. 8:19–23 (the "waiting" and "groaning" of the creation for salvation subjected to futility). It can do this because it participated in the life given by the Creator.

44. Gen. 2:7: καὶ ἐνεφύσησεν εἰς τὸ πρόσωπον αὐτοῦ πνοὴν ζωῆς καὶ ἐγένετο ὁ ἄνθρωπος εἰς ψυχὴν ζῶσαν; cf. John 20:22: ἐνεφύσησεν καὶ λέγει αὐτοῖς, Λάβετε πνεῦμα ἅγιον; creation becomes the type of salvation. Also compare the τετέλεσται of Jesus (John 19:30) on the eve of the Great Sabbath (1931) with Gen. 2:1f.

45. Gen. 1:26f.; 5:1; cf. Ps. 8:6; Rom. 1:18ff.

46. Ps. 36:10 (LXX 35:10): ὅτι παρὰ σοὶ πηγὴ ζωῆς, ἐν τῷ φωτί σου ὀψόμεθα φῶς;

If the divine Word that communicates life to the world withdraws "the light of life"[47] from his creatures, they all fall back into the night of death into nothingness. But for human beings "life" means more: as *imago Dei* they are created to be illuminated by the Word of God, "and the life was the *light of men*" (v. 4b). As the power of life the Logos has endowed only human beings with the knowledge of God, which at the same time represents self-knowledge, responsibility, and obedience to God's commandment; however, the first human couple squanders life and light and delivers itself over to darkness, to death. John indicates this in the next sentence:

The light shines in the *darkness*,
But the *darkness* could not grasp it. (v. 5)

The drama of human history has begun. It is also a history of disaster, but at the end the Word of God that brings light and salvation will establish itself in the face of all powers of nothingness: the darkness could neither "grasp" the light nor "seize" it. Here the poet is playing with the ambivalence of καταλαμβάνειν.[48] It is not said where this power of darkness that is hostile to life comes from. But the hearers still have v. 3 ringing in their ears: nothing was created without the Logos. The "fall," that deep disruption in creation and history that is part of God's mystery, is presupposed between vv. 3 and 5 and again in v. 10. Like the whole apostolic testimony, John knows no theodicy — the incarnation replaces it. God does not need justification; his only justification is that of the sinner because of the vicarious sacrifice of Christ: therefore the Word of God *must* become man.

In vv. 6-8 the Evangelist introduces the first insertion of John the Baptist. With "a man appeared, sent from God, his name was John," he transports us into the center of salvation history. In the Synoptics the Baptist is identical with the Elijah redivivus as the last and greatest prophet.[49] John knows this but disapproves of it and changes his function.[50] The aorist ἐγένετο, which emphasizes

---

cf. Hos. 10:12: τρυγήσατε εἰς καρπὸν ζωῆς, φωτίσατε ἑαυτοῖς φῶς γνώσεως; Prov. 14:27: πρόσταγμα κυρίου πηγὴ ζωῆς; and John 4:14.

47. Ps. 56:14 (LXX 55:14): τοῦ εὐαρίστησαι ἐνώπιον τοῦ θεοῦ ἐν φωτὶ ζώντων; Job 33:30: ἀλλ' ἐρρύσατο τὴν ψυχήν μου ἐκ θανάτου ἵνα ἡ ζωή μου ἐν φωτὶ αὐγῇ αὐτόν. Cf. Ps. 56:14. See Gese, "Der Johannesprolog," p. 191, and cf. John 8:12.

48. Cf. John 1:5: καὶ ἡ σκοτία αὐτὸ οὐ κατέλαβεν and 12:35: περιπατεῖτε ὡς τὸ φῶς ἔχετε, ἵνα μὴ σκοτία ὑμᾶς καταλάβῃ.

49. Cf. Mark 9:13 = Matt. 17:12; 11:14; Luke 1:17; Mal. 3:23; Sir. 48:10. See M. Hengel, *Judaica, Hellenistica et Christiana, Kleine Schriften II* (WUNT 109; Tübingen: Mohr-Siebeck, 1999), pp. 18f, 26, 28.

50. 1:25 — he is neither the Messiah nor the Elijah redivivus nor the eschatological prophet according to Deuteronomy 18 (cf. 3:28).

---

the unique occasion, has its parallel in 1:14. Their common feature is that both John the Baptist and Jesus are contemporary Jews with an eschatological significance. The first, however, has only the one task of bearing witness to the second, so that people may believe in *him*, Jesus, as the light. The next clause, "he [the Baptist] was not the light," may refer to Baptist communities toward the end of the first century who saw John as the redeemer sent by God;[51] however, the polemical motif should not be over-emphasized.

Vv. 6-8 refer to the prophetic witness to the light of the Word before its manifest appearance. Thus John the Baptist appears initially as the concluding witness of Israel for Jesus who therefore defines his function in 1:23 with the quotation of Isaiah 40:3 (LXX).

In the second insertion (v. 15) he becomes the first witness to the incarnation of the preexistent word now visibly present as a person and thus appears as the *first disciple of Jesus* who by his testimony leads his own disciples to him.[52]

V. 9 takes up the motif of light once again, and again the Logos is the subject: "He was the true light," which, coming into the world, "enlightens every man." The Word does not remain at a divinely exalted distance from the world that it has created. It enters this world as divine *address*, i.e., as a "revelation" that time and again makes claims on human beings. God's blessing has given to man the responsibility for his creation (Gen. 1:28-30). Man "represents" the "Cosmos" that the Word enters. It is the human world. The Logos comes to human beings because the Creator loves his creatures and does not want to leave them to themselves, to the darkness of their hearts. They remain dependent on him. According to John, *God's nature is love*.[53] This is at work from the beginning. In other words, again we have the partnership of man with God created by the address of the Word. Here we can happily talk of "spiritual light," enlightened reason, wisdom, a vigilant conscience, and a capacity for hearing: they are gifts of the Creator through his Word and are what first make human beings human. The Logos is "true light" because all true "insight," all responsible action comes from him. Man is God's partner because he should be susceptible to the voice of God's Logos. However, this "that enlightens every man" points to a primal state that humankind has lost, for the "divine image" in human beings has been badly damaged, their "in-

---

51. Cf. Luke 3:15. In the Pseudo-Clementine homilies (I 54:8; 60.1) the disciples of the Baptist saw their master as the Messiah. Cf. H. Lichtenberger, "Täufergemeinden und frühchristliche Täuferpolemik im letzten Drittel des 1. Jahrhunderts," *ZThK* 84 (1987): 36-57.

52. See 1:29-37; 3:23-36. The first insertion, John 1:6-8, is related to the μαρτυρία of the Baptist, 1:19-27; the second, 1:15, to 1:28-36. See Gese, "Der Johannesprolog," pp. 196f.

53. 1 John 4:7-10, 18f. (v. 8: Θεὸς ἀγάπη ἐστίν); cf. John 3:16; 6:51; 10:11; 13:1; 15:13. The proof of this love is the incarnation of the Logos and his atoning death for the whole of mankind.

sight" has been obscured by sin, their susceptibility has been deadened by disobedience. Between the enlightenment by the Logos and the reality of human life in the world there is the deep rift already indicated in v. 5 and presupposed by the Evangelist not only in the Prologue but in the whole Gospel. This rift is the condition for the necessity of incarnation in v. 14. In the prologue in heaven in Goethe's *Faust*, Mephisto accuses God himself because of the unsuccessful creation of man:

> I've no remarks to make about the sun or planets
> I merely see how mankind toils and moils.
> *Earth's little gods* still do not change a bit,
> are just as odd as on their primal day.
> Their lives would be a little easier
> *if You'd not let them glimpse the light of heaven....*
> *they call it Reason and employ it only*
> *to be more bestial than any beast.*[54]

C. The *third strophe* in vv. 10 and 11 expresses the fundamental resistance to the address by the Word of God in the human world:

> He was in the world
> and the world came into being through him
> yet the world did not recognize him.
>
> He came into his own,
> And his own people did not receive him.

On the one hand vv. 9 and 10 *correspond*: the Word of God has come into the world; *the* "transcendent" has become "immanent" — and yet they *contradict* each other. V. 9 says that with its coming the Word *illuminates* every man, but v. 10 states that the human world has not *recognized* this Word,[55] — it has rejected it. It "loved darkness rather than light" (3:19) and "the glory of men more than the glory of God" (12:43).[56] In its self-glorification it did not want to recognize the true light, to hear its "address." Here we have the serpent's original sin, that "you will be as God."[57] This "worldwide" rejection in which the evangelist recalls the creation of the world through this Word may have especially in view the failed beginnings of the history of humankind in Genesis 3–11. They are the paradigm for the conduct of the whole "human world."[58]

V. 11 refers to a new "stage of revelation":

> He came into his own,
> And his own people did not receive him.

The terms τὰ ἴδια and οἱ ἴδιοι are a reference to Israel, God's own possession, the people chosen by him. To them God speaks the promise, "If you will obey my voice...you shall be *my own possession* among all peoples."[59] But even God's own possession, the people chosen since Abraham,[60] turns away from God's word and command: "Did not Moses give you the law? Yet *none of you* keeps the law" and: "It is Moses who accuses you, on whom you set your hope." But "if you do not believe his writings, how will you believe in me?" asks the Johannine Christ.[61]

---

54. *Faust I and II*, pp. 9f, vv. 280-86.
55. Gese, "Der Johannesprolog," p. 165: "Das Erkennen, das der 'Kosmos' nicht vollzieht, ist im Sinne des hebräischen Begriffs jā⁴ das anerkennende, das sich zum Logos bekennende Erkennen, das der Erleuchtung, dem Sehen, der Wahrnehmung (v. 9) wie eine Antwort folgen müßte. Die Menschheit, und mit ihr der Kosmos, sieht wohl, aber erkennt nicht."
56. Cf. 5:44; 7:7, 18.
57. Gen. 3:5. Mephisto writes this verse in the album of a young student beginning his studies and asking for advice: "Eritis sicut deus scientes bonum et malum" and adds: "Follow the ancient saw, and my cousin the serpent and I warrant your likeness to God will some day perplex you" (*Faust I and II* p. 52 vv. 248-50).
58. Mankind has chosen to be subjected to the ἄρχων τοῦ κόσμου τούτου 12:31; 14:30; 16:11; see above n. 18. His existence and seductive power is presupposed but not explained. Men remain responsible for their "loving darkness rather than light" and for their "evil deeds," 3:19; cf. 8:41: "You do what your father did." The "Jews" are here the paradigm for the whole mankind. 8:44: "You are of your father the devil, and your will is to do your father's desires. He was a murderer *from the beginning* and has nothing to do with the truth, because there is no truth in him. When he lies he speaks according to his own nature, for he is a liar and the father of lies." His lies seduced Adam and Eve (Gen. 3:1-7) and handed them over to death, cf. Gen. 4:6ff. and 1 John 3:12. Because primeval man and his descendants chose the lie instead of God's truth, they cannot acknowledge the word of God as their creator. Cf. Rom. 1:18–3:20, 23.
59. Exod. 19:5; cf. Deut. 7:6; 10:14f; Pss. 135:4; 33:12; Mal. 3:17. Εἰς τὰ ἴδια and οἱ ἴδιοι has a personal meaning of special familiarity (cf. 19:27). Israel, the people elected by God as his possession is a *creatura verbi* and belongs to the *familia Dei*. See Sir. 24:3-12: God sends his beloved wisdom, which is identical with the Torah (24:23), to Israel his heritage, to the beloved town Jerusalem, and to mount Zion.
60. See Gese, "Der Johannesprolog," p. 166: "Es sollte keine Frage sein, daß nach der Menschheit (v. 10) hier in v. 11 nur von Gottes Eigentumsvolk, Israel, die Rede sein kann, zu dem der Logos 'kam' (ἦλθεν), was auf den heilsgeschichtlichen Vollzug im Unterschied zur sozusagen 'natürlichen' Gegebenheit (ἦν) verweist. Dem Kommen entspricht das Aufnehmen, die die personale Verbundenheit gegenüber dem Erkennen stärker zum Ausdruck bringende Kategorie." The "coming" to the ἴδιοι is the expression of a new, especially personal bestowal founded on election.
61. 7:19; 5:45, 47; cf. 3:14f.

D. The *fourth strophe*, vv. 12 and 13, indicates the turning point, an alternative that represents an incomprehensible miracle. Among the ἴδιοι, the members of the chosen people, there were some who, in contrast to the majority, "accepted" the Word and gave it credence. These are the ones (ὅσοι) who hear the Word, trust it, and allow their lives to be governed by it.

With πιστεύειν the Evangelist is taking up a dominant key word; he uses it by far the most frequently in the New Testament.[62] But this πιστεύειν, obedient trust, is already fundamental for the people who are God's possession. The key-word occurs for the first time in the paradigmatic faith of Abraham,[63] and above all in Deutero-Isaiah, which in 43:10, for example, sounds completely Johannine: ἵνα γνῶτε καὶ πιστεύσητε . . . ὅτι ἐγώ εἰμι; "that *you may know and believe that I am*."[64] Along with Moses and all the prophets, Abraham, who "rejoiced" that he was to see the day of the incarnation,[65] and Isaiah, who saw the glory of the Incarnate One, are examples of such "believers."[66]

This word empowers those who trust it "to become God's beloved children."[67] Because they followed the call of the Word through the prophets: "Return, faithless *children*, I will heal you."[68] The promise "They will be called *chil-*

---

dren of the living God" is fulfilled in them.[69] God will be the father of his elected (but now disobedient) people.[70]

The disputed v. 13 explains this being a child of God. In reality it does not come about through natural begetting and descent in the association of a people, but through birth from God: ἀλλ' ἐκ θεοῦ ἐγεννήθησαν (v. 13d).[71] We are reminded of John the Baptist's preaching of repentance in the logia tradition: "Do not say 'We have Abraham for our father.' God can raise up children for Abraham from these stones."[72] Birth from God, the gift of being a child of God, remains beyond the control of natural human beings of "flesh and blood." In this artistic four-member sentence the Evangelist describes the desires of the σάρξ for physical and national self-assertion, which has no significance for being a child of God.

The demand for the "birth from God" is also prepared for in the Old Testament. Thus we find the "begetting" (or the "birth") of Israel from God in the "Song of Moses":

You have abandoned the God who gave birth to (or begat) you and forgotten the God who fed you.[73]

We also find the "begetting" (or the "birth") of Israel from God in the beginning of the book of Isaiah:

The Lord has spoken: *Sons have I begotten* and brought up, but they have rebelled against me.[74]

Their disobedience does not abolish divine election, but it makes necessary prophetic admonition and promission leading forward to incarnation.

---

62. In the Gospel John has πιστεύειν 108 times, in the letters 9 times. In the whole of the NT we find it 241 times. The noun πίστις appears only once in the letters (1 John 1:10c). The use of γινώσκειν (cf. 1:10c) is comparable: 56 times in the Gospel, 26 times in the letters, and 221 times in the whole of the NT. The noun γνῶσις is lacking, too.

63. Gen. 15:6 (LXX): ἐπίστευσεν Ἀβραμ τῷ θεῷ καὶ ἐλογίσθη αὐτῷ εἰς δικαιοσύνην; cf. Rom. 4:3; Gal. 3:6. See also the faith of Israel after the miraculous crossing of the Red Sea, Exod. 14:31: καὶ ἐπίστευσαν ἐν τοῖς λόγοις αὐτοῦ. Ps. 115:1 (MT 116:10): ἐπίστευσα διὸ ἐλάλησα (cf. Paul in 2 Cor. 4:13); Isa. 28:16; etc. For faith as trusting in the name of the Lord see Isa. 50:10 (πεποιθέτω ἐπὶ τῷ ὀνόματι τοῦ κυρίου) and the numerous examples of πεποιθέναι (*bṭḥ*) in connection with God, especially in the Psalms and Isaiah. But see also the many examples of Israel's unbelief: Ps. 105:24 (MT 106); Ps. 77:22, 32 (MT 78); Jer. 25:8; Deut. 9:23; etc.

64. Cf. John 8:24: ἐὰν γὰρ μὴ πιστεύσητε ὅτι ἐγώ εἰμι, 8:28: τότε γνώσεσθε ὅτι ἐγώ εἰμι. Cf. Deut. 32:39 and Isa. 7:9: καὶ ἐὰν μὴ πιστεύσητε, οὐδὲ μὴ συνῆτε. See also above n. 63.

65. John 8:56; cf. Gen. 15:9ff. and the Jewish exegesis of Abraham's vision; see Hengel, "Schriftauslegung," p. 265.

66. John 12:41; cf. Isa. 6:1ff., the quotation of Isa. 6:10 in 12:40, and Isa. 53:1 in 12:38. See Hengel, "Schriftauslegung," pp. 265f. The "speaking" of Isaiah about the δόξα of Christ is related to Isaiah 53.

67. Unlike the OT and Paul, John does not speak about "sons of God" (τέκνα θεοῦ): 1:12; 8:39; 11:52; 1 John 3:1f, 10; 5:2. For John the title "Son" is only true of the one sent by the Father into the world. But in John 20:17 the Risen One says to Mary Magdalene: "Go to my brethren and say to them: I am ascending to *my Father and your Father*."

68. Jer. 3:22: ἐπιστράφητε υἱοὶ ἐπιστρέφοντες καὶ ἰάσομαι τὰ συντρίμματα ὑμῶν; cf. v. 11; 4:22; Isa. 30:1, 9.

69. Hos. 2:1: κληθήσονται υἱοὶ θεοῦ ζῶντος. Cf. Deut. 14:1: υἱοί ἐστε κυρίου τοῦ θεοῦ ὑμῶν; Isa. 43:6; 45:11; see G. Fohrer, *ThWbNT* VIII, pp. 352f.

70. Exod. 4:22; Jer. 31:19f.; Hos. 11:1. Therefore Israel can call him "our Father": Isa. 63:16; 64:7; Mal. 2:10; see M. Hengel, "Abba, Maranatha, Hosanna und die Anfänge der Christologie," in *Denkwürdiges Geheimnis. Beiträge zur Gotteslehre. Festschrift für Eberhard Jüngel zum 70. Geburtstag*, ed. I. U. Dalferth, J. Fischer, and H.-P. Großhans (Tübingen: Mohr-Siebeck, 2004), pp. 145-83.

71. For this formula see John 3:3-8 and 1 John 2:29; 3:9; 4:7; 5:1-4, 18, and in relation to the OT, Gese, "Der Johannesprolog," pp. 166f, 197f.

72. Luke 3:8 = Matt. 3:9; Rom. 4:12; Gal. 3:14; John 8:39ff.

73. Deut. 32:18: θεὸν τὸν γεννήσαντά σε (γ°ⁱlaďkhā) ἐγκατέλιπες καὶ ἐπελάθου θεοῦ τοῦ τρέφοντός σε. Therefore, the Israelites are faithless sons (v. 20), υἱοὶ οἷς οὐκ ἔστιν πίστις ἐν αὐτοῖς; cf. 32:5.

74. Isa. 1:2 (LXX): υἱοὺς ἐγέννησα (MT: *giddaltî*) καὶ ὕψωσα (*rômamtî*), αὐτοὶ δέ με ἠθέτησαν.

In Psalm 87 Zion appears as the foundation beloved by YHWH. He himself records the peoples in Zion's register of citizens because all are "born in here."[75] Isaiah 66 describes the eschatological miraculous birth of the people of God in connection with the epiphany of the *kabôd* YHWH announced by the word of God:

Before she [Jerusalem] was in labor she gave birth;
before her pain came upon her she was delivered of a son
. . .
Shall a nation be born in one moment?
For as soon as Zion was in labor she brought forth her sons.[76]

Even when most of his own children "received him not" and became faithless, some of them remained faithful and proved themselves as true "sons of God" and even witnesses of the Logos, beginning with Abraham via Moses and all prophets up to John the Baptist the last witness in Israel and first disciple of the Logos incarnate. At the same time their testimony refers to the fulfillment of all promises given to them in the Logos incarnate.

The reference to the miraculous birth of the true people of God brought about by the Word — and opposed to all the efforts of the σάρξ — concludes the revelation of the *logos asarkos* in creation, the human world, and Israel. The Logos psalm can now concentrate on the deepest paradoxical miracle — the incarnation.

We can — indeed, we must — ask, isn't the incarnation of the Word already indicated from v. 3 onward, wherever the activity of the Logos as life and light is spoken of — his coming into the world, the rejection and his acceptance — except that the incarnation is not yet mentioned? In reality it is the case that this concise sketch of salvation history, which in four strophes moves to the decisive point, the incarnation, anticipates as a type the activity and fate of the incarnate Word with this movement. John loves such ambivalences. Thus the Prologue becomes the *testimony to a theology of the whole Bible*, which has an utterly christological orientation. It is the Incarnate One who illuminates his own "preparing revelation" in the Scriptures given to Israel.[77]

---

75. Ps. 87:5f. (LXX 86): *zeh yullad šam*.
76. Isa. 66:7-9; cf. vv. 11-13; 49:21; 54:1ff.; 62:4f.; as well as the marriage between YHWH and his people in Hos. 2:22f.
77. John 2:22: after the resurrection οἱ μαθηταὶ αὐτοῦ . . . ἐπίστευσαν τῇ γραφῇ καὶ τῷ λόγῳ ὃν εἶπεν ὁ Ἰησοῦς. Cf. 12:16; 20:9; see also 1:45; 3:14; 5:32, 45; etc.

The Incarnation (Verses 14-18): The "Logos ἔνσαρκος"

E. The *fifth strophe*, vv. 14 and 16, brings the decisive four words "the Word became flesh" and associates this with the first-person plural of the confession of the disciples: "and dwelt among us and we saw his glory . . . and from his fullness have we all received, grace upon grace." The mere fact that the Logos is mentioned as subject only in 1:1 and here shows that everything moves toward these words: v. 14 summarizes the whole Gospel. In order to interpret this one sentence the Evangelist could not continue the Synoptic tradition; he had to write a different Gospel that sets out to inculcate in readers the truth of this one sentence.

Here *the* miracle takes place that is unimaginable for human beings: in his Word God himself becomes human; the timelessly eternal and almighty God who, as the hymn in 1 Timothy puts it, "dwells in light inaccessible, whom no man has seen nor can see,"[78] becomes human at a fixed point of time and space in a remote and insignificant region, Galilee, and a little known and despised village, Nazareth.[79] I have already shown the weighty connotations of the word σάρξ/*bāśār* and how this brief sentence "And the word became flesh" already contains within it a Johannine *theologia crucis*. It was as much "a stumbling block to the Jews and foolishness to the Greeks" as the Pauline word of the cross. In Christology John stands on Paul's shoulders.[80] We find the closest parallel in Romans:

What the law, weakened by the *flesh*,
could not do, God has done,
sending his own Son
in the likeness of sinful flesh.

This πέμψας ἐν ὁμοιώματι σαρκὸς ἁμαρτίας comes closest in content to our σάρξ ἐγένετο.[81] Both John and Paul have in common the fact that the eter-

---

78. 1 Tim. 6:16: φῶς οἰκῶν ἀπρόσιτον, ὃν εἶδεν οὐδεὶς ἀνθρώπων οὐδὲ ἰδεῖν δύναται; cf. 1:17; John 1:18; 5:37.
79. Galilee is mentioned in John most often: seventeen times; in Mark, twelve times; in Luke, thirteen times; in Matthew, sixteen times. According to the Pharisees neither the Messiah nor a prophet can come from Galilee: 7:41f., 52. For Nazareth see John 1:45f. This insignificant village is first mentioned in the Gospels.
80. J. Wellhausen, *Das Evangelium Johannis* (Berlin: G. Reimer, 1908), p. 121 = *Evangelienkommentare* (Berlin/New York: Walter de Gruyter, 1987), p. 721; Hengel, *Johanneische Frage*, p. 299.
81. Rom. 8:3; cf. Gal. 4:4; Phil. 2:6ff. See also John 3:16, 18; 1 John 4:9; Rom. 8:32.

nal God himself comes as a human being to lost human beings who have turned away from him. According to John he comes to them as the personified divine "Word," as the "only-begotten Son of the Father full of grace and truth." These are concepts that are also of central importance for Paul, above all χάρις, as a keyword of his theology.[82] In John it appears only in the Prologue, but there it occurs four times as an expression of the fullness of divine salvation given through the Son.

He differs from Paul in that he narrates his message, which is Christology through and through, as the story of Jesus, whereas Paul concentrates on the formal kerygma of cross and resurrection.

Here v. 14 sketches out the quintessence of the Johannine narrative: in becoming flesh the Word overcomes with divine sovereignty the "infinite qualitative difference" between God and man (to use Kierkegaard's famous phrase) in our favor, by exposing himself as a human being "of flesh and blood" to the antigodly powers in this world for our salvation. As Karl Barth remarked: "The Logos takes the side of his adversaries."[83] In other words, he "dwelt among us." The aorist ἐσκήνωσεν (like ἐγένετο and the following ἐθεασάμεθα) underlines that the incarnation was a *fact* that happened "once for all" (Rom. 6:10) in the past. The rather unusual verb σκηνοῦν we find again only in Revelation for the future "dwelling" of God in the midst of his delivered people.[84] Σκηνοῦν reminds us also of σκηνὴ τοῦ μαρτυρίου (*miškan* √*škn*), the "tent of the meeting" as the place of the presence of God in ancient Israel, which was replaced by the temple. The ἐν ἡμῖν introduces the confessing community of disciples into the Prologue. During this limited time of fellowship with him their community saw the divine glory that the Logos made flesh mediates — even in his lowliness.

The letter of 1 John supplements the solemn ἐθεασάμεθα: we have seen, or, better, "contemplated by our eyes" with the antidocetic "touching" (ψηλαφᾶν) by the hands (1:1). It expresses there the "physical" reality of incarnation *and* the corporeal seeing of the risen Christ. The "seeing" of the incarnate Logos's δόξα and the physical seeing of his presence do not contradict but belong inseparably together for the Evangelist. With this statement he possibly prepares the Beloved Disciple as the decisive witness for Christ.[85]

---

82. In the genuine letters we find it sixty-six times; in the Deutero-Paulines, thirty-four times; in the rest of the NT, fifty-five times.

83. Barth, *Erklärung*, p. 110.

84. Σκηνοῦν: See Liddell/Scott, p. 1608: pitch a tent, live or dwell in a tent, generally: settle, take up one's abode; cf. W. Michaelis, *ThWNT* VIII, p. 388. See Rev. 7:15; 21:3: Ἰδοὺ ἡ σκηνὴ τοῦ θεοῦ μετὰ τῶν ἀνθρώπων, καὶ σκηνώσει μετ' αὐτῶν.

85. John 19:26, 35; 20:8, 20; 21:7, 24. See also Hengel, *Johanneische Frage*, pp. 183f. The Christology in the Gospel as in the letters of John is strongly antidocetic; cf. U. Schnelle,

This paradoxical "seeing the glory" of the Incarnate One by the community of disciples becomes one of the basic themes of the Gospel: beginning with the testimony of John the Baptist,[86] it is completed in the use of the verbs ὑψωθῆναι and δοξασθῆναι. Here the "being exalted" points to his crucifixion[87] and the "being glorified" to his resurrection.[88] The "glory" consists in his being made manifest as the "only-begotten" from the Father.

Μονογενής describes the Son in his unique relation to the Father,[89] he from now on replaces the Logos. His δόξα, which the disciples saw, results from his unity with the Father. We could sum up the message of the Son with a statement from the Farewell Discourses: "The Father himself loves you, because you have loved me and have believed that I came from the Father" (16:27). With this twofold μονογενής the Prologue prepares for the Nicene Creed: τὸν υἱὸν τοῦ θεοῦ μονογενῆ, τὸν ἐκ τοῦ πατρὸς γεννηθέντα πρὸ πάντων τῶν αἰώνων, γεννηθέντα οὐ ποιηθέντα ("the only begotten Son of God, begotten from the Father before all eternities . . . begotten not made").[90] Harnack was wrong when he insisted that "not the Son but only the Father belongs in the gospel as Jesus preached it."[91] The Jesus of all four Gospels preaches the Father *who sent the Son*, but John does so most intensively. Jesus' mission by the Father is an indispensable part of his message. Like his consciousness of being Son it belongs to the mystery of his person and his messianic activity.[92]

The reference to the "glory of the only-begotten from the Father" that the disciples see in the λόγος ἔνσαρκος thus interprets v. 1, "and the Word was with God and the Word was God." Love, the inner being of the Father, becomes visible in him.[93]

In conclusion v. 16 emphasizes that this revelation from the fullness of the Son that leads to eternal life is an utterly unmerited gift:

Antidoketische Christologie im Johannesevangelium (FRLANT 144; Göttingen: Vandenhoeck, 1987).

86. John 1:32, 51; 2:11; 11:40; 17:1ff., 5, 22, 24.

87. John 3:14; 8:28; 12:32, 34.

88. John 7:39; 8:54; 12:16, 23, 28; 13:31f.; 17:1ff.

89. We find μονογενής with a christological meaning only five times in the Johannine corpus, twice in the Prologue: 1:14, 18; cf. 3:16, 18; 1 John 4:9. It is not in the apostolic Fathers, but later in Diogn. 10.2, which is dependent on John. The same is true of Justin, *Dial.* 105.1f.; cf. also 98.5. Its use in Wisdom 7:22 is a preliminary stage.

90. See n. 31 above.

91. *Das Wesen des Christentums* (Leipzig: Hinrichs, ⁴1901), p. 91; cf. his criticism of Paul and John (p. 114).

92. See Hengel, "Abba, Maranatha, Hosanna," *Kleine Schriften* IV, 496-534.

93. See above n. 53. Cf. also 2 Cor. 3:18 and 4:6.

For from his *fullness*
have we all received
grace upon grace.

Again we are reminded of a Pauline statement: "For in him the *whole fullness of the deity* dwells bodily." For Colossians 2:9, the revelation of this fullness represents the reconciliation of the universe, the restoration of peace between the Creator and his creatures in the death of Christ. The fullness of "grace upon grace" given through incarnation has the same goal. The radical character of salvation as *gift*, which the Evangelist emphasizes by the fourfold use of χάρις, points to an ultimate unity between the two greatest theologians, Paul and John.

F. By contrast, a difference becomes evident at the beginning of the Epilogue in vv. 17 and 18. In John the battle over the relationship between Law and grace that Paul has to fight has been decided. So when this Epilogue says, "The law was given by Moses, grace and truth became (reality) through Jesus Christ," it is not expressing an abrupt opposition but (certainly very different) "stages" of revelation, those of preparation and consummation.[94] The λόγος ἄσαρκος has itself given Israel the Law "through Moses"; this in fact begins with the same words as the Prologue, ἐν ἀρχῇ. Thus, like the prophets, Moses is a witness to the word of God that is at work as creator of the world and later in Israel: "the fullness of grace and truth" (*rab ḥesed we'emet*) is already attested in Exodus 34 through Moses as a predicate of the God who reveals himself in the Logos.[95] In other words, χάρις is already at work in the Law given to Israel. However, it finds its saving consummation in the person of Jesus Christ, whose name is mentioned here in v. 17b for the first time and is identified with the Logos made flesh — in him salvation has become reality in its abundant fullness.[96]

---

94. In the whole Prologue there are three "stages of revelation": Eltester, "Der Logos und sein Prophet," p. 132: "Nach meiner Auffassung eines geradlinig fortschreitenden Gedankengangs gelangen wir ... nach dem Abschnitt über die Schöpfung als der *revelatio generalis* (V. 3-5,9f.), nach dem Auftreten des Logos asarkos im Alten Testament als der *revelatio specialis* (V. 11-13) zur letzten Stufe der Offenbarungsbewegung, auf welcher der Schöpfer als logos ensarkos diese Erde betritt. Der Wechsel der Aussage von der dritten in die erste Person macht es klar, daß nach der lehrhaften Darstellung nunmehr die christliche Gemeinde ... sich bekennend um den Fleischgewordenen schart. Sie tut dies im Rückblick, wie die Praeterita zeigen, die den Vers beherrschen."

95. Exod. 34:6 = Ps. 86:15; cf. related texts like Num. 14:18 and Ps. 103:8. The LXX translates πολυέλεος καὶ ἀληθινός, but the author of John, like the author of the Apocalypse, has knowledge of the Hebrew text — see above n. 17. Cf. also Ps. 92:3: "to declare thy grace (*ḥesed*) in the morning and thy truth (*'emet*) in the night."

96. See also the christological and typological interrelation of χάρις and ἀλήθεια, which

---

The statement "No one has seen God at any time" likewise points us toward the encounter between God and Moses in Exodus 33, where God qualifies Moses' request to see his glory: "I will make all my goodness pass before you ... *but my face you cannot see*, for man shall not see me and live."[97] Isaiah, too, sees and attests only the δόξα of the preexistent Logos.[98] Solely the only-begotten, who, himself in substance God, as the Son "rests in the Father's bosom" (μονογενὴς θεὸς ὁ ὢν εἰς τὸν κόλπον τοῦ πατρός) like a beloved child,[99] has made visible the Father's countenance, his essence determined most inwardly by love. He has "made known this love" (ἐκεῖνος ἐξηγήσατο).[100]

In the Farewell Discourses Jesus gives upon Thomas's question, "Lord, we do not know where you are going, how can we know the way?" (14:5), his famous answer is, "I am the way, the truth and the life. No one comes to the Father, but by me" (14:6). This is already the message of the Prologue where we meet the keywords *life* and *truth* and where the way of the Logos is prepared. Then Jesus continues, "If you have known me you will also know my Father, and from now on you know him *and have seen him*." Philip does not understand and asks: "Lord, show us the Father, and we shall be satisfied." Jesus has to explain: "He who *has seen me has seen the Father*. Do you not believe (πιστεύεις) that I am in the Father and the Father in me?"[101] The summit of religious experience transcending all human possibilities, the *visio Dei*, is given in the faith in Jesus, for in him the Father is present. Faith in him that is also confessing knowledge of him becomes identical with the vision of God.[102] The epilogue of

---

presupposes the knowledge of the Prologue in the Paschal Homily of Melito of Sardis, ed. O. Perler, SC 123 (1966), I, pp. 48f.

97. Exod. 33:18-23; cf. Exod. 19:21; Judg. 13:22; Isa. 6:5.

98. John 12:41: ὅτι εἶδεν τὴν δόξαν αὐτοῦ, καὶ ἐλάλησεν περὶ αὐτοῦ; cf. Isa. 6:1ff, but John 5:37: The Jews have not seen the εἶδος of God.

99. See O. Hofius, *Johannesstudien* (WUNT 88; Tübingen: Mohr-Siebeck, 1996), pp. 24-32, and already R. Meyer, *ThWNT* III, pp. 824-26 and Gese, "Der Johannesprolog," pp. 169-77. The background is Prov. 8:30f.: Wisdom as the beloved child of God.

100. Cf. Job 28:27 (LXX): God himself εἶδεν αὐτὴν καὶ ἐξηγήσατο αὐτὴν (τὴν σοφίαν). At the end of the Prologue this statement is inverted: The Logos has made visible the invisible Father by revealing his love.

101. John 14:6-10.

102. John does not need to contradict here the restriction of 2 Cor. 5:7: διὰ πίστεως περιπατοῦμεν, οὐ διὰ εἴδους; see John 20:29, the last word of the Risen One: μακάριοι οἱ μὴ ἰδόντες καὶ πιστεύσαντες. The true believers of the later generations after the disciples "see" with their spiritual eyes enlightened by the paraclete; cf. 14:17, 26; 15:26. In 2 Cor. 4:4ff Paul expresses a similar thought. This "spiritual seeing" with the eyes of faith presupposes the "physical seeing" of Jesus by the disciples: John 1:14; 19:35; 20:8, 20; cf. 1 Cor. 9:1; 15:3-8. For confessing knowledge and faith see the comments by H. Gese quoted above (n. 55).

the Prologue appears like an anticipation of the climax of the Farewell Discourses in John 14.

Common to both texts is that the incarnate Son of God discloses the vision of God impossible in the old covenant, that this takes place through his message which brings about faith, and that, while being wholly *one* with the Father in his divine being, is yet not identical with him as a person. The Son "in the bosom of the Father," an image from the Jewish wisdom tradition that expresses the unity of the Father with the Son stamped by love,[103] here surpasses the earlier notion of the sharing of a throne by Father and Son, the sitting at the right hand of God according to Psalm 110:1.[104] We do not find this text, which is quoted so often in the New Testament, in the Johannine corpus; for John it is no longer a sufficient expression of the *unity* of the Father with the Son.[105]

Resuming the metaphor of the Son in the bosom of the Father, which is related to the godlike preexistent Son, the Incarnate One says, "I am in the Father and the Father in me."[106] In the high-priestly prayer he takes up this "ontological" unity again, now including the community of all later believers:

The *glory* which thou hast given me I have given to them,
That they may be one, even as we are one.
I in them and thou in me
That they may become perfectly one,
so that the world may know that thou hast sent me
and hast loved them even as thou hast loved me.[107]

Here the lost creatures, the world of human beings, have been brought home: the goal of the incarnation, that ἐκεῖνος ἐξηγήσατο, the revelation of God's love has been achieved. Light *has* overcome darkness. The Prologue as the introit to the Fourth Gospel already indicates this goal, the gift (χάρις) of eternal true life in the vision of God, fellowship with the triune God — Father, Son, and Spirit. This confession binds John and Matthew together in their ap-

proach, the two so very different Gospels that stand as pillars at the entrance to the New Testament.[108]

The message of the Synoptics and the Fourth Gospel comes from the same root: the personal mystery of Jesus as the Son and that certainty of God the loving Father which the Son also teaches his disciples by addressing God as *Abba* in prayer, a form of address that became the confessing prayer-cry of the primitive community.[109] In one sense the Fourth Gospel is basically an exposition of this form of address by the Son, "dear Father," for all men and women. Jesus' personal mystery is also the last starting point of the Prologue.

Seven Conclusions

1. The Prologue is the most influential christological text in the New Testament. It leads us into Johannine Christology and cannot be separated from it. Moreover, it showed the early church the way to christological truth.

2. At the same time the Prologue is a witness to a theology of the whole Bible — a "salvation history" that brings together Old and New Testaments.[110] Creation, redemption, and consummation must be seen together. We may not read John with Marcionite eyes. Already in the Prologue we can recognize that οἰκονομία εἰς τὸν καινὸν ἄνθρωπον . . . Χριστόν of which Ignatius speaks a few years later, that οἰκονομία which plays a central role in the Fathers.[111] Here it can mean the whole of God's saving work from the creation to the consummation of the world, but also its climax in the incarnation.

3. We already encounter in Paul the roots of this "high Christology" criticized since the deistic Enlightenment. It does not lie in a pre-Christian Gnostic redeemer myth nor in philosophical speculation, but in biblical Jewish thought. It has developed with intrinsic consistency. A mere "rabbi and prophet," indeed even a Messiah as a ψιλὸς ἄνθρωπος and exponent of the Torah, could not bring real redemption, universal atonement, new creation, and the overcoming of evil. That could be brought about only by God, who, as a sign of his boundless love in Jesus of Nazareth, himself came to human beings to free them from the

---

103. See above n. 99. For the unity of the Son with the Father stamped by love see the last testimony of the Baptist, 3:35: ὁ πατὴρ ἀγαπᾷ τὸν υἱὸν καὶ πάντα δέδωκεν ἐν τῇ χειρὶ αὐτοῦ. Cf. 17:24: ὅτι ἠγάπησάς με πρὸ καταβολῆς κόσμου.
104. See Hengel, *Studies in Early Christology*, pp. 119-226.
105. Hengel, *Studies in Early Christology*, pp. 212ff., 225. Justin (like the later Greek Fathers) is rather reluctant to quote Ps. 110:1; he prefers Ps. 110:3f. (LXX 109:3f.) to v. 1 (see pp. 124, 126-28).
106. 14:10f; cf. 14:20.
107. John 17:21-23 (quotation vv. 22f.); cf. 10:38; 14:10, 20.

108. See the paraclete promises, especially 14:16 and the unique triune baptism formula: Matt. 28:19 and, dependent on it, Didache 7.
109. Mark 14:36; Gal. 4:6; Rom. 8:15; see Hengel, "Abba, Maranatha, Hosanna," n. 92.
110. See M. Hengel, "'Salvation History': The Truth of Scripture and Modern Theology," in *Reading Texts, Seeking Wisdom: Scripture and Theology*, ed. D. F. Ford and G. Stanton (London: SCM Press, 2003), pp. 229-44.
111. Ignatius, *Eph.* 20:1; cf. 6:1; 18:2 and a bit earlier, probably contemporaneous with the Gospel of John, the Deutero-Pauline Eph. 1:10; 3:9.

slavery of sin and death.[112] There was an inner consequence and necessity in the notion of preexistence and incarnation. With good reason the Prologue of John is the Gospel for Christmas Day in the Anglican *Book of Common Prayer*.

4. The roots of this Christology lie in the personal mystery of Jesus, in the relationship of the Son to the Father that is the foundation for his activity and suffering and includes the miracles of the resurrection and outpouring of the Spirit. Here we have come up against the limits of all our historical analysis and reconstruction. Attempts to reconstruct the historical effectiveness of Jesus are necessary for the sake of the historical truth, but always lead only to "approximations," not to a certainty that can constitute faith. We have the Jesus tradition, which is fundamental to the origin of Christology only in the form of the "apostolic testimony" in which the "messianic claim" of Jesus has fused with the first witnesses' experience of Easter and the Spirit. In the Gospel of John the radical concentration on this personal mystery has decisively transformed the Synoptic Jesus tradition. This concentration on the unique relationship and unity of the Son as the personified Word of God to the Father, his sending into the world, the incarnation, which includes the passion, takes place most impressively in the Prologue.

5. In the contemporaneous hymn fragment 1 Timothy 3:16 we encounter the incarnation as the mystery of God:[113]

Great indeed, we confess, is the *mystery of religion* [i.e., of Christian faith]:
He [God] *was made manifest in the flesh*
vindicated in the spirit
seen by the angels
preached among the nations
believed on in the world
taken up in glory.

The text relates to Christ as mediator between God and human beings. His being made manifest in the flesh has contacts with the basic theme of the Prologue. Granted, the word μυστήριον does not appear in the Fourth Gospel; nevertheless its content, like that of the Prologue, the incarnation, and glorification of the Son of God as bringer of eternal life can be understood only as *mystery of God*.

112. John 8:34: πᾶς ὁ ποιῶν τὴν ἁμαρτίαν δοῦλός ἐστιν τῆς ἁμαρτίας; cf. 8:21, 24 and 32; ἡ ἀλήθεια (Jesus Christ himself, 14:6) ἐλευθερώσει ὑμᾶς.

113. ὁμολογουμένως μέγα ἐστὶν τὸ τῆς εὐσεβείας μυστήριον· ὃς (cf. v. 15, θεός) ἐφανερώθη ἐν σαρκί, ἐδικαιώθη ἐν πνεύματι . . .

Just as the Evangelist addresses the personality of the Logos and the way in which he is like God only briefly in 1:1f, so in 1:14 he notes the incarnation without defining it directly in its "ontological" relationship of the "divinity" and "humanity" in Jesus Christ. He and the earliest church do not yet speak in so many words about different "natures" of Christ.[114] Nor has he given a completely clear solution of the problem of the unity with the Father and subordination to the Father. He affirms both and that would become a long-lasting problem. John does not develop his Christology with a speculative interest, but with a soteriological interest for the sake of *real salvation* for mankind.

6. The controversies over the definition of this message determined christological thought in the next five hundred years, and above all in the fifth and sixth centuries, led to the splitting off of the Oriental churches. However much these struggles were burdened with a human desire to be right,[115] no matter how much since the Enlightenment people have believed that they have liberated themselves from all "orthodoxy," we should remember that at that time too people were fighting for the *truth* of the Christian faith, the right understanding of the self-communication of God, the Father, in his Son Jesus Christ — over the mystery of the triune God and the reality of redemption through the incarnate Son of God and the paradox of the *Unum enim ex Sancta Trinitate Christum esse . . . ; Deum vero carne passum* and *of Mary Dei genetricem matremque Dei verbi ex ea incarnati*.[116]

The man Jesus alone, as teacher of higher ethics and a human example, cannot open the way to the Father; our sins continue to separate us from him. Only as the *Deus incarnatus* who has come to us in order vicariously to free us from the fate of sin and death can he give us the certainty of salvation. Therefore the incarnation belongs to the foundations of our faith and at the same time remains God's mystery. In 431 C.E. Cyril of Alexandria wrote to the Council in Ephesus "that the Word . . . has become man in an inexpressible and in-

114. As far as I can see, Melito of Sardis is first to speak of the φύσις and οὐσία of Christ, *Peri Pascha* 8 (55-58), ed. O. Perler, SC 123 (1966), p. 64:

καὶ ὡς ἄνθρωπος ταφείς,
ἀνέστη ἐκ νεκρῶν ὡς θεός,
φύσει θεὸς ὢν καὶ ἄνθρωπος.

Cf. frag. VI (de incarnatione): τῆς καθ' ἡμᾶς ἀνθρωπίνης φύσεως . . . θεὸς γὰρ ὢν ὁμοῦ τε καὶ ἄνθρωπος τέλειος ὁ αὐτός, τὰς δύο αὐτοῦ οὐσίας ἐπιστώσατο ἡμῖν. Melito already uses philosophical terminology here but is clearly dependent on John.

115. See now H. Chadwick, *East and West: The Making of a Rift in the Church* (Oxford: Oxford University Press, 2003).

116. *Ep. Iohannis II ad senatores Constantinopolitanos*, in H. Denzinger, *Enchiridion Symbolorum* (Freiburg: Herder, ²⁶1947), p. 96, nr. 201.

comprehensible way."[117] This mystery is described paradoxically at Chalcedon in 451 C.E. by the fourfold definition of the relationship between the divine and human "natures" in the *one* person of Christ as "unconfused, immutable, undivided and inseparable."[118]

7. The last appropriate form of grasping this mystery is therefore *liturgy*, *worship* — for example, in the Christmas hymns, the praise of God's love for sending the Son. On his death in 1560 Philipp Melanchthon left behind a note listing reasons "why one need not fear death."[119] The last sentences run: "You will come into the light, see God, contemplate God's Son. You will learn those wonderful mysteries that you could not understand in this life: Why are we created as we are and *in which the union of the two natures in Christ consists.*" Ὁ λόγος σὰρξ ἐγένετο; The Prologue seeks to be a signpost pointing us to the knowledge of the love of God that has been made manifest in Christ, "the only Son of the Father," and to his worship in the Spirit — and in truth.

---

117. Denzinger, p. 56, nr. 111a: ἀδιαιρέτως τε καὶ ἀπερινοήτως γέγονεν ἄνθρωπος.
118. Denzinger, p. 70f., nr. 148: ἕνα καὶ τὸν αὐτὸν Χριστὸν υἱὸν κύριον μονογενῆ ἐν δύο φύσεσιν ἀσυγχύτως, ἀτρέπτως, ἀδιαιρέτως, ἀχωρίστως γνωριζόμενον.
119. W. Scheible, *Melanchthon: Eine Biographie* (Munich: Beck, 1997), p. 263.

The Poetical Structure of John's Prologue (according to Hartmut Gese)

A I. 1a   Ἐν ἀρχῇ ἦν ὁ λόγος,   a
       b   καὶ ὁ λόγος ἦν πρὸς τὸν θεόν   b
       c   καὶ θεὸς ἦν ὁ λόγος,   a
       2   οὗτος ἦν ἐν ἀρχῇ πρὸς τὸν θεόν.   b
   II. 3a   πάντα δι' αὐτοῦ ἐγένετο,   a
       b   καὶ χωρὶς αὐτοῦ ἐγένετο οὐδὲ ἕν.   b

B I. 3c/4a ὃ γέγονεν ἐν αὐτῷ ζωὴ ἦν,   a
       b   καὶ ἡ ζωὴ ἦν τὸ φῶς τῶν ἀνθρώπων.   b
   5a   καὶ τὸ φῶς ἐν τῇ σκοτίᾳ φαίνει,   a
   b   καὶ ἡ σκοτία αὐτὸ οὐ κατέλαβεν.   b

   E¹ I. 6a Ἐγένετο ἄνθρωπος,   a₁
         b   ἀπεσταλμένος παρὰ θεοῦ,   a₂
         c   ὄνομα αὐτῷ Ἰωάννης·   b
      II. 7a οὗτος ἦλθεν εἰς μαρτυρίαν   a₁
          b ἵνα μαρτυρήσῃ περὶ τοῦ φωτός,   a₂
          c ἵνα πάντες πιστεύσωσιν δι' αὐτοῦ.   b
      III. 8a οὐκ ἦν ἐκεῖνος τὸ φῶς,   a
           b ἀλλ' ἵνα μαρτυρήσῃ περὶ τοῦ φωτός.   b

   II. 9a   Ἦν τὸ φῶς τὸ ἀληθινόν,   a
       b   ὃ φωτίζει πάντα ἄνθρωπον,   b₁
       c   ἐρχόμενον εἰς τὸν κόσμον.   b₂

C I. 10a   ἐν τῷ κόσμῳ ἦν,   a₁
       b   καὶ ὁ κόσμος δι' αὐτοῦ ἐγένετο,   a₂
       c   καὶ ὁ κόσμος αὐτὸν οὐκ ἔγνω.   b
   II. 11a εἰς τὰ ἴδια ἦλθεν,   a
       b   καὶ οἱ ἴδιοι αὐτὸν οὐ παρέλαβον.   b

Martin Hengel

D	I.	12a	ὅσοι δὲ ἔλαβον αὐτόν,	a
		b	ἔδωκεν αὐτοῖς ἐξουσίαν	b₁
		c	τέκνα θεοῦ γενέσθαι,	b₂
		d	τοῖς πιστεύουσιν εἰς τὸ ὄνομα αὐτοῦ,	b₃
	II.	13a	οἳ οὐκ ἐξ αἱμάτων	a₁
		b	οὐδὲ ἐκ θελήματος σαρκὸς	a₂
		c	οὐδὲ ἐκ θελήματος ἀνδρὸς	a₃
		d	ἀλλ' ἐκ θεοῦ ἐγεννήθησαν.	b
E	I.	14a	Καὶ ὁ λόγος σὰρξ ἐγένετο	a₁
		b	καὶ ἐσκήνωσεν ἐν ἡμῖν,	a₂
		c	καὶ ἐθεασάμεθα τὴν δόξαν αὐτοῦ,	b
	II.	d	ὡς μονογενοῦς παρὰ πατρός,	a
		e	πλήρης χάριτος καὶ ἀληθείας.	b
	E²	I. 15a	Ἰωάννης μαρτυρεῖ περὶ αὐτοῦ	a₁
		b	καὶ κέκραγεν λέγων·	a₂
		c	Οὗτος ἦν ὃν εἶπον·	b
		II. d	Ὁ ὀπίσω μου ἐρχόμενος	a
		e	ἔμπροσθέν μου γέγονεν,	b₁
		f	ὅτι πρῶτός μου ἦν.	b₂
	III.	16a	ὅτι ἐκ τοῦ πληρώματος αὐτοῦ	a
		b	ἡμεῖς πάντες ἐλάβομεν	b₁
		c	καὶ χάριν ἀντὶ χάριτος·	b₂
F	I.	17a	ὅτι ὁ νόμος διὰ Μωϋσέως ἐδόθη,	a
		b	ἡ χάρις καὶ ἡ ἀλήθεια	b₁
		c	διὰ Ἰησοῦ Χριστοῦ ἐγένετο.	b₂
	II.	18a	θεὸν οὐδεὶς ἑώρακεν πώποτε·	a
		b	μονογενὴς θεὸς	b₁
		c	ὁ ὢν εἰς τὸν κόλπον τοῦ πατρὸς	b₂
		d	ἐκεῖνος ἐξηγήσατο.	b₃

"We Beheld His Glory!" (John 1:14)

Craig S. Keener

Most scholars today concur that the Fourth Gospel includes both history and theology. Even many patristic interpreters, who often harmonized John with the Synoptics (hence apparently stressing history), recognized John as a "spiritual" Gospel, emphasizing its interpretive aspects. The Gospel clearly interprets theologically the eyewitness claim that apparently stands behind it (cf. 21:24); perhaps most conspicuously, in the Fourth Gospel as a whole the eyewitness claim of water and blood from Jesus' side (19:34–35) is made to climax a motif of water running through the narrative (1:26, 33; 2:7–9; 3:5, 23; 4:10, 13–14; 5:2; 7:37–39; 9:7; 13:5).[1]

John's Prologue supplies us with something of an interpretive grid for the Gospel, and it may also suggest both an eyewitness claim and a theological interpretation, starting from the phrase, "we beheld his glory" (1:14). Although I shall develop at greatest length the character of John's theological interpretation, I must comment first on what John professed to interpret, because this historical substance is central to his theological perspective. His theology is inseparable from his interest in historical events concerning Jesus.

"We Beheld"

Perhaps not surprisingly, in a variety of genres of ancient literature, the first-person plural normally implied the narrator's inclusion in the action.[2] Both historians and biographers were eager to mention their own direct knowledge of events in the (usually) few places where they possessed it.[3] Of course, bias often shaped how even eyewitnesses interpreted events (e.g., Thucydides 1.22.2–

---

1. In several of these passages, Jesus supersedes or fulfills traditional rituals associated with the water, esp. purification rituals (see Keener 2003, passim, esp. 441–48, 509–13, 542–44, 858, 903–4, 908–10; earlier Keener 1997, 139–62).

2. E.g., Philostratus, *Vit. soph.* 2.21.604 shifts to the first person because the author was now present (2.21.602).

3. See, e.g., Polybius 29.21.8; Cornelius Nepos 25 (Atticus), 13.7; 17.1.

3), and eyewitness accounts sometimes diverged even on public events that the sources all claimed to have witnessed.[4] Usually participants employed first-person language when noting their eyewitness testimony; even when employing the third person, however, writers who inserted themselves into narratives were claiming their presence and direct knowledge of events or reports (e.g., Eunapius, *Lives* 494).

Naturally, "we" becomes fictitious in a fictitious narrative,[5] but such narratives were rarely tied to events surrounding a recent historical person as closely as John's narrative is (which, when the speeches are excepted, both parallels the Synoptics at points and is generally "Synoptic-like" elsewhere; see e.g., D. Moody Smith 2007; Keener 2007). "We" nearly always attests a real speaker's presence and was barely ever fictitious outside of novels (see Nock 1972, 828). Novels about historic characters (such as Pseudo-Callisthenes' *Alexander Romance* and Xenophon's *Cyropedia*) are exceptional,[6] biographies and novels generally being distinguishable genres in antiquity.[7]

Although "we" could refer to humanity in general here, the parallel with Moses beholding God's glory (developed below) suggests that "we" refers to those who witnessed and understood Jesus' ministry;[8] the first-person plural functions with an analogous authority claim elsewhere in Johannine literature.[9]

With many others, I believe that the later claim in the Gospel attesting that blood and water flowed from Jesus' side (19:34–35) indicates an eyewitness claim concerning a specific historical event with theological implications (see Keener 2003, 1154–57).[10] This is a third-person claim, but third-person and first-person claims sometimes appeared together in the same documents in ancient literature; thus, for example, Polybius employs first-person claims when he was an observer (e.g., 29.21.8) but prefers third-person claims when he was an active participant in the narrative.[11] I have argued elsewhere, along with many other interpreters, that the Fourth Gospel reflects an eyewitness tradition or source, so I shall not belabor that point further here (see Keener 2003, 81–115). Such eyewitness material is congruent with John's factual accuracy, even on many points of detail increasingly noted in recent work (see, e.g., Anderson 2006a; von Wahlde 2006).

However one interprets apparent eyewitness claims in the Gospel, the claim to behold Jesus' "glory" in the events of his historical ministry is necessarily also theological. John refers not to a single, visible transfiguration such as appears in the Synoptics, but overall to Jesus' ministry (see the first and last "signs" in 2:11; 11:4) and passion (12:16, 23–24; cf. 13:31; 17:1, 5). He employs the language of theophany (as we shall argue below), but he applies it to "signs" that differ from the character of visible theophanies in Israel's Scriptures. Thus what the eyewitnesses "beheld" is not only the events themselves (since John did not believe that all who witnessed them interpreted this as his glory; cf., e.g., 11:45–46; 14:17; 17:24–25), but their meaning (e.g., the promise of a theophany recalling Jacob's to Nathanael in 1:50–51). Some of this meaning was available to them only in retrospect (2:22; 12:16).

Such a perspective does not by itself explain fully the divergences from the Synoptics. It does, however, suggest from the beginning that John is interested not only in the events but in their theological interpretation. As scholars have often argued, the content of John's narratives generally resembles those in the Synoptics; because of this character, they stand a good chance of representing an independent tradition no less historical than what we find in the Synoptics.[12] But whereas the speeches often contain ideas attested elsewhere in the Jesus tradition, even in terms of Christology (see Keener 2003, 280–320), these speeches may function the way speeches often did in ancient historiography, as interpretive events providing perspective on the history surrounding them (see Keener 2003, 53–80).

---

4. E.g., Arrian, *Alex.* 4.14.3; cf. the Gospels' Easter accounts.

5. E.g., Lucian, *Ver. hist.* 1.5–2.47 (entitled "A True Story"; explicitly identified as fictitious, however, in 1.2–4).

6. Philostratus's later *Life of Apollonius* might also fit this category; so also two fictitious eyewitness accounts of the Trojan War (Merkle 1994, 183–84). But novels as a whole were apparently most popular in the late second and early third centuries (Bowie 1994, 452–53; Stephens 1994, 414), and even then, perhaps less popular than historiographic works (Stephens 1994, 415).

7. For the Gospels, including John, as ancient biographies, see esp. Burridge 1992. Although biographers often depended on legend (as they themselves conceded for characters of the distant past; those writing about more recent persons tended to be more reliable), they were not freely composing novels (often focused on humorous and generally amorous adventures) from whole cloth (see Keener 2003, 8–11).

8. Cf. Paul's comparison of the apostolic ministry with Moses in 2 Cor 3:7–18, treated again below, although Paul's experience of Jesus was largely if not wholly "postresurrection."

9. Of greatest relevance is 1 John 1:1–2, where the author distinguishes the first-person plural who testify of what they saw and touched of Jesus from the audience that depends on this testimony (perhaps emphasizing the historic Jesus of the Johannine Gospel tradition above purely pneumatic claims to have received revelations from him; see 1 John 4:1–6).

10. Authors or narrators could include themselves in narratives using the third person, if their ideal audience already knew their identity; e.g., Thucydides 1.1.1; 2.103.2; 5.26.1; Xenophon, *Anab.* 2.5.41; 3.1.4–6 and passim; Caesar, *Gallic War* 1.7; 2.1; 3.28; 4.13; 5.9; 6.4; 7.17 and passim; *Civil War* 1.1 and passim; Polybius passim (see below).

11. E.g., Polybius 31.23.1–31.24.12; 38.19.1; 38.21.1; 38.22.3; cf. 39.2.2. Caesar mixes occasional first-person phrases (e.g., *Gallic War* 2.9) with his general third-person usage (*Gallic War* passim).

12. See Keener 2003, 3–52; for the state of scholarship on John and the Synoptics, see esp. Smith 2001.

JOHN, JESUS, AND HISTORY: ASPECTS OF HISTORICITY

What does John mean by his claim in 1:14 that "we saw his glory"? In addressing this question, I shall focus especially on the theological perspectives that supplement rather than repeat what I already included in my commentary, to ensure that this essay is a distinctly new contribution.

VISION OF GOD IN JOHN AND HIS MILIEU

We may start this discussion with one of the Fourth Gospel's earliest interpreters. Most scholars view 1 John as one of the earliest interpretations of the theology in John's Gospel; this is true whether, as most scholars hold, the authors are distinct or, as I and some other scholars have argued, the same final author is responsible for both.[13] I begin with three claims in 1 John that would be readily intelligible to John's first audience: (1) those who continue in sin have not "seen" God (1 John 3:6), a claim relating to the past vision of God; (2) those who contemplate seeing him thereby become pure like he is pure (3:3), a claim that might relate to the present vision of God (in a limited sense; cf. 4:20); (3) God's children will be fully transformed into his likeness at his coming (3:2), a claim relating to the future vision of God.

Most members of John's first audience would have heard of visions of the divine before reading his Gospel; John is distinctive not for advocating knowing or seeing God but rather for claiming that the locus of revelation is in Jesus. The theme of seeing the divine was pervasive in Greek and Hellenistic Jewish spirituality. For example, Middle Platonists such as Philo of Alexandria and later Maximus of Tyre emphasized the soul's vision of the divine, an experience of the divine that increasingly divinized the soul. In the mid-second century C.E., Maximus urged his audience to strip away the layers of sense perception to see God (*Or.* 11.11). He regarded this as necessary because divine beauty, while perfect in the unchanging heavens, appears much less clearly in the lower realms of the senses (*Or.* 21.7–8). Philo was a first-century Jewish philosopher who drew on Middle Platonism and other sources.[14] Because Philo emphasized God's absolute transcendence, he believed that one best experiences the divine ecstatically through mystical vision.[15] Only the pure soul may envision God;[16] as in Scripture, this vision is utterly dependent on God's self-revelation (*Abraham* 80).

In many Hellenistic and Roman sources, the soul was of heavenly origin and cultivated its heavenly character by meditating on the divine, on what was heavenly.[17] This prepared the soul for its heavenward ascent after death.[18] That ideas such as these were also common among Jewish readers literate in Greek is suggested by their inclusion in the Wisdom of Solomon.[19] This work claims that the body weighs down the soul with earthly cares, distracting it from heavenly matters (Wis 9:15–16).[20] It goes on to argue that the only way people can understand heavenly matters is the divine gift of wisdom and God's spirit from heaven (Wis 9:17).

John's portrayal of Jesus' heavenly revelation (John 3:11–13) resembles such themes from the Wisdom of Solomon.[21] The correspondence is not surprising in view of John's claim that God revealed his character through wisdom enfleshed, Jesus Christ (1:1–18; see the discussion below). Other early Christians also developed the divine vision theme: for example, the letter to the Colossians employs analogous imagery to invite believers to look to the exalted Christ rather than to human rituals (Col 2:16–3:3).[22]

Jewish mystics emphasized visionary ascents to heaven,[23] probably sometimes cultivated by the same means through which philosophers sought to experience the divine. Some of these "ascents" probably produced many of the apocalyptic journeys reported in the Enoch and other apocalyptic literature. One traditional model was Moses, who in some sources ascended to heaven to receive the Torah.

---

13. Keener 2003, 123–26 (although after my commentary's publication I discovered that I had inadvertently omitted several pages of discussion concerning the scholarship on this question); for Johannine authorship, see 81–115. Those who do not share this assumption will at least assign both to the "Johannine community."

14. The preservation of his writings suggests that at least in Alexandria, and probably elsewhere in the Diaspora, some Jewish intellectuals shared his views; other Jewish works (such as Wisdom of Solomon and 4 Maccabees) show that many Jewish intellectuals heavily imbibed from the well of Hellenistic philosophy.

15. Isaacs 1976, 50; Dillon 1975; Hagner 1971, 89–90. On parallels to ecstatic vision, see also Kirk 1934, 23. On the impossibility of full vision of God in this life, see Philo, *Rewards* 39.

16. *Confusion* 92; for biblical examples, see *Names* 3–6; *QG.* 4.138; *Confusion* 146; *Dreams* 1.171; *Abraham* 57.

17. E.g., Porphyry (a much later Platonist), *Marc.* 6.103–108; 7.131–134; 10.180–183; 16.267–268; 26.415–416; cf. also Col 3:1–2.

18. For the soul's postmortem ascent, see, e.g., Maximus of Tyre, *Or.* 41.5; Menander Rhetor 2.9, 414.21–23; this can be portrayed as divinization (2.9, 414.25–27), which goes beyond the closest early Christian parallels to the idea (2 Cor 3:18; 2 Pet 1:4).

19. Its wide circulation is attested by its inclusion, along with other books of the Apocrypha, in some manuscripts of the Greek Bible.

20. Analogous language appears in the Greco-Roman philosophic tradition; see, e.g., Musonius Rufus (Lutz 1947) 18A, pp. 112.20, 27–28 (a first-century Stoic); Maximus of Tyre, *Or.* 1.5.

21. See Wis 9:10; 18:15; cf. Bar 3:29–32.

22. Relevant to ancient philosophic approaches, the same context invites hearers to meditate on things above (Col 3:1–2) rather than to contemplate sins, which characterize earthly appetites (3:5–11).

23. See, e.g., Chernus 1982; Himmelfarb 1988; Kirk 1934, 11–13.

John is emphatic, however, that the only one who has ascended to heaven and can fully reveal heavenly things is the one who first came down from heaven (John 3:11–13; see Keener 2003, 559–63). This affirmation need not rule out the sorts of heavenly visions reported in the book of Revelation (e.g., 4:1–2), probably circulating in the same community, but it filters claims to heavenly revelation through the Spirit who exalts Christ (e.g., John 16:13–15; Rev 4:2; 5:5–6). Jesus is the heavenly revealer, and no claims to heavenly revelations that contradict him may be admitted.

Such an approach to John's understanding of divine "vision" is not new. Both Augustine and Eastern Orthodox thinkers, familiar with the philosophic tradition, emphasized the importance of not merely knowing about but *contemplating* the divine character.

The Vision of God in Israel's Scriptures

From what we have observed so far, it may seem as if John's emphasis on spiritual vision stems purely from Greek sources about the soul's meditation on the divine (even if this emphasis was also adopted by many of his Jewish contemporaries). From this connection we might infer that John's interests are purely abstract and ahistorical. Such a conclusion would, however, be premature at best.[24]

John's discussion of the vision of God is intelligible in a Greek setting, and Greek philosophic sources significantly contribute to our understanding of his language. Yet his Gospel explicitly articulates a biblical rationale for his approach. As we shall explain more fully below, John draws a multifaceted parallel between Moses' vision of God's glory on Sinai and the disciples' vision of God's glory in the word made flesh (1:14–18). Because a prologue normally sets the tone for the work that follows, it is significant that two elements of his vision motif must be clear to his audience from the start. First, Christ is the fullest revelation of God (1:18); as in earlier Scripture, God's character is revealed in concrete history. Second, Exodus provides John's paramount interpretive grid for understanding the vision of God.

Later, in a transitional section summarizing Jesus' works and teachings just before the passion narrative, John also interprets the vision of Christ through the grid of Isaiah's call (John 12:37–41). Both Isaiah (John 12:41) and Abraham (8:56)

---

24. This would be true even if John had not provided a biblical basis for his claim. Most Jews writing in the Greek language used Greek images and categories to varying degrees. After centuries of interaction with Hellenism, Judaism had learned to articulate its ideas in forms intelligible in a Hellenistic milieu. But a distinction remains (with a few extreme exceptions) between pagan Hellenism, on the one hand, and Judaism that was to various degrees Hellenized, on the other. Purely Greek sources lack traditional Jewish language (except sometimes in magical papyri); documents that included both Greek and Jewish language (like John's Gospel were *Jewish* (see, e.g., Claussen 2007, 36).

witnessed Christ's glory in advance.[25] John undoubtedly identifies the latter vision with Isaiah's experience of God enthroned (Isa 6:1–8) in the immediate context of the quotation he offers (Isa 6:9–10, in John 12:40).

The two texts John uses at fullest length to explain the vision of God in Christ (Exod 33:18–34:7; Isa 6:1–8) are both theophanies, and both were widely known in Jewish circles. Some used such theophanies as models for mystical ascent to secure "visions" of God's throne. For John, however, seeing God's character in Christ in history is itself the deepest vision of God. That is, John's theological vision is grounded in the historical mission of Jesus.

God's Revelation Is in Christ

Although some pagan intellectuals preferred the unmediated vision of God, even they generally allowed idols and other physical entities to provide reminders of his character (e.g., Maximus of Tyre, *Or.* 11.12). John, a Jewish-Christian monotheist, draws on a tradition closer to home.[26] For John, vision of God is never unmediated; humanity is already in darkness and must come to the light where God has offered it, in Christ (John 3:19–21). John could draw on earlier traditions to support this view. In Scripture, humanity itself was in God's image (Gen 1:26, connoting being God's children; cf. Gen 5:1–2), contrasted with idols.

But in articulating his conception of divine revelation in the historic person of Jesus, John probably draws especially on an idea that was apparently fairly widespread in contemporary Greek-speaking Judaism, namely, of Wisdom or the Logos as God's image.[27] Scholars have long noted John's Wisdom Christology, highlighted in the opening Prologue that sets the tone for his Gospel.[28] Here it is also a Torah Christology: Jesus as the "Word" is greater than Moses and reveals God more completely than the law (which is also God's "Word") did (1:17).[29] Wisdom was often identified with the law in Jewish tradition (Bar 3:29–4:1; Sir 24:23; 34:8; 39:1).[30]

---

25. For early Jewish discussion of patriarchal visions of the future era, see e.g., 4 Ezra 3:14; 2 Bar. 4:3–4; L.A.B. 23:6; 4Q544, 10–12; 4Q547, 7; Sifre Deut. 357.5.11; b. B. Bat. 16b–17a, bar.; 'Abot R. Nat. 31A; 42, §116B; further in Keener 2003, 767–68.

26. Although some philosophers' rationale for divine images could inform the later Eastern Christian tradition of icons, that tradition emphasizes its connection instead with the incarnation, drawing heavily from Johannine theology.

27. E.g., Wis 7:24–27; L.A.B. 23:6; Philo, *Confusion* 97, 147; *Dreams* 1.239; 2.45; *Sobriety* 133; *Eternity* 15; *Flight* 101; *Heir* 230; *Planting* 18; *Spec. Laws* 1.81; *Creation* 16, 36, 146; cf. Col 1:15; Heb 1:3.

28. See, e.g., Witherington 1995b; Ringe 1999; Keener 2003, 350–55.

29. See esp. Epp 1975; Keener 2003, 354–63.

30. See further 4 Macc 1:16–17; later rabbis developed this theme more elaborately (e.g., Sifre Deut. 37.1.3; Gen. Rab. 17:5; 31:5; 44:17; see further Epp 1975, 133–36; Keener 2003, 354–55).

Like Wisdom in some early Jewish sources, Jesus appears as God's image, the one who makes God fully known (1:18; see also 5:37–38; 14:7–9). Wisdom as God's image mediated the divine image to the world (see Wis 7:22, 25–26). In Philo, the Logos as God's image imprints his image not only on people but also on all creation.[31] Thus it is not surprising that in 1 John, as we have noted, those who behold Jesus become like him, both in the past (1 John 3:6), present (3:3), and future (3:2; cf. 2:28).[32] The beatific vision of God that some ancient thinkers associated with the time of death or the end-time[33] is for John's circle of Christians (at least in 1 John) a matter of both future and realized eschatology. The defining point here for John is in fact not eschatology (i.e., *when* they see God) but Christology (i.e., *where* they see God: in Jesus who had come in the flesh; cf. 1 John 4:2).

John was not the first Christian writer to adapt such language to communicate Jesus for his milieu; at least Paul did so earlier. Because Jesus is God's "image" (2 Cor 4:4–6),[34] those who behold him are being transformed into the same image (2 Cor 3:18), as Moses was transformed by beholding God's glory (2 Cor 3:7; see Keener 2005, 169–71). Just as John compares the eyewitnesses of Jesus' glory with Moses in Exod 33–34 (see discussion of John 1:14–18 below), so Paul compared Christ's agents with Moses (2 Cor 3:6–4:4).[35]

For both Pauline and Johannine theology, therefore, transformation through vision was not simply good Greek philosophy (although it would be intelligible there); it followed the model of Moses. The glory of the earlier covenant transformed Moses (Exod 34:29–35); the greater glory of God's word made flesh also transforms its agents. For John, all people not transformed remain children of the devil, sharing his deceptive and violent character (John 8:44); those who embrace Christ, however, share the imprint of his character, born from above as children of God rather than of the devil (John 1:12–13; 3:3–6).

For John, there is no unmediated vision of God. If believers wish to experience the complete vision of God, they must do so not in a vacuum, nor merely by Platonic meditation on supreme goodness, nor by their own *merkabah* mysticism or visionary ascents to God's throne. Rather, believers experience the vision of God through the enfleshed Jesus on whom John's Gospel focuses, whom John

---

31. *Dreams* 2.45; cf. *Planting* 18, 20, 22.
32. Although the disciples' historical vision of Christ was not repeatable in the strictest sense (see John 20:29), even in the Gospel it presumably does offer a model for believers' continuing experience of God in Christ (cf. 14:7, 9, 17; 16:16).
33. With death, e.g., 4 Ezra 7:98; Maximus of Tyre, *Or.* 9.6; 10.3; 11.11; with the end-time, see 1 En. 90.35.
34. The Wisdom language in Col 1:15 is even more emphatic in this regard. For Wisdom language there, see, e.g., Lohse 1971, 48; Bruce 1976, 94; cf. also Glasson 1969.
35. For Paul, this glory is mediated through weak vessels (2 Cor 4:7–12); for John, too, glory is revealed in weakness (see discussion of John 1:14–18 below).

---

presents as the only way to come to the Father (John 14:6; cf. also 14:2–9). As divine Wisdom incarnate, Jesus is the ultimate revelation of God's character and as the mediator of God's presence.

Examining his work more broadly, we see that John's focus on beholding Christ belongs to the related Johannine notion of the "knowledge of God" which serves almost the same purpose as his "vision of God" motif (see Keener 2003, 243–51). Certainly John regards this experience as theologically significant. Scripture already depicts Israel's covenant relationship with God as "knowing" him (Exod 6:7); often it uses the phrase to distinguish those faithful to the covenant from those who are not (e.g., Judg 2:10; 1 Sam 2:12; Jer 22:16; 24:7; Hos 2:20; 5:4; 6:3; 8:2; 13:4). The same experience would characterize the promised new covenant (Jer 31:34; even Gentile nations in Isa 19:21; cf. also Exod 7:5); for John, "knowing God" marks off true believers from those who merely pretend adherence to the covenant. Israel was God's flock (e.g., Pss 95:7; 100:3; Isa 40:11); for John, all those who follow Jesus are his flock, and they "know" him (John 10:3–4, 14–15).

This emphasis on the remnant having a unique covenant relationship with God comports well with John's polemical distinction between Jewish followers of Jesus (probably along with their Gentile converts), to whom he writes, and the rest of their ethnic community. The same language of "knowing God" served an analogous purpose for the Qumran community, who also viewed themselves as the authentic remnant of Israel.[36] But for John, the present experience of knowing God rests on knowledge of the Jesus who came historically, according to Johannine tradition (John 1:10, 26; 6:69; 8:19; 9:29; 14:17; 16:3).[37]

John thus grounds authentic religious experience in God's own gracious revelation in history. This is true especially of believers' experience through the Spirit, who comes to testify about Jesus (14:26; 15:26; 16:13–15; 1 John 3:24–4:6).[38]

Jesus' Enfleshment and Death and the Sinai Theophany

Not only is divine vision mediated through the enfleshed Christ for John; it also focuses on the cross, the epitome of Christ's enfleshment, demonstrated in his mortality. In John's Prologue, which introduces his approach, Jesus is God's *logos*, his supreme revelation. As noted above, his wisdom imagery may also facilitate the identification of Jesus with God's law (see John 1:17–18). That is, what God

---

36. On knowledge of God in the Qumran Scrolls, see, e.g., 1QS 4:22; 10:12; 11:3; 1QM 11:15; 1Q27 1:7; for further discussion, see Flusser 1988, 57–59; Keener 2003, 239–43.
37. Perhaps even John's motif of spiritual "abiding" (John 14:17; 15:4–10) is connected by analogy with the historical experience of earlier disciples (John 1:38–39; 4:40).
38. See further discussion of this point in Dietzfelbinger 1985, 395–408; Keener 2003, 977–79.

revealed of himself by his "word" to Israel, he was now revealing in person in a more accessible way.

John fairly conspicuously compares the ultimate revelation of God's character in the flesh with God's revelation of his character on Mount Sinai.[39] This is clarified by the compounding of allusions to an account of Moses' vision of God's glory in the setting of his second receiving of the law:[40]

JOHN 1:14–18: THE WORD	EXOD 33–34: THE LAW
"Tabernacled" among us (1:14b)	Moses pleads for God to grant his continued presence (33:15–16)
"We [the eyewitnesses] beheld his glory" (1:14c)	Moses beheld God's glory (33:18–19)
The glory was "full of grace and truth" (1:14e)	The glory was "abounding in covenant love and truth" (34:6)
The law came through Moses, but "grace and truth" through Jesus Christ (1:17)	Grace and truth were present at the law-giving (34:6), but Moses' revelation was partial (33:20, 23)
No one has seen God, but God the unique Son has revealed him (1:18)	No one can see God, so Moses sees only part of God's glory (33:20, 23)

The parallel themes highlight the contrasts. Grace and truth were present in the law, but John declares that they came more fully in Christ (1:17). This is because Christ is God's word—his Torah, become flesh. Moses saw only part of God's glory; in Jesus, all of God's character is unveiled (1:18; see also 14:8–9, probably adapting Exod 33:18).

How is this glory revealed? When God revealed his "glory" to Moses, he showed him his "goodness" (Exod 33:19); he revealed his character, with an emphasis on his love and faithfulness. God's just anger extended as far as three or four generations, but his covenant love and faithfulness lasts for thousands of generations, probably a Hebrew expression for forever (Exod 34:7; cf. 20:6; Deut 5:10; esp. clear in Deut 7:9). His mercy is far greater than his anger, and Moses, knowing this, effectively pleads for God to forgive his people (Exod 33:14–17; 34:9–10).

In John's Gospel, God reveals his character to humanity as his word becomes human and shares human existence (1:14). God reveals his glory through Jesus' ministry of compassion, explicit in his first and final "signs" (2:11; 11:4, 40),[41] but the ultimate revelation of glory in Jesus is in the cross (and consequent and inseparable exaltation; 12:16, 23–24; 13:31–32), the epitome of both the divine message's enfleshment and of God's love and faithfulness earlier revealed at Sinai. Moses saw God's glory on Sinai, and Isaiah saw it in the temple (John 12:41). Yet the Johannine witness (see 19:34–35), and through such witness later believers (see 20:31), see it in the cross (cf. 2 Cor 3:7–11). Platonists might meditate on divine transcendence and Jewish mystics on God's majestic throne, but Johannine theology meets God most climactically in the brutal suffering of an unjust Roman execution by slow and shameful torture.

Conclusion

The claim "we beheld his glory" in John 1:14 compares the vision of Jesus with a central biblical theophany. Connected as it is with Jesus' enfleshment (and an eyewitness claim concerning it), it claims to find theological meaning in the historical Jesus and ultimately in his passion. This passage suggests to us that John does not draw a clear line separating his history from his theology (as if some "events" he reports belong to the one and others to the other); still less does he promise us success in separating these into distinct sources or layers. Instead, he offers both (and the latter as a definitive interpretation of the former) as part of his "witness."

Johannine theology also draws on Greco-Roman and Jewish ideas of vision available in the milieu, but it insists on a historical, Christocentric locus for this vision. In contrast to the disembodied, mental encounter with the divine preferred by many Hellenistic thinkers, John emphasizes an encounter that climaxes various divine revelations in biblical history (to Abraham, Moses, and Isaiah). Like most of his contemporaries, he undoubtedly accepts biblical reports of such revelations as both historically genuine and theologically accurate. In this light, John's focus of the revelation in the Jesus who came in the flesh, evidenced and exemplified in the story he reports in his Gospel, suggests that he would make the same claim for his own narrative.

---

39. John's allusion to Exod 33–34 might counter a charge of ditheism attached to Exod 32 (where his people violate the idolatry prohibition even when Moses is receiving the law). Countering a ditheism charge (cf. m. Sanh. 4:5; Sifre Deut. 329.1.1; b. Sanh. 38ab; Pesiq. Rab. 21:6; 3 En. 16:2), John contrasts artificially making something created into God (see John 5:18; 10:33) with God coming down and tabernacling, reflecting a contrast he may find in Exod 32–34.

40. See, e.g., Boismard 1957, 135–45, esp. 136–39; Hanson 1976; Mowvley 1984; Keener 2003, 405–26.

41. Taken together, these texts also constitute Moses allusions: Jesus turns water to wine instead of blood (the first plague) and raises the dead rather than striking the firstborn (the last plague).

The Sheep of the Fold
The Audience and Origin of the Gospel of John

EDWARD W. KLINK III

2

EARLY CHRISTIAN COMMUNITY: A STUDY OF THE COMMUNITY CONSTRUCT AND ITS FUNCTIONAL POTENTIAL IN EARLY CHRISTIANITY

The quest for the early Christian "community"

The quest for the historical Jesus that occupied much of the nineteenth century largely gave way to the quest for the early church in the twentieth century.[1] As we saw in chapter 1, the focus on the communities of the early church, though undefined, was considered by the initial form critics to be the only historical remnant left to be sought. The historical results determined by the form critics were in many ways sociological in nature. The basic methodology used by Bultmann and the other early form critics was an idea taken from the sociology of literature, namely that certain specific types of literature or genres (*Gattungen*) are bound to and shaped by specific types of social life-settings (*Sitze in Leben*).[2] Literary genre is a social category of communication.[3] the questions being asked of the text were sociological. The communities in which the Gospel texts were created had various functions which determined the forms and overall use of the Jesus tradition and its eventual Gospel text form.

Although the initial sociological emphasis in form criticism looked promising, the sociological potential was never developed. Thomas Best argues that, "it cannot be denied that even form criticism, with all its talk of the *Sitz-im-Leben* (life-setting) of the text, was a literary and theological[4] discipline which produced hardly any concrete historical, social, or economic information about the traditions which it studied."[5] Whether it should be attributed to the world wars[6] or the theological revival of the 1920s,[7] the use and application of the social sciences to the text of the Gospels would have to wait. Even redaction criticism focused on the religious milieu of the evangelists and their particular theological emphasis rather than on the social situation.

Since the 1970s, and in light of the almost fifty-year absence of social history and sociological perspectives, what could be called a reform movement within historical criticism took place and has been broadly called social-scientific criticism.[8] Social-scientific criticism has offered what it believes to be new and improved questions to the Gospels.[9] In place of the traditional questions of occasion and purpose of the Gospel text, which are ideational or theological terms, situation and strategy are being offered.[10] Situation refers to the social circumstances and interaction that motivated the writing of a text. Examples of causality commonly used include social disorder or conflict, threats to group cohesion and commitment, problems with group boundaries, conflicts over legitimate authority, events to be celebrated, and communities to be galvanized to action.[11] Strategy, on the other hand, refers to the fact that the text is specifically designed by its producer not simply to communicate ideas but to move a specific

---

[1] See a good discussion of the quest for the early church in reference to the origin of the Gospel of John by Brodie, *The Quest for the Origin of John's Gospel*, pp. vii-viii, 5–21, 137–52.
[2] Holmberg, *Sociology and the New Testament*, pp. 1–2.
[3] We will discuss the implications of Gospel genre in chapter 3.
[4] See Watson, "Toward a Literal Reading of The Gospels," in *GAC*.
[5] Best, "Sociological Study of the New Testament: Promise and Peril of A New Discipline," *SJT* 36 (1983), pp. 181–82.
[6] Holmberg, *Sociology and the New Testament*, p. 2.

[7] Robert Morgan and John Barton, *Biblical Interpretation*, OBS (Oxford: Oxford University Press, 1988), pp. 145–46. See also the discussion by Robin Scroggs, "The Sociological Interpretation of the New Testament: The Present State of Research," *NTS* (1980), pp. 164–65, where the theological "pendulum," as Scroggs called it, had been taken from the liberals as unfashionable and been given to the Neo-orthodoxy emphasis upon theology and the word.
[8] It is important that we recognize the distinction between sociological and social-scientific criticism. Although they have related beginnings, they have developed into two distinct sub-disciplines. A history of sociological and social-scientific criticism is well beyond the scope of this book. For an excellent and comprehensive survey of social-scientific criticism see John Elliott, *What is Social-Scientific Criticism?* GBSNTS (Minneapolis: Augsburg Fortress, 1993). For sketches that highlight the trends of sociological criticism as it was developing see Edwin A. Judge, *The Social Pattern of Christian Groups in the First Century: Some Prolegomena to the Study of New Testament Ideas of Social Obligation* (London: Tyndale, 1960); Leander E. Keck, 'On the Ethos of Early Christians," *JAAR* 42 (1974), pp. 435–52; Jonathan Z. Smith, "The Social Description of Early Christianity," *RSR* 1 (1975), pp. 19–25; Gerd Theissen, *Studien zur Soziologie des Urchristentums*, WUNT 19 (Tübingen: Mohr Siebeck, 1979); Robin Scroggs, "The Sociological Interpretation of the New Testament," pp. 164–79; Gerd Theissen, *The Social Setting of Pauline Christianity: Essays on Corinth*, ed. and trans. John H. Schütz (Philadelphia: Fortress Press, 1982).
[9] Although social-scientific questions are not new, as its relation to form criticism showed above, the overall methodological approach that is attempting to apply pure social-scientific models on the text of the Gospels is itself an innovative enterprise.
[10] Elliott, *What is Social-Scientific Criticism?*, pp. 54–55. The concepts "situation" and "strategy" were first used by Elliott in his *A Home for the Homeless: A Sociological Exegesis of 1 Peter, Its Situation and Strategy* (Philadelphia: Fortress Press, 1981).
[11] Elliott, *What is Social-Scientific Criticism?*, p. 54. See also the earlier discussion by Klaus Berger, *Exegese des Neuen Testaments: neue Wege vom Text zur Auslegung*, Uni-Taschenbücher 658 (Heidelberg: Quelle & Meyer, 1977), pp. 111–27.

audience to some form of action.[12] "Social-scientific criticism thus aims at discovering how a given document was designed as an author's motivated response to a specific situation and how it was composed to elicit a specific social response on the part of its audience."[13]

It is in this way that the term "community" becomes used to denote the group situation in which and for which a document's strategy is functioning. The classical use of "community" was in a more general sense, denoting the earliest "Christians"[14] and the group movement that they began following Jesus' departure. In this more general sense it can refer to the most ancient membership of the Christian religion. "Chronologically, it refers to Christian beliefs and practices of the first three or four decades after the crucifixion, and it partially overlaps Pauline Christianity."[15] Several of the older studies reflect this understanding of "community,"[16] many of which focus on Paul (Acts 15; Gal. 2).[17] Of course, the more recent understanding of "community" is not the general early movement, but the various "groups" affiliated with belief in Jesus in the first century. In this more specific sense the term is used to describe a group of "Christians" in a specific, geographic location, or, as it is used with the biblical texts, a group of Christians who are reflected in a NT document. It is in this sense that we have returned to our discussion in chapter 1 concerning the developing concept of "community." While Paul was the primary "community" focus in the older studies, modern research has commonly assumed that for the post-Pauline era the Gospels, and maybe the Deutero-Pauline letters and some of the Catholic letters, are our primary sources, not to mention bits of information from non-Christian sources[18] or the sparse and questionable information to be gleaned by Christian authors in the early to mid-second century. It is primarily the Gospels, though, that are being used to discover the nature and issues within the various Christian communities. Thus for historical critics, who claim that the meaning of any text is dependent on the historical circumstance in and for which it was written, the "community" behind the Gospel texts became as hermeneutically important as the texts themselves. But a problem already exists in reference to the study of early Christianity and its "communities": the paucity of sources.

The success of such an enterprise is only as likely as the sources that are available. The difficulty in grasping the occurrences of the period and the "groups" in which things occurred is compounded by the lack of directly relevant material. In many ways, the historian of early Christianity is researching a movement that is "shrouded in historical darkness."[19] Martin Hengel summarizes it best:

All too often we are only left with traces: names of people without specific details, isolated events, sporadic accounts or obscure legends – as from Talmudic literature, except where suddenly larger fragments emerge, resting on individually lucky discoveries. We constantly come up against gaps and white patches on the map; our sources are uncertain and we have to content ourselves with more or less hypothetical reconstructions. All this is true of ancient history in general and even more of the history of early Christianity in particular, above all its first 150 years.[20]

Even the sources we do have are only the creation of Christians themselves; their own internal literature created for their own purposes.[21] What has become apparent is that the limited sources reduce our access to the "world" behind the Gospels, including the audience for whom they were created. Once a specific audience was assumed, the text was scavenged for clues to the nature and circumstances of this "community." Using insights from form and redaction criticism modern scholars began to evaluate the material to differentiate between the authentic and

---

12 Elliott, *What is Social-Scientific Criticism?*, p. 54.
13 *Ibid.* In this sense there is also a rhetorical thrust that can be deduced.
14 The use of the term "Christian" is not meant to impose institutionalization upon the first-century "Jesus movement," as if by "Christian" we imply the homogeneous institution later called the "church." Rather, we will use the term to refer to the "communities" in the first-century movement that centered themselves, in whatever fashion, upon Jesus of Nazareth.
15 Joseph B. Tyson, *A Study of Early Christianity* (New York: Macmillan, 1973), p. 273.
16 A good example of this procedure can be found in Adolf Harnack, *The Expansion of Christianity in the First Three Centuries*, 2 vols., trans. James Moffatt, TTL 19 (London: Williams & Norgate, 1904), vol. I, pp. 54–55. See also A. J. Mason, "Conceptions of the Church in Early Times," in H. B. Swete (ed.), *Essays on the Early History of the Church and the Ministry*, 2nd edn (London: Macmillan, 1921), pp. 3–56.
17 Johannes Weiss, *Earliest Christianity: History of the Period A.D. 30–150*, 2 vols., trans. Frederick C. Grant (New York: Harper & Brothers, 1959), vol. I, p. 1. This is supported more recently by Frederick J. Cwiekowski, *The Beginnings of the Church* (Dublin: Gill and Macmillan, 1988), p. 100.
18 Although Judge, *The Social Pattern of Christian Groups in the First Century*, p. 16, argues that the non-Christian sources are all plagued with a "Roman slant."
19 Taken from Elisabeth Schüssler Fiorenza, *In Memory of Her: A Feminist Theological Reconstruction of Christian Origins* (London: SCM Press, 1983), p. 160.
20 Hengel, *Acts and the History of Earliest Christianity* (Philadelphia: Fortress, 1979), pp. 4–5. A similar despair is given by Burton L. Mack, *A Myth of Innocence: Mark and Christian Origins* (Philadelphia: Fortress Press, 1988), pp. 3–4.
21 Wayne Meeks, *The First Urban Christians: The Social World of the Apostle Paul* (New Haven: Yale University Press, 1983), p. 1. Meeks considers the hermeneutical key of interpreting the Gospels to be getting inside their social-functioning worldview that is apparent in their sectarian literature.

inauthentic material; the traditional material and the redacted or interpreted material. Such a procedure allows one to see the intentional data, as well as the unintentional data, made manifest by the context in the communication; as well as the unintentional data, made manifest by the context in and for which it was created.[22] Thus, with the onslaught of form criticism, and with it the preliminary death of the historical Jesus and the historically pure Gospels, the primitive Christian church and its various and dispersed communities became the focus of interpretation. These later groups in the early Christian movement are seen as the co-authors of the Christian scriptures, having not merely passed on the Jesus Tradition, but intentionally adapted[23] it for the sake of their own contextually determined needs.[24]

This returns us to the Gospel community debate and the appraisal of the Gospel community reconstructions by this book. Several problems arise with an approach that attempts to discover the specific "community" in and for which a Gospel was written. First, there is a problem in establishing what is exactly meant by the term "community." The use of the term "community," as a category for audience is unhelpful since, as was discussed in chapter 1, it has several possible uses and meanings. The use of a "community" model is not inappropriate, but it must be defined and defended. Its abstract sense has allowed it to be a catch-all term for Gospel audiences; unfortunately, this catch-all has become an assumption one begins with when reading the Gospels. This chapter will argue that the current "definition" of the term has been applied too loosely. Are we to assume that a "community" was a sectarian or isolated audience? Or is it simply in reference to a local audience in a specific geographic location? Is there any historical evidence of a real JComm? Thus, if the term itself is difficult to grasp, the actual historical circumstances of the early "communities" are even more elusive. This first issue, then, is external to the Gospel text, for it requires the application of models.

The second issue is internal: there is a dangerous circularity involved in defining the audience behind the text without anything but the text. Once the form critics made common the reference to Gospel "communities," various approaches to the Gospel "language" as self-referential became an important issue. The limited purview of the Gospel authors has allowed community interpreters to place limits on the reference of Gospel language. The Gospels were speaking on behalf of their individual communities, just as the individual communities can be seen as speaking through the Gospels. At that point "the one document per community fallacy," as James Dunn describes it,[25] wedded the external (community formation) and the internal (community language) issues into a single hermeneutical approach.

Therefore, this chapter will assess both of these issues and argue that the entire approach is problematic. We will accomplish this in three parts. First, concerning the external definition of community, we will investigate the various "models" used in assuming a "community" audience for the Gospels, and will argue for a more complex model for understanding "community" in the early Christian movement. Second, in reference to the community language internal to the text, we will examine the "sectarian" nature of the Gospel of John by testing the nature and function of its "language." Third, we will conclude our quest for a definition of an early Christian "community" by examining the evidence for Gospel "communities" in the patristic writings, using specifically the evidence and argument presented by Margaret Mitchell against *GAC*.

Definition of the early Christian community: its variation and type

In the exegetical method we are appraising, where a Gospel community is reconstructed from the text and placed within a first-century context, the definition of "community" is simply too loose to be of any explanatory value. Since we have no evidence of what these so-called "communities" looked like, we are limited in ascertaining their function. As with all reconstructions, models must be used in order to establish the potential form and function of these "communities." This is central to the Gospel

---

[22] Marc Bloch, *The Historian's Craft*, trans. Peter Putnam (Manchester: Manchester University Press, 1954), pp. 60ff. See also the discussion by Harvey, *The Historian and the Believer* (New York: Macmillan, 1966; repr. Urbana: University of Illinois, 1996), pp. 214–21.

[23] The authority to adapt the Jesus tradition is usually assumed to have been given by the Spirit. In the context of the early church, according to Gary M. Burge, *The Anointed Community: The Holy Spirit in the Johannine Tradition* (Grand Rapids: Eerdmans, 1987), p. 224, "the Spirit was known as a revelatory aid . . . recalling the words of Christ (anamnesis) and leading into new frontiers of truth."

[24] According to Meeks, *The First Urban Christians*, p. 2, "Since we do not meet ordinary Christians as individuals, we must seek to recognize them through the collectives to which they belonged and to glimpse their lives through the typical occasions mirrored in the texts. It is in the hope of accomplishing this that a number of historians of early Christianity have recently undertaken to describe the first Christian groups in ways that a sociologist or anthropologist might. Without wishing to abandon previous accomplishments in philology, literary analysis, history of traditions, and theological insight, these scholars have sought in social history an antidote to the abstractions of the history of ideas and to the subjective individualism of existential hermeneutics."

[25] James D. G. Dunn, *Christianity in the Making: Vol. 1: Jesus Remembered* (Grand Rapids: Eerdmans, 2003), pp. 150–51.

community debate. Recent research has advanced our understanding not only of potential "community" forms, but also their functional potential through sociological analysis.[26] This research has attempted to view groups and their societal relations from a new perspective, critiquing the objective categories normally applied to these movements. This research will be especially helpful in our discussion below concerning the sectarian nature of Christian groups, but for now it will help us apply judicature between the various "subjective" descriptions of group form. Since the possible early churches or "communities" are assumed to be derivative of other known and existing social and group formations, it will be valuable to begin there. Thus, our goal is to attempt to define more closely the term "community" and its possible form in the early Christian movement.

Models of "community" in the early Christian movement

The information within the NT reveals the existence of many and variously located communities in the early Christian movement. Although around thirty Christian groups are mentioned in Acts and the Pauline letters, many other groups may also be implied.[27] Certainly these supposed Gospel "communities"[28] varied depending on group size, location, and resources. Our most immediate problem is that we have no idea what the Gospel "communities" would have looked like; everything between a single, isolated "community" and a network of "groups" has been posited.[29] Problems exist in the vague terminology currently used to describe the early Christian groups. Although recent research has attempted to define these possible audiences by looking at known group formations in the first century, such a procedure gives little more data concerning the specific Gospel "communities." For example, in order to determine the sociological form of the early Christian communities, various models of ancient group formation have been drawn on for comparison:[30] the ancient household,[31] the synagogue,[32] clubs, voluntary associations, and religious cults,[33] and philosophical schools.[34] Interestingly, the school model has been the most well-known model applied to the FG.[35] Although it is appropriate to assume that the early Christians

---

[26] Most helpful here is John M. G. Barclay, *Jews in the Mediterranean Diaspora: From Alexander to Trajan (323 BCE–117 CE)* (Edinburgh: T. & T. Clark, 1996) and Philip A Harland, *Associations, Synagogues, and Congregations: Claiming a Place in Ancient Mediterranean Society* (Minneapolis: Fortress, 2003).

[27] Judge, *The Social Pattern of Christian Groups in the First Century*, p. 12. Although it is beyond the scope of this work to look specifically at the definition and usage of Christian ἐκκλησία, we are assuming it existed as a sociological and functional entity. For a discussion of the term ἐκκλησία and its pre-Christian and Christian understanding see Robert Banks, *Paul's Idea of Community: The Early House Churches in their Historical Setting* (Exeter: Paternoster, 1980), pp. 34–37, 43–51; Meeks, *The First Urban Christians*, pp. 74–110; K. L. Schmidt, TDNT, vol. III, pp. 501–36; L. Coenen, NIDNTT, vol. I, pp. 291–307.

[28] Several terms are used synonymously in scholarly literature to describe the audiences of the Gospels or the "church(es)" they represent. Thus, we will use terms like group, congregation, association, and "community" in a synonymous manner.

[29] For the purpose of the Gospel community debate, the hermeneutical difference between a single group and a network of groups is minimal; the assumption is the same: one document is representative of one audience.

[30] The most recent and comprehensive work on the social history of early Christianity is by Ekkehard W. Stegemann and Wolfgang Stegemann, *The Jesus Movement: A Social History of Its First Century*, trans. O. C. Dean, Jr. (Minneapolis: Fortress Press, 1999).

[31] There is evidence in the NT that the early Christians met in one another's homes (Acts 10:1ff.; 16:15, 32ff.; 18:8ff.; 1 Cor. 1:14, 16; 16:15–19; Rom. 16:5, 23; Col. 4:15). For research on house churches see Floyd V. Filson, "The Significance of Early House Churches," *JBL* 58 (1939), pp. 105–12; Hans-Joseph Klauck, *Hausgemeinde und Hauskirche im Frühen Christentum* (Stuttgart: Katholisches Bibelwerk, 1981); C. Osiek and David L. Balch, *The Family in the New Testament: Households and House Churches, FRC* (Louisville: Westminster John Knox, 1997).

[32] It is generally assumed that between 70 and 135 CE Christianity became a religion based very largely on the geography and organization of the Hellenistic synagogue. See Martin Hengel, "Die Synagogeninschrift von Stobi," *ZNW* 57 (1966), pp. 145–83; Wayne A. Meeks, *The First Urban Christians*, pp. 80–81.

[33] For research on Greco-Roman associations see Edwin Hatch, *The Organization of the Early Christian Churches*, 4th edn, Brampton Lectures for 1880 (London: Longman & Green, 1892), pp. 26–55; Georg C. F. Heinrici, "Die Christengemeinde Korinths und die religiösen Genossenschaften der Griechen," *ZWT* 19 (1876), pp. 464–526; Judge, *The Social Pattern of Christian Groups in the First Century*, pp. 40–48; Robert L. Wilkin, "Toward A Sociological Interpretation of Early Christian Apologetics," *CH* 39 (1970), pp. 1–22; Abraham J. Malherbe, *Social Aspects of Early Christianity*, 2nd and enl. edn (Philadelphia: Fortress, 1983), pp. 87–91.

[34] The comparison of the "school" model to the Christian communities was made as early as the second century by Justin Martyr who presented Christianity as a "true philosophy," followed similarly by other apologists of the second and third centuries. At the same time, Tertullian was strictly opposed to such a designation for the Christian organization (*Apol.* 38–39). According to Stegemann and Stegemann, *The Jesus Movement*, pp. 273–74, Tertullian combined various concepts that could have been used with other Roman associations as well as with schools of philosophers. Nevertheless, Tertullian was attempting to prove the harmlessness of the Christian groups and, when doing so, specifically denies that Christian communities were identical with the *collegia* or philosophical schools. See Wilkin's understanding of the Christian defense in school-like terms in Robert L. Wilkin, "Collegia, Philosophical Schools, and Theology," in Stephen Benko and John J. O'Rourke (eds.), *The Catacombs and the Colosseum* (Valley Forge: Judson, 1971), pp. 268–91.

[35] The "school" model is different in degree from the other primary community models, which are based upon a community of location and organization. The difference is that behind the documents stands a teacher, whose scholastic influence is primary and who, for all purposes, is the school. The geographic community model is less hierarchical, less established around one individual, and is more tradition based, often assumed to be the tradition of a local church group. The concept of the JComm by Martin Hengel, *The Johannine Question*, for example, is based upon the school model. For Hengel, behind all the Johannine documents stands one head, "an outstanding teacher who founded the school ... in Asia Minor and developed a considerable activity extending beyond the region and who – as an outsider – claimed to have been a disciple of Jesus, indeed – in the view of the school – a disciple of a quite special kind" (p. 80). Culpepper, *The Johannine School*,

would have organized themselves in a way consonant with their tradition and cultural distinctives, it is impossible to know exactly how they did so.

Although several models might be helpful in revealing ancient analogies to "community" forms, none of them is able to explain what any one of the Gospel "communities" may have been. Even if we were to argue that the household model was the initial phase of community building, especially in the Jewish context, and when available, more substantial synagogue-like and permanent structures for meeting would be established, we would not be able to place any of the Gospels in that development. The various "communities" would have probably used aspects from each of the four models, depending on their geographic location, their missionary undertakings, their local activities and fellowship needs, and their connection with other groups of Christians. The early Christian communities, as recorded in our sources, amalgamated various aspects of the numerous group models in their culture to the needs of their own specific Christian "community." But our analysis of the concept of a Gospel "community" must move beyond analogy.

The above discussion has helpfully laid out the potential groups or associations found in the early Christian movement. But that alone is not sufficient. No one model can be proven coterminous with the "community" (audience) behind a Gospel; nor can any description of that "community" be accomplished from an objective, external perspective.[36] It is at the point of external description that the definition of a Gospel "community" normally ends. A local group (or network) is assumed as a Gospel "community," fitting some or all aspects of the models mentioned above, and is then "filled-out" from data found in the Gospel texts. Using an analogy from scientific hypotheses, once the community interpreters have "determined" their constant (a local, physical group or network of groups) then the variables (community history, members represented) can be defined by using textual data. But such a procedure has already inappropriately assigned an external model as the constant when no such definition of "community" can be verified. What is needed, then, is a reevaluation of this "constant." This will require a more complex model that takes an internal approach to "community" form. This is not to deny that external models are helpful, only that in this case such an approach is limited in analytical value. As Meeks admits, "the associations offer as little help as does the household in explaining the extralocal linkages of the Christian movement."[37] What is lacking is an attempt to weigh the significance of each Gospel's own portrayal of their form – an assessment which involves internal perceptions without assuming an external model as constant. Thus, we now turn from external analogies to internal perception.

Definition of Gospel "community": a new proposal

In the essay entitled "Can we Identify the Gospel Audiences?," in *GAC*, Stephen Barton discusses the problematic nature of defining the notoriously ambiguous term "community."[38] Barton claims that although social scientists are trained to use the term with caution, NT scholars are more liberal in their use. The term "community," according to its use by social scientists, is one of the most elusive terms to define. The social anthropologist Anthony Cohen states the case plainly, "'Community' is one of those words – like 'culture,' 'myth,' 'ritual,' 'symbol' – bandied around in ordinary, everyday speech, apparently readily intelligible to speaker and listener, which, when imported into the discourse of social science, however, causes immense difficulty."[39] Cohen warns that past understandings of community have been "based entirely upon a highly particularistic and sectarian definition."[40] The definition of community is not to be understood from an external perspective (first-century models), it is defined from the inside; its boundaries are marked by their symbolic meaning for the participants.[41] In reference to this Cohen states:

---

[36] Even the social-historical work of Stegemann and Stegemann, *The Jesus Movement*, p. 274, reveals the problem in defining an early Christian group from an "outside view."

[37] Meeks, *The First Urban Christians*, p. 80.

[38] Barton, "Can We Identify the Gospel Audiences?," in *GAC*, pp. 173–94.

[39] Anthony Cohen, *The Symbolic Construction of Community*, KI1 (London: Routledge, 1985), p. 11. Cohen is also referred to by Barton, "Can We Identify the Gospel Audiences?" See also Pierre Bourdieu, *Language and Symbolic Power*, ed. John B. Thompson, trans. Gino Raymond and Matthew Adamson (Cambridge: Polity Press, 1991), especially pp. 220–51, for a more theoretical discussion of the difficulty of defining sociological and anthropological terms.

[40] Cohen, *The Symbolic Construction of Community*, p. 12. Cohen argues that such an understanding has been a misinterpretation of the earlier writers like Durkheim, Weber, Tönnes, and Simmel.

[41] Concerning community and group identity see T. Schwartz, "Cultural Totemism: Ethnic Identity Primitive and Modern," in G. De Vos and L. Romanucci-Ross (eds.), *Ethnic Identity: Cultural Continuities and Change* (Palo Alto: Mayfield, 1975), pp. 106–31; and J. A. Boon, *Other Tribes, Other Scribes: Symbolic Anthropology in the Comparative Study of Cultures, Histories, Religions, and Texts* (Cambridge: Cambridge University Press, 1980). We will deal with this "symbolic meaning" for the participants in the so-called JComm when we deal with John's antilanguage.

the community is not approached as a morphology, as a structure of institutions capable of objective definition and description. Instead, we try to understand "community" by seeking to capture members' experience of it. Instead of asking, "what does it look like to us? What are its theoretical implications?", we ask, "What does it appear to mean to its members?" Rather than describing analytically the form of the structure from an external vantage point, we are attempting to penetrate the structure, to look *outwards* from its core.[42]

What was axiomatic in the past is that the supposed structure of the community implied certain functions and results. While it is true that the borders of the community, its differentiation from the other groups that allows it to be its own entity, define the community's essence, the process of establishing the border must occur from the inside, not the outside.[43] Recent sociological research on the symbolic construction of community can assist us as we attempt to establish a method that allows a group behind the text to define the nature of its community. In broad categories the term "community" has two major uses: territorial and relational. The territorial concept points to a context of location, physical territory, and geographic continuity. The relational concept points to the quality or character of human relationships, without reference to location.[44] In both the social sciences and the Gospel "community" reconstructions, the two concepts are not sharply exclusive. Although it is rarely discussed in NT scholarship, the nature of community is related to the historically difficult tension between community and society. But as we will see below, most "community" reconstructions assume a relational concept, a symbolic construction of community (and world). It is this concept that we will define more closely.

As we noted above in our discussion of community models, the term "Gospel community" does not describe any group known to exist in history. There is absolutely no evidence of a specific Gospel community standing behind the Gospels; we have created the Gospel "community" model for the sake of analysis.

> They are analytical and not empirical terms; concepts invented to help the analyst think about change and human associations. As such, they are products of human imagination and not

---

[42] Cohen, *The Symbolic Construction of Community*, p. 20. [43] *Ibid.*, pp. 50–63.
[44] Joseph R. Gusfield, *Community: A Critical Response*, KCSS (Oxford: Basil Blackwell, 1975), pp. xv–xvi.

descriptions of a real world. No permanent human association of institutions can be found which contains all the attributes of community…[45]

The use of such models goes back to Max Weber's ideal types.[46] The various terms used to describe the Gospel "communities" in the history of its use – group, school, circle, church – are forms of that first-century type. As Gusfield makes clear, "One of the great dangers in the use of ideal-types is *reification* – treating an abstract, analytical term as if it were descriptive and empirical… In this process the type (an idea) has been transformed into a thing."[47] This applies directly to the current definitions of Gospel "communities." The text is only allowed to reveal what the community ideal type behind the Gospel allows, as was determined by its assumed structure and functional ability. Thus, in reference to the community reconstructions, the question needs to be asked: Who is defining the boundaries of the assumed Gospel communities? If the boundaries of the Gospel communities are defined by an inappropriate, externally imposed grid of understanding, confusion and distortion will most certainly exist. The amount of community constructions for each of the Gospels seems to imply that there is widespread uncertainty concerning the boundaries of these "communities."

This book is proposing that the current "ideal type"[48] of Gospel community is mistaken. The notoriously ambiguous term, to use Barton's terminology, has produced ambiguous results. For the sake of analysis, and in light of the fact that no known "group" is known to have lived behind the Gospels, a more preferred determination of the Gospels' own audience, as viewed from the inside, would define "community" in its relational sense, in contrast to its geographical sense. Since the concept of community denotes a quality of human relations rather than a quantity of population, we need to describe the kind of social bonding that exists. Gusfield tells a joke that explains well this social interaction:

> The story is told of a dying Jew who in his last hour asks to be converted to Christianity. His sons plead against it but the old man wins out, is converted and given the last rites of the Church. The children cannot understand why their father, always a devout and Orthodox Jew, should renounce his life-long faith and they

---

[45] *Ibid*, p. 11.
[46] Max Weber, *The Methodology of the Social Sciences*, trans. Edward A. Shils and Henry Finch (New York: Free Press, 1949).
[47] Gusfield, *Community*, p. 13 (emphasis original).
[48] The term "type" is singular instead of plural since the various community reconstructions all define "community" in a geographic sense.

prevail on him to explain. With his dying breath the old man rises up in bed and shouts, "Better one of them should die than one of us."[49]

Two aspects of the story are useful for our definition of "community." The first is the exclusivity of the dying man's loyalties. The distinction between "them and us" is sharp. It is the intrinsic nature of his being "one of us" that makes his death-bed conversion so strange. The humor of the joke comes when one realizes that the dying man's wish remained consistent with his participation as "one of us." The second useful aspect is the dying man's attempt to define himself as something other than what he has been – to create communal membership through symbolic construction.[50] It reveals how people identify themselves and others as belonging to one or another association. The fact that the dying man's sons, and for the joke to be understood the readers, assumed that the transition from Jew to Christian would have been real and not hypothetical shows the reality of such a symbolic construction. There was no need for physical evidence – that the man had never been in a Christian church, or been baptized, or that the man was Jewish by birth – all that was assumed to be needed was mental conversion (a symbolic construction).

A symbolic-constructed community places one in several areas of communal interaction. It is too simple to define a community member by only one aspect of community, let alone by a geographical location. "Community" is not an organized group of associates; it is an analytical category used by observers for description. "It becomes a 'class for itself' when organization develops and a self-consciousness emerges among members and they come to act collectively toward mutual [community] goals."[51] This fits well with the definition Cohen argued for above: "We try to understand 'community' by seeking to capture its members' experience of it."[52] In this way we can begin to see the one-sided nature of the terms Johannine community, or Markan community, or Matthean community, or Lukan community. The "community" reconstruction model only defines a Gospel community as one "type" of community: an enclosed, particular, even sectarian "group" of Christians in which the Gospel document arose and remained. Such a definition is too limited to provide adequate analysis; not to mention the complete lack of historical evidence for such a "community." Although it provides a helpful external model, it

[49] Gusfield, *Community*, p. 23. [50] *Ibid.*, p. 24.
[51] *Ibid.*, p. 26. See the related discussion of Jewish "community" by Barclay, *Jews in the Mediterranean Diaspora*, p. 414.
[52] Cohen, *The Symbolic Construction of Community*, p. 20.

fails to take into account internal aspects of "community" and potential interaction with other "communities." Thus, there are other aspects of a "community," that a geographic definition cannot explain.

Post-World War II research on the establishments of national units in the retreat of colonial powers and the focus of attention on efforts of new governments to promote and develop a consciousness of nationhood provides a helpful link to our discussion of the early Christian concept of community. As Gusfield explains, "The crucial quality of communal interaction is the recognition that a common identity of communal membership implies special claims which members have on each other, as distinct from others."[53] In reference to the concept of nation, another notoriously ambiguous term,[54] Benedict Anderson has proposed the following definition: "It is an imagined political-community – and imagined as both inherently limited and sovereign."[55] As Anderson explains: "It is imagined because the members of even the smallest nation will never know most of their fellow-members, meet them, or even hear of them, yet in the minds of each lives the image of their communion."[56] But even the largest nation is limited, because it has finite, even if elastic, boundaries beyond which lie other nations. In this sense a nation is a type of "community." Again, Anderson explains:

> it is imagined as a community, because, regardless of the actual inequality and exploitation that may prevail in each, the nation is always conceived as a deep, horizontal comradeship. Ultimately it is this fraternity that makes it possible, over the past two centuries, for so many millions of people, not so much to kill, as willing to die for such limited imaginings.[57]

And later,

> The idea of a sociological organism moving calendrically through homogenous, empty time is a precise analogue of the idea of the nation, which also is conceived as a solid community moving steadily down (or up) history. An American will

[53] Gusfield, *Community*, p. 29.
[54] Hugh Seton-Watson, *Nations and States: An Inquiry into the Origins of Nations and the Politics of Nationalism* (Boulder, Col.: Westview Press, 1977), author of the best and most comprehensive English-language text on nationalism, explains: "Thus I am driven to the conclusion that no 'scientific definition' of the nation can be devised; yet the phenomenon has existed and exists" (p. 5).
[55] Anderson, *Imagined Communities: Reflections on the Origin and Spread of Nationalism*, rev. edn (London: Verso, 1991), p. 6.
[56] *Ibid.* [57] *Ibid.*, p. 7.

never meet, or even know the names of more than a handful of his... fellow Americans. He has no idea of what they are up to at any one time. But he has complete confidence in their steady, autonomous, simultaneous activity.[58]

We have used the concept of "nation" as an analogy for the concept of "community" in order to show the potential for defining the Gospel communities in light of an internal perspective. Rather than reading the Gospels as documents for one of several Christian "communities," a reading strategy that applies a territorial model that limits the receiving audience to a geographic and special location, we propose to apply a relational model, one of a symbolic construction, as the primary mode of thinking and assuming involvement in an early Christian "community." This "community," rather than existing as one local group or networked group, often viewed as sectarian in nature, is much more connected than normally assumed. It is not an isolated "communal world" of its own but part of a much larger social system. Like a nation, the early Christians saw themselves as related to one another, as horizontal comrades. They may not have even known one another, for their group was ever-growing and thus elastic, as well as spread over a huge geographic region, but they had an imagined connection that was symbolically constructed.

Such a proposal is not difficult to reconcile with the diversity and conflict normally perceived to have existed in early Christianity. As Cohen explains, the "commonality" which is found in community need not be uniformity.[59] An important explanation by Cohen is worth quoting in full:

It does not clone behaviour or ideas. It is a commonality of forms (ways of behaving) whose content (meanings) may vary considerably among its members. The triumph of community is to so contain this variety that its inherent discordance does not subvert the apparent coherence which is expressed by its boundaries. If the members of a community come to feel that they have less in common with each other than they have with the members of some other community then, clearly, the boundaries have become anomalous and the integrity of the "community" they enclose has been severely impugned. The important thrust of this argument is that this relative similarity or difference is not a matter for "objective" assessment: it is a matter of feeling, a matter which resides in the minds of the members themselves. Thus, although they recognize important differences among themselves, they also suppose themselves to be more like

each other than like the members of other communities. This is precisely because, although the meanings they attach to the symbols may differ, they share the symbols. Indeed, their common ownership of symbols may be so intense that they may be quite unaware or unconcerned that they attach to them meanings which can differ from those of their fellows.[60]

Thus we find the potential for difference within commonality. Gusfield is helpful here. In a section entitled, "Pre-Conditions of Community," Gusfield explains that too often suggested pre-conditions for communal development do not result in communal formation, in fact, in some cases different and even opposite sources can be associated with communal emergence.[61] A homogeneous culture, for example, has often been posited as a mark of community. Languages, moralities, and common histories are assumed to produce a sense of being unique and different in comparison to other groups. This common perception, however, does not specify the boundaries of homogeneity. As Gusfield notes:

Why don't Europeans develop strong communal ties, since they possess much of a common history and customs as compared to non-Europeans? Why did American Jews of German origin develop a strong communal identity with American Jews of Russian origin when their "cultures" were so opposite? What appears crucial are the situations in which the culture does or does not appear homogeneous; the perception among an aggregate of people that they constitute a community. This "consciousness of kind" is not an automatic product of an abstract "homogeneity."[62]

The second area often posited as a mark of community is common territory. "It has so frequently been posited as an essential condition for community that the term is sometimes coterminous with territory, as in the 'local community,' 'community studies,' 'community power structure.'"[63] According to this text, the concept of community is part of a system of symbols used by members and observers as a way of explaining or justifying a member's behavior. "It is the behavior governed by criteria of common belonging" that established the community, not the geographic region in which it occurs.[64]

---

[58] *Ibid.*, p. 26. [59] Cohen, *The Symbolic Construction of Community*, p. 20.
[60] *Ibid.*, pp. 20–21. [61] Gusfield, *Community*, p. 31. [62] *Ibid.*, p. 32. [63] *Ibid.*
[64] *Ibid.*, p. 33. Admittedly, the relation between territorial size and communalism remains a central issue in social theory. For our purposes, it is only important to state that the symbolic construction of early Christianity was assumed to spread much further than the borders of one Christian "group."

This understanding of difference within commonality makes sense of the evidence we have in other NT documents. Early Christianity was not devoid of a universal Christian sense or awareness. Three times Paul alleviates tension between what would seem to be different groups functioning under the symbolic Christian construction (1 Cor. 12:13; Gal. 3:28; Col. 3:11). Elsewhere Paul urges his readers to have concern for members in other areas within "church," even those whom they may not know personally (1 Cor. 8–9). This in no way implies that there was no intra-group conflict, just that it was intra-group and not inter-group. While we must be careful in our description of what first-century Christians saw as common between themselves in a comprehensive way, or how they dealt with their differences (which is why some prefer to speak of Christianities), this does not imply that the various versions within Christianity were any less Christian or that they saw other "Christians" as equal to a completely other religious system (e.g. Gentiles, or even Jews).[65] A recent collection of essays by Judith Lieu also confirms the more complex model of early Christianity.[66] According to Lieu, "the creation, at least rhetorically, of a self-conscious and distinctive identity is a remarkable characteristic of early Christianity from our earliest sources and from Christianity's equally characteristic literary creativity."[67] After critiquing the use of external models to denote various "communities," Lieu argues that such models are incapable of accounting for the evidence both within and outside the NT documents.[68] Although our understanding of the exact "identity" of early Christians must remain opaque, it seems that "Christians" may have viewed themselves as a new *genus*, a third "race."[69] In fact, Paul's theoretical construct of a new ἄνθρωπος (Col. 3:10) is the ultimate pattern and goal of all Christians. As Lieu explains, Paul's "letters bear eloquent testimony to the practical context, the creation of new communities both out of individuals and out of existing networks or households of both Jewish and non-Jewish background without, theoretically, giving priority to either."[70] The research of Lieu and others shows how a more complex model of identity and "community" fits well with this text and its critique of the "communities" behind the Gospels.

Such a proposal also fits well with Peter Berger's description of a "plausibility structure" (symbolically constructed world) in his *The Sacred Canopy*: a work commonly used to describe the "group" consciousness of a Gospel "community." Although Berger makes a general distinction between an entire society which serves as a plausibility structure and situations in which only a sub-society serves as such, he never provides definitions to the forms or functions in which a "sub-society" might exist.[71] Certainly individual groups could have their own plausibility structure, but, as we have argued, the Gospels do not reflect such a use, as the use of other Gospels makes clear. Thus, when Philip Esler claims, in reference to the model presented by Berger, that "The importance of this model for New Testament criticism *depends on the view* that the New Testament documents were, by and large, written *for particular* early Christian communities and that *these communities may be regarded as social worlds* of the kind Berger describes," he has misapplied Berger's model.[72] Berger never shows how to make a distinction between a sub-society, which would certainly be characteristic of the early Christian movement, and particular early Christian communities that are "part of" that sub-society. Such a move by Esler is a misuse of Berger's "plausibility structure" model.[73]

Finally, recent research in Jewish "communities" reveals a striking similarity to our proposed definition of "community." John Barclay, in a monograph devoted to *Jews in the Mediterranean Diaspora*, argues that a more complex analysis of "Judaism" is needed than has traditionally been suggested. Barclay argues that recent research has reacted against the generalizations spawned by previous generations of scholars.[74] What is interesting for our purposes is Barclay's portrayal of the unity of Diaspora Judaism, even amidst all the diversity in the different locations

---

[65] This more nuanced understanding of difference within commonality also makes sense of the patristic evidence we have concerning defenders of the early church, issues of heresy, and a universal gospel.

[66] Judith Lieu, *Neither Jew Nor Greek? Constructing Early Christianity*, SNTW (London: T. & T. Clark, 2002).

[67] *Ibid.*, p. 171. Averil Cameron, *Christianity and the Rhetoric of Empire: The Development of Christian Discourse*, SCL 45 (Berkeley: University of California Press, 1991), p. 21, argues similarly: "But if ever there was a case of the construction of reality through text, such a case is provided by early Christianity ... Christians built themselves a new world. They did so partly through practice – the evolution of a mode of living and a new communal discipline that carefully distinguished them from their pagan and Jewish neighbours – and partly through a discourse that was itself constantly brought under control and disciplined."

[68] Lieu, *Neither Jew Nor Greek?*, pp. 172–82.   [69] *Ibid.*, pp. 183–84.

[70] *Ibid.*, p. 184. Lieu admits that "The fragility of the construct, both practically and theoretically, is equally clear."

[71] Berger, *The Sacred Canopy: Elements of A Sociological Theory of Religion* (Garden City, NY: Doubleday, 1967), pp. 48–49.

[72] Esler, *The First Christians in their Social Worlds: Social Scientific Approaches to New Testament Interpretation* (London: Routledge, 1994), p. 6 (emphasis added).

[73] See a similar critique by Stephen Motyer, *Your Father the Devil? A New Approach to John and "the Jews,"* PBTS (Carlisle: Paternoster, 1997), pp. 30–31.

[74] Barclay, *Jews in the Mediterranean Diaspora*, p. 400.

catalogued earlier in the monograph. According to Barclay although "Jewish identity could be presented differently according to context . . . such varying Jewish profiles do not necessarily represent different 'Judaisms': one and the same socio-religious phenomenon can wear many masks."[75] The reason for this is two-fold: ethnic bonds and social and symbolic resources; the latter of which is especially pertinent to our study. According to Barclay, these "social and symbolic resources" allowed Diaspora Jews to bond at the local community level, but also at the wider level of "networks which joined Jews of *diverse communities* together."[76]

What is most surprising in this regard is how well Barclay's findings mesh with Martyn's proposal for a unified Judaism that was organized enough to produce the *Birkat ha-Minim*, that is, the systematic excommunication of Jewish-Christians from Jewish synagogues.[77] According to Martyn, "clearly [this] is a formal agreement or *decision* reached by some *authoritative Jewish group* . . . We are not dealing with an *ad hoc* move on the part of the authorities. . ."[78] Of course, even though Martyn's proposal is rarely accepted in total, as we will discuss in chapter 3, the very idea that Martyn's Judaism was able to view itself as a single unit, even after centuries of strife, causing some scholars to prefer the term "Judaisms," makes his following assumption, that the Christians were isolated, closed "communities," extremely difficult to reconcile. For such a "formal decision" to have occurred, it would not only have required that Judaism had come to recognize "Christianity" as diametrically opposed to itself, but more importantly that Judaism had come to recognize "itself," with all its diversity both ideologically and geographically, as a unified movement with various "groups" working in some synthesized fashion, having communication and general agreement between them. And all of this, or at least its recognition and response to Christianity, would have had to occur in less than seventy years, since "Christianity" had come into existence, the last thirty of which were after the core and center of the Jewish faith, the temple, had been destroyed. Why, if Judaism could have been so organized and unified, according to Martyn, could not Christianity have had a similar recognition of identity? If Jewish sources can

be viewed as depicting the larger Jewish movements and thought-world, then in principle the Christian sources can as well.

Returning to the unity of Judaism, Barclay discusses several unifying resources, each of which we will discuss and relate to early Christianity. The first Jewish resource is the link with Jerusalem, the "homeland," and the temple. Both before 70 CE and certainly after the temple was primarily a conceptual reality for Diaspora Jews. But it was a significant concept, for it was the "base" of Judaism, as can be witnessed by the annual collection of dues required for the temple prior to 70 CE. Although some in early Christianity may have seen Jesus as a replacement for the temple (John 2:21), Jerusalem was still an important "base" for early Christians. The fact that Paul went to Jerusalem more than once (Gal. 2:1) implies a wide recognition of the functional centrality of a Christian leadership. A second Jewish resource is the Law/Scriptures. The importance of "the Scriptures," as evidenced by the unequivocal use of the term γραφή, is no less important to early Christians. The use of the Jewish Scriptures (OT) and a devout spreading of an oral tradition about Jesus and his disciples are evident in the early movement, even in local worship.[79] The third Jewish resource is the figure of Moses. Certainly the figure of Jesus in early Christianity is of equal if not greater standing than Moses is to Judaism (see John 9:28). The existence of four Gospel *bioi* about Jesus makes this abundantly clear. Even some of the earliest followers of Jesus were forced (honored) to bear his name: "Christians."[80] Finally, the fourth Jewish resource is practical distinctions. Barclay describes how regular practices in daily life focused Jews on their distinctiveness, and hence their unity. For Jews this can be seen in their rejection of alien, pluralist, and iconic cults, the separatism at meals, the circumcision of males, and the Sabbath observance.[81] Early Christians also had found unity in their rejection of other "religious" groups' perspectives; in fact, it might be argued that "the Jews" were one of the groups that were rejected. The important Christian meal became the Eucharist, which also had separatist components (1 Cor. 11:17–34). The NT makes clear that circumcision of the "heart" became of great importance, which was symbolized in Christian baptism. In conclusion, we have argued that taken cumulatively, there were several symbolic resources for early Christians that incorporated them into a "community" much larger than their own local community. Just as Jews in the Mediterranean Diaspora were able to form a "web of social and

---

[75] *Ibid.*, p. 401. Barclay is not alone in his dislike of "Judaisms." See E. P. Sanders, *Jewish Law from Jesus to the Mishnah*. Five Studies (London: SCM Press, 1990), pp. 255–56; and Richard Bauckham, "The Parting of the Ways: What Happened and Why?," *ST* 47 (1993), pp. 135–41. According to Barclay, it would appear that models drawn implicitly from Christian denominations or from contemporary varieties in Judaism have led the historian astray at this point (p. 401, n. 2).
[76] Barclay, *Jews in the Mediterranean Diaspora*, p. 413 (emphasis added).
[77] Martyn, *History and Theology in the Fourth Gospel*, pp. 46–66.   [78] *Ibid.*, p. 47.

[79] See the classic discussion of this by Oscar Cullmann, *Early Christian Worship*, trans. A. Stewart Todd and James B. Torrance, SBT 10 (London: SCM Press, 1953).
[80] This probably occurred only in Greek- and Latin-speaking contexts.
[81] Barclay, *Jews in the Mediterranean Diaspora*, pp. 428–42.

religious commitments"82 that allowed interconnection amidst diversity, so also the Christian "communities" could see beyond their geographic borders to a reality greater than their own.

Of course, this does not imply a complete unity between different geographic communities, for certainly individual boundaries defined themselves over and against other communities. Again, what is needed is a more complex analysis. Although there may never have been a single, identifiable "Christian" identity; that does not imply that each "community" was its own "Christianity." Certainly Christian "communities" can not simply be defined by their individual ideological stances, as if they never saw themselves as part of a larger "community." Thus, for each group one needs to determine in what ways they viewed themselves as part of the broader "Christian" community, and in what ways they attempted to correct it (and other "deviant" forms of Christianity). Thus, using the FG as an example, certainly John saw a boundary that some groups might have extended beyond (John 15; cf. 1 John 2), yet he also maintains some general flexibility that would agree with several "communities." Again, turning to an earlier essay by John Barclay we find similar evidence within Judaism:

individual Jewish communities could clearly take some definitions for granted and a certain unity of mind is sometimes perceptible *both within individual communities and across geographical and temporal bounds*. Philo tells us his own opinion on who has "deserted the ancestral customs," but also indicates the viewpoint of "the masses" in the Jewish community in Alexandria with which he is largely in accord. We can also discern certain topics (e.g. engagement in "idolatrous" worship and eating unclean foods) on which there appears to have been a fair degree of unanimity across different Jewish communities in our period. Thus *we need not suppose that every case of "deviating" behavior had to be negotiated from scratch in the community as to its "deviant" or "non-deviant" status*.83

This is not to deny that early Christianity's highly fluid conditions had less "taken-for-granted norms," as Barclay describes it, than a more established Judaism, and that the future of Christianity was determined by

---

82 *Ibid.*, p. 442.
83 Barclay, "Deviance and Apostasy: Some Applications of Deviance Theory to First-Century Judaism and Christianity," in Philip F. Esler (ed.), *Modeling Early Christianity: Social-Scientific Studies of the New Testament in its Context* (London: Routledge, 1995), p. 119 (emphasis added).

power contests, as no historian can deny, but it does imply that these struggles were not fought only by individual "communities" and without a concept of a larger "Christian" movement.84 Thus, far from seeing John or any of the Gospels as attempting to completely supplant the other Gospels ideologically, as if the only relationship that can exist between these documents (and their "communities") is either complete acceptance or rejection, one may begin to see areas of common "unity of mind" and other areas of differing boundaries. The very fact that we even have a "Synoptic problem" would seem to point in this direction. Each Gospel does provide a definition of "Christianity" that is unique, but it is not in complete isolation or disagreement with other "versions" of other early Christians. The very fact that some evangelist would use large sections of Mark for their own presentations would seem to argue against a reading of each Gospel as representative of a limited audience. A more complex model is needed, one that accounts for the use of two or more "Gospels" for any given audience.

Definition of community: conclusion

This book is proposing that a more complex model be applied to the assumed audiences of the Gospels. Rather than defining a Gospel audience based upon a territorial or ideological model of community, we propose to define the audience based upon a relational model of community. This would, in the words of Bauckham, make the Gospels intended for "any and every Christian" reader in the first century. The key word for our purposes is not "any and every," but "Christian." Using a relational model, the Gospels would have been appropriate reading material for several geographic communities throughout the Roman Empire. Readers who were not even aware of the other's existence could participate together in the story told by the Gospels, based upon their related symbolic construction. "People who do not know each other nevertheless see themselves in the same category and share the same friends and enemies."85 For the early Christians, the Gospels were a story that many, if not most, could share. Even amidst the diversity, and often a redefining of friends and enemies, they all saw themselves as partakers in the same story.86

---

84 *Ibid.*, p. 125.   85 Gusfield, *Community*, p. 49.
86 This concept of a more worldwide church goes against the sectarian division model used by several interpreters, including David Sim, "The Gospels for All Christians? A Response to Richard Bauckham," who presented a major critique against Bauckham and

Anti-Judaism, the Jews, and the Worlds of the Fourth Gospel

Judith Lieu

No defense is needed for identifying "anti-Judaism" as a necessary, and not merely a possible, topic to be addressed in any exploration of the Gospel of John and Christian theology. It is no longer possible, as has sometimes happened, to dismiss the topic as a chimera, projecting upon the distant past a phenomenon, particularly when termed "anti-Semitism," inapplicable to antiquity, a child of modern views of race, and an anxiety driven by contemporary social and political concerns. The *Judaism* part of the term is certainly a problem, and to that we shall return, but the strenuous scholarly efforts devoted to the question, symbolized by the 612 pages of the Leuven volume that have self-confessedly failed to halt further efforts, suggest that those who give glib dismissals have not first listened to what is being said.[1] In any case, although contemporary concerns, above all reflection on the Shoah, have demanded attention to the issue, sensitivities to the problem are perhaps less recent than is sometimes assumed: Hilgenfeld's explicitly entitled essay of 1893, "Der Antijudaismus des Johannes-evangeliums," was not the first to address the issue.[2] Certainly it continues to be a common experience when teaching the Fourth Gospel that, while some students are from their prior experience already deeply aware of the problem of its attitude to "the Jews," for others this comes as a surprising, but usually uncomfortably compelling, discovery. Two aspects of this discomfort should be emphasized, for they will continue to demand our attention. The first is that it is inseparable from a need to articulate quite how readers/respondents understand "Christianity" in relation to "Judaism," however either of those terms are defined and whether or not such definitions can be unreflectively applied to the first century.[3] Second, there is the hermeneutical challenge, particularly for those for whom the Bible, or the New Testament, has a clear moral authority, of a text whose moral heritage is, at the least, ambivalent. Some will have met that challenge elsewhere, in ideological, and particularly in feminist, criticism, and it is no surprise that some of those writing on this particular question, anti-Judaism in John, have also explored feminist readings of the New Testament. Indeed, the spectrum of feminist approaches to the Bible, which has often been sketched, might also be used as a template for approaches to our concern; there too we find a range from the argument that what appears to be negative is, in context, not so, to the prioritizing of a lodestone of Gospel truth as a measure of the "authenticity" of the rest, or to the radical questioning of the canon. To these two sources of discomfort we may add a third: that is, the nature of this text as a public and as a liturgical document — that for many people the text is received, often only received, aurally (alas!).[4]

Historical Debate

The topic is, then, of central theological significance. Yet, from the perspective of biblical scholarship, the primary starting-point must be, as expressed by Stephen Motyer, "the significance of history." This, as he notes, is inseparable from — indeed it is conceptually prior to — the hermeneutics of translation hinted at already (which he lists as the first aspect of the problem). A common solution, followed by Motyer, provides for the Gospel, as originally intended, a particular social, religious, and historical location; this, it can be argued, determines its meaning and how it is to be read. One approach is to address this

---

This paper was circulated in advance at the conference and was written as a response to the paper by Dr. Stephen Motyer. The first part of the paper is shaped by Motyer's paper, and I am grateful to him for giving the lead. It has been only slightly edited for publication. Page references to Motyer refer to his paper as printed here, pp. 143-67.

1. R. Bieringer, D. Pollefeyt, and F. Vandecasteele-Vanneuville, eds., *Anti-Judaism and the Fourth Gospel: Papers of the Leuven Colloquium 2000* (Assen: Van Gorcum, 2001); for the failure to reach an "answer" see the editors' introduction, pp. 3-44. Both Dr. Motyer and I were contributors to that volume.

2. A. Hilgenfeld, "Der Antijudaismus des Johannes-evangeliums," *ZWT* 36 (1893): 507-17.

3. Clearly they cannot, yet there are almost unavoidable in treating the issue; moreover, the truism of there being multiple "judaisms" in the first century will not suffice to escape it.

4. As noted by Stephen Motyer in his discussion of translations, pp. 146-47, 151-53.

through theories of layers of source and redaction, or of tradition and its reuse, a form of literary archaeology, which may then locate the variation in John's language in a (number of) particular context(s).[5] Another approach, more in tune with recent biblical scholarship, takes the Gospel in its (final) received form and reads it and the way it works as "narrative." This is implied in Stephen Motyer's reading with its interest in how the Gospel might be *received* "whether designed or not" (p. 149). Here, there is a direct correlation between the "implied audience" as it can be narrative-critically constructed and the actual or hermeneutically normative audience: in contrast to some narrative-critical readings this presupposes that we both can and should move to an "original" setting which has, it is assumed, hermeneutical priority. (We should note that this would not go without challenge in contemporary biblical criticism: some would doubt whether we can access an original setting; others would reject the assumption that such a setting has hermeneutical priority over other contexts in which the text has or can be read. For the moment, however, we may leave aside these challenges.)

Clearly, if the earliest contextualization of the Gospel is to have hermeneutical priority, its reconstruction must persuade. Yet here, biblical scholars have failed to reach a consensus, although to explore this in sufficient detail would take more time and space than is possible here. Admittedly, Motyer's reconstruction is relatively broad-brush, eschewing the very specific account of approaches based on a hypothetical "history of the community" (see below). Nevertheless, I find myself uncomfortable with a straightforward statement of "the needs of Jews of many types (including the Samaritans) in their intense effort to come to terms with the disaster of the Jewish War" (p. 149), which provides the foundation of Motyer's reading. It is easy to imaginatively reconstruct what we might *expect* those needs to have been, but establishing what they *were*, especially in, perhaps, Samaria or the Diaspora, is another question, and such (few) sources as we have do not give a uniform picture. Secondly, I am not persuaded that the conflict in John focuses around "the intensity of their devotion to Torah" or "to the Law"; the word "Law" is surprisingly infrequent in the Gospel. Consequently I find it difficult to agree that "there can be little doubt that such Jews would have recognized themselves in the Fourth Gospel in the late first century, and *felt themselves* to be addressed by it" (p. 151).[6] If such disagreements are valid and unexpected among specialists in the field, then it is difficult to see how we can offer to others an original historical context as an answer to the theological problem.[7]

Before developing this further we should also note that while reading through the lens of a reconstructed original context does endeavor to address the way in which "the Jews" are portrayed, and the possible reasons for this, it does not address the most intractable question. Motyer quotes Adele Reinhartz's description of her own experience as a reader, that "each johannine usage of the term 'Jew' felt like a slap in the face."[8] He rightly concludes that paragraph by approving the simple observation that whatever John means, what he says is "the Jews," or, better, in Greek, οἱ Ἰουδαῖοι (*hoi ioudaioi*) — English offers a particular problem in having lost the etymological link between "Jew" (*ioudaios*) and "Judea" (*ioudaia*).[9] Why does John say "the Jews" some seventy times, compared with a mere five in Matthew? It is, of course, true — and part of the dilemma of interpretation — that he says other things: "rulers," "Pharisees," "crowd," even "Jerusalemites."[10] Yet, on the whole — and, again, one of the problems is that we can only say "on the whole" (cf. 4:22) — whenever the narrative moves toward hostility it also moves toward the use of *hoi ioudaioi*. A semantic analysis that registers not just the occurrences of the term itself but the constructions within which it is used and the terms with which it is associated will be struck by the number which imply negativity — fear, murmuring, seeking to kill. Why is this, not least in a text supposedly designed to appeal and to persuade? The objection sometimes made that in the first century we cannot speak of "Judaism," since anything we might so label was too much characterized by diversity to carry a single "-ism" suffix, does not really succeed in countering speaking of John's anti-Judaism because it only underlines that, and fails to explain why, John uses an apparently undifferentiated term, *hoi ioudaioi*. That remains a historically perplexing question, and perhaps also a theologically perplexing one.

However, our task here is to focus rather more on the hermeneutical issues.

---

sentation, might it not be easier to forgive an author a certain ham-fistedness (to put it mildly) in seeking a noble intention, than to envisage an unintentional textual *telos* of "meeting needs"?

7. I wish to emphasize this, because, understandably, systematic theologians do sometimes adopt a historical contextualization they find in *some* secondary literature, and build on it to develop a theological argument, without fully realizing its fragility.

8. A. Reinhartz, "'Jews' and Jews in the Fourth Gospel," in Bieringer et al., eds., *Anti-Judaism and the Fourth Gospel*, pp. 341-56, p. 341, quoted by Motyer, p. 144.

9. The point here is that some interpreters comment that John must *mean* the religious authorities, as if that observation deals with the problem. Arguments that the term has a geographical focus in John have proved unpersuasive, and do not reflect normal first-century usage.

10. For example, John 7:1, 2, 11, 15, 20, 25, 26, 31, 32, 45.

---

5. For example, U. C. von Wahlde, "The Terms for Religious Authorities in the Fourth Gospel: A Key to Literary Strata?" *JBL* 98 (1979): 231-53.

6. We should note that Motyer is careful to maintain a strategic agnosticism on whether this might be the author's intention. However, given the partisan character of the Gospel's pre-

Stephen Motyer illustrates the logic behind the hermeneutical process when he offers his own reconstruction of the context of the Gospel's reception as an alternative to the reconstruction of its origin frequently proposed: "However, historically we are *not bound* to decide that there is an ineradicable hostility towards Jews and Judaism in the Fourth Gospel. Other historical *constructs* are available, *arguably* ones with as much if not more historical *plausibility* than the dominant reconstruction . . ." (pp. 148-49; emphasis mine). The dominant reconstruction, that the Gospel plays out a two-level drama reflecting the Johannine group's experience of expulsion from the synagogue, is regularly seen as "explaining" the hostility and so as solution to it; Stephen Motyer rightly recognizes it, instead, as part of the problem because it retains the givenness of hostility.[11] Yet this invites further questions: what is the hermeneutical status of a historical reconstruction that can only be qualified by the language of plausibility? And, if this is only a case, and it is difficult to see how it can ever be more, of "*arguably* as much if not more" *plausibility* than other recontextualizations, what do we mean if we claim to be assigning moral primacy to the "original" intention, voice, or even reception? Might we not be in danger of favoring a recontextualization that saves us from the ethically and theologically harsher alternative simply because it does so save us; and if we do so, is this because of a doctrine of the biblical text as something that "cannot" be ethically ambivalent?

We may, indeed, extend this observation. The entirely appropriate language of "construct" in this exercise directs us toward constructionist views of history. Certainly, in historiographical debate constructionism is highly contentious, not least because of the ethical ambiguity frequently inherent therein. In the study of the distant past, where controls are rarely available, the relationship between text and history, or a view of history as text, render these dilemmas more intractable. Is the (his)story Stephen Motyer tells, particularly as textualized through the translations of "*hoi ioudaioi*" that he offers, the same text as the Gospel, or is it another, perhaps parallel, text?[12]

Thirdly, we have sharply focused here a pressing hermeneutical concern which, in theory, is impressed upon us in each of the Gospels to the extent that they tell the past through the prism of the present, but that is particularly stark in John (although also in a different form in Matthew). If it is the case that the Fourth Gospel blurs the boundary between the identities of the Jews of John's time and of those of Jesus' time, then can we avoid reproducing this in any translation or rendering? It is, in the quotation given earlier, the Jews of the late first century who would, so the argument goes, recognize themselves as addressed by the Gospel. Stephen Motyer suggests translating 9:22 ". . . they were afraid of *the more hard-line Jews in the synagogue leadership*. For *these Jews* had determined that anyone who confessed Jesus as the Christ should be expelled from the synagogue" (p. 153; italics his). Yet, besides introducing a restrictive (implicitly only "some") where none is semantically, even if it is narratively, indicated, this probably reproduces a view of synagogue structures and authority relevant more in the 90s than in the 30s of the first century. So, who is it who sought to kill Jesus (5:18), and why? Stephen himself does suggest that although the offense of John's language about the Jews can be reduced it cannot be eliminated because "these Jews were acting out of intense loyalty to the Law, *in opposing Jesus*" (p. 154; emphasis mine). Here, we must suppose, this refers to the "Jesus of history;" but that assertion would demand another investigation into the still debated question by whom and why Jesus was opposed in the context of the Galilee and Judaea of the 20s-30s, and the answers we would find might not be those that John offers: it does not seem to be the case that those Jews who opposed ("the historical") Jesus did so "because he made himself equal to God" (5:18). We are not absolved from the fundamental hermeneutical dilemma both of conveying, in translation and otherwise, and of reflecting on the significance of, the projection onto the Jesus-story of the historically and geographically focused issues of a later period. The ethical priority we, with Stephen Motyer, might wish to give to the first voice remains a hermeneutical challenge simply because that first voice is already distant from the voice of Jesus which, narratively, it claims to reproduce. Indeed, through his use of the "remembering" motif, John acknowledges this more clearly than do the other Evangelists (2:17; 22; 12:16).[13] Put in other terms, how is truth served in the statement of 5:18 that "the Jews sought all the more to kill him"?

Much of this has, indeed, been long familiar, and certainly since the advent of redaction criticism, which sought to acknowledge the independent voice of each of the Evangelists. So we recognize each of the Evangelists, and not John alone, as theologians. The nettle that has to be grasped more firmly, and certainly in our present discussion of John and Judaism, is that this theology is articulated through the telling of the story of Jesus. How do faith claim and biographical mode come together? (I use "biographical mode" as a shorthand and without conceding that technically this is an adequate and sufficient analysis of the genres of the Gospels).

---

11. This reconstruction was popularized by J. L. Martyn, *History and Theology in the Fourth Gospel*, 3d ed. (Louisville: Westminster John Knox, 2003 [1968]). For a critique see also Judith M. Lieu, "Anti-Judaism in the Fourth Gospel: Explanation and Hermeneutics," in Bieringer et al., eds., *Anti-Judaism and the Fourth Gospel*, pp. 127-43, at pp. 133-35.

12. See Motyer, pp. 152-53, and the next paragraph.

13. See J. M. Lieu, "Narrative Analysis and Scripture in John," in *The Old Testament in the New Testament: Essays in Honour of J. L. North*, ed. S. Moyise (JSNTSup 189; Sheffield Academic Press, 2000), pp. 144-63, at pp. 152, 155-56.

The conference out of which this book has come was tasked to explore the place of John's Gospel within Christian theology, past and present. In speaking of the "significance of history" and of the rights of the "first voice," Stephen Motyer, understandably and properly, affirms the task of the biblical scholar, and part of our agenda is surely to explore what is the role of that task and how its own voice is to be heard within Christian theology. We are, comparatively speaking, a young discipline, born, as often has been rehearsed, in a particular Western intellectual and ecclesiastical context. For most of its history — indeed, arguably from (and perhaps from before) the "publication" of the Gospels — the church has had comparatively little interest in what has come to be seen as their biographical mode. Both John's "anti-Judaism," insofar as it is itself a construct, and our attempts to interpret it are not exclusively functions of the modern investment in that mode, i.e., in a quasi-historical reading of their story, but they are deeply implicated within it.

Theological Structure

Thus far it has become clear that any concentration on the Fourth Gospel as story (or even as biography) invites the concomitant questions, Whose story? — that of Jesus? of the author? of the community? of the Jews (but which ones)? Also, how "true" a story? These questions both have transformed recent study of the Gospel and perhaps have problematized it. Yet we may also examine how the Gospel functions in other ways, or, put differently, we may suspend the assumption that the genre both is known and is determinative of reading; we may then ask how "the Jews" belong in those other invited ways of reading. In what follows three such readings that appear to be invited by the Gospel itself will be explored.

To preface this are the familiar statistics whose significance we need to determine: *ioudaioi* (singular only in 3:25; 4:9; 18:35) appears forty-six times between 1:19 and 12:11, and twenty-three times in the passion narrative (only one of which is in the resurrection narrative [20:19]). It is not found in the Prologue (1:1-18) nor in the Farewell Discourses (13–17, *except* for 13:33).[14] All but seven uses are by the narrator; the exceptions are 4:9 (Samaritan woman); 11:8 (the disciples, reminding us of something that the narrator has already told us [8:59; 10:31]); 18:35 (Pilate); and four uses by Jesus: 4:22; 13:33; 18:20, 36.

---

[14]. As noted earlier, this lies at the heart of the problem and marks a sharp contrast with the Synoptics; the only NT parallel is Acts. There is nothing quite similar outside the NT. There are also seven references to Judea, the feminine form (including 3:22, "the Judean/Jewish land").

The Two-Level Drama

The Fourth Gospel tells a narrative; it also constructs a worldview. How do these impact on each other? Or, put differently, as well as the often-claimed two-level drama of the Jesus of the 20s-30s and the Johannine author or community of the 90s referred to above, there is another two-level drama. This is the earthly drama of the story of Jesus whose first appearance is as an adult in some sort of relationship with John the Baptist, who gathers followers, acts, and speaks, who encounters opposition and dies, and who subsequently appears to his disciples. Alongside this there is what some have termed the cosmological drama, the story of the Son who is sent by the Father, or who comes from (descends from) heaven, in order to give testimony or to do the will of the one who sent him, and who returns to the Father. The first, the "earthly" drama, is largely told by the narrator of the Gospel, and Jesus is a character within it. The second, the "cosmological" drama, is more complex; although also told through the narrator's own voice (e.g., 1:1-18; 3:16-21, 31-36),[15] it is particularly told through Jesus' own discourses, both in public and to his disciples. This means that we can read Jesus' discourses both as events within the earthly drama, but also as shaping the cosmological drama by means of the narrative world that they create.

This, at first fairly simple, account becomes more complex once we begin to address the detail: where, for example, are we to locate the promised coming of the Paraclete, and how does that relate to the promised future coming not only of Son but of Son and Father to the believer (14:16-17, 18-23)? Before long, some theologians in the early church would want to ask how the cosmological drama provides the pattern for the eternal activity of, and the relationships between, Father and Son. More important for our immediate purposes, how do these two narratives impact upon and intersect with each other? Often noted, for example, is the question of how the return of the Son to the Father through the glorification on the cross is to be related to the resurrection and appearance narratives of chapter 20, and also to the highly problematic 20:17. It is clear that the earthly and the cosmological tales cannot simply be mapped one upon the other, as if one provided the template by which the other was to be told or read; equally clearly, it is within the merging of these particular "two horizons" that our problem belongs.

Given the predominance of *hoi ioudaioi* on the mouth of the narrator, they evidently belong to the "earthly narrative." The way that they merge with and sometimes replace, or are replaced by, other, more specific, groups confirms this (for example, the "Jews" of 18:14 refer back to the "chief priests and

---

[15]. Assuming the speaker in these last two to be the narrator, although this is not certain.

Pharisees" of 11:47-53). There are appropriate questions to be asked of the way in which they are represented in this "earthly narrative," some of which we have already asked, and the specific term remains perplexing. We know, perhaps, that Jesus is a Jew, although only by inference, and also, indeed, if she is a trustworthy character, because the Samaritan woman explicitly tells us so (4:9); it is, however, possible that we are expected to react to her words with the same sort of ambivalence or knowing superiority as we may to "the Jews" who think that they know the father (and mother) of Jesus, son of Joseph (6:41-42). It is on this earthly level that "the Jews" oppose and seek to kill Jesus. Yet, presumably, it is also on this level that Jesus says "salvation is from the Jews" (4:22).[16]

In what sense do the Jews belong to the cosmological narrative? The passage just quoted (6:41-42) focuses the question, for their objection at that point is to Jesus' claim that he has "come down from heaven," a formulation that belongs to the cosmological drama.[17] For this reason Adele Reinhartz locates the Jews firmly in the cosmological drama as well, and she sees in them the main focus of the exclusivity claimed by and for Jesus, an exclusivity that mirrors the exclusive claims of Jewish covenantal theology.[18] Thus, it is on this level that she sets the controversy of 8:31-59, one of the most difficult passages of the Gospel. She draws this conclusion because for her the scriptural story as a whole, its grand narrative, is a cosmological narrative, presumably because it claims an absolute, and not a contingent, place within God's dealings with all creation.

However, it would also be possible to argue that John does not understand things in this way; rather, at the cosmological level it is "the world," the *kosmos* (κόσμος), that represents the arena of and the respondents to the mission of the Son. The term *kosmos* appears as frequently as does *ioudaioi*, but it is rarely used by the narrator; although it is found on the mouth of other characters in the narrative, it is particularly Jesus' term, most notably in the Farewell Discourses (13-17),[19] although most of its main contours are already in place before those chapters.[19] Indeed, it seems to be the case that the Farewell Discourses bring the disciples into Jesus' cosmological story as that has already been sketched through the earlier discourses.

The relationship in John between "the Jews" and "the *kosmos*" has been much debated. They explicitly intersect at a few key points. In 18:20 Jesus defends himself by saying that he has spoken openly "to the world" by teaching "where all the Jews gather",[20] in 8:23 he tells "the Jews" that they are from below and "of this world," just as he is from above and not "of this world" (cf. 7:4-7).[21] These points of intersection have led to debates as to whether "the Jews" are a cipher for "the world," or, alternatively, whether "the world" is a cipher for (real) Jews, who constituted "the world" as experienced by the putative Johannine community in its own context.[22] The former solution makes much of the absence of "the Jews" from the Farewell Discourses where the disciples, representatives of the Johannine community and perhaps of the contemporary situation, are in view. It can then move in one of two directions:[23] one is simply to replace "world" with the language of "universal" in a way that leaves opaque whether actually this means nothing more than "(perhaps local) gentiles"; the other is to withdraw from any specifics of time and place and to speak about "unbelief," a trajectory that would take us toward the reading of the Gospel most associated with Rudolf Bultmann: "Solche Feindschaft gegen das Leben und gegen die Wahrheit macht also das Wesen der 'Juden' aus, und daraus entspringt ihr Unglaube. . . . Im Sinne des Evglisten findet diese Feindschaft jedoch ihre symbolhaften Ausdruck in der 5,18 zuerst aufgetauchten Absicht der Juden, Jesus zu töten . . ."[24]

A key verse here is 8:47, where Jesus charges his interlocutors, "Therefore you do not hear, because you are not of God." These are identified by the narrator in the following verse as "the Jews," although, typically of Johannine narrative (dis)continuity, they have been hidden by the general third-person plural since 8:31 where they were surprisingly characterized as "the Jews who had believed in him," and, equally typically, their riposte in v. 48 shows no obvious logical link with Jesus' preceding words. Within the earthly narrative his charge is a denial of the Jews' claim to Abrahamic status;[25] within the cosmological narrative it denies them a place within the life-giving purposes of the Son's story.

---

16. However, 4:22 is ambiguous in its "level" because of the move into the first-person plural, a Johannine characteristic for a change of voice or perspective (cf. 3:11).

17. See also 6:51-52 and below, nn. 21, 34.

18. A. Reinhartz, "The Gospel of John: How 'the Jews' Became Part of the Plot," in *Jesus, Judaism and Christian Anti-Judaism: Reading the New Testament after the Holocaust*, ed. P. Fredericksen and A. Reinhartz (Louisville: Westminster John Knox, 2002), pp. 99-116, at p. 105.

19. It appears sixty times in the mouth of Jesus, thirty-eight in the Farewell Discourses; it is used by other speakers five times and by the narrator twelve times, including four in the prologue and five in 3:16-19, on which see n. 15 above.

20. On this verse see J. M. Lieu, "Temple and Synagogue in John," *NTS* 45 (1999): 51-69.

21. At 6:51 Jesus declares that the bread he will give is "my flesh for the life of the world," to which "the Jews" (see n. 34) respond, "How can this man give us his flesh to eat?"

22. In support of this second reading, in 15:18-16:4 the hatred of the world is manifested in exclusion from the synagogue.

23. See J. Zumstein, "The Farewell Discourses (John 13:31-16:33) and the Problem of Anti-Judaism," in Bieringer et al., eds. *Anti-Judaism*, pp. 461-78, who in practice merges these two.

24. R. Bultmann, *Das Evangelium des Johannes* (Göttingen: Vandenhoeck & Ruprecht, 1968[19]), p. 243 on 8:44.

25. Some would say "covenantal" but John does not use explicit covenantal categories.

Particularly important too is the Prologue; this begins with the cosmological story, although here it is the story of the Logos through whom all things were created. Its arena is initially the *kosmos* (1:9-10), but it then moves to "his own" (*idia; idioi*, v. 11).[26] Too often, interpreters move immediately to declare that "his own" represents Israel, whose failure to "receive him" will be told in the story that follows (5:43), and who will be "replaced" by a new "his own" (albeit "in the world," 13:1). To draw this conclusion, however, is to ignore the text's invitation to its readers to reflect on the polyvalence of the terms chosen, not "Israel" (or even "Jews"), but "his own"; in the light of all that has been said in the previous ten verses, are not "his own" there also to be found within the *kosmos*?

Some have seen in this supposed "universalizing" of the Jews as *kosmos* a solution to the Gospel's so-called anti-Judaism.[27] Yet, as others have rightly argued, this does not offer an easy solution: on the contrary, to cast "the Jews" in the role of "unbelief" may — as has often happened — be to deny them any other role in any other story; so doing, it distances them from the actual ambiguities and differentiation of all human experience. At the same time it too easily creates a caesura between these "symbolic" Jews and the flesh-and-blood Jews who have suffered through centuries of Christian slander and persecution. Yet what is surely the case is that the Jews are not universalized; neither are they simply ciphers for unbelief. There is a particularity about the Jesus story, and, for John, there is a truth that transcends the particularity but that can only be told through it; "the ultimate problem is the nature of the gospel genre and its participation in historical specificity and in redemptive myth."[28]

Johannine Dualism and Determinism

The dualism of the Johannine worldview is integrally related to its cosmological drama, but may also be considered separately from it. It is a dualism of above and below, of light and darkness, of truth and falsehood, of salvation and judgment. This is discussed in greater detail elsewhere in this volume and the detail can be left to others. To what extent do the Jews belong to, or, even, to what extent are the Jews the victims of, the Johannine dualistic worldview? On the one hand, they are located within it, for, as we have seen, they are "not of God" but are "from below" (8:47, 23). So, for example, Nicodemus, identified as a ruler of the Jews, who comes by night, the absence of light (3:2; cf. 11:9-10 with 12:35)? On the other hand, they have no antithetical counterpart: they are not obviously a negative pole within a fixed scheme of oppositions. To some extent this is also true of "the world," to which the only real contrast is "not of the world" (8:23).[29] Although it could be argued that Jesus, or even his disciples, are the counterpart of "the Jews" in narrative terms, this is never made explicit, and it may even be undermined. Although I am not persuaded that, in the questions of the disciples in chapter 14, "the Jews" find a voice in that of the disciples, and one is a devil," echoed in 13:18, or in the light of the narrator's careful sandwiching of Judas's diabolic inspiration between Jesus' controlling foreknowledge and act (13:2-3, 26-27).[31] Yet this only postpones the problem, for what does it mean theologically for divine act to precede human response? "The one who is of God, hears the words of God; therefore you do not hear because you are not of God" (8:47).

Origen's deep and detailed exegesis of John 8, in which he records and tackles Heracleon's exegesis, illustrates well the hermeneutical challenge this poses (*In Iohannem* 20). Are people determined by some originating principle,

---

26. It is true that the two stories intersect with vv. 6-8 (perhaps added to an earlier "hymn") and the appearance of "the man named John"; but the language used of John in these verses mirrors that to be used of the Son. In contrast to his later appearance in the narrative (1:19-28), he is not here set in a "Jewish" framework.

27. The same goal has been reached by a different method in Manfred Diefenbach's recent application of theories of dramatic role, although he endeavors to demonstrate that "the Jews" represent not "unbelief" but "disbelief" or "belief otherwise." For Diefenbach this means that "the Jews" are not *personally* responsible; within the narrative drama they are not characters but role-representatives, there to adopt a position: M. Diefenbach, *Der Konflikt Jesu mit den "Juden": Ein Versuch zur Lösung der johanneischen Antijudaismus-Diskussion mit Hilfe des Antiken Handlungsverständnisses* (NTA nf 41; Münster: Aschendorff, 2002).

28. Lieu, "Anti-Judaism in John: Explanation and Hermeneutics," p. 138.

29. "Of the world" is not set in opposition to "of heaven"; 3:31 uses "earth" over against "heaven."

30. Contrast Motyer, pp. 157-60; in 14:17, 24 the present tenses, "you do know" and "you do hear" sharply contrast with Jesus' denial that "the Jews" hear or know (8:43, 47).

31. Although, as always, this is double-edged: the association of *Ioudas*, the betrayer, devil-inspired, with the Jews (*Ioudaioi*) was to have a long *Wirkungsgeschichte* of its own. See, for example, Cyril of Alexandria, *In S. Iohannem* 6 on John 8:44 who compares Cain who deceitfully took Abel into the plain with the Jews "who deceived by sending the traitor in the form of a friend," who himself deceitfully greeted Jesus (cf. n. 36); similarly, his comment on 13:28-30 (Book 9) continually moves between Judas and the Jews. See also H. Maccoby, *Judas Iscariot and the Myth of Jewish Evil* (London: Halban, 1992).

so that their response to Christ is actually dependent upon that principle, being of God or not of God, rather than merely establishing it? For Heracleon the Jews represent those who cannot hear because of their "essence" (*ousia*), being sons of the devil by nature (the *choikoi* or "earthly"); yet, so he claims, there are also those who become sons of the devil not by nature but by will (the *psychikoi* (20.198-219). Origen challenges this, and to do so he struggles to exploit the imbalance in Johannine dualism which speaks of birth from God but not of *birth* from the devil (for which he also appeals to 1 John 3:8-9). Assurance and the priority of divine saving act are provided by the language of *birth* from God (1 John 3:9); human choice and willful sinfulness establish the perpetrator as "*of the devil*." To establish his point that a "*becoming*" is involved and necessary, Origen has to appeal to Matthew 5:43-45 (those who love their enemies and so become sons of their Father in heaven). This last is a strategy, however, that most contemporary Johannine exegetes will feel unable to copy, and it serves rather to underline the problem of the Johannine scheme (*In Iohannem* 20.106-7, 141-51). Can they take more comfort from Origen's repeated appeal to the narrative audience, the Jews of 8:31, who had the possibility, which (presumably) they have rejected, of abiding in him, but perhaps have not done so irrevocably?[32] I would hesitate to do so, and this is perhaps one of those gaps (or overlaps) between earthly drama and cosmological drama discussed earlier.[33]

Again, we would do wrong to turn "the Jews" into a cipher for the enduring theological dilemmas of divine omniscience and human choice. For this is not a matter of ciphers, easily replaced by other symbols that may become more powerful in new settings. Johannine dualism is not a conceptual system *fortuitously* told through this particular story. Sociologically, it has often been suggested that Johannine dualism is a function of sectarianism; the challenge remains how it is to be read theologically.

A Re-Telling of Scripture

John's pervasive indebtedness to the Scriptures is sometimes claimed as evidence of its "Jewishness" — even with the *non sequitur* conclusion being drawn

---

[32] Before we too enthusiastically become Origenists, at least in Johannine exegesis, we should note his reflections on 11:47-48, where he speaks of the people becoming not a people, those of Israel no longer Israel, and where he comments how "even now" there are those who "through the preservation of physical Judaism wish to destroy the spiritual teaching of Christ" (*In Iohannem* 28.93-97).

[33] Other exegetical traditions (e.g. midrashic) would make much of the gaps, but their potential is still to be fully explored in Christian exegesis.

---

that this means that it cannot be anti-Jewish. That apologetic conclusion may be understandable given the way that assertions about the Gospel's essentially Hellenistic character were used in nineteenth- and early twentieth-centuries (especially German) scholarship to buttress a view of Christianity that had separated from and had no essential unity with Judaism; in recent years, however, recognition of John's essential "Jewishness," perhaps most ingrained of all the Gospels, has gone hand-in-hand with sensitivity to its "anti-Jewishness." This indebtedness is marked not only by the claims (albeit, relatively few) to fulfill "Scripture" (ἡ γραφή), but also by allusions to an interplay of scriptural themes and passages (such as the Shepherd of chapter 10), by echoes of contextually appropriate scriptural and extra-scriptural associations (for example, Tabernacles and chapter 7), but also by extended "re-tellings" of scriptural stories. There is the story of Wisdom retold in the Prologue; the story of the wilderness wanderings and the gift of manna retold in chapter 6; and the story of Cain, which lies behind part of chapter 8. The Jews also become characters, "victims" of and within the scriptural intertextuality, as it would now be called. "Murmuring" over Jesus' claim to be the new manna, they fulfill the role of those who, although they ate, murmured and died (6:41-49 [*N.B.* v. 41, "the Jews"]; cf. Exod. 16:2).[34] The story of those whose father is the devil, is the story of Cain, murderer of his brother, the righteous Abel, and destined to be replaced by Seth (8:41-47).[35] These interweavings of scriptural tales spread across the Gospel (and first Epistle). The Johannine "remembering" included the remembering of Scripture "written about him" (12:16); Scripture becomes a screen through which Jesus can be remembered, and his story, and that of the Jews, told. How do we deal with Scripture's power to create new stories? If Origen read John 8:44 alongside Matthew 5:43-45, Cyprian read it alongside Matthew 6:3 and Isaiah 1:3, "offspring who do evil, children who deal corruptly," a familiar passage in early Christian anti-Jewish polemic: for him the conclusion follows that by dominical authority "the Jews" can no longer call God their Father (*De orat. dom.* 10). This was to be a route many early Christian writers would take, finding in Scripture the authoritative story of promise and of the loss of promise. Other patristic writers would recognize and take up the allusion to Cain, with destructive results.[36] Again, it was not fortuitous that Jesus' contemporaries should be set within such retellings of Scripture; it is integral to the givenness of

---

[34] The appearance of "the Jews" in Galilee in 6:41 and 52 (see also above) is one of the arguments against a purely geographical reading of the term.

[35] For these two see Lieu, "Temple and Synagogue," p. 65.

[36] So, for example, Cyril of Alexandria, *In S. Iohannem* 6 on 8.44-45, who argues that Cain is the father of the Jews, and Satan the father of Cain, Abel being the type of Christ. See R. Mellinkoff, *The Mark of Cain* (London: University of California, 1981).

his story within the tradition of and alongside the authoritative template found in Scripture. The contemporary hermeneutical challenge is how we give an account of and respond to such ways of reading.

Conclusion

These three ways of reading the Fourth Gospel may not be incompatible with each other. They do, perhaps, begin, but only begin, to explain John's use of the undifferentiated "Jews," for they take us into constructed worlds that may have to be called "myth." They are not intended to refute or to replace the "historical" or biographical reading either of Jesus or of the Johannine community, for these too need to be recovered. However, they confirm that we shall be unable to find in an always tentative original setting a palliative for the uses to which the Gospel was later put. They also suggest that merely to ask, Who are the Jews in John? is inadequate; in addition to the questions of what the Gospel says, and why it says it, there is the question of *how*. It is for this reason that John's language may resist more irenic translation. John's attitude to and uses of "the Jews" cannot be reduced to an optional topic, easily isolated from other possible areas of interpretative interest, neither is it one that can be abstracted from the very fiber of the text. It directs us to the fundamental theological impulses of the Gospel, which will emerge only through close exegetical dialogue with the text and with the trajectories that run through it from behind as well as into the future. Here the biblical scholar must also find her theological voice.

INTRODUCTION

New Testament exegetes, like scholars in many other fields, are increasingly concerned with the relationship between the text and the reader. In attempting to describe and account for that relationship, they have been turning to the work of reader-response critics such as Stanley Fish and Wolfgang Iser.[1] Although the assumptions and insights of reader-response criticism have been applied to most if not all of the New Testament, this approach has been most influential in the study of the gospel narratives.[2] The present study is intended as a contribution to the ongoing conversation about readers and readings of the Gospel of John. Its specific focus will be the implied reader's construction and utilization of the gospel's story in reading and making sense of the Fourth Gospel as a whole.

The Fourth Gospel has been and continues to be subject to a multiplicity of readings. The vigorous debates over Johannine eschatology, christology, symbolic language, and meaning testify to the openness of this text to multivalent readings and attempts at consistency-building. Behind many of these attempts, however, lie three related, though often unarticulated, assumptions. First, the text is a narrative. Second, this narrative is, to borrow a narratological term from Gérard Genette, a "signifier."[3] Like other narrative texts, this signifier tells a story.[4] This story may be termed the "signified" or the narrative content of the narrative text.[5] Finally, the "signified" or story of the Johannine narrative has

---

[1] There has been some debate, however, about whether what New Testament scholars call reader-response criticism is in fact that. See Stanley E. Porter, "Why Hasn't Reader-Response Criticism Caught on in New Testament Studies?" *Journal of Literature and Theology* 4 (1990) 278–92. For a different analysis of the impact of reader-response criticism, see Stephen D. Moore, *Literary Criticism and the Gospels: The Theoretical Challenge* (New Haven: Yale University Press, 1989).

[2] See, for example, Jeffrey Lloyd Staley, *The Print's First Kiss: A Rhetorical Investigation of the Implied Reader in the Fourth Gospel* (SBLDS 82; Atlanta: Scholars Press, 1988), and the essays in *Reader Perspectives on the New Testament*, ed. Edgar V. McKnight, *Semeia* 48 (1989).

[3] Gérard Genette, *Narrative Discourse: An Essay in Method* (Ithaca: Cornell University Press, 1980) 27.

[4] That the gospels are first and foremost stories is emphasized by Frank Kermode, who argues against foregrounding of the source-critical enterprise by suggesting that "the critic who attends to the story rather than to some lost narrative it replaced perhaps is attending to the first requirement of the Gospels." See Kermode, "John," *The Literary Guide to the Bible* (ed. Robert Alter and Frank Kermode; Cambridge: Harvard University Press, 1987) 441–42.

[5] Genette, *Narrative Discourse*, 27. One could also use Chatman's distinction between discourse (the narrative) and story, although this terminology would be confusing in the

a plot, that is, a sequence of actions "rendered" toward achieving particular emotional and artistic effects."[6] Although the plot of the Fourth Gospel's story of Jesus can be described and charted in many different ways,[7] its central element is the conflict between hero—Jesus—and villain—Jesus' opponents—over Jesus' identity, a conflict which reaches its climax and resolution in the Passion. The death of Jesus expresses the antagonists' ultimate rejection of his claims, and hence the failure of Jesus' attempts to persuade them otherwise. Jesus' death evokes sorrow in his followers (20:1) and also, potentially, in the readers, until it is dramatically reversed by his resurrection appearances in chapter 20. The markers within the text that signal this plot are the characters named and described within the gospel and the actions attributed to them, as well as geographical and temporal details that root the plot in space and time.

This narrative content, or story, may be said to constitute a historical tale, for two reasons. First, its setting—early first-century C.E. Palestine—is that of the historical Jesus. Second, though episodic (20:30) and dramatic, it is meant to be read as a "true" account of events which really happened. This is emphasized by the narrator, who in 21:24 expresses his[8] concern that the readers consider as true the testimony of "the disciple who is testifying to these things and has written them...."[9] The historical tale is accessible to all readers of the Fourth Gospel and might be described as the primary "signified" or content towards which the gospel as signifier is generally thought to point.

But even a first reading of this gospel raises the suspicion that it does more than tell a historical tale. For example, there are details which, though clearly part of the historical tale told by the gospel, may seem out of context in the life of the historical Jesus himself. These include references to the exclusion of Jesus' followers from the synagogue (9:22; 16:2), an event which is generally dated to the latter part of the first century, at least fifty years after the crucifixion event. Raymond E. Brown[10] and J. Louis Martyn,[11] among others, drew on such details and other features of the gospel to read a second story in the Johannine narrative. This is the story of the Johannine community at the end of the first century C.E. in the Greek Diaspora.[12] This story too has a plot, which revolves around the conflict between the Johannine community and the synagogue in its city over issues of belief and unbelief. Because its setting is the life of the Johannine church, this story may be called an ecclesiological tale.

The historical tale is perceived by means of a realistic reading of the gospel narrative, in which, for example, the signifier "Jesus" in the narrative is taken to signify the character Jesus in the story, the "disciples" in the narrative signify Jesus' disciples in the story, and so on. In contrast, the ecclesiological tale is perceived by means of what may be termed a representational reading of the narrative text. For example, the signifier "Jesus" in the narrative is taken to represent the Christian preacher in the ecclesiological tale; the "disciples" are thought to represent the post-Easter Johannine community; the "Jews" represent the late first-century synagogue in conflict with the church.[13]

In fact, it may be suggested that for readers interested in the gospel for what it reveals about the Johannine community, the historical tale itself becomes a signifier, with the ecclesiological tale as its narrative content. The encounter between Jesus and the Samaritans, signified by the narrative in John 4, for example, in turn signifies the acceptance of Samaritan believers into the Johannine community.[14] The experience of Jesus and his followers in the historical tale signifies the experience of the community. Hence the conflict between Jesus and the Jews in John 9 can be read as a paradigm for the strained relations between Johannine Christians and their Jewish antagonists after the expulsion of Jewish Christians from the synagogue.[15] The words of the Johannine

---

[6] M. H. Abrams, A Glossary of Literary Terms (3d ed.; New York: Holt, Rinehart and Winston, 1971) 127. For a list of other definitions, see Culpepper, 79–80.

[7] For a brief survey of the ways in which the plot or structure has been described, see Fernando F. Segovia, "The Journey(s) of the Word of God: A Reading of the Plot of the Fourth Gospel," The Fourth Gospel From a Literary Perspective, ed. R. Alan Culpepper and Fernando F. Segovia, Semeia 53 (1991) 26–31.

[8] Although we do not know the identity of the "real" author, the implied author of the gospel is the Beloved Disciple, hence the use of the masculine pronoun. This does not necessarily mean that the "real" author was male, but in my view this is likely, despite the fact that, as scholars have noted, the Fourth Gospel places stories about women at crucial points in the narrative. See Elisabeth Schüssler Fiorenza, In Memory of Her (New York: Crossroad, 1986) 326, and AB 1.xcii–xcviii.

[9] Cf. also 19:35. All quotations are from the New Revised Standard Version (1989), unless otherwise noted.

[10] Raymond E. Brown, The Community of the Beloved Disciple (New York: Paulist, 1979).

[11] J. Louis Martyn, History and Theology in the Fourth Gospel (2d ed.; Nashville: Abingdon, 1979). For a recent discussion and summary of the state of the question, see John Ashton, Understanding the Fourth Gospel (Oxford: Clarendon, 1991) 166–74.

[12] For a discussion of provenance, see AB 1.ciii–civ.

[13] This is Martyn's reading of John 9. See Martyn, History, 37–62.

[14] Brown, Community, 36–40.

[15] Martyn, History, 29–30, 38–62, 156–7; Brown, Community, 22; compare Reuven Kimelman, "Birkat Ha-Minim and the Lack of Evidence for an Anti-Christian Jewish Prayer in Late Antiquity," Jewish and Christian Self-Definition (ed. E. P. Sanders; Philadelphia: Fortress, 1981) 2.226–55, 391–403.

Jesus, while directed to a specific audience within the narrative, are taken to address the situation of the Johannine community.[16] In this way, says Martyn, "The text is also a witness to Jesus' powerful presence in actual events experienced by the Johannine church."[17] If the historical tale is the primary tale told by the narrative text, the ecclesiological tale may be labeled the sub-tale which moves beneath its surface.

Rich as these two tales are, however, they do not exhaust the levels of the narrative content of the Fourth Gospel. Rather, specific hints in the gospel intimate that its story goes well beyond the temporal and geographical boundaries of the historical and ecclesiological tales. These hints appear as early as 1:1, those famous words with which our gospel begins: "In the beginning was the Word, and the Word was with God, and the Word was God." This passage, and many others like it, point to the presence of yet another story in this gospel, with its own set of dramatis personae and its particular emotional impact upon the reader. This tale has the cosmos as its setting and eternity as its time frame. Its hero is the pre-existent Word who becomes flesh, having been sent by God his Father into the world to bring salvation. The villain is the "ruler of this world" (14:30), "the evil one" (17:15), Satan (13:27), or the devil (8:44; 13:2).[18] As in the historical tale, the struggle between hero and villain reaches its climax in the Passion narrative. The death of Jesus on the cross marks not his failure but his success: it signifies the successful completion of his mission, the "casting out" of the ruler of this world (12:31), and the beginning of the hero's return to his Father from whom he had come forth. The appropriate emotional response to this death is not sorrow but joy (16:20). Furthermore, Jesus' death and departure from the world is not a rupture in the relationship between Jesus and his followers, but rather a new phase, marked by the presence of the paraclete, whom Jesus will send after his departure (16:7).

Because of its cosmic setting, this sequence of events may be said to constitute a cosmological tale, in no sense less "true" than the historical and ecclesiological tales. The cosmological tale intersects and parallels the historical and ecclesiological tales at many points. Indeed, it may be said that the cosmological tale provides the narrative framework into which the other tales are set. The two- to three-year time span of Jesus' earthly mission—the "story time" of the historical tale—and the period of the Johannine church—the "story-time" of the ecclesiological tale—are placed in the continuum of the Word's pre-existence with God and the eventual return of the Word and his disciples to God's realm, that is, the "story time" of the cosmological tale.[19] The geographical settings of the historical and ecclesiological tales, namely, Palestine (including Judea, Samaria and Galilee) and the Diaspora respectively, have their place in the cosmos, the geographical setting of the cosmological tale. Furthermore, the three tales intersect at many different points. To give just one example, the Jewish villains of the historical tale are spiritual kin not only to the messengers who informed the Jewish community in John's city of the Jamnian decision to exclude Christians from the synagogue, or to the members of the local Gerousia who enforced this decision,[20] but also to the diabolical villain of the cosmological tale (cf. 8:44).[21]

These observations suggest that the cosmological tale is the meta-tale, which provides the overarching temporal, geographical, theological, and narrative framework for the other two tales. The cosmological tale shares certain features of the other two tales. Like the historical tale, it reads the gospel narrative realistically. The "Jesus" of the narrative does not signify or represent someone other than the Jesus of the historical tale. Rather, the Jesus of the historical tale is seen to *be* the very Word of the cosmological tale. The physical and temporal setting of the historical tale is not representative of another place and time, as in an ecclesiological reading of the gospel, but rather is situated in the larger context of the cosmos, according to the cosmological tale. Like the ecclesiological tale, however, the cosmological tale constitutes an implicit commentary on the historical tale; as such, it adds depth and texture to the gospel narrative and richness to the reading experience.

That there is a narrative schema with cosmic dimensions operative in the Fourth Gospel has not gone completely unnoticed by Johannine scholars. Indeed, this point has been developed in detail by Rudolf Bultmann, who saw its origins in a Gnostic myth of the Redeemer.[22] But whereas Bultmann, his

---

[16] The two stories are linked not only through parallelism but also through the signifier "Beloved Disciple." This signifier in the narrative text points to Jesus' favorite disciple in the historical tale, the one who reclined next to him at the last supper (13:23, 25) and to whom Jesus gave over the care of his mother (19:27). The analysis of Brown (*Community*, 31–34, 89) suggests that the "Beloved Disciple," unlike other signifiers in the Fourth Gospel, is to be understood as the same signified within the ecclesiological tale as within the historical tale. That is, the same person who was Jesus' favored disciple within the historical tale was the founder or leader of the Johannine community.
[17] Martyn, *History*, 30.
[18] Cf. C. J. Coetzee, "Christ and the Prince of this World in the Gospel and the Epistles of St. John," *Neot* 2 (1968) 104–21.

[19] For a definition and discussion of "story-time," see Genette, *Narrative Discourse*, 33–35; Culpepper, 53–75.
[20] This is according to Martyn, *History*, 61.
[21] This is seen also in 13:27, in which Judas, the agent of Jesus' betrayal in the historical tale, is directly associated with Satan, who entered into him.
[22] See Rudolf Bultmann, *Theology of the New Testament* (New York: Charles Scribner's Sons, 1955), Vol. 2, Part III; also his commentary, passim. The relationship between cosmology and

supporters, and his detractors argued about the implications of this myth for historical and source criticism of the Fourth Gospel,[23] only recently have scholars begun to pay attention to its role in the narrative and its impact on the reader. Robert Kysar, for example, comments that John's story of Jesus "is indeed a story of a human on the plane of history; but it is at the same time the story of one who comes from beyond the world and from the beginning of all existence."[24] Fernando Segovia has argued that the "mythological, cosmic journey" of the Word of God provides a framework for the other journeys which structure the plot of this gospel.[25] These works and others which touch on aspects of the cosmological tale[26] suggest the need for a more comprehensive study of the cosmological tale, its place and function in the gospel narrative, and its utilization by the implied reader constructing a coherent reading of the gospel as a whole. It is to this need that the present study is addressed.

Before commencing, however, it will be useful to define the key terms, assumptions, and aims which will inform our study. We shall assume the objective existence of a real reader—a flesh and blood person engaged in the act of reading—and a real text, namely the Fourth Gospel, as found in the critical edition of Nestle-Aland.[27] Furthermore, we shall consider this gospel to be a work of fiction, a "self-consciously crafted narrative...resulting from literary imagination."[28] Although the possibility that the Fourth Gospel may contain historical data should not be dismissed, this issue is not germane to the present study. Finally, taking our cue from Seymour Chatman,[29] we shall assume that this text contains three literary constructs accessible to the real reader.

The first is the implied author. The implied author is the image of the author which readers construct as they read the gospel and to whom they attribute the literary strategies of the narrative. In the gospels, the voice of the implied author is that of the narrator who tells the story and speaks to the reader.[30] The attribution of the gospels to the four evangelists, which usually heads any version or translation of the gospel texts which readers are likely to read, also implies an identification of the narrators as the evangelists.[31] Hence the terms evangelist, narrator, and implied author can all be used to refer to aspects of the image of the author to whom the reader attributes the narrative elements and techniques of the text.[32]

The second is the narrative content or story. As a narrative text, the Fourth Gospel tells its story by means of its narration of particular events that follow one another in a particular sequence. The story has an independent existence apart from the narrative only in the mind of the reader, and may be constructed by different real readers in different ways.[33]

The third is the implied reader. Like the implied author and the story, the implied reader exists only in the mind of the real reader and, in the case of the Fourth Gospel, may be identified with, or identical to, the narratees, the party to whom the narrator is addressing his or her words.[34] The implied readers may be reconstructed from the text as those who are capable of understanding the text, its language, its devices, and its message. Hence the implied reader may be defined as the image of the intended reader which a real reader constructs in reading the text.[35]

---

apocalyptic is discussed by Barnabas Lindars, "The Apocalyptic Myth and the Death of Christ," BJRL 57 (1974–5) 366–87. Although Lindars focuses primarily on the Synoptic gospels, many of his comments are applicable to the Fourth Gospel as well.

[23] See Schnack. 1.543–57.
[24] Robert Kysar, *John's Story of Jesus* (Philadelphia: Fortress, 1984) 18.
[25] Segovia, "Journey," 23–54.
[26] See, for example, Godfrey C. Nicholson, *Death as Departure* (SBLDS 63; Chico, Calif.: Scholars Press, 1983); Karl Martin Fischer, "Der johanneische Christus und der gnostische Erlöser," *Gnosis und Neues Testament* (ed. Karl-Wolfgang Troeger; Berlin: Gerd Mohn, 1973) 235–266; Wayne A. Meeks "The Man from Heaven in Johannine Sectarianism," JBL 91 (1972) 44–72 (reprinted in Ashton, 141–73); M. de Jonge, *Jesus: Stranger from Heaven and Son of God* (SBLSBS 11; Missoula, Mont.: Scholars Press, 1977); D. Bruce Woll, *Johannine Christianity in Conflict* (SBLDS 60; Chico, Calif.: Scholars Press, 1981).
[27] *Novum Testamentum Graece* (26th ed.; Stuttgart: Deutsche Bibelstiftung, 1979).
[28] These words, which Mary Ann Tolbert has applied to the Gospel of Mark, apply equally well to the Fourth Gospel and, no doubt, to the First and Third Gospels as well. See Tolbert, *Sowing the Gospel: Mark's World in Literary-Historical Perspective* (Minneapolis: Fortress, 1989).
[30] For more detailed discussion on scripture as fiction, see Robert Alter, *The Art of Biblical Narrative* (New York: Basic, 1981) 24–27.

[29] Chatman, *Story and Discourse*, 146–51.
[30] Culpepper, 16.
[31] See Culpepper (213), who at times uses the terms narrator and evangelist interchangeably. The identification of the narrator with the evangelist is especially clear in the Gospel of Luke, in which the narrator provides a rationale in the first person for the writing of his narrative (Luke 1:1–4).
[32] In using the term "evangelist" in this sense, however, it is important to keep in mind that the reference is not to the evangelist as a historical person but to the image of the evangelist that the reader would construct through a reading of the gospel narrative. For discussion of the issue of authorship, see AB 1.lxxxvii–ciii. For detailed discussion of the term "implied author," cf. Culpepper, 15–16.
[33] See Wolfgang Iser, *The Implied Reader* (Baltimore: The Johns Hopkins University Press, 1974) 279.
[34] Culpepper, 208. Note, however, that the identity of the implied reader and narratee is not to be assumed in the case of other texts, such as the Gospel of Luke, in which the narratee is Theophilus, but the implied reader is likely not a single individual but rather a community.
[35] For an introduction to the multiplicity of readers, see Gerald Prince, "Introduction to the Study of the Narratee," *Reader-Response Criticism: From Formalism to Post-structuralism* (ed.

The present study will therefore examine the ways in which one construct of the Fourth Gospel, namely, the implied reader, would derive a second construct, the story or stories embodied in the Johannine narrative, in order to discern the intentions of the third construct, the implied author. Its focus will therefore be on the activity of the implied reader. But who is this implied reader and what does he/she do?

Many scholars have tried, whether explicitly or implicitly, to identify the implied readers of the Fourth Gospel in their attempts to label the original real readers whom the real author meant to address in writing this gospel.[36] Such attempts focus on what, according to the gospel, the readers are expected and not expected to know, and examine assumptions that are apparently held in common by implied author and implied reader.[37]

One key to the identity of the implied reader is 20:30–31:

Now Jesus did many other signs in the presence of the disciples, which are not written in this book. But these are written so that you may come to believe [πιστευσητε] [or: may continue to believe—πιστευητε] that Jesus is the Messiah [Christ], the Son of God, and that through believing you may have life in his name.

The textual variant in 20:31 casts some doubt as to whether the addressees are already Christians whom the implied author wishes to edify and strengthen in their faith, or non-Christians whom the implied author aims to persuade. Many scholars argue, however, that in the context of the gospel as a whole, it is the former who are the primary addressees of this gospel.[38] Furthermore, it would seem that these addressees were not themselves eye-witnesses to the life of the historical Jesus. Rather, they formed part of a community, probably the community of the evangelist himself, which belonged to the era after the death and resurrection of Christ.[39]

This conclusion can be supported from evidence throughout the Fourth Gospel narrative.[40] It is important to note, however, that the gospel in general, and 20:30–31 in particular, do not explicitly limit their intended audience to a specific community. Rather, they suggest an open definition of the implied readers as those who see themselves as being personally addressed by the verbs in 20:30–31 which are in the second person plural: "you may believe" [πιστευητε], "you may have life" [ζωην εχητε] "in his name." Such a general definition creates an opening for the real reader to identify with the implied reader. That is, any reader who is open to the message of the gospel and takes seriously the implied author's statement of purpose in 20:30–31 may in fact see himself or herself as being directly addressed by the gospel narrative as well as challenged by its theological perspective.[41] Hence the particular narrative techniques and elements of the text, including the multi-layered narrative itself, will affect not only the implied readers but all of the real readers who identify with them.

In addition to defining who "readers" are, reader-response critics attempt to describe what readers do, that is, the moves the readers make in constructing meaning from, or finding meaning in, the text.[42] Perhaps the most fundamental of these is the observation that the reader will strive to come up with a harmonious or coherent interpretation or reading of the text.[43] As Wolfgang Iser notes, the reader is engaged in

---

Jane P. Tompkins; Baltimore: Johns Hopkins, 1980) 7–25. Prince uses the term "virtual reader" for Iser's implied reader. For a discussion of "gaps," see Iser, *Implied Reader*, 274–80.

36 An identification of the real "original" reader and the implied reader is assumed by many studies of the addressee and purpose of the gospel. For summaries of the various positions, see Culpepper, 211, and Robert Kysar, *The Fourth Evangelist and his Gospel* (Minneapolis: Augsburg, 1975) 147–65.

37 Culpepper, 212.

38 The major manuscripts supporting the present subjunctive are Bezae, Alexandrinus and those of the Byzantine tradition. The aorist subjunctive is supported by Vaticanus, Sinaiticus, and possibly also P66. This reading is followed in Nestle's critical edition. Harald Riesenfeld ("Zu den johanneischen ἵνα-Sätzen," ST 19 [1965] 220) suggests that the normal usage of the ἵνα clause is the present subjunctive, a conclusion which would tend to support the theory that the Gospel is directed towards Christians. It must be pointed out, however, that theories of purpose cannot be hung on this point alone, both because the gospel is not consistent in its use of tenses, and also because the aorist subjunctive does not necessarily have to have a future connotation. See Rudolf Schnackenburg, "Die Messiasfrage im Johannesevangelium," *Neutestamentliche Aufsätze: Festschrift für Josef Schmid* (ed. Josef Blinzler; Regensburg: Pustet, 1963) 257; AB 2.1056.

39 For a recent look at the purpose of the gospel, see D. A. Carson, "The Purpose of the Fourth Gospel: John 20:31 Reconsidered," *JBL* 106 (1987) 639–51. Carson concludes that, contrary to the opinion of most recent scholarship, the gospel may in fact have an evangelistic intent.

40 See Brown, *Community*, 13–24.

41 Similar inclusion of the implied readers and those real readers who see themselves as addressed by the gospel is to be found in 4:48, which castigates not only the centurion but "you," plural [ζητε] for requiring signs and wonders in order to believe, and in 20:29, in which Jesus gently rebukes Thomas, "Have you believed because you have seen me? Blessed are those who have not seen and yet believe."

42 For a good summary of these moves, see Steven Mailloux, "Learning to Read: Interpretation and Reader-Response Criticism," *Studies in the Literary Imagination* 12 (1979) 93–108; Mailloux, *Rhetorical Power* (Ithaca: Cornell University Press, 1989) 39–53.

43 Iser is challenged on this point by Terry Eagleton, who labels this notion an "arbitrary prejudice." Where Iser appears, to the present reader, to be making a statement concerning the psychology of reading ("readers strive for coherence"), Eagleton accuses him of delivering an

the process of grouping together all the different aspects of a text to form the consistency that the reader will always be in search of. While expectations may be continually modified, and images continually expanded, the reader will still strive, even if unconsciously, to fit everything together in a consistent pattern.[44]

In their efforts at consistency building, readers, implied and real, utilize two sets of data in responding to and making sense of a given text.[45] They use data intrinsic to the text, following the clues of the text in order to fill in the gaps between words, sentences, paragraphs, chapters, and ideas within the text. They also bring extrinsic data to the text, including cultural, linguistic, biographical, and other information from outside the world of the text.[46] These extrinsic data contribute to the "horizon of expectations" which the implied reader (as well as the real reader) will bring to the text. Although the horizon of expectations is not controlled by the implied author, that author, through the narrative itself, can manipulate, frustrate, or modify it in order to create an effect on the reader.[47]

Although both real and implied readers apply intrinsic and extrinsic data to their readings, a real reader will not read the text in the same way that the implied reader is expected to do. On the contrary, a given real reader's reading, while using the same intrinsic data as are available to the implied reader and perhaps even identifying with the implied reader, will depend to some degree on the purpose for which he or she is reading the text, as well as on the specific extrinsic data which he or she brings to bear on a reading of the text. For example, many Christian readers of the gospels are interested in deriving some guidance for their lives in the present.[48] On the other hand, Jewish readers may be interested in learning about the symbols and images used by their Christian friends, or in investigating the issue of anti-Judaism in the gospels.[49]

When New Testament exegetes read the text, it is often with a view to determining the "meaning" of the text for its original audience. This entails, whether explicitly or implicitly, the process of reconstructing the way in which the implied readers might have read the text, that is, filled in the gaps left by the narrator/implied author. This task in itself points out yet another kind of gap, which is the very real distance in time, space, and cultural milieu, which exists between the exegete and the implied reader inscribed in the gospel narratives. This last gap, perhaps more appropriately, this gulf, places the reader-response critical enterprise, as often practiced in the field of New Testament studies, in the service of historical-critical concerns.[50] Not only do these texts, and their implied authors, draw on the literary conventions, symbols, and norms of another age and another time to convey a message to the implied readers, but those readers would do the same in decoding, that is, in reading and receiving the message of, the texts. The exegete attempts to take on the role of the implied reader as a receptor and decoder of the signals of the implied author encoded in the text.[51] In doing so, however, he or she also interacts with the work of other scholars, and generally attempts to set his or her work in the context of contemporary New Testament scholarship. The norms, assumptions, and language of scholarship therefore become elements in the extrinsic data which the exegete uses to interpret the gospels, even while the exegete is trying—whether implicitly or explicitly[52]—to reconstruct the implied reader's reading of the text at hand.

---

[44] Iser, *Implied Reader*, 283.
[45] Ibid, 284.
[46] It is the ever-presence of extrinsic data—information, biases, points of view—which readers inevitably bring to the text which is responsible for "subjectivity," an element which reader-response critics, as well as other sorts of literary critics, have difficulty taking into account. For one critic's attempt to do so, see Stanley Fish, *Is there a Text in this Class?* (Cambridge: Harvard University Press, 1980) 1–17.
[47] For discussion of "horizon of expectations," see Hans Robert Jauss, "Literary History as a Challenge to Literary Theory," *New Literary History* 2 (1970–71) 7–31, and *idem*, "Theses on the Transition from the Aesthetics of Literary Works to a Theory of Aesthetic Experience," *Interpretation of Narrative* (ed. Mario J. Valdés and Owen Miller; Toronto: University of Toronto Press, 1978) 140–41.
[48] For example, see Thomas Boomershine, *Story Journey: An Invitation to the Gospel as Storytelling* (Nashville: Abingdon, 1988).
[49] See Samuel Sandmel, *Anti-Semitism in the New Testament?* (Philadelphia: Fortress, 1978); Adele Reinhartz, "The New Testament and Anti-Judaism: A Literary-Critical Approach," *JES* 25 (1988) 524–37.
[50] Moore (*Literary Criticism*, 72), suggests that "recent literary exegesis of the Gospels...has found this reader-in-the text approach especially congenial." For this reason, "New Testament reader-response criticism is a more narrowly focused and more unified phenomenon than its nonbiblical counterpart."
[51] This is impossible to do in any complete way, as it is difficult if not impossible for modern readers, including exegetes, to put aside completely their own concerns and reading strategies. This may be part of what underlies the view of Iser (*The Implied Reader*, xii), who sees the implied reader as a blend between the reader inherent in the text and the real reader who responds to the text. He states that "this term incorporates both the prestructuring of the potential meaning by the text, and the reader's actualization of this potential through the reading process."
[52] This focus on the implied reader, in his or her guise as the intended audience, is not the exclusive province of reader-response critics. Rather, the entire corpus of New Testament

authoritarian instruction to the readers, that they "*must* construct the text so as to render it internally consistent" (emphasis added). For Eagleton's critique of Iser and other reader-response critics, see his *Literary Theory: An Introduction* (Oxford: Basil Blackwell, 1983) 61–90.

The present study of the Gospel of John will focus primarily on intrinsic data, that is, on the clues provided within the gospel itself. This is not done out of imitation of New Critics, who see every text as a closed entity requiring no outside information for its interpretation.[53] Rather, this focus on the text reflects what Wayne Meeks has called "the self-referring quality of the whole Gospel, [which is a] closed system of metaphors."[54] In making sense of this closed world, the real reader, to a certain degree at least, is on the same footing as the implied reader, since both must rely primarily on the information gleaned from the text itself.

Furthermore, although the narrative sequence of the gospel, that is, the order in which ideas, events, and metaphors are presented, is important for its interpretation and will be one of the principal elements of the narrative used by readers to construct coherent meaning,[55] the gospel itself leaves the way open for a holistic reading as well. Whereas in a first reading the readers' expectations are continually challenged and revised as they proceed sequentially through the text, upon rereading the same text, readers are influenced not only by the narrative sequence but also by material from the text as a whole.

While some genres, such as mystery novels, are aimed primarily at the first-time reader, the gospels are intended by their implied authors to be read and reread many times. This is surmised from the fact that in almost every case the reader is given information at the end of the gospel which prompts a re-evaluation of the entire gospel.[56] In the case of the Fourth Gospel, this information is found in 20:30-31.

These verses are not only a fitting conclusion to a sequential reading of the gospel[57] but also serve as an invitation to reread the gospel in light of the perspective expressed in them.[58] Although the narrator has provided clues regarding the "correct" interpretation of the signs narratives throughout the course of his narration, in 20:30-31 the reader is addressed directly and told of the implied author's reason for telling his story, namely, to encourage christological understanding, which leads to faith and eternal life. This perspective will inform the reader's second and subsequent encounters with the text. As Iser notes,

In every text there is a potential time sequence which the reader must inevitably realize, as it is impossible to absorb even a short text in a single moment. Thus the reading process always involves viewing the text through a perspective that is continually on the move, linking up the different phases, and so constructing what we have called the virtual dimension. This dimension, of course, varies all the time we are reading. However, when we have finished the text, and read it again, clearly our extra knowledge will result in a different time sequence; we shall tend to establish connections by referring to our awareness of what is to come, and so certain aspects of the text will assume a significance we did not attach to them on a first reading, while others will recede into the background.[59]

---

scholarship is testimony to the centrality, and the difficulty, of this endeavor. See, for example, Paul S. Minear, *John, The Martyr's Gospel* (New York: Pilgrims, 1984) 14–23.

[53] For an introduction to New Criticism, see Eagleton, *Literary Theory*, 47–53.

[54] Meeks, "Man from Heaven," 68. Although the generally self-referential nature of this gospel focuses attention on the gospel itself as the primary resource for the exegesis of a given passage, it also points beyond itself on occasion. There are clear references and allusions not only to biblical passages, but also to events and ideas which were apparently known from other sources, literary or non-literary. For example, 3:24 implies that the imprisonment of John the Baptist was common knowledge, though it is not recounted in this gospel. Similarly, 7:42 creates dramatic irony by referring to Bethlehem as the birthplace of the Messiah, another detail not mentioned in this gospel. Furthermore, many of the terms used in the gospel, while given particular Johannine definitions and nuances, were apparently part of the thought world shared by both author and intended audience. This is especially clear with regard to the christological titles such as Logos, Christ, Son of Man, Son of God, Prophet, and King of Israel. In exegeting the Fourth Gospel, many scholars do take seriously the extra-Johannine background, but give precedence to intra-textual factors. See, for example, Schnackenburg, "Excursus III: The Titles of Jesus in John 1," Schnack. 1.507-14.

[55] On the importance of sequential reading, see Iser, *Implied Reader*, 278.

[56] See Mark 16:1–9, in which the "messianic secret" is finally revealed, Matt 28:20, in which the Risen Lord asks his disciples to teach others "to observe all that I have commanded you," including, presumably, Jesus' commandments as recorded in the First Gospel, and Luke 24:45, in which the Risen Lord opens the minds of his disciples to understand the scriptures, as well as Jesus' words (24:44). In these passages, the messages imparted to characters within the narratives affect the implied readers, who can now reread the texts in the light of their new insight.

[57] In this study we will accept the viewpoint of a majority of Johannine scholars that chapter 21 is an epilogue to the body of the text. See AB 2.1077–82 for detailed discussion. Since the gospel apparently did not circulate without chapter 21, however, it would have been read by the implied readers and utilized in making sense of the gospel as a whole. This would not, however, detract from the force of 20:30-31 as the conclusion and statement of purpose conveyed by the implied author to the implied reader. Indeed, the concluding verse of chapter 21 would not replace 20:30-31 but, by repeating that the function of the book was to record a selection of Jesus' acts, would rather serve to remind the reader of the earlier passage.

[58] This would have been reinforced by the liturgy, if the gospels were already read during worship at this time. For a historical survey of the role of the Bible in liturgy, see S. J. P. van Dijk, "The Bible in Liturgical Use," *The Cambridge History of the Bible* (ed. G. W. H. Lampe; Cambridge: Cambridge University Press, 1969) 2.220–52.

[59] Iser, *Implied Reader*, 280–81.

The study will begin in chapter one by looking in detail at the cosmological tale as it comes to expression in this gospel. The tale will be reconstructed on the basis of the clues or signals of the gospel narrative, and its identity as a tale will be explored. Chapter two will examine the role of the cosmological tale in the narrative strategy of the Johannine narrator as well as its effect on the reader. The remainder of the study will focus on one particular passage as a more detailed test case of the way in which the implied reader may have used the cosmological tale as an interpretive key. The passage is the παροιμία (*paroimia*)—cryptic discourse or riddle—of the Shepherd and the Sheep in John 10:1–5. Accordingly, the third chapter will provide a survey of scholarly attempts to solve this riddle, most of which have understood it in the context of the historical and/or ecclesiological tales. The fourth chapter will develop a cosmological reading of the passage based on clues within the Fourth Gospel. The study will conclude by examining the implications of the study for our understanding of Johannine literary technique on the one hand, and the historical situation of the implied audience on the other. Finally, in an appendix, we will examine relevant material from outside the gospel which may provide insight into some of the extrinsic data which implied readers may have brought to their reading of the *paroimia*.

There are other indications of the implied author's anticipation of multiple readings of the text on the part of the implied reader. In 11:2, for example, the reader is told of an event—Mary's anointing of Jesus—which is described in chapter 12. Furthermore, the gospel emphasizes at several points that even the disciples did not understand the full import of Jesus' words upon first hearing them. In 2:22, we are told that the saying of Jesus recorded in 2:19 ("Destroy this temple, and in three days I will raise it up") was remembered, and presumably understood, by the disciples only after Jesus' resurrection. The comprehension of Jesus' words will also be aided by the paraclete, who, according to 14:26, "will...remind you of all that I have said to you." If the disciples, who had the privilege of being eye-witnesses to the works and words of Jesus, did not comprehend everything first time around (cf. 16:28-29), surely the implied readers of the gospel would not have been expected to do so. For this reason, while attention will be paid in the present study to sequential features of the text, material will not be considered out of narrative sequence as well.

As a real reader, what I offer in this study is my own reading, my own attempt to reconstruct the reading experience of the implied reader as it pertains to the gospel story. The study will of necessity have points of contact with both formalism, because of its focus on constructs inherent in the text itself, and historical criticism, since it is concerned primarily with the implied reader and only secondarily with a specialized group of contemporary readers of this ancient text, namely New Testament exegetes. Yet it is unrealistic and artificial to attempt to isolate reader-response criticism from other kinds of concerns. Indeed, it would seem that one of the important contributions of reader-response criticism to New Testament studies is a greater clarity on the reading strategies not only of ancient readers but of contemporary readers including New Testament exegetes themselves. Included among these strategies is the necessity to construct and engage the implied reader in the course of one's reading and exegesis of the text. As Stephen Moore suggests, "to read any literary text...is always in some sense to read through its reader construct, to dialogue with it, and through it to dialogue with its author construct."[60] For this reason, the reading of the implied reader, which is the focus of the present and many other reader-oriented gospel studies, should not be seen in contrast to the readings of contemporary readers, but rather as one of the factors constitutive of those readings.

It is my hope that the reading which I offer in these pages will help to illuminate the attempts of other readers to read this most enigmatic of gospels in a meaningful way.

---

60 Stephen Moore, *Literary Criticism*, 72.

1

Why John Calls Jesus "the Word"

Introduction

This book depends entirely on, and argues for, the view that John's decision to call Jesus "the Word," the Logos (ὁ λόγος), was influenced by the Targums, the Aramaic translations of the Hebrew Scriptures, many or most of which were prepared for recitation in the synagogue after the reading of the Hebrew text. In hundreds of cases in these Targums, where the MT refers to God, the corresponding Targum passage refers to the divine *Word*. Considered against this background, calling Jesus "the Word" is a way of identifying him with the God of Israel. This book also argues that understanding the Logos title as based on the Targums is crucial to understanding not only John's Prologue, but the body of the Gospel as well, for if we understand the Logos as a divine title, we can see that John's statements about the Word (the Word was with God, the Word was God, and the Word became flesh) presage themes throughout the Gospel.

My reader is probably more familiar with other explanations for the Logos title: (1) that it is based on "the word of the LORD" in the OT, through which God reveals himself and accomplishes his will in the world, just as he does through his Son in the NT; (2) that it is developed from the idea of Wisdom personified in the OT and in the intertestamental Wisdom literature, and (3) that it is adapted from the Greek philosophical concept of the Logos, especially as found in the writings of the Alexandrian Jew Philo. Each of these views is plausible, and each is described in the next section. A fourth view, Bultmann's gnostic hypothesis, is not considered plausible and will not be discussed here.[1]

Three Plausible Proposals

OT Word of the Lord

In the first view, the OT or use of "the word of the LORD" (דְּבַר־יהוה) is considered sufficient to explain John's use of "the Word" for Christ. For instance, C. H.

---

[1] For a refutation of the gnostic view, see Craig A. Evans, *Word and Glory: On the Exegetical and Theological Background of John's Prologue* (JSNTSup 89; Sheffield: JSOT Press, 1993).

Dodd, though an advocate of the third view, nevertheless noted that there is "a very strong case to be made out, stronger than has sometimes been recognized, for the view that the Logos of the Prologue is the [OT] Word of the LORD."² Likewise, William Hendriksen wrote, "Already in the Old Testament the Word of God is represented as a Person", citing Ps 33:6, which can be related to John 1:1 ("by the word of the LORD the heavens were made").³ In addition, Donald A. Carson suggested that John chose the title as fitting Christ's work of revelation, to which he was uniquely suited, being the only one to have been to heaven; he paraphrases John 1:1, "In the beginning God expressed himself." Carson contends that God's word is so important in the OT in creation, revelation, and deliverance; that John 1:1 ("In the beginning") alludes directly to Gen 1, where the phrase "and God said" is so prominent that this word is sometimes personified (e.g., Ps 107:20). All this makes "it suitable for John to apply [the Word] as a title to God's ultimate self-disclosure, the person of his own Son."⁴

Franklin W. Young pointed to Isa 55:10–11 as an attractive possibility for an OT or background to Christ as God's Word, with a focus more on agency:

> As the rain and the snow *come down* from heaven, And do not return there without watering the earth, . . . and furnishing . . . *bread to the eater*, So shall *my word* be which *goes forth* from my mouth; It shall *not return to me empty, without accomplishing what I desire*.⁵

Young noted that one could view "my word" here as a description of Christ's work as described in John 6: he came down from heaven to do the Father's will (v. 38); he is the bread upon whom people must feed to have life (vv. 48, 50); and he will not return until he accomplishes the Father's will (v. 44). The LXX for "accomplish" in Isa 55:11 is a form of συντελέω, which Young compares to the Lord's final saying on the cross, "It is finished" (τετέλεσται; John 19:30).⁶ The LXX of Isa 55:10 has ῥῆμα for "word," but λόγος could have been used just as well, and John does not necessarily use the LXX for his OT citations and allusions.⁷

Delbert Burkett gave further support for this view by relating John 7:34, "You will seek me but will not find me . . ." (similarly 8:21) to Amos 8:11–12, which predicts a famine for hearing the words of the LORD: "They will wander from sea to sea . . . to seek the word of the LORD, but they will not find it"⁸ This passage is especially striking in that the context indicates that the sign of the fulfillment of this judgment is that "I will make the sun go down at noon, and darken the earth in broad daylight" (Amos 8:9; cf. Matt 27:45; Mark 15:33; Luke 23:44). That John does not mention this darkening of the land does not necessarily count against this allusion if (as I assume) John's intended audience is already familiar with the synoptic tradition.

As impressive as Burkett's argument is, John 7:34 can also be used to furnish equally striking support for each of the other views to be discussed. Support for the notion that the Logos title is based on the OT "word of the LORD" can also be found in John 14:6, where Jesus calls himself "the truth" and later says that the Father's "word is truth" (17:17), echoing Ps 119:60, "the sum of your words is truth." Thus, "Jesus is the truth" implies "Jesus is the [OT] word."

Andreas J. Köstenberger offered four lines of support for the idea that the OT or word of the LORD is preferable to either Wisdom or Philo's Logos as a basis for the Logos title:

> (1) the evangelist's deliberate effort to echo the opening words of the Hebrew Scriptures by the phrase "in the beginning"; (2) the reappearance of several significant terms from Gen 1 in John 1 ("light," "darkness," "life"); (3) the Prologue's or allusions, be it to Israel's wilderness wanderings (1:14: "pitched his tent") or to the giving of the law (1:17–18); and (4) the evangelist's adaptation of Isa. 55:9–11 for his basic Christological framework.⁹

Wisdom in the Wisdom Literature

Interpreters have also made a reasonable case for the second view—that the idea of Wisdom as developed in Proverbs, Sirach, Baruch, and Wisdom of Solomon provides a possible background to John's Logos.¹⁰ Thomas H. Tobin, though an advocate of the third view, summarized the connection to Wisdom as follows:

> Both the logos of the hymn in the Prologue [of John] and wisdom in Jewish wisdom literature are with God in the beginning; both are involved in the creation of the world; both seek to find a place among humankind; both are within a Jewish tradition of speculation about the deeper meanings of the early chapters of Genesis. In addition, many of the parallels between the logos in the hymn and the figure of wisdom are found in passages which like the hymn are poetic in character (Prov 8:22–31; Sir 24). The parallels are not simply conceptual but also stylistic.¹¹

---

²C. H. Dodd, *The Interpretation of the Fourth Gospel* (Cambridge: Cambridge University Press, 1953), 273.

³William Hendriksen, *The Gospel of John* (Edinburgh: Banner of Truth Trust, 1954), 70.

⁴Donald A. Carson, *The Gospel according to John* (Grand Rapids: Eerdmans, 1991), 96, 115–16.

⁵Franklin W. Young, "A Study of the Relation of Isaiah to the Fourth Gospel," *ZNW* 46 (1955): 228.

⁶Ibid. Similarly, Delbert Burkett, *The Son of the Man in the Gospel of John* (JSNTSup 56; Sheffield: JSOT Press, 1991), 131–32.

⁷See Günter Reim, *Studien zum alttestamentlichen Hintergrund des Johannesevangeliums* (Cambridge: Cambridge University Press, 1974), 1–98, which studies or quotations in John as designated by the author. In these quotations John does not necessarily follow the LXX, and it follows that the same would hold for allusions, as we will see in ch. 2. Consider, for example, "full of grace and truth" in John 1:14, which depends on a non-LXX rendition of Exod 34:6.

⁸Burkett, *Son of the Man in the Gospel of John*, 151.

⁹Andreas J. Köstenberger, *John* (Baker Exegetical Commentary on the New Testament; Grand Rapids: Baker, 2004), 27.

¹⁰This view was initially proposed by J. Rendel Harris, *The Origin of the Prologue to St. John's Gospel* (Cambridge: Cambridge University Press, 1917).

¹¹Thomas H. Tobin, "Logos," *ABD* 4:354. Tobin made similar comments in an article "The Prologue of John and Hellenistic Jewish Speculation," *CBQ* 52 (1990): 252–69. As many

Especially of interest in connection with John 1:14 is Sirach's image of Wisdom as dwelling in a tent among men:

> I (Wisdom) dwelt in the highest heavens,
>   and my throne was in a pillar of cloud.
> Alone I compassed the vault of heaven
>   and traversed the depths of the abyss.
> Over waves of the sea, over all the earth,
>   and over every people and nation I have held sway.
> Among all these I sought a resting place;
>   in whose territory should I abide?
> "Then the Creator of all things gave me a command,
>   and my Creator chose the place for my tent.
> He said, 'Make your dwelling in Jacob,
>   and in Israel receive your inheritance.'" (Sir 24:4–8 NRSV)

"Dwelt" in v. 4 and "make your dwelling" in v. 8 are from κατασκηνόω, often used in the LXX to translate the Hebrew verb שָׁכַן, used for God's dwelling among his people. John 1:14 uses the similar verb σκηνόω. Likewise, "tent" in v. 8 is σκηνή, used in the LXX for the tabernacle. Similarities to John 1:14 are thus obvious. Of course, there is a major difference as well, since John says that all things were created through the Word, whereas in the wisdom passage, Wisdom is said to be "created" by "the Creator of all things."

Baruch 3:36–37 also is reminiscent of John 1:14: "(God) found the whole way to knowledge, and gave her to his servant Jacob and to Israel, whom he loved. Afterward she appeared on earth and lived [συνανεστρέφω] with humankind" (NRSV).

The view that John's Word depends on Wisdom in the Wisdom Literature has much in common with the view that the Logos title depends on the OT or word of God, since Wisdom is specifically equated with God's written word. Immediately following the quote just given about Wisdom living with humankind, we read of Wisdom, "She is the book of the commandments of God, the law that endures forever. All who hold her fast will live, and those who forsake her will die" (Bar 4:1 NRSV). Thus, Wisdom "appeared upon earth" as the Torah given to Israel.

In Proverbs the message of Wisdom is essentially the same as that of the Law and the Prophets: fear God, heed his commandments, and live. Craig Keener thinks that John combined the idea of Torah (OT or word in its most complete sense) and Wisdom to present Jesus as Torah, because his life exhibited perfect obedience to (thus was a revelation of) the Torah.[12]

In terms of the close verbal parallels to John's Prologue, the Wisdom background can be seen as an improvement over the OT or word background. There is

---

do, Tobin regards the sections of John's Prologue that mention the Logos as part of an originally independently circulating hymn to which some material was later added before it was incorporated in the Gospel.
[12] Craig S. Keener, *The Gospel of John: A Commentary* (2 vols.; Peabody, Mass.: Hendrickson, 2003), 360–63.

---

nothing as explicit as "and Wisdom became flesh," but Dodd notes that the fact that Wisdom is immanent among men "provides a kind of matrix in which the idea of incarnation might be shaped." In addition, he notes that the Wisdom literature comes closer to the proposition "the Word was God" because "the functions assigned to Wisdom are often clearly those which are elsewhere assigned to God Himself."[13] For example, while the passages quoted above speak of Wisdom dwelling among humankind (specifically, Israel), the OT speaks of the LORD himself dwelling among humankind.

Glory is an attribute of Wisdom, and Wisdom is associated with the glory of God (Wis 7:25; 9:11; Sir 14:27). Wisdom is also unique (Wis 7:22, using μονογενής as in John 1:14, 18), which leads Martin Scott to conclude, "Just as the glory of the unique Sophia is seen as she comes into the world, so too the glory of the unique Logos is seen as he comes among human beings as a human."[14] However, Wis 7:22 says that Wisdom has a *spirit* that is μονογενής, and there is no Wisdom text that uses phraseology anything like "the glory of the unique Wisdom is seen as she comes into the world."

Other texts in John could be used to support a personified Wisdom background to "the Word" in John. In 15:10, Jesus says, "If you keep my commandments, you will abide in my love." Because Jesus defines love for him as keeping his commandments (14:15, 21; 15:14), 15:10 could also be interpreted, "If you love me, you will abide in my love," agreeing with Prov 8:17, where Wisdom says, "I love those who love me, and those who diligently seek me shall find me." This last phrase could also be connected to John 7:34 ("You [the Jews] will seek me but will not find me"), the same verse Burkett connected to Amos 8:11–12 to support the OT or word view (see above). John 7:34 could support the view that outside the Prologue, the Gospel of John depicts Jesus as Wisdom; they will not find him because they do not seek diligently. Proverbs 14:6 makes a similar point about wisdom, though the verb "find" is not actually used: "The scornful seeks wisdom, but there is none." With Jesus understood as Wisdom, this verse would imply that they do not find him because they are scoffers (cf. Luke 16:14, where the Pharisees are scoffing at him).

While the personified Wisdom interpretation might be preferable to the OT word interpretation, as it accords better with the statement "the Word was God," it has the disadvantage that John uses "Word," not "Wisdom." The switch to "word" is sometimes explained as due to the avoidance of the feminine gender of the word "wisdom" (both in Greek and Hebrew, not to mention Aramaic). Further, "word" is an appropriate substitute for "wisdom" on the grounds that either (1) personified Wisdom is the wisdom of the OT or word or (2) Philo's Logos incorporates Wisdom and brings us closer to "the Word was God." This leads us to a discussion of the Logos in Philo.

---

[13] Dodd, *Fourth Gospel*, 275.
[14] Martin Scott, *Sophia and the Johannine Jesus* (JSNTSup 71; Sheffield: JSOT Press, 1992), 107.

The Logos in Philo

One of the most prominent advocates of the third view was C. H. Dodd, who wrote that "With Wisdom we are already half-way to Philo's Logos." Dodd argued for the following parallels between the Logos in Philo and John's Prologue.[15]

In the beginning was the Word.

"Before creation, God conceived in His mind the κόσμος νοητός [the world perceptible to the mind], which is His λόγος." This plan of the world is analogous to that of an architect before he builds a city. "Discerned only by the intellect," this plan can only be called "the Word of God" (*On the Creation of the World* 24).

The Word was with [πρὸς] God.

"God sent forth His younger son, the κόσμος αἰσθητός, but kept the elder, κόσμος νοητός = λόγος (see above), παρ᾽ ἑαυτῷ (with him)." God decided that this older son "should remain in His own keeping" (*That God Is Unchangeable* 31).

The Word was God.

"The anarthrous θεός may be used of the λόγος while ὁ θεός is reserved for the Self-existent." Dodd cites *On Dreams* 1.229–30 where Philo is commenting on Gen 31:13, which in the LXX reads, "I am (the) God [ὁ θεός] who appeared to you (Jacob) in the place of God" (ἐν τόπῳ θεοῦ, without the definite article, for MT Bethel). What Moses calls "God" without the article is "His chief Word." Dodd could have cited this text also under "the Word was with God," since Philo is wondering why God does not say to Jacob "in my place," but rather "in the place of God', as though it were another's" (*On Dreams* 1.228). This apparent "other" is the Logos.

All things came into being through him.

In *On the Cherubim* 127 Philo says that God is the cause of the world coming into existence, while "its instrument (is) the word of God, through which it was framed."

In him was life.

Dodd did not find a direct parallel, but pointed to *On Flight and Finding* 97, where Philo interprets the command to flee to a city of refuge as a command to flee "to the supreme Divine Word, who is the fountain of Wisdom, in order that he may draw from the stream and, released from death, gain life eternal as his prize."

In *On the Posterity of Cain* 68–69, Philo says, "he that lives an irrational [ἀλόγως] life has been cut off from the life of God."

The Word is true light.

In *On Dreams* 1.75, Philo refers to God as light, and the highest model of light: "For the model or pattern was the Word which contained all His fullness—light, in fact." *On the Creation of the World* 33 speaks of the adversary relationship between light and darkness. In *On the Confusion of Tongues* 60–63, Philo calls the incorporeal light "the eldest son," elsewhere called "His first-born" which is also elsewhere called the Logos.

To those who received him, he gave the right to become children of God.

Philo notes that Moses calls the Israelites "sons of God" in Deut 14:1: "But if there be any as yet unfit to be called a Son of God, let him press to take his place under God's First-born, the Word" who is called by many names, such as "the Name of God, and His Word, and the Man after His image," so that at least "we may be sons of His invisible image, the most holy Word" (*On the Confusion of Tongues* 145–47).

No man has seen God at any time . . . .

Commenting on Exod 24:10, which in the LXX reads, "they saw the place where the God of Israel stood" (cf. the MT: "they saw the God of Israel"), Philo says that those who choose Moses as their guide will see this place. It is natural to "desire to see the Existent if they may, but, if they cannot, to see at any rate his image, the most holy Word" (*On the Confusion of Tongues* 96–97).

Tobin has also advocated Philo's Logos over wisdom as the source of John's Logos title. He reasons that the fact that we find λόγος and not σοφία in John 1 shows that the author has moved beyond wisdom speculation to the kind of Logos speculation found in Philo, in which the "*logos* overshadows wisdom in importance," is "a reality which existed with God before creation", is described with "the anarthrous *theos* (God)" connected to "in the beginning" from Gen 1:1, was the instrument of creation, and is associated with light and with becoming children of God.[16]

Despite these parallels, Philo's Logos falls short in providing a complete explanation for the Logos of John 1, specifically, "the Word became flesh." Dodd maintains, however, that this sentiment is more understandable in Philo than in the Wisdom literature since in Philo the Logos is not a word but "creative reason," which in some sense is "immanent in man, as the equivalent of the divine, essential humanity."[17]

---

[15] Dodd, *Fourth Gospel*, 276–77. In what follows, the quoted summaries of Philo are from Dodd, and the quotes from Philo are from LCL (in these quotes "word" always stands for *logos*).

[16] Tobin, "Logos," 4:354. Tobin had already noted, however, that not just the λόγος in Philo, but wisdom in the wisdom speculation was light and was associated with life and with becoming children (actually, "friends") of God (ibid.).

[17] Dodd, *Fourth Gospel*, 281.

Dodd also explained why the word λόγος is not used in this Philonic sense in the Gospel itself: "It is only in the Prologue that the evangelist deals with cosmology." Even so, he maintained that the Logos theology pervaded the Gospel. As evidence, he noted: (1) "truth" as used in the Gospel is very close to λόγος in Philo; (2) the metaphysics of John is not unlike Philo (Jesus' use of ἀληθινός for true light, true bread, true vine); (3) the term "Son of Man" is best understood as true man (ἄνθρωπος ἀληθινός) or "the Idea of Man," identified in Philo with the Logos. Thus, "the substance of a Logos-doctrine similar to that of Philo is present all through the gospel."[18]

Returning to John 7:34, we have noted previously how this text ("You will seek me, but will not find me") can be related either to OT Word or to wisdom texts so as to provide striking support for either of the two previously discussed views. But if one was inclined to explain the Logos title as deriving from Philo, one can also find support for this view in John 7:34.

In *Questions and Answers on Genesis* 3.27, Philo explains the meaning of Gen 16:7 ("An angel of the Lord found her by a spring of water . . ."), in the course of which he says, "If the divine Logos is to be found, he seeks it"—"he" being "the soul that progresses" who is not "completely foolish." In *On Flight and Finding* 5, Philo identifies the angel of the LORD who found Hagar (Gen 21:17) as the divine Word [θεῖος λόγος].

In *On Flight and Finding* 120, Philo discusses the possible combinations of seeking and finding: (1) some neither seek nor find; (2) some both seek and find; (3) some seek but do not find; (4) some do not seek yet find. John 7:34 would put Jesus' hearers in the third category, but Philo's discussion of the second category is actually more pertinent to John's Gospel. In a discussion of the manna in the wilderness, Philo says that the Israelites' question concerning the manna (Exod 16:15, "What is it?") was an inquiry of those seeking to know about "What it is that nourishes the soul", adding that they "became learners and found it to be a saying of God [ῥῆμα Θεοῦ], that is the Divine Word [καὶ λόγον θεῖον], from which all kinds of instruction and wisdom flow in perpetual stream" (*On Flight and Finding*, 137). Such a view of the manna as divine word could be seen as underlying John 6, where Jesus, called the divine Word in the Prologue, presents himself as the true manna (vv. 32ff), after being both sought and found (vv. 24–25). In closing his discussion of seeking and finding, Philo quotes Moses from Deut 4:29, that if Israel seeks the LORD with all their soul, they will find him (*On Flight and Finding*, 142). Deuteronomy 4:29 assumes that Israel has been exiled for their sins, and promises restoration, which is of relevance to John if, as most interpreters believe, the Gospel is also written from a post-AD 70 perspective, so that Palestinian Jews have experienced a recent exile and would naturally hope for a restoration such as Deut 4:29 anticipates.

While Philo ascribes spiritual motives to the Israelites' seeking to know what the manna is, implying that this is why they found what they sought, Jesus says that his hearers seek him for baser motives: "You seek me, not because you saw

---

[18] Dodd, *Fourth Gospel*, 278–79.

---

miracles, but because you ate of the loaves, and were filled" (John 6:26). He goes on to direct their attention to spiritual nourishment and their need to feed upon him, the one whom John has called "the Word." Their rejection of this invitation means that they will fall not into Philo's second category but into his third: "You will seek me but will not find me."

Summary

In this chapter, we have reviewed the plausible arguments for three views of the source of John's Logos title. A wrong hypothesis will typically be harder to recognize as wrong, the closer it is to the correct one. It is easy to assume that data which is *consistent* with a particular hypothesis confirms that hypothesis and thereby to overlook the fact that the data might also be consistent with another hypothesis. We saw that John 7:34 could be interpreted to support any of these three views, which diminishes its value in supporting any one of them in particular. Further, John 7:34 can just as plausibly be interpreted as consistent with a Targum derivation of the Logos title. I make the case for such an understanding in ch. 8, but at this point I will simply mention that the Targum view takes "the Word" as a divine title denoting the name of God. Consequently, one may, for example, relate John 7:34 directly to Deut 4:29 (the passage mentioned by Philo, and noted above, which promises that if Israel seeks the LORD with all their heart, they will find him) or Isa 55:6 ("Seek the LORD while he may be found"), two passages that imply the possibility of seeking God but not finding him.

Methodologically, when faced with multiple possible interpretations, one must identify the one that best explains all the data. When there are competing views, it is necessary to explain why one's favored view is better than the others. As we have seen, Dodd did so when advocating Philo's Logos, except that he did not consider the "Word" language of the Targums, even though (as we shall see) he acknowledged that the targumic Word was conceptually similar to Philo's Logos. Often interpreters completely overlook the Targum view. We will address the arguments of those who do consider this view in ch. 12, when we will be in a better position to critique them.

A PRELIMINARY CASE FOR DERIVING THE LOGOS TITLE FROM THE TARGUMS

What Are the Targums?

"Targum" is a Hebrew word (also used in Aramaic) meaning "translation," and it is used especially for Aramaic translations of the Hebrew Scriptures that were read in the synagogues on the Sabbath and on feast or fast days. Scholars usually assume that the practice of translation was necessitated by the loss of Hebrew fluency by Jews growing up in exile. Nehemiah 8:7–8 says that after Ezra's reading of the law, the Levites explained the law to the people: "They read from the book, from the law of God, translating [or explaining] to give the sense so that they understood the reading" (v. 8 NASB). Other versions say not that they translated, but that they made clear, or read clearly or distinctly.[19] In any case, the NASB translation of Neh 8:8 seems to be a good summary of the goal of the Targums. Translations developed over time, and at some point began to be written down, though in the synagogue they were recited, not read, so as not to be put at the same level as the Hebrew Scriptures. The written Targums were subject to modification from one generation to another, while the Hebrew Scriptures were preserved as they were received. All of the extant Targums seem to date from the second century C.E. and later, yet a number of the translations would preserve readings that were current in the first century, as is evident from various passages from the NT itself.[20] For the Targums of individual books or sets of books described below, the relevant volumes of The Aramaic Bible provide suitable introductions with bibliographies (Collegeville, Minn., Liturgical Press; Edinburgh, T&T Clark). This ongoing project, started in 1987, aims to provide English translations for all the Targums.

Targums Jonathan and Onqelos

Targum Jonathan (*Tg. Jon.*) covers the Former and Latter Prophets (Joshua, Judges, Samuel, Kings, Isaiah, Jeremiah, Ezekiel, and the minor prophets). Tradition ascribed this Targum to Jonathan ben Uzziel, who lived in the first century C.E., although it is more likely a product of many hands and continued to be modified into the fourth century. *Targum Onqelos* (*Tg. Onq.*) covers the Pentateuch and, like *Jonathan*, probably has many authors. *Onqelos* and *Jonathan* are considered "official" Targums in the sense that they are supposed to represent rabbinic Judaism after C.E. 70. They apparently originated in Palestinian Judaism, but their latest editions were done in Babylon.

The Palestinian Targums of the Pentateuch[21]

Targums considered "Palestinian" (*Pal. Tgs.*) are *Neofiti 1* (*Tg. Neof.*), *Pseudo-Jonathan* (*Tg. Ps.-J.*), and the *Fragmentary Targums* (*Frg. Tgs.*). In the case of *Tg. Ps.-J.*, both "Palestinian" and "Targum" need qualification. Michael Maher suggests that *Ps.-J.*, though based on a Targum, is not a proper "Targum" in that (1)

---
[19] The Hebrew is מְפֹרָשׁ (pual), "to be made distinct."
[20] See, e.g., J. T. Forestell, *Targumic Traditions and the New Testament: An Annotated Bibliography with a New Testament Index* (SBL Aramaic Studies 4; Chico, Calif.: Scholars Press, 1979).
[21] For introductory material for *Tg. Neof.*, see Martin McNamara, *Targum Neofiti 1: Genesis* (ArBib 1A; Collegeville, Minn.: Liturgical Press, 1992), ix–50, 231–49; also see Alejandro Díez Macho, *Neophyti 1: Targum Palestinense MS de la Biblioteca Vaticana* (5 vols; Madrid: Consejo Superior de Investigaciones Científicas, 1968, 1970, 1971, 1974, 1978), for the Aramaic text of *Tg. Neof.*, various introductory studies, and Spanish (Díez Macho), French (Roger Le Déaut), and English (Martin McNamara and Michael Maher) translations. For *Tg. Ps.-J.*, see Michael Maher, *Targum Pseudo-Jonathan: Genesis* (ArBib 1B; Collegeville, Minn.: Liturgical Press, 1992), 9–14, 167–85.

---

it shows signs of being a scholarly work meant to be read and studied in private by other scholars rather than recited publicly in the synagogue as a translation of the Hebrew Scriptures; and (2) it approaches the genre "rewritten Bible" because of the extensive embellishments which have little or nothing to do with translating the relevant Hebrew text. "Palestinian" is also problematic because that term is supposed to distinguish these Targums from the "official" Targum of the Pentateuch, namely, *Tg. Onq.* Yet it is clear that in a great many cases *Tg. Ps.-J.* agrees with *Tg. Onq.* against the *Pal. Tgs.*[22] This fact underscores the importance of the discovery of *Tg. Neof.* sixty years ago; until then we did not have "Palestinian" renderings of a great number of passages in the Pentateuch.

The name *Pseudo-Jonathan* came about due to the fact that at one time (e.g., J. W. Etheridge's nineteenth-century translation) the author was considered to be the same Jonathan who was thought to have authored *Tg. Jon.*, the Targum of the Prophets. This conclusion seems to have resulted from mistaking the initials TJ (ת״י), likely meaning "*Targum Jerusalem*," for "*Targum Jonathan*." When the mistake was realized, the text then became known as *Targum Pseudo-Jonathan*. Of course, of course, Jonathan did not write the Targum of the Prophets, either, but the Targum of the Prophets is not called *Pseudo-Jonathan*.

The *Frg. Tgs.* are not fragments of manuscripts of complete Targums but rather portions of Palestinian Targums of the Pentateuch that were selected and copied out according to some unknown principle. The two major types are called P (after the Paris MS 110) and V (after MSS from the Vatican, Nürnberg, and Leipzig).[23] In this book, *Frg. Tg. V* indicates a reading found in one or more of the MSS of this type.

Targum Neofiti, thought to be a copy of a Targum from about the fourth century, is therefore the only complete Palestinian Targum of the Pentateuch. Actually, as Martin McNamara notes, because of the extensive marginal and interlinear glosses (*Tg. Neof.* [mg.] / [int.]), it is a witness also to three other types of Palestinian Targums.[24] *Neofiti* glosses tend to agree with the *Frg. Tgs.* (where extant) more closely than does the body of the text. *Neofiti* was discovered in the Vatican library in 1949, about the same time as the Dead Sea scrolls were discovered in the caves of Judea. It had been overlooked for some time because it was considered to be just another copy of *Tg. Onq. Neofiti*, so called because it was produced by a college for Jewish converts to Catholicism (thus neophytes).

Fragments of Targum manuscripts from the famous Cairo Synagogue Genizah (*CTgs.*), not to be confused with the *Frg. Tgs.*, often agree with one or more of the Palestinian Targum readings.[25] McNamara's volumes on *Tg. Neof.* in The Aramaic Bible series include readings of interest from these fragments.

---
[22] Maher, *Pseudo-Jonathan: Genesis*, 1–8.
[23] See Michael L. Klein, *The Fragment-Targums of the Pentateuch according to Their Extant Sources* (2 vols.; AnBib 76; Rome: Biblical Institute Press, 1980), 1:12–42.
[24] McNamara, *Neofiti 1: Genesis*, 15.
[25] These fragments are published in Michael L. Klein, *Genizah Manuscripts of Palestinian Targum to the Pentateuch* (2 vols.; Cincinnati: Hebrew Union College, 1986).

Besides having odd-sounding names, the Palestinian Targums are characterized by more paraphrase and inclusion of legendary material than *Tg. Onq.* They also tend to be of more significance for NT studies, including (as we shall see) the concept of the divine Word.

Other Targums

Targums of the other OT books, with the exception of Ezra-Nehemiah and Daniel (originally written partly in Aramaic), also exist and are relevant for our study. The *Tosefta Targum of the Prophets* (*Tos. Tg.*) consists of Targums of individual verses in the Prophets which have a more "Palestinian" character than *Tg. Jon.* and may be witnesses to a now (mostly) lost Palestinian Targum of the Prophets.[25]

There is some evidence that there may once have been a Palestinian Targum to the Prophets that contained large units of material added into the translation. The evidence is that some manuscripts of the known Targum to the Prophets preserve such additional material in their margins. Similarly, medieval scholars such as Rashi and Kimhi cite prophetic traditions in Aramaic designated as Targum Yerushalmi (i.e., Palestinian Targum) as do some manuscripts such as Codex Reuchlinianus. The best explanation for this material is that they once belonged to a complete Palestinian Targum to the Prophets, but during the early middle ages when the more literal Jonathan Targum to the Prophets became the dominant targum in the West, the aggadic material was extracted to preserve it alongside the newly authoritative translation, while the Palestinian Targum itself was lost.[27]

The Aramaic texts of the Targums are available online, through the "Comprehensive Aramaic Lexicon" project (CAL) of the Hebrew Union College in Cincinnati. The texts are displayed a verse or chapter at a time, with some morphological information. Online dictionaries and concordance searches are also available on the website.[28] Etheridge's nineteenth-century English translations of *Tg. Onq.*, *Tg.*

Ps.-J., and *Frg. Tg. V* (labeled "Jerusalem"),[29] along with recent English translations of the Targums of Psalms, Lamentations, Ruth, and Song of Songs, are available online through "The Newsletter for Targumic and Cognate Studies."[30]

The Divine Word in the Targums

In the Targums, the divine Word is usually indicated by a form of the Aramaic word מֵימְרָא (*Memra*), which, when so used, is not a translation of anything in the Hebrew text; rather, the phrase "the Word of the LORD", is often a circumlocution, or substitute, for the Tetragrammaton (the "four letters," יהוה, or YHWH), the pre-eminent OT name for God.[31] "The Word of the LORD" is actually more than a circumlocution, since "Lord" by itself was already in use as a substitute for the divine name, as is clear from a comparison of the MT and the LXX. In recitation of the Targums, when the Hebrew *Adonay* was used, rather than another Hebrew word meaning "Lord," the hearers would know that the Tetragrammaton was meant.[32]

"*Memra*" is the emphatic (definite) form of מֵימַר (*memar*), from the root אמר. Aramaic *memar* may be used simply as a translation of a Hebrew word for "word" (usually the etymologically related אֹמֶר or דִּבּוּר). When the word is used as a circumlocution for the divine name, it is of particular interest with relation to the Logos title. When so used, in English translations of the Targums it is often transliterated consistently as *Memra*, even though the underlying Aramaic spelling changes depending on whether or not the word is emphatic or has pronominal suffixes.

Another important word used in "the Word of the LORD" as a way of rendering MT. "the LORD" is דִּבְּרָא (*Dibbera*), also spelled דִּבּוּרָא (*Dibbura*). This word is

---

have been compiled and made available as user databases for *BibleWorks* by Jay Palmer: see http://bibleworks.oldinthenew.org/?cat=37 (Accessed: July 21, 2009).

[29] J. W. Etheridge, *The Targums of Onkelos and Jonathan Ben Uzziel on the Pentateuch, with Fragments of the Jerusalem Targum from the Chaldee* (2 vols.; London: Longman, Green, Longman, 1862, 1865; repr., 2 vols. in 1, New York: Ktav, 1968).

[30] Online: http://targum.info/; accessed June 30, 2009. The site has links to various English translations of Targums; these include Etheridge, *Targums of Onkelos and Jonathan Ben Uzziel*; Edward M. Cook, "The Psalms Targum: An English Translation" (2001); Christian M. M. Brady, "Targum Lamentations" (printed ed.: *The Rabbinic Targum of Lamentations: Vindicating God* [Studies in the Aramaic Interpretation of Scripture 3; Leiden: Brill, 2003]); Samson H. Levey, "Targum to Ruth" (1998); and Jay C. Treat, "The Aramaic Targum to Song of Songs" (2001).

[31] In English translations of the Hebrew Bible, the Tetragrammaton is traditionally rendered LORD, with capital letters indicating the name of God as opposed to the Hebrew word *Adonai*, "Lord." In the Targums the Tetragrammaton is represented in various ways besides יהוה, such as ה, יי, יוי, or ייי. The ˚ seems to be used as a syllable place holder, such that ייי represents the 3 syllables of Hebrew *Adonay*, "represents the 2 written vowels of the Tetragrammaton as it is usually found in MT, while the ו in יוי indicates the long ō vowel of *Adonay*. ה would represent the Hebrew definite article and be an abbreviation for "the Name."

[32] Aramaic רִבּוֹן is used for human masters in the Targums but sometimes also for God (e.g. *Tg. Neof.* Exod 23:17). "Marana-tha" ("Lord come!") in 1 Cor 16:22 is based on another Aramaic word, מָר, or מָרֵי, also found in the Targums occasionally for God, e.g. *Tg. Ps.* 35:23.

---

[26] Rimon Kasher published 150 such texts in *Tosefot Targum to the Prophets* [Hebrew; תוספתות תרגום לנביאים] (Sources for the Study of Jewish Culture 2; Jerusalem: World Union of Jewish Studies, 1996).

[27] Paul V. M. Flesher, ed., "Palestinian Targum to the Prophets," in *Dictionary of Judaism in the Biblical Period: 450 B.C.E. to 600 C.E.* (ed. Jacob Neusner and William Scott Green; 2 vols.; New York: Simon & Schuster Macmillan, 1996), 2:467. Articles in this dictionary are unsigned, but p. ix indicates that Flesher was responsible for editing articles on the Targums.

[28] Online: http://cal.cn.huc.edu/; accessed June 30, 2009. Users of the CAL text should be aware that marginal readings in *Tg. Neof.* that only indicate the addition of *Memra* are not indicated in that text (or in programs such as BibleWorks that use this text). Therefore some of the marginal readings in *Tg. Neof.* noted in this book will not be found in the CAL text. The CAL texts were produced independently and thus may differ on occasion from published texts. *BibleWorks 7* has the Aramaic texts of the Targums, although version 6 omitted the *Pal. Tgs.* of the Pentateuch. *Accordance 8* has the Aramaic texts and is in the process of producing English translations. *Logos Bible Software* has a Targum module based on the CAL material, including the *Pal. Tgs.*, for use in the Libronix Digital Library System. Public domain English translations of *Tg. Song* (Adam Clarke) and *Tg. Isa.* (C. W. H. Pauli)

used primarily in the *Pal. Tgs.* of the Pentateuch and appears infrequently compared to אמימר. Yet, among its relatively few uses are several that give key support to the view that the Logos title in John does in fact depend on the Word of the LORD terminology from the Targums. *Dibbera/Dibbura* is generally overlooked by those considering the Targums as possible background for the Logos title, though its use was noted as long ago as the nineteenth century by Ferdinand Weber and B. F. Westcott.[33]

To some extent, *Memra* and *Dibbera* are used interchangeably, as can be seen from several examples: (1) Gen 3:8 says that Adam and Eve heard the sound of the LORD God walking about in the garden; in v. 10 Adam says, "I heard the sound of you." In *Pal. Tgs.* Gen 3:8, 10, Adam and Eve hear the sound/voice of "the Word of the LORD" strolling about in the garden. Both *Memra* (*Tgs. Neof.* and *Ps.-J.* Gen 3:8, 10; *Frg. Tg. P* Gen 3:8) and *Dibbera* (*Tg. Neof.* [mg.] and *Frg. Tg. P* Gen 3:10) are used. (2) In giving instructions for the building of the ark of the covenant, the LORD says, "there I will meet with you, and from above the mercy seat, from between the two cherubim that are on the ark of the testimony, I will speak with you about all that I will command you concerning the sons of Israel" (Exod 25:22). In place of "I will meet you," *Tg. Neof*, *Tg. Ps.-J.*, and *Tg. Onq.* all read "I will appoint my *Memra*."[34] In reporting the fulfillment of this purpose in Num 7:89, *Tgs. Neof.* and *Ps.-J.* say that from above the mercy seat, between the two cherubim, the *Dibbera* used to speak to Moses. Also, in Num 17:[4] God describes the place before the ark as the place where he meets with Moses, and again *Tg. Neof*, *Tg. Ps.-J.*, and *Tg. Onq.* say that his *Memra* meets Moses there. (3) Leviticus 1:1 says, "The LORD called to Moses and spoke to him." The *Tg. Ps.-J.* Lev 1:1 says the *Dibbera* of the LORD called to him and the *Memra* of the LORD spoke to him. *Targum Neofiti* and *Frg. Tg. V* also use *Dibbera* as subject of the verb "call," and both of the *Frg. Tg.* traditions use *Memra* as subject of the verb "spoke." When "Word" (capitalized) appears in Targum passages in this book, *Memra* is meant, unless otherwise indicated (e.g. by adding *Dibbera/Dibbura* in brackets).

But despite the overlap between the two terms, *Dibbera* is used in a more specialized sense than *Memra*. Etan Levine notes that *Memra* is used for more or less the full range of God's activities in the world; *Memra* "conveys the *being* and *doing* of *YHWH*," across the entire spectrum.[35] Samson H. Levey notes the *Memra* "is

---

[33] Ferdinand Weber, *System der Altsynagogalen palästinischen Theologie aus Targum, Midrasch, und Talmud* (1880); repr. in *Jüdische Theologie auf Grund des Talmud und verwandter Schrifen* (ed. Franz Delitzsch and Georg Schnedermann; 2d ed.; Leipzig: Dörfling & Francke, 1897), 180, cited in Robert Hayward, *Divine Name and Presence: The Memra* (Totowa, N.J.: Allenheld, Osmun, 1981) 2, 11 n. 5; B. F. Westcott, *The Gospel according to St. John: With Introduction and Notes* (1880; repr., London: James Clarke & Co, 1958), xvi. Westcott noted that in *Tg. Onq.* "the action of God is constantly though not consistently referred to 'His Word.'... It may be noticed that the term *Debura* (דבורא) occurs in this sense as well as *Memra*" (ibid.).

[34] Evans noted the association of the *Memra* with the tabernacle in *Tg. Neof.* Exod 25:22; 29:43; 30:6, 36 (*Word and Glory*, 118).

[35] Etan Levine, *The Aramaic Version of the Bible: Contents and Context* (BZAW 174; Berlin: de Gruyter, 1988), 59–60.

everything that God is supposed to be, and its manifold activity encompasses the entire spectrum of divine endeavor," but "the *Dibbur* is the divine word, limited to speech, articulation, proclamation."[36]

Since *Dibbera* by itself means divine speech, it is not necessary to say "the *Dibbera* of LORD." Thus, in Num 7:89, cited above, the *Pal. Tgs.* say, "From there the *Dibbera* (*not* the *Dibbera of the* LORD) used to speak with (Moses)." This is potentially significant since in the Prologue John calls Jesus "the Word," not "the Word of the Lord" or "the Word of God" (although this term is used for Jesus in Rev 19:13). George Foot Moore argued against the idea of relating *Memra* to John's Logos because

memra does not occur without a genitive—"the word of the Lord," "my word," etc., or a circumlocution for the genitive, "a *memar* from before the LORD." "the *Memra*," "the Word," is not found in the Targums, notwithstanding all that is written about it by authors who have not read them.[37]

However, John called Jesus "the Word" based on both *Memra* and *Dibbera*, this objection loses its force. As shown below, several passages in John 1 seem to be illumined by passages in the *Pal. Tgs.* of the Pentateuch, where Jesus in the NT corresponds to the *Dibbera*, "the Word," of the Targums.

In its "common" meaning, דבר is used for the Ten Commandments, which are the ten "words" in Hebrew, rendered in the LXX with both λόγοι. (Exod 34:28; Deut 10:4) and ῥήματα (Deut 4:13). *Targum Pseudo-Jonathan* Deut 4:12–13 illustrates the two usages: "You heard the voice of the Word [דברא]... And he declared to you his covenant,... the ten words [דבריא]."[38] *Dibbera* is also not used in pronominal expressions such as "my Word." דברי is also found once as a biblical Hebrew word, if the pointing is correct, where again it has the connotation of divine speech: "The word [הדבר] is not in them (the false prophets)" (Jer 5:13).

An objection to examining targumic passages containing *Dibbera* with passages in John could be made on the basis that "*Dibbura* in *Tg. Ezek.* is usually held to be a late and secondary insertion within the Targumic versions."[39] Against this view I would draw attention to the use of *Dibbura* in *Tg. Ezek.* 1:25. Levey notes how *Tg. Ezek.* (part of *Tg. Jon.* of the Prophets) avoids use of the term "Messiah," despite a

---

[36] Samson H. Levey, *The Targum of Ezekiel* (ArBib 13; Collegeville, Minn.: Liturgical Press, 1987), 15.

[37] George Foot Moore, "Intermediaries in Jewish Theology: Memra, Shekinah, Metatron," *HTR* 15 (1922): 61 n.24.

[38] Cf. Ernest G. Clarke, *Targum Pseudo-Jonathan: Deuteronomy* (ArBib 5B; Collegeville, Minn.: Liturgical Press, 1998), 18, where v. 13 is mistakenly rendered "the ten *Memras*."

[39] Andrew Chester, *Divine Revelation and Divine Titles in the Pentateuchal Targumim* (Texte und Studien zum antiken Judentum 14; Tübingen: J. C. B. Mohr [Paul Siebeck], 1986), 115. Chester cites in agreement Paul Billerbeck (Str-B 2:316–19), Vinzenz Hamp (*Der Begriff "Wort" in der aramäischen Bibelübersetzungen. Ein exegetischer Beitrag zum Hypostasen-Frage und zur Geschichte der Logos-Spekulationen* [Munich: Neuer Fiber-Verlag, 1938], 93–97), and Domingo Muñoz-León (*Dios-Palabra. Memrá en los Targumim del Pentateuco* [Granada, 1974], 668–79). In Klein's opinion, "Muñoz León's argument for the lateness of *dibberah* relative to *memra* is not convincing" (*Genizah Manuscripts*, 2:70).

number of opportunities to use it, and where one might expect it to be used. For example, in *Tg. Ezek.* 34:23–24; 37:24–25, "my servant David" is translated literally, whereas "David their king" in Jer 30:9 and Hos 3:5 is rendered "the Messiah, son of David, their king" in *Tg. Jon.* In Levey's view, "Merkabah Mysticism" is substituted for "Messianic activism" in *Tg. Ezek.* in order to avoid Roman persecution of Jewish nationalism. Levey ascribes this substitution to the work of Rabbi Johanan ben Zakkai.[40] The Merkabah is the divine chariot seen by Ezekiel, and it is in this context that *Dibbura* is used (the angels' wings were silent before the Word).

Since the term *Dibbura* is used only here in all of *Tg. Jon.* of the Former and Latter Prophets, it would seem reasonable to ascribe the unique use of *Dibbura* in *Tg. Ezek.* 1 also to Johanan ben Zakkai. But Johanan ben Zakkai was a contemporary of Johanan ben Zebadiah, better known as John son of Zebedee, the traditional author of the Gospel named for him. It could be, then, that *Tg. Ezek.* preserves an early usage of *Dibbura* which does not appear elsewhere in *Tg. Jon.*, and that the use of *Dibbura/Dibbera* in the *Pal. Tgs.* of the Pentateuch dates at least as far back as the first century.

For an example of *Memra* being used in the Targums where the MT refers to God, apparently to guard the transcendence of God, consider Exod 34:5. The MT reads, "The LORD came down in the cloud," whereas a marginal gloss of *Tg. Neof.* for this passage reads, "The Word of the LORD was revealed." Two devices safeguard the transcendence of God here: (1) changing the anthropomorphic "came down" to "was revealed"; (2) changing "the LORD" to "the Word of the LORD."

Anthropomorphic references to God's hand, arm, etc., were also frequently changed to "Word" in targumic translations. For instance, in the MT of Exod 33:22, God says to Moses, "I will cover you with my hand," while *Tg. Onq.* reads, "I will shield you with my Word." Such a practice could be considered an extension of the substitution of "command" for "mouth," as in *Tgs. Onq.* and *Ps.-J.* Exod 17:1, where Israel journeyed "according to the word of the LORD" (MT, "according to the mouth of the LORD"). A substitution like this may be done for the sake of idiom, not simply to remove the anthropomorphism. In such cases, *Memra* in the Targums could be understood literally as God's word, that is, command. The Word may also be used for anthropopathisms, as in *Tg. Isa.* 63:5, "By the Word of my pleasure I helped them" (MT: "my wrath sustained me").

There is some dispute about whether the Targums have avoidance of anthropomorphisms as a goal, not only because the Targums do not consistently avoid anthropomorphisms, but also because some language that has been interpreted as anti-anthropomorphic is also used of kings or people in general, meaning we may be dealing with language of respect or idiomatic renderings.[41] Still, as Andrew Chester says, "the Pentateuchal Targumim change a very great number of expressions which bear directly upon the understanding of God, and a substantial number of which in Old Testament scholarship are generally labeled 'anthropomorphisms.'"[42] The targumists may not have been concerned so much with avoiding anthropomorphisms per se as with avoiding wrong impressions about God on the part of the synagogue hearers. Thus anthropomorphisms which would not mislead ordinary people could be translated literally. "The main point is their concern for the most appropriate way to speak of God in the synagogue setting."[43] Similarly, Robert Hayward notes that some anthropomorphisms remain in the Targums, but the targumist "can act quite drastically" when "anthropomorphic language of the Bible might lead to misconceptions about God", citing the example of *Tg. Jer.* 14:8–9, where Jeremiah's question to God, "Why are you like a stranger in the land . . . like a mighty man who cannot save?" is changed so that the inhabitants of Judah are strangers in the land, whom God is able to save.[44]

As for the transcendence of God, McNamara explains the "extremely frequent use" of "the Word of the LORD" to refer to God as due to "the religious mentality which produced the Targums [which] shrank from speaking of God as acting directly in the world and spoke instead of his *Memra* doing so."[45] This aspect of the targumic Word is conceptually similar to Philo's Logos. Similarly, J. Stanley McIvor writes, "The Targumist ensures that God is God and remains 'high and lifted up'"; he achieves this purpose through various means, such as "by removing God from the scene of direct action or direct contact with human beings" and "by rephrasing many expressions which might suggest that there was something human about God."[46] In Isa 57:15, the one who is "high and lifted up" says, "I dwell in a high and holy place, *yet also with the contrite and lowly of spirit.*" That is, he is both transcendent and imminent. But in the Targum, he is "high and lifted up" —period:

For thus says the high and lofty One who dwells *in the heavens*, whose name is Holy; *in the height he dwells*, and *his Shekhinah is holy. He promises to deliver the broken in heart* and the humble of spirit, *to establish the spirit of the humble, and to help the heart of the broken.*[47]

At the same time, the nearness of God is rendered literally throughout some Targums, such as *Tg. Onq.* and *Tg. Ps.*

---

[40] Levey, *Targum of Ezekiel*, 4.

[41] See e.g., Michael L. Klein, "The Translation of Anthropomorphisms and Anthropopathisms in the Targumim," Vetus Testamentum Supplements 32 (1979): 162–77; and "The Preposition *qdm* ('before'), a Pseudo-anti-anthropomorphism in the Targum," *Journal of Theological Studies* 30 (1979): 502–7.

[42] Chester, *Divine Revelation*, 298. See all of Chester's ch. 6 for a discussion of various views on how anthropomorphisms were dealt with in the Targums, and why.

[43] Ibid., 383.

[44] Robert Hayward, *Targum Jeremiah* (ArBib 12; Collegeville, Minn.: Liturgical Press, 1987), 22–23.

[45] Martin McNamara, "Logos of the Fourth Gospel and *Memra* of the Palestinian Targum (Ex 12⁴²)," *Expository Times* 79 (1968): 115. Attributing God's actions to his Word was just one of many stratagems employed by the targumists to this end.

[46] *The Targum of Chronicles* and *The Targum of Ruth* (trans. J. Stanley McIvor (Chronicles) and D. R. G. Beattie (Ruth); ArBib 19; Collegeville, Minn.: Liturgical Press, 1994), 24–26. The second and third quotes given here are italicized in the original.

[47] Bruce D. Chilton, *The Isaiah Targum* (ArBib 11; Wilmington, Del.: Michael Glazier, 1987), 111. Italic font in The Aramaic Bible series indicates differences in meaning from (and additions to) the MT.

The targumic Word is frequently employed in passages that speak of God's interaction with his creation, including humankind (especially his people), a fact consistent with the view that such usage is meant to guard the transcendence of God. In such passages, what the MT ascribes to God the Targums often ascribe to his Word. Above, we noted Levey's description of the targumic Word: "It is everything that God is supposed to be, and its manifold activity encompasses the entire spectrum of divine endeavor."[48] Levey was not promoting any connection between the Logos of John and the targumic Word, but what he said agrees closely with what John says about the Word. "It is everything that God is supposed to be" agrees with "the Word was God" (John 1:1), or as REB translates it, "What God was, the Word was." As for the divine Word encompassing "the entire spectrum of divine endeavor," we see in John's Gospel that the Son's activities encompass the entire spectrum of divine activity in the OT. John says explicitly that creation was accomplished through the Son (1:3), but in addition John shows us that the redemption of Israel from Egypt was accomplished through the Son who came down from heaven, the law was given through the Son, Israel was led through the wilderness by the Son, as his bride, and Israel had life by believing in the Son (as shown in chs. four through eight below). The Targums employ Word in describing the works of God in all these categories.

Of course, it would be going too far to say that since the divine Word "is everything that God is supposed to be," therefore "the Son is everything that the Father is supposed to be." The Son is not the Father; the Son is in relationship to the Father, a relationship of love, trust, dependence, and submission. This relationship between the Father and the Son is not the same as that between God and his Word in the Targums, where reference to the divine Word is simply a way of speaking of God himself under certain circumstances, and sometimes "my Word" in the Targums is equivalent to "myself" in the MT.[49] In many contexts, one could view the divine Word as a projection of the transcendent God into his creation. But the Son in John and the Word in the Targums share the same relationship with God in the fact that they both speak the words of God, interact with his people, and accomplish his will in the world.

The divine Word is also associated with the divine name. The targumic paraphrase "the Word of the LORD" for YHWH in the MT is sometimes further developed as "the name of the Word of the LORD," as we can see for example in various renderings of Gen 15:6:

MT	Tg. Onq.	Tg. Ps.-J.	Tg. Neof.
Abram believed in the LORD.	He believed in the Word of the LORD.	He had faith in the Word of the LORD.	Abram believed in the name of the Word of the LORD.

Faith in Jesus, or faith in his name, is a key issue in John's Gospel, analogous to faith in the divine Word, or the name of the divine Word, in the Targums. This will be explored in more detail in ch. 8.

A close association between the divine Word and the divine name is also seen in Tg. Isa. 48:11. In the MT, God says, "For my own sake, for my own sake I will act." In the Targum, this becomes, "For the sake of my name, for the sake of my Word." Similarly, Tg. Neof. Num 6:27 says, "so shall they put my name, my Word, upon the sons of Israel." The association of the divine Word with the name of God is also of interest for John's Gospel, which expresses the theme that the Father's name (i.e., the Tetragrammaton, YHWH) is given to the Son and that the Son's mission is to make known or manifest the Father's name to his people (John 17:6, 11–12, 26). Similarly, John 1:18 says that while no man has seen God (the Father), the Son has explained him. "Explained" is the Greek word from which comes our word "exegesis" (ἐξηγέομαι). In light of this, it is interesting to note what Chester wrote of the targumic Word and glory of the Shekinah as used in the Targums of the Pentateuch: "In a sense, both these terms are used as an *exegesis* of the divine names, especially the tetragrammaton."[50]

It is my contention that understanding the Logos title of the Gospel of John is based on targumic "Word" best fits the OT background to John 1:14 and its context, can also explain at least in part the evidence put forth for the other views, and leads to the recognition of a close connection between John's Prologue and the body of his Gospel. That is, John's Gospel as a whole can be seen as showing us what it meant by the statement that "the Word [that is, YHWH Son] became flesh and dwelt among us, and we beheld his glory." We will see that the so-called *Pal. Tgs.* to the Pentateuch are of greatest interest with respect to this subject.

Evidence from John 1

In this section, we look at various passages from John 1 that can be understood to support the view that the Logos title is based on the divine Word of the Targums. Since we are looking only at ch. 1, the case will be made only in a preliminary way. After examination of those passages, we will also be able to see, in a preliminary way, how John has adapted the divine Word of the Targums to the person of Jesus Christ.

---

[48] Levey, *Targum of Ezekiel*, 15. Levey also said that the targumic Word was used for "safeguarding divine dignity, shielding the deity from unseemly expressions and mundane matters" (ibid.).

[49] For MT "by myself I have sworn," *Tgs. Onq.* and *Ps.-J.* Gen 22:16 and *Tg. Isa.* 45:23; *Tg. Jer.* 22:5; 49:13 have "by my Word I have sworn." In Deut 18:19, God says, "I myself will require it of him"; *Tg. Ps.-J.* says, "my Word will require it"; *Tg. Neof.* says, "I, in my Word, will require it." In Isa 44:24 God says that he is "the one who stretches out the heavens by myself"; *Tg. Isa.* has "by my Word" with obvious relevance to John 1:1. Similarly, in 1 Sam 2:35, God says he will raise up a faithful priest "who will act according to what is in my heart and soul." *Tg. 1 Sam.* has, "who will act according to my Word and according to my pleasure."

[50] Chester, *Divine Revelation*, 374. "Shekinah" is a word used to refer to the divine presence manifested locally in some way. As discussed in ch. 2, "Shekinah" and "Word" are overlapping concepts.

THE JEWISH TARGUMS AND JOHN'S LOGOS THEOLOGY

The Word Was with God, and the Word Was God (John 1:1)

"The Word of the LORD" (or, "My Word," etc.) in the Targums is usually a translation of names and titles of God in the MT; it is a divine title. Hundreds of times, the targumic Word corresponds to the divine name or some other designation of God in the MT. The divine Word of the Targums is thus a circumlocution for God, a way of saying "God" or the Tetragrammaton. McNamara points out that such a use constitutes metonymy, that is, calling something by an attribute or feature associated with it.[51] "The Word of the LORD" can be taken literally in many cases, but often it simply means "the LORD." We can compare it to the expression "the name of the LORD" in Isa 30:27, "Behold, the name of the LORD comes from afar," where the reference is to God coming in judgment (NLT: "Look! The LORD is coming from far away").

While "the Word of the LORD" is a metonym for "the LORD," its use is not random or arbitrary (though it is inconsistent). As already noted, it tends to be used when God is interacting with his creation, so that God can be viewed as transcendent, yet still immanent. Thus, "the Word of the LORD" is metonymy used under particular circumstances, such as in the act of creation itself, as noted below. God remains transcendent over creation; his Word creates. In terms of language, the very words "his Word" imply a certain distinction between God and his Word, even though conceptually that Word is something like a projection of God himself into the creation. While this targumic relationship between God and his Word is not nearly as developed as the relationship between the Father and the Son, who are distinct persons, yet in both cases the Word is God, and yet to some extent distinct from God.

The targumic Word is explicitly called God in many passages. In Gen 17:7–8, where God says to Abraham, "I will establish my covenant . . . to be God to you," and "I will be their God," *Tg. Neof.* has "to be, in my Word, God to you" and "I will be to them in my Word a savior [or redeemer] God." Similar expressions are found in *Tg. Neof.* Exod 6:7; 29:45; Lev 11:45 [mg.]; 22:33; 25:38; 26:12, 45; Num 15:41 [mg.]; Deut 26:17.[52] In *Tg. Neof.* Lev 26:12, the context of the promise of the Word of the LORD being a savior God is that the LORD will make the glory of his *Shekinah* dwell among them (v. 11). For MT "I will walk among you," *Tg. Neof.* has "My Word will go among you." *Targum Pseudo-Jonathan* Lev 26:12 also refers to the divine Word as a savior God. *Targum Neofiti* Deut 26:17 is also of interest, in light of Pilate's presentation of Jesus as king in John 19: "This day you have made the Word of the LORD your God to be King over you, so that he may be for you 'a savior God, [promising] to walk in ways that are right before him" (also *Frg. Tg. V, CTg. AA*).

Tgs. Onq. and *Jonathan* usually render God's promises to be God to individuals or to Israel literally. However, *Tg. Onq.* Gen 28:21 has Jacob vow, "The Word of the LORD will be my God," and in *Tg. Onq.* Exod 19:17 (also *Frg. Tg. P*), Moses brings the people to meet the Word of the LORD (MT: to meet God), to which we might compare the declaration of Thomas to Jesus the Word, "my Lord and my God" (John 20:28).[53] In *Tg. Onq.* Deut 4:24, Moses says, "the LORD your God, his Word, is a consuming fire, a jealous [or zealous] God." *Targum Pseudo-Jonathan* Deut 4:24 says, "the LORD your God, his Word is a consuming fire; the jealous God is a fire, and he avenges himself in jealousy." When Jesus cleansed the temple, the disciples were reminded of the zeal of a man, David (John 2:17; Ps 69:9). Identifying Jesus as the Word who is God points more significantly to divine zeal in the cleansing of the temple.

Creation through the Word, Who Was in the Beginning with God (John 1:1-3, 10)

Targum Onqelos and *Tg. Ps.-J.* of Gen 1 do not ascribe creation to the divine Word, but the Word of the LORD is the subject of verbs in the creation account seventeen times in *Tg. Neof.* and twenty-five times in *Frg. Tg. P*.[54] In *Frg. Tg. V*'s abbreviated account, the divine Word is the subject of the verb "create" only in v. 27, but v. 28 is quoted in Gen 35:9 of the same Targum, with the Word of the LORD as subject of "blessed" and "said" (*Tg. Neof.* [mg.] here agrees with *Frg. Tg. V*, but, interestingly, *Frg. Tg. P* Gen 35:9 has "God" as subject).

Further, where the MT of Gen 1 says "and it was so," *Tg. Neof.* and/or *Frg. Tg. P* say that it was so "according to his Word" (*Tg. Neof.* Gen 1:7, 9, 11, 15, 24, 30) or "through the decree of his Word" (*Tg. Neof.* [mg.] Gen 1:24; *Frg. Tg. P* Gen 1:7, 9, 11, 15, 24). *Targum Neofiti* Gen 1:3 says "there was light according to the decree of his Word," while *Frg. Tg. P* says "there was light through his Word."

Outside of the creation account itself, *Tg. Neof.* [mg.] Gen 3:1 says that the serpent was more clever than all the beasts of the field which "the Word of the LORD" created. In *Tg. Neof.* Gen 14:19, Melchizedek says, "Blessed is Abram before God Most High, who by his Word created the heavens and the earth," and Abram echoes this description of God in v. 22. Both *Tg. Neof.* Exod 20:11 and 31:17 say "In six days the LORD created the heavens and the earth," and in both passages, the gloss "and the Word of the LORD perfected" suggests an alternate text which could have read either "In six days the Word of the LORD created and perfected" etc.

---

[51] McNamara, *Targum and Testament: Aramaic Paraphrases of the Hebrew Bible: A Light on the New Testament* (Grand Rapids: Eerdmans, 1972), 99; "*Logos* of the Fourth Gospel and *Memra* of the Palestinian Targum," 115.

[52] Listed in McNamara, *Neofiti 1: Genesis*, 141 n.16.

[53] Westcott cited *Tg. Onq.* Gen 28:21 and Exod 19:17 as part of his argument for the superiority of the Targum background to Philo's Logos (*St. John, xvi*).

[54] *Tg. Neof.* Gen 1:1 (created), 3 (said), 4 (separated), 5 (called), 6 (said), 8 (called), 9 (said), 10 (called), 11 (said), 16 (created), 20 (said), 22 (blessed), 24 (said), 25 (created), 27 (created), 28 (said); 2:2 (completed). *Targum Neofiti* Gen 1:1 actually reads "the Son of the LORD," which McNamara says "is due most probably to a late, even sixteenth-century, correction. . . . The original Palestinian Targum probably read: 'From the beginning in wisdom the *Memra* of the Lord created'" (*Neofiti 1: Genesis*, 52 n.2). *Fragmentary Targum P* agrees with *Tg. Neof.* at Gen 1:3, 4, 5, 6, 8, 9, 10, 11, 16, 20, 22, 24, 25, 27, 28; 2:2 (variant). In addition, the Word of the LORD is subject in *Frg. Tg. P* Gen 1:7 (created), 14 (said), 17 (placed), 21 (created), 26 (said), 28 (blessed), 29 (said); and 2:3 (blessed and created). Of these nine, *Tg. Neof.* has "the Glory of the LORD" as subject five times (Gen 1:17, 28, 29; and 2:3 [twice]).

CHAPTER 2

Jesus' Origin and Identity

To determine what we can, historically and theologically, say about Jesus, we shall now look more closely at the question of who Jesus was and where he came from. The Gospel of Luke 3:23 states that Jesus was about thirty years old when he was baptized by John the Baptist in the river Jordan. The three synoptic gospels describe that after this took place, he spent time in the wilderness in preparation for the task awaiting him. Afterwards, he began to wander about in Galilee with his message that the kingdom of God was at hand.[1] This probably took place in the year 28 CE.[2]

Regarding the question of who Jesus was and where he came from, much more has been said in early Christianity. We will begin to examine the New Testament, because this includes the oldest testimonies. Afterwards, 'gnostic' and related sources will come up for discussion.

2.1 The letters of Paul

The earliest Christian documents that we have at our disposal are the letters of Paul; in section 1.2 we noted that probably the oldest of these letters is his first letter to the Thessalonians, generally regarded as dating from around 50 CE. The remaining letters known to be by him date from the 50s of the first century. The letter to the Philippians might be an exception, as it could have been written around 62 CE.

Paul pays exceptionally little attention to the life of Jesus in his letters; he never mentions Jesus' baptism nor the beginning of his appearance.

---

1   Matthew 3:13–4:17; Mark 1:9–15; Luke 3:21–4:15.
2   Gerd Theissen and Annette Merz (1997), *Der historische Jesus: Ein Lehrbuch* (2nd edn). Göttingen: Vandenhoeck & Ruprecht, p. 186.

It is, however, possible to conclude from a few of Paul's texts how he thought about Jesus' origin. In his letter to the Galatians (generally dated around 56 CE[3]) he writes, 'But when the fullness of time had come, God sent his Son, born of a woman, born under the law' (Galatians 4:4). With this text, Paul does not give the impression that he is saying something completely new to the Galatians, because in that case he would have to justify this statement, which he does not do at all. He does not deem it necessary to explain that he is referring to Jesus as the Son sent forth by God, nor from where God has sent his Son. Some scholars understand this expression to mean that God sent forth his Son in the same way that he sent forth Moses and the prophets to the people of Israel;[4] this means that God has given them a special task and it does not say anything about the place from which they have been sent. But because Paul mentions the sending of the Son of God even before he makes mention of his birth, he will certainly have intended that the Son of God was with God before he was sent forth to be born as man.[5] Because Paul undoubtedly shared the Old Testament conception that God lives in heaven,[6] we can conclude that, in his view, God's Son also originated from heaven and that he already was there before he came to earth.[7] The theological term for this is 'pre-existence'. We must note, however, that Paul does not state that God's Son already carried the name of Jesus in heaven (or in his pre-existence). Paul mentions no speculation whatsoever about the nature of Jesus' pre-existence.

Moreover, Paul states in Galatians 4:4 regarding Jesus' origin that he is 'born of woman' and 'under the law'. After having first referred to Jesus' divine origin, he subsequently names his earthly origin. He considers it unnecessary to elucidate Jesus' earthly origin by mentioning, for example, the name of Jesus' mother or his place of birth. Paul's

---

3   The view that the letter to the Galatians was written in 48 or 49 is less likely; in that case it would not have been addressed to the ethnic Galatians in the north of the Roman province Galatia (in present-day Turkey), but to the inhabitants of the south of this province. For this view, see for example H. N. Ridderbos (1953), *The Epistle of Paul to the Churches of Galatia: The English Text with Introduction, Exposition and Notes*. Grand Rapids MI: Eerdmans, pp. 22–35.
4   Thus James D. G. Dunn (1998), *The Theology of Paul the Apostle*. London, New York: T&T Clark, pp. 277–278, who refers to Exodus 3:12–15; Judges 6:8; Psalm 105:26; Jeremiah 1:7; 7:25, etc.; see also James D. G. Dunn, *Christology in the Making: An Inquiry into the Origins of the Doctrine of Incarnation*. London: SCM Press, pp. 38–44.
5   Cf. Romans 8:3, where Paul writes that God sent his Son in the likeness of sinful flesh; there he uses the verb *pempein*, whereas in Galatians 4:4 he uses *exapostellein*.
6   See, e.g., Psalm 115:16; Ecclesiastes 5:1; Romans 1:18.
7   See, e.g., Franz Mussner (1974), *Der Galaterbrief*. Freiburg: Herder, pp. 271–272; Joachim Gnilka (1994), *Theologie des Neuen Testaments*. Freiburg: Herder, p. 24; Hurtado, *Lord Jesus Christ*, pp. 118–119.

statement that Jesus is born 'under the law', means that he is born in a Jewish environment in which one lived in obedience to the law of Moses. Paul reminds the Galatians of Jesus' birth 'under the law' to point out the purpose of this: in order to redeem those who were under the law, so that we might receive adoption as children (Galatians 4:5). Paul was engaged in a fierce controversy with the Galatians concerning the position of the law of Moses, because, in his opinion, they wrongly wanted to subject themselves to all sorts of requirements of this law. It can be deduced from this letter that after Paul, other (so-called 'Jewish Christian') preachers had tried to persuade the Galatians to live according to the Mosaic law, and apparently with success. A drastic measure was, for example, that they made circumcision compulsory for non-Jewish men in the Christian church. With this letter, Paul wants to convince the non-Jewish Galatians that, if they want to believe in Jesus Christ, the literal maintenance of all kinds of regulations from the law of Moses does not fit in with this. The thoroughness with which he demonstrates this, stands in clear contrast to the conciseness of the formulation with which he, without further explanation or justification, designates Jesus as 'the Son of God' and alludes to God who sent his Son.[8] This proves that in the Galatian congregations, this was not a topic to be brought up for discussion.

A text in Paul's letter to the Philippians (dating from about 54 or 60–62) also testifies to Jesus' origin, but in completely different terms. Many exegetes think that Paul quotes a hymn here, but this opinion is not shared by everyone.[9] Paul admonishes the congregation that the same mind be in them that was in Jesus Christ and describes him thus,

who, though he was in the form of God,
did not regard equality with God
as something to be exploited,
but emptied himself,
taking the form of a slave,
being born in human likeness.
And being found in human form,
he humbled himself
and became obedient to the point of death –
even death on a cross. (Philippians 2:6–8)

The most probable explanation of this description of Jesus Christ is that he first, in his pre-existence with God, was equal to God, and that he subsequently 'emptied' himself, pointing to his descent from heaven to earth, where he became equal to man, and lived as a servant. To this must be added that this text has also been explained with regard to Jesus' life on earth, where he lived as a second Adam, created in God's image. On this point of view, differing from the first Adam, Jesus did not want to be like God (cf. Genesis 3:5) and humbled himself as a servant.[10] Exegetes such as Gordon D. Fee and Larry W. Hurtado discuss this interpretation, but do not consider it to be plausible. It is indeed more probable that Paul points to Christ's coming from his pre-existence, after which he became equal to man.[11] If this explanation is correct, then it seems that Paul in this letter also assumes Jesus' divine and heavenly origin. If, furthermore, it is correct that Paul here quotes an existing hymn, it can be deduced that, even before Paul wrote his letter, the outlook existed that Jesus originated from God and that he, before his earthly existence, was equal to God.

A third text, in which Paul mentions Jesus' human origin and thereby at the same time designates him as the Son of God, appears in the salutation of his letter to the Romans (dating from 56 or 57 CE). There he writes that the gospel that he proclaims, concerns

his (namely God's) Son, who was descended from David according to the flesh and was declared to be Son of God in power according to the spirit of holiness by his resurrection from the dead, Jesus Christ our Lord. (Romans 1:3–4)

Because various terms of this passage do not return in any of Paul's letters, exegetes think that he used an older confession here. Given the reference to the lineage of David, the king of Israel, and since 'the spirit of holiness' is a Hebrew formulation that Paul does not use anywhere else in his letters, it is supposed that this confession originates from Jewish Christians in Palestine for whom Hebrew was a familiar language.[12] In this confession it is twice stated that Jesus was God's Son. Differentiation is made between his human origin ('according to the flesh') from the lineage

---

8 See also Galatians 1:16; 2:20.
9 Gordon D. Fee (1995), *Paul's Letter to the Philippians*. Grand Rapids MI: Eerdmans, pp. 39–46; 192–194, is not convinced that Paul quotes an older hymn.
10 Thus Dunn, *Christology in the Making*, pp. 114–121; Dunn, *The Theology of Paul the Apostle*, pp. 281–288. The expression 'in the form of God' would then be equivalent to 'in the image of God' (Genesis 1:26–27).
11 Fee, *Philippians*, pp. 202–203; Hurtado, *Lord Jesus Christ*, pp. 119–123; see also Martin Hengel (1976), *The Son of God: The Origin of Christology and the History of Jewish-Hellenistic Religion*. Philadelphia: Fortress Press, pp. 1–2; Bert Jan Lietaert Peerbolte, 'The Name above all Names (Philippians 2:9)', in George H. van Kooten, ed. (2006), *The Revelation of the Name YHWH to Moses: Perspectives from Judaism, the Pagan Graeco-Roman World, and Early Christianity*. Leiden: Brill, pp. 187–206.
12 See, e.g., Otto Michel (1977), *Der Brief an die Römer* (14th edn). Göttingen: Vandenhoeck & Ruprecht, pp. 72–73.

Jesus, Gnosis and Dogma

of David,[13] and his spiritual identity ('according to the spirit of holiness') as the Son of God, who arose form the dead and is dressed with power. Here it is not written, as it is sometimes assumed, that Jesus has become God's Son since his resurrection from the dead, but that he has since then been indicated as 'God's Son *in power*', meaning that he obtained a higher, more powerful position after his resurrection from the dead.[14] In comparison with the two texts of Paul that we previously discussed, it is remarkable that this text does not point to Jesus' pre-existence.

A few other texts from Paul's letters confirm that he himself assumed Jesus Christ to be pre-existent with God the Father before he appeared on earth as a human being. In 1 Corinthians 8:6 he writes,

yet for us there is one God, the Father, from whom are all things and for whom we exist, and one Lord, Jesus Christ, through whom are all things and through whom we exist.

Of this statement too, it is assumed that Paul quotes a traditional formula.[15] However this may be, if Paul casually writes, without further explanation, that everything came into being through the Lord Jesus Christ, this implies that, in his view, God created the world with the assistance of Jesus Christ, which points to his pre-existence.[16] Furthermore, Paul declares in 1 Corinthians 10:4 that the rock from which the Israelites drank water in the wilderness was Christ himself. Therefore, they drank their 'spiritual drink' from Christ. So Paul assumes that the pre-existent Christ travelled along with the Israelites.[17] In 2 Corinthians 8:9, he writes, in an appeal to give generously to an offertory for the congregation of Jerusalem,

For you know the generous act of our Lord Jesus Christ, that though he was rich, yet for your sakes he became poor, so that by his poverty you might become rich.

From this text too, we can deduce that Paul points to Jesus' riches when he was with God in heaven, prior to becoming poor by becoming man.[18]

Jesus' Origin and Identity

This tour through a few of Paul's letters shows in the first place that, without further explanation, Paul could allude to Jesus' heavenly origin as something that, in his view, was not under discussion. Secondly, it shows – and this is confirmed by other texts from his letters[19] – that Paul could designate Jesus as the Son of God without having to explain or defend this as something new. Because his 'undisputed' letters date from the 50s (with perhaps an extension to 62 CE), it follows that the designation of Jesus as the Son of God, historically speaking, goes back to the 40s at least.

In chapter 8 we shall deal with the question of from where this idea of Jesus as the pre-existent Son of God derived. With regard to Jesus' identity, there is however another surprising designation to be found in Paul's letters. It happens several times that Paul quotes an Old Testament text about the LORD (Yahweh) and applies this to Jesus.[20] In Romans 10:13, he cites Joel 2:32, 'Everyone who calls on the name of the Lord shall be saved.' From Romans 10:9, it turns out that by 'the Lord' Paul means Jesus in this context, while Joel means the LORD God. In Romans 14:11, Paul writes, 'As I live, says the Lord, every knee shall bow to me, and every tongue shall give praise to God.' This is a free quotation from Isaiah 45:23, where the prophet speaks in the name of the LORD. However, in Paul's argument, he means Christ when he writes 'Lord' (see Romans 14:8–9). Philippians 2:9–11, which is the second part of the hymn that we encountered before, alludes to the same text from Isaiah 45:23. Here, Paul writes,

Therefore God also highly exalted him
and gave him the name
that is above every name,
so that at the name of Jesus
every knee should bend,
in heaven and on earth and under the earth,
and every tongue should confess
that Jesus Christ is Lord,
to the glory of God the Father. (Philippians 2:9–11)

---

13 This tradition also occurs in Matthew 1:1–16; Luke 1:27; 1:32; 2:4; 3:23–31.
14 See, e.g., James D. G. Dunn (1988), *Romans 1–8*. Dallas TX: Word Books, pp. 5–6; 11–16.
15 Wolfgang Schrage (1995), *Der erste Brief an die Korinther (1Kor 6,12–11,16)*. Solothurn, Düsseldorf: Benzinger Verlag, Neukirchen-Vluyn: Neukirchener Verlag, pp. 221–222.
16 Schrage, *Der erste Brief an die Korinther (1Kor 6,12–11,16)*, pp. 243–244; Hurtado, *Lord Jesus Christ*, pp. 123–124.
17 See Exodus 17:6; Numbers 20:7–11, and Schrage, *Der erste Brief an die Korinther (1Kor 6,12–11,16)*, p. 394.
18 See Margaret E. Thrall (2000), *The Second Epistle to the Corinthians II*. London, New York: T&T Clark, pp. 532–534.
19 Romans 1:9; 5:10; 8:3; 8:29; 8:32; 1 Corinthians 1:9; 15:28; 2 Corinthians 1:19; 1 Thessalonians 1:10. In the letters in Paul's name that have probably been written by a pupil of Paul, the designation 'the Son (of God)' for Jesus seldom occurs: only in Ephesians 4:13 and Colossians 1:13.
20 See David B. Capes (1992), *Old Testament Yahweh Texts in Paul's Christology*. Tübingen: J. C. B. Mohr.

According to numerous commentaries, 'the name that is above every name' is an allusion to the name Yahweh (or LORD).[21] This is confirmed by the end of this hymn, which says that Jesus Christ is Lord to the glory of God the Father.

Another Old Testament quote in which the Lord is named and which is applied to Jesus, is 1 Corinthians 1:31, 'Let the one who boasts, boast in the Lord,' which refers to Jeremiah 9:22–23 in the Greek translation. David B. Capes declares that in still two other passages Old Testament texts about Yahweh are applied to Jesus. 1 Corinthians 2:16 reads, 'For who has known the mind of the Lord so as to instruct him? But we have the mind of Christ,' and 1 Corinthians 10:26, 'the earth and its fullness are the Lord's.'[22] We must add, however, that other Old Testament quotes in which the LORD is named, are applied by Paul to God 'the Father'.[23] This shows that he is not consistent in his identification of the LORD with Jesus. In our discussion of the gospels, we shall see, however, that this identification, which sometimes occurs in Paul's writings, is not just limited to his letters.

2.2 The Gospel of Mark

The Gospel of Mark is generally assumed to have been written in the 60s of the first century or round about the year 70 CE. It is widely accepted to be of later date than the undisputed letters of Paul. This gospel teaches its readers apparently little about Jesus' origin, birth and baptism. It starts with a short description of the ministry of John the Baptist and his announcement of the coming of Jesus; John then speaks about Jesus as someone stronger than he himself, who will baptize with the Holy Spirit (1:1–8). Subsequently, Jesus' baptism by John in the river Jordan is described; afterwards the heavens opened and the Spirit descended upon him as a dove and a voice came from heaven and spoke, 'You are my Son, the Beloved; with you I am well pleased' (1:11). Because the voice from heaven obviously means the voice of God, Jesus is, according to this account, declared to be God's beloved Son at the moment of his baptism. This corresponds with the letters of Paul, insofar as in those Jesus is also called God's Son. The Gospel of Mark offers no opinion on whether Jesus is being regarded as God's Son from that moment and therefore adopted as God's Son at his baptism, or whether he actually was so beforehand.

21 See, e.g., Fee, *Philippians*, pp. 221–222.
22 Capes, *Old Testament Yahweh Texts*, pp. 136–149; Cf. Isaiah 40:13; Psalm 24:1.
23 Romans 4:7–8; 9:27–29; 11:34; 15:9–11; 1 Corinthians 3:20; 2 Corinthians 6:18.

Differing from the later Gospels of Matthew and Luke, the Gospel of Mark tells nothing about the circumstances of Jesus' birth. Only in Mark 6:1–3, mention is made of the residents of Jesus' home town, saying of him in surprise, 'Is not this the carpenter, the son of Mary and brother of James and Joses and Judas and Simon, and are not his sisters here with us?' The readers know from Mark 1:9, which tells that Jesus came from Nazareth in Galilee, that Jesus' hometown is Nazareth.[24] It is remarkable that in Mark 6:3 Jesus is called the son of Mary and that his father is neither mentioned here, nor in the rest of the Gospel of Mark. No suggestion is made, however, that there was something special about Jesus' birth.

After Mark's account of Jesus' baptism, he continues with a short record of Jesus' stay in the wilderness and of his preaching of the imminent kingdom of God (1:12–15).

Even though this gospel does not contain specific stories of Jesus' origin, it does give some indications of his very special identity. In addition to the account of Jesus' baptism, Jesus is designated as the Son of God on a few other occasions. However, for this designation we cannot point to Mark 1:1, even though it reads, according to most manuscripts, 'The beginning of the good news of Jesus Christ, the Son of God'. The words 'the Son of God' are not present in all manuscripts, and a comparison of the manuscripts shows us that the version without these words is the most original.[25] Of importance, however, is Mark 3:11, which reads that the unclean spirits cried out to Jesus, 'You are the Son of God', and Mark 5:7, where a possessed man cried out, 'What have you to do with me, Jesus, Son of the Most High God?' These incidents remind the reader of the exclamation of a possessed man in Mark 1:24, 'What have you to do with us, Jesus of Nazareth? Have you come to destroy us? I know who you are, the Holy One of God.'[26] We see that according to the Gospel of Mark the demons knew of Jesus' divine origin and authority.

In the story of Jesus' transfiguration, which tells that Moses and Elijah appeared to him and to three of his disciples, a voice came out of the cloud and spoke, 'This is my Son, the Beloved; listen to him' (9:7). The voice out of the cloud is surely intended as the voice of God, who thus, according to this gospel, confirms what was also said to Jesus at his baptism.

24 This is confirmed by Mark 1:24, where a possessed man addresses Jesus as 'Jesus of Nazareth'. This designation also occurs in Mark 10:47; 14:67; 16:6.
25 Bart D. Ehrman (1993), *The Orthodox Corruption of Scripture: The Effect of Early Christological Controversies on the Text of the New Testament*. New York, Oxford: Oxford University Press, pp. 72–75; Bruce M. Metzger (1994), *A Textual Commentary on the Greek New Testament* (2nd edn). Stuttgart: Deutsche Bibelgesellschaft, United Bible Societies, p. 62.
26 For the title 'the Holy One of God' compare John 6:69, where Peter calls Jesus thus; see section 1.3.

According to Mark 13:32, Jesus said about the horrors of the end of this world and about his own coming, 'But about that day or hour no one knows, neither the angels in heaven, nor the Son, but only the Father.' Some exegetes believe that it is hardly conceivable that Jesus spoke about himself as 'the Son' in the absolute sense. They, therefore, think that this saying originated from the early church.[27] Others think that Jesus perhaps did say this, but that he spoke of 'the Son' in the sense of 'the Son of Man',[28] a term which he, according to this gospel, regularly used to describe himself (the last time in 13:26), and which we will examine further. The objection to the latter opinion is that 'the Son' is found nowhere else as a shortened form of 'the Son of Man', and that 'the Son' in Mark 13:32 is named in contrast to 'the Father', meaning God the Father, of course.[29] On this basis, it is more probable that 'the Son' is a shortened designation of 'the Son of God (the Father)'. There are also exegetes who believe that Jesus really did say this, because it is unthinkable that the first church attributed to Jesus, whom they worshipped as divine, ignorance about the last day.[30] Yet it is very well possible that the first Christians, even though they worshipped Jesus as divine, regarded him subordinate to God the Father, so that he did not have all of the knowledge of the Father at his disposal.[31] By this approach too, Jesus could have made this statement. However this may be, this verse in the Gospel of Mark is a confirmation of the view that Jesus was 'the Son', which apparently means 'the Son of God'.

When Jesus was captured and subsequently interrogated by the high priest, he was asked, 'Are you the Messiah, the Son of the Blessed One?' (14:61). 'The Blessed One' is a Jewish designation of God and because, according to this account, the high priest uses this term here, it means he is reacting to the rumour that Jesus as Messiah was also the Son of God. In his answer, Jesus confirms this by saying, 'I am' (14:62), a statement to which we will get back further on in this section and in the discussion of the Gospel of John.

Finally, it is recorded that a centurion of the Roman army, when he saw how Jesus on the cross breathed his last, exclaimed, 'Truly this man was God's Son!'(15:39). The expression used in Greek can also be translated as 'this man was a son of God' or 'the son of a god'. Yet, in the context of the Gospel of Mark, this statement is clearly intended as an allusion to all the other texts where Jesus was called the Son of God.

So we see that this gospel repeatedly presents Jesus as the Son of God. We will consider the background and meaning of this title in chapter 8. First, we will return to the title 'Son of Man' (literally: 'the son of the human being'), which Jesus regularly uses in this gospel to indicate himself. In various statements, he refers to himself in this way when he announces his suffering, dying and resurrection,[32] but he also says that the Son of Man has authority to forgive sins and that he is lord of the Sabbath (2:10, 28). Moreover, according to this gospel, Jesus says that the Son of Man will be ashamed of whoever is ashamed of him and his words when he comes in the glory of his Father with the holy angels (8:38). Just as in a few other verses (13:26, 14:62), Jesus speaks of his coming (in the sense of 'second coming') as the Son of Man from heaven. To be sure, it is possible simply to interpret the title 'Son of Man' as 'human being', as in Psalm 8:4, which reads, 'What is man, that thou art mindful of him? and the son of man, that thou visitest him?' (KJV).[33] Another possibility is to connect this designation with the heavenly figure of whom Daniel says, 'As I watched in the night visions, I saw one like a human being [the Son of man, KJV] coming with the clouds of heaven' (Daniel 7:13). In the Book of Parables, that is the Second vision of the first book of Enoch, this figure regularly appears as a heavenly being residing directly under God ('the Lord of the spirits'), and ruling in heaven from his throne.[34]

---

27   E.g., Joachim Gnilka (1999), *Das Evangelium nach Markus (Mk 8,27-16,20)* (5th edn). Zürich, Düsseldorf: Benzinger Verlag, Neukirchen-Vluyn: Neukirchener Verlag, p. 207.
28   E.g., Rudolf Pesch (1977), *Das Markusevangelium 2*. Freiburg: Herder, p. 310.
29   This absolute use of 'the Son' in relation to God the Father by Jesus also occurs in Matthew 11:27 and Luke 10:22. For this, see section 2.3.
30   Vincent Taylor (1959), *The Gospel According to St. Mark*. London: MacMillan & Co, p. 522; B. M. F. van Iersel (1961), *'Der Sohn' in den synoptischen Jesusworten: Christusbezeichnung der Gemeinde oder Selbstbezeichnung Jesu?*. Leiden: Brill, pp. 117-123; Meier, *A Marginal Jew* I, 169; Craig A. Evans (2001), *Mark 8:27-16:20*. Nashville TN: Word Books, p. 336. Cf. also section 1.2.
31   Compare for this 1 Corinthians 15:23-28, from which it is apparent that Christ is subordinate to God the Father and that the moment in which all enemies will be subjected to Christ and the end will come is not settled, but depends on the battle yet to be fought.
32   Mark 8:31; 9:9, 12, 31; 10:33, 45; 14:21, 41.
33   See, e.g., Hurtado, *Lord Jesus Christ*, pp. 290-306. Joseph A. Fitzmyer (1979), *A Wandering Aramean: Collected Aramaic Essays*. Missoula: Scholars Press, pp. 143-160 concludes that it is not apparent from contemporaneous Aramaic texts that at that time the term 'son of man' was a special title.
34   1 Enoch 46:3-4; 48:2; 62:5, 7, 9, 14; 63:11; 69:29; 70:1; 71:17 (in 60:10 and 71:14 Enoch is addressed as 'Son of Man'). The parables of the book of Enoch have only been passed down in Ethiopic (OTP 1). Given that no Aramaic fragments of this have been found in Qumran and on the basis of the alleged historical context, J. C. Hindley (1967-68), 'Towards a date for the Similitudes of Enoch: An Historical Approach', *New Testament Studies* 14, 551-565, argued for a date which will be written at the beginning of the second century CE. J. T. Milik (1976), *The Books of Enoch: Aramaic Fragments of Qumrân Cave 4*. Oxford: Clarendon Press, pp. 91-96, dated the Parables to around 270

Because in the Gospel of Mark Jesus refers to himself in similar terms as the Son of Man from heaven, it is almost impossible not to connect these statements to this heavenly figure from the first book of Enoch.[35] This implies that the term Son of Man points to Jesus' heavenly identity.

After this examination of the designations Son of God and Son of Man, we will once more go through the Gospel of Mark to point to a few other texts which allude to Jesus' special origin and identity.

From the beginning of this gospel, a special light is shed upon Jesus. Mark 1:2–3 holds a combined quote from Exodus 23:20, Malachi 3:1 and Isaiah 40:3, 'See, I am sending my messenger ahead of you, who will prepare your way; the voice of one crying out in the wilderness: "Prepare the way of the Lord, make his paths straight"'. In the context of Exodus and Malachi, it is God the LORD speaking here. In the Gospel of Mark, these words have been so understood to mean that God sent his messenger John the Baptist ahead of Jesus to prepare his way. While it is written in Malachi 3:1, 'See, I am sending my messenger to prepare the way before *me*' – and this '*me*' refers to the LORD – Mark 1:2 reads, 'who will prepare *your* way', which refers to Jesus. The same application to Jesus of a text about the LORD is seen in the following quotation from Isaiah 40:3 in Mark 1:3. The 'voice' alludes to the voice of John the Baptist, whose mission was to 'prepare the way of the Lord' and 'make his paths straight'. Where Isaiah 40:3 speaks of 'the way of the LORD' and of 'the paths of our God', these words, in the context of Mark, point to the way and paths of Jesus. So, from the very beginning of this gospel, Jesus is implicitly identified with God the LORD.[36]

---

35 See Simon J. Gathercole (2006), *The Preexistent Son: Recovering the Christologies of Matthew, Mark, and Luke*. Grand Rapids MI, Cambridge: Eerdmans, pp. 253–271.

36 See Rudolf Pesch (1976), *Das Markusevangelium* 1. Freiburg: Herder, pp. 77–78; Robert A. Guelich (1989), *Mark 1–8:26*. Dallas TX: Word Books, p. 11; Joachim Gnilka (1998), *Das Evangelium nach Markus (Mk 1–8,26)* (5th edn). Zürich, Düsseldorf: Benzinger Verlag, Neukirchen-Vluyn: Neukirchener Verlag, pp. 44–45.

CE or slightly later. If one of these datings is correct, then the term 'Son of Man' in these Parables can not be used as an explanation for this title in the New Testament gospels. Matthew Black (1985), *The Book of Enoch or I Enoch: A New English Edition*. Leiden: Brill, pp. 181–189, however, states that the Parables do date back to before 70 CE, just as E. Isaac, in James H. Charlesworth, ed. (1983), *The Old Testament Pseudepigrapha* 1. London: Darton, Longman & Todd, p. 7. The translation 'Son of Man' conveys different Ethiopic expressions. See the notes in the translation of Isaac in Charlesworth, ed., *The Old Testament Pseudepigrapha* I, 34–50; also C. Colpe (1972), '*ho huios tou anthrōpou*' B III 2a, in Gerhard Friedrich and Geoffrey W. Bromiley, eds, *Theological Dictionary of the New Testament* 8. Grand Rapids MI: Eerdmans, pp. 423–427, and Black, *The Book of Enoch or I Enoch*, pp. 206–207, who elucidates that all Ethiopic expressions stem from the same original Hebrew or Aramaic term 'Son of Man'.

In Mark 1:8, John the Baptist states that Jesus will baptize with the Holy Spirit. For the prophets of the Old Testament, it is the LORD who will give his Spirit.[37] This means that Jesus will assume the role of the LORD.

Mark 2:1–12 tells of Jesus saying to a lame man laid in front of him, 'Son, your sins are forgiven' (2:5). The scribes who heard this, considered it blasphemy, because only God can forgive sins. Jesus, perceiving their objection, said to them, 'Which is easier, to say to the paralytic, "Your sins are forgiven", or to say, "Stand up and take your mat and walk?" But so that you may know that the Son of Man has authority on earth to forgive sins' – he said to the paralytic – 'I say to you, stand up, take your mat and go to your home' (2:9–11) – which the paralytic subsequently did. Since the traditional view of the scribes that only God can forgive sins[38] is not contradicted here, and Jesus as the Son of Man forgives the lame man his sins, it can be concluded that, according to this story, Jesus has divine authority and therefore acts on behalf of God.[39]

Mark 4:37–41 describes that Jesus is on a boat in the Sea of Galilee where he, to the amazement of his disciples, rebukes a heavy storm. Their question, 'Who then is this, that even the wind and the sea obey him?' (4:41) is not explicitly answered in this story. In the composition of this gospel, however, the answer is given by a possessed man in the land of the Gerasenes, who shortly thereafter addresses him as 'Jesus, Son of the Most High God' (5:7). From the perspective of the Old Testament, it is God (or the LORD) who stills turbulent waters.[40] Thus the evangelist suggests that Jesus is clothed with the power of God.

Mark 6:47–51 once more declares that Jesus is more powerful than the wind and the sea. The story reads that during the night he walked on the water towards his disciples, while they were rowing against the wind. In the Old Testament, it is God who tramples the waves.[41] Furthermore, two other allusions to the Old Testament suggest that Jesus is described as the LORD in this story. It was his intention 'to pass by' his disciples (6:48). In the Old Testament, it is said of the LORD that he passes by Moses and Elijah,[42] which refers to his appearing to them. Moreover, Jesus answers his disciples by saying, 'Take heart, it is I [*egō eimi*; literally: "I am"]; do not be afraid' (6:50). In the Old Testament, it is often the LORD who says in the same words, 'It is me (or I am with you), fear not.'[43] Especially in

---

37 Isaiah 44:3; Ezekiel 36:25–27; Joel 2:28–29.

38 E.g., Exodus 34:6–7; Psalm 103:3, 10–12; 130:3–4; Isaiah 43:25; 44:22; Daniel 9:9.

39 Cf. Gnilka, *Das Evangelium nach Markus (Mk 1–8,26)*, p. 101.

40 E.g., Psalm 65:7–8; 77:17; 89:10; 93:3–4; 107:29.

41 E.g., Job 9:8; Psalm 77:20; 34:6; 1 Kings 19:11.

42 Exodus 33:19–22; 34:6; 1 Kings 19:11.

43 Genesis 26:24 LXX (LXX = Septuagint); 46:3 LXX; Isaiah 41:10 LXX; Jeremiah 1:8 LXX; 1:17 LXX; 26:28 LXX / 46:28 MT (Masoretic text); 49:11 LXX / 42:11 MT.

Jesus, Gnosis and Dogma

the Greek translation of the book of Isaiah, the words 'I am' are spoken several times by the LORD.[44] These words also recall the name of the LORD in Exodus 3:14, 'I am who I am', reproduced in the Greek translation as 'I am the One Who Is'. As stated earlier, in our discussion of the Gospel of John we will further examine the meaning of the words 'I am' coming from Jesus' lips.

The story of Jesus' entry in Jerusalem (11:1–11) is also of importance. At first it is ambiguous if Jesus' statement about the colt, 'the Lord needs it' (11:3), refers to himself, to God or to the owner of the colt. However, when he rides into Jerusalem, he is greeted with the words of Psalm 118:26, which read, 'Hosanna! Blessed is the one who comes in the name of the Lord!' (11:9). This implies that this story closely associates him with the LORD.

The Gospel of Mark gives another concealed indication of Jesus' extraordinary origin, just before the end of its description of Jesus' public appearance (12:35–37). Jesus poses the question how the scribes could say that the Messiah is a son of David. David himself, inspired by the Holy Spirit, declared, 'The LORD said to my Lord, "Sit at my right hand, until I put your enemies under your feet"' (12:36; Psalm 110:1). Jesus then asks how it is possible that David called the Messiah Lord, while the Messiah is at the same time David's son. To these mysterious words neither reaction, nor explanation follows. Yet, the hidden purport is clear enough.[45] By now, the readers of this gospel know that Jesus is the Messiah.[46] It follows that he spoke about himself and about his future exaltation to God's right hand, in a concealed manner. In his view, David had already prophesized this. This teaching meant therefore, that Jesus, as Messiah, surpassed David so that David called him 'my Lord', even though Jesus was descended from David. The question is, however, how Jesus surpassed David. Did this – considered from David's point of view – relate only to the future, as Jesus' exaltation unto the right hand of God still lay in the future?[47] Or did Jesus – or the Gospel of Mark – suggest that David, when he composed the psalm, called the Messiah 'my Lord', because he acknowledged him as such, even though his exaltation was still to come? In that case, the Messiah precedes David in time and this gospel suggests in enigmatic language that the origin of Jesus

Jesus' Origin and Identity

as Messiah should not be looked for in his birth, but in days long gone.[48] In that case this passage would be an important but concealed testimony of Jesus' pre-existence. I indeed think that this text has to be explained in this way. For this point of view, it is of little importance whether Jesus himself really said this in these words. However, I do think that the exegetes who plead for the authenticity of this instruction could be right.[49]

If it is correct that in the Gospel of Mark Jesus is described as the LORD, who apparently already existed before he came to earth as a human being, then the texts speaking of Jesus' 'coming' deserve special attention. Thus the demons said to him in Mark 1:24, 'Have you come (*ēlthes*) to destroy us?' It is possible to apply this 'coming', to Mark 1:14, where the same Greek verb (*ēlthen*) is used to state that Jesus came to Galilee. It is also possible that Jesus' 'coming' refers to his previous heavenly existence, just as in other writings the angels say that they have come, for example to a human being on earth.[50] In addition, when Jesus says about the proclamation of his message, 'for that is what I came out to do (*exēlthon*)' (1:38), this can be interpreted in this sense, although a more down to earth explanation is not excluded.[51] The same goes for Jesus' sayings, 'I have come not to call the righteous, but the sinners' (2:17) and 'but the Son of Man came not to be served but to serve' (10:45).[52]

---

44 Isaiah 43:10, 25; 45:18–19, 22; 46:4; 48:12, 17; 51:12; 52:6.
45 Riemer Roukema (2006), 'De Messias aan Gods rechterhand', in G. C. den Hertog, S. Schoon, eds, *Messianisme en eindtijdverwachting bij joden en christenen*. Zoetermeer: Boekencentrum, pp. 92–107 (92–95).
46 See Mark 1:1; 8:29 and section 1.3.
47 Thus Joachim Jeremias (1971), *Neutestamentliche Theologie* I. Gütersloh: Gerd Mohn, p. 247.

48 Thus, e.g., Oscar Cullmann (1957), *Die Christologie des Neuen Testaments*. Tübingen: J. C. B. Mohr, p. 133; Pierre Bonnard (1963), *L'Evangile selon Saint Matthieu*. Neuchâtel: Delachaux et Niestlé, pp. 330–331; Julius Schniewind (1968), *Das Evangelium nach Matthäus*. Göttingen: Vandenhoeck & Ruprecht, p. 223; William L. Lane (1974), *The Gospel According to Mark: The English Text with Introduction, Exposition and Notes*. London: Marshall, Morgan & Scott, p. 438; Joseph A. Fitzmyer (1985), *The Gospel According to Luke (X–XXIV)*. New York: Doubleday, p. 1312.
49 Roukema, 'De Messias aan Gods rechterhand', pp. 92–95; Taylor, *The Gospel According to St. Mark*, pp. 490–493; Ernst Lohmeyer (1967), *Das Evangelium des Markus* (17th edn). Göttingen: Vandenhoeck & Ruprecht, pp. 261–263; David M. Hay (1973), *Glory at the Right Hand: Psalm 110 in Early Christianity*. Nashville TN: Abingdon Press, pp. 110–111; Pesch, *Das Markusevangelium 2*, p. 254; Michel Gourgues (1978), *A la droite de Dieu: Résurrection de Jésus et actualisation du Psaume 110:1 dans le Nouveau Testament*. Paris: Gabalda, p. 142; Fitzmyer, *The Gospel According to Luke (X–XXIV)*, pp. 1309–1313.
50 Sevenster, *De Christologie van het Nieuwe Testament*, pp. 103–104; Gathercole, *The Preexistent Son*, pp. 53; 84; 101; 113–147; 150–152, etc. I consider James D. G. Dunn's criticism of Gathercole's interpretations exaggerated. (http://www.bookreviews.org/pdf/5607_6160.pdf, consulted 1 May 2007). Dunn however, would not even hear of Jesus' pre-existence in Paul (see the previous section), so his criticism was to be expected.
51 Thus Ernst Lohmeyer (1967), *Das Evangelium des Markus* (17th edn). Göttingen: Vandenhoeck & Ruprecht, p. 43; Walter Schmithals (1979), *Das Evangelium nach Markus Kapitel 1–9,1*. Gütersloh: Mohn, Würzburg: Echter Verlag, p. 134.
52 Sevenster, *De Christologie van het Nieuwe Testament*, p. 103; Gathercole, *The Preexistent Son*, pp. 154–158; 167–168.

Jesus, Gnosis and Dogma

In this discussion of the Gospel of Mark, I have not always examined the question of whether a saying or act of Jesus is really authentic. For the many stories, this cannot be determined any more, and from a historical-critical point of view it is often considered doubtful. For this investigation, the answer to this question is not of vital importance. What matters is how the author of the Gospel of Mark portrayed Jesus 'theologically'. We have seen that he traces Jesus' origin, in his capacity of Messiah, to the time before David. Jesus is regularly called Son of God and he calls himself the Son of Man. It is told that he forgives sins with divine authority and that he rebukes the turbulent sea. A few Old Testament quotations closely associate Jesus with the name of the LORD. On a few occasions he said, 'It is I,' which alludes to the name of the LORD. The texts in which his 'coming' are mentioned, can be explained as references to his heavenly origin. It is obvious that in this gospel, Jesus is not merely characterized as a very special man, although he most certainly was.

2.3 The Gospel of Matthew

As has already been remarked in section 1.3, a large part of the Gospel of Mark, often in a slightly different form, is echoed in the Gospel of Matthew; it is generally accepted that the author of the Gospel of Matthew assimilated the Gospel of Mark in his own book about Jesus. The Gospel of Matthew is generally dated around 80–90 CE.[53] All sorts of passages about Jesus' origin and identity examined in the previous section are included in this gospel too. This means that here also, Jesus sees the Holy Spirit descend upon him at his baptism and is called 'my beloved Son' by a voice from heaven (3:16–17). Also elsewhere in this gospel he is repeatedly described as the Son of God; sometimes, compared to the text of Mark, this title has even been added to the story.[54] Jesus regularly calls himself the Son of Man and speaks even more often than in the Gospel of Mark about the purpose for which he has come.[55] In this gospel too, Jesus teaches that the Messiah is David's Lord and therefore it suggests that in time he precedes David (22:41–46).

---

53 Ulrich Luz (2002), *Das Evangelium nach Matthäus (Mt 1–7)* (5th edn). Düsseldorf, Zürich: Benzinger Verlag, Neukirchen-Vluyn: Neukirchener Verlag, pp. 103–104.
54 Thus in Matthew 14:33, where Jesus' disciples in the boat, after he has walked on the sea towards them, and the wind had died down, say, 'Truly you are the Son of God'; and in Matthew 16:16, where Peter says, 'You are the Messiah, the Son of the living God.'
55 Sayings on his 'coming' which are not written in Mark do appear in Matthew 5:17; 10:34–35.

Jesus' Origin and Identity

Using the Gospel of Mark as his starting point, Matthew has added other stories and sayings of Jesus. In the first place, it is striking that the Gospel of Matthew contains some stories about Jesus' origin, birth and earliest childhood. Over forty-two generations his genealogy is traced back to David and Abraham. Furthermore, it is mentioned that Joseph, penultimate on the list, was the husband of Mary who gave birth to Jesus, called the Christ (1:1–17). Directly following this, it is made clear why it is not written that Joseph fathered Jesus by Mary; an angel explains to Joseph that the child conceived in her is from the Holy Spirit. The evangelist sees in this the fulfilment of a prophecy of Isaiah (1:18–23; Isaiah 7:14). This implies that, according to this gospel, Jesus is conceived by the Holy Spirit and born of Mary while she was yet a virgin. This story of his miraculous birth testifies to the extraordinary intervention of God and therefore of Jesus' exceptional origin and identity. Although one might expect that someone who is said to be conceived by God's Holy Spirit is, for this reason, called 'Son of God', this explanation is not explicitly given in this gospel. Yet it is true that as a small child Jesus was already called 'my Son' by God, when it is told that he returns with his parents from Egypt to Israel. The evangelist regards this as a fulfilment of the prophecy: 'Out of Egypt I have called my Son' (2:15; Hosea 11:1).[56] Furthermore, the fact that Jesus was called Emmanuel, which means 'God with us' (1:23), testifies to his exceptional identity.

The Gospel of Matthew describes much more emphatically than the Gospel of Mark that Jesus came as the shepherd to look for the lost sheep of Israel and to have mercy on those who have no shepherd.[57] Young S. Chae makes a reasonable case for the evangelist seeing in this a fulfilment of the prophecy of Ezekiel that the LORD himself will search for his sheep and as a shepherd look for his flock (Ezekiel 34:11–16). In this gospel Jesus predicts that he, as the coming Son of Man, will separate the sheep from the goats (25:31–46). This image refers to Ezekiel 34:17–22, which reads that the LORD will judge between the sheep, the rams and the he-goats. Chae concludes that in Matthew Jesus not only obtains the characteristics of David, whom God, according to Ezekiel 34:23, will appoint over his flock, but that he is also described as shepherd in terms of the LORD himself.[58]

---

56 In Hosea 11:1 the people of Israel are originally meant by 'my son'.
57 Matthew 2:6; 9:36; 10:6, 16; 15:24; 25:31–46; 26:31; cf. Mark 6:34; 14:27.
58 Young S. Chae (2006), *Jesus as the Eschatological Davidic Shepherd: Studies in the Old Testament, Second Temple Judaism, and in the Gospel of Matthew*. Tübingen: J. C. B. Mohr, pp. 173; 205–233; 387–395. For the LORD as shepherd see also, e.g., Psalm 23:1-4; 74:1; 78:52; 79:13; 80:1; Isaiah 40:11; Jeremiah 23:1–5; 31:10; 50:19; Micah 2:12; 4:6–7.

Furthermore, Matthew has some passages in common with the Gospel of Luke, which do not, or not in the same form, appear in the Gospel of Mark. Exegetes presume that in those cases Matthew and Luke go back to an older source, named Q.[59] In this source also, Jesus is named 'the Son of God' and he speaks of himself as the Son of Man. In the story of Jesus' temptation in the wilderness, the devil says to him: 'If you are the Son of God ....'[60] In another passage Jesus praises God in the following words,

I thank you, Father, Lord of heaven and earth,
because you have hidden these things from the wise and the intelligent
and have revealed them to infants;
yes, Father, for such was your gracious will.
All things have been handed over to me by my Father;
and no one knows the Son except the Father,
and no one knows the Father except the Son
and anyone to whom the Son chooses to reveal him.[61]

In these words Jesus designates himself as 'the Son'. He indicates that he and God the Father know each other in a unique, intimate way and that only he as the Son is able to share the knowledge of God his Father with others.[62] Therefore, the high position Jesus occupies according to Q and according to the Gospel of Matthew (and also that of Luke) is evident.

A few remarkable sayings of Jesus, originating from Q, occur at the end of a scathing speech to the Pharisees. According to this gospel, Jesus first says here,

Therefore I send you prophets, sages, and scribes,
some of whom you will kill and crucify,
and some you will flog in your synagogues
and pursue from town to town. (23:34)

Here Jesus is speaking with divine authority, as it were, since according to this text he is responsible for sending prophets, sages and scribes to the people of Israel.[63] These and the following words (23:35–36) have a parallel in Luke 11:49–51, but there Jesus states that God's Wisdom has spoken thus. In Matthew 23:34, the reference to the figure of God's Wisdom[64] is absent and Jesus speaks in his own name. In this way, the evangelist identifies him as the incarnation of God's Wisdom. Subsequently, Jesus says:

Jerusalem, Jerusalem, the city that kills the prophets and stones those who are sent to it! How often have I desired to gather your children together as a hen gathers her brood under her wings, and you were not willing. (23:37)

These words explicitly addressed to Jerusalem, are surprising in the context of this gospel, because it does not say that Jesus has been to Jerusalem previously. Yet he says to the city, 'How often have I desired to gather your children together.'[65] The evangelist, therefore, has Jesus say something that we can expect from the mouth of a prophet on behalf of God, who by the voice of his prophets has so often addressed Jerusalem. Jesus says this however – according to this gospel – not after the prophetic introduction, 'Thus says the Lord,' but in his own name. Therefore, he speaks as if he were the LORD, or at least the Wisdom of the LORD himself.[66]

---

59 J. M. Robinson, P. Hoffmann, J. S. Kloppenborg, eds (2000), *The Critical Edition of Q: Synopsis including the Gospels of Matthew and Luke, Mark and Thomas with English, German, and French Translations of Q and Thomas*. Leuven: Peeters, Minneapolis: Fortress.
60 Matthew 4:3, 5; Luke 4:3, 9.
61 Matthew 11:25–27; cf. Luke 10:21–22.
62 Cf. the absolute use of 'the Son' in Matthew 24:36 and Mark 13:32 (see section 2.2).
63 Cf., e.g, Jeremiah 35:15; 2 Chronicles 24:19; 36:15–16, where it is the LORD who sends his prophets.
64 See, e.g., Proverbs 1:20–33; 8:1–9:18; Ecclesiasticus 24:1–22; Enoch 42 and chapter 8 in this book; also Gathercole, *The Preexistent Son*, pp. 199–201.
65 More or less the same is true of the parallel in Luke 13:34; Jesus had only been to Jerusalem as a newborn baby and a twelve-year-old according to Luke (Luke 2:22–52). According to the Gospel of John, Jesus had been to Jerusalem more often during his public appearance (John 2:13; 5:1; 7:10; 12:12).
66 Ulrich Luz (1997), *Das Evangelium nach Matthäus (Mt 18–25)*. Zürich, Düsseldorf: Benzinger Verlag, Neukirchen-Vluyn: Neukirchener Verlag, p. 380, assumes that Matthew 23:37–39 originated from an early Christian prophet who spoke in the name of the exalted Lord Jesus. Sherman E. Johnson, George A. Buttrick (1951), 'The Gospel According to Matthew', in George A. Buttrick et al., eds, *The Interpreter's Bible VII*. New York, Nashville TN, pp. 229–625 (540) and M. Eugene Boring (1995), 'The Gospel of Matthew: Introduction, Commentary, and Reflections', in Leander E. Keck et al, eds, *The New Interpreter's Bible VIII*, Nashville TN, pp. 87–505 (438) refer here to Jesus as the incarnation of God's Wisdom. Gathercole, *The Preexistent Son*, pp. 210–221 also explains Matthew 23:37 as a reference to Jesus' attempts to bring together Jerusalem before he became a human being.

2.4 The Gospel of Luke

Like the Gospel of Matthew, the Gospel of Luke is also often dated about 80–90 CE.[67] Because this gospel has many passages in common with Mark and Matthew, it corresponds to a large degree with these gospels regarding Jesus' origin and identity. In this gospel too, Jesus is described as the Son of Man, as the Son of God and as the Messiah who is David's Lord (20:41–44).

Characteristic for the Gospel of Luke are, among other things, the stories about Jesus' birth. In contrast to the Gospel of Matthew, an angel here announces not to Joseph but to Mary that she is to conceive by the Holy Spirit. The angel, named Gabriel, instructs her to give her son the name Jesus. He announces that Jesus will be called the 'Son of the Most High' and 'Son of God', and that God will give him the throne of his father David. Jesus will reign over the house of Jacob for ever and there will be no end of his kingdom, says Gabriel according to Luke (1:26–34). To be sure, the view that Jesus is conceived by the Holy Spirit and born of the Virgin Mary is shared by the Gospel of Luke and the Gospel of Matthew, but we see that the stories are told very differently. In contrast with the Gospel of Matthew, the Gospel of Luke does show a relationship between Jesus' conception by the Holy Spirit and his designation as 'Son of God'. In this way the Gospel of Luke wants to point to Jesus' divine origin and identity.

This is also evident when the angel Gabriel tells ageing Zechariah about his son John (the Baptist), saying that he will prepare the way for the Lord (1:17). Later, Zechariah uses these words when he says of his newborn son, 'And you, child, will be called the prophet of the Most High; for you will go before the Lord to prepare his ways' (1:76). These words remind one of the prophecy in Malachi 3:1, where Malachi speaks in the name of the LORD of a messenger who will prepare the way for him. It is also reminiscent of the prophecy in Isaiah 40:3 which we have already discussed in our examination of the Gospel of Mark.[68] Considering that in the Gospel of Luke, John the Baptist is regarded as Jesus' forerunner,[69] these Old Testament prophecies about the way of the LORD are understood here too as the way of Jesus. Directly afterwards, Zechariah speaks of 'the tender mercy of our God, when the dawn from on high will break upon us' (1:78). The term translated here with 'dawn', *anatolē*, means on the one hand sunrise, but in the Septuagint it is also a designation for the messianic saviour, to be translated as 'offspring' or 'branch'.[70] With this term Zechariah points to Jesus, of whom he says that he comes 'from on high', therefore from heaven.[71]

Jesus' unique identity is confirmed when the angels announce to the shepherds at Bethlehem that a Saviour is born unto them who is called Christ the Lord (2:11). Since elsewhere in this gospel the name 'the Lord' is used for God,[72] here Jesus is again closely associated with God. In the continuation of the Gospel of Luke, Jesus is regularly called 'the Lord',[73] in this respect, this gospel differs from the Gospels of Mark and Matthew, where the explicit use of 'the Lord' meaning Jesus hardly ever occurs.[74]

In the account of the appearance of John the Baptist, Jesus' baptism is all but mentioned in passing. Here, all the emphasis is put on the Holy Spirit who descended upon Jesus as a dove and on the voice sounding from heaven (3:21–22). It is doubtful, however, what this voice said according to the original text of the Gospel of Luke. Most manuscripts read, 'You are my Son, the Beloved; with you I am well pleased' (3:22), which literally corresponds to Mark 1:11. Yet, various manuscripts dating from the second to the fifth centuries here read, 'You are my son, today I have begotten you.' These words come from Psalm 2:7, where they are spoken by the LORD to the king. When they are applied to Jesus, they suggest that he became God's Son on the day of his baptism and that he was not so before. As we will see in section 9.4, a persuasion existed in early Christianity holding that God the Father adopted Jesus as his own Son at his baptism, but this view has been rejected by the church. Some exegetes consider it probable that Luke 3:22 originally read, 'You are my Son, today I have begotten you.' They believe that copyists of the manuscripts have replaced these words with the text from the Gospel of Mark, which did not so much suggest that only at his baptism Jesus was begotten or adopted to be God's Son.[75] If Luke 3:22 indeed originally

---

67 Joseph A. Fitzmyer (1981), *The Gospel According to Luke (I–IX)*, New York: Doubleday, pp. 53–57; François Bovon (1989), *Das Evangelium nach Lukas (Lk 1,1–9,50)*. Zürich, Düsseldorf: Benzinger Verlag, Neukirchen-Vluyn: Neukirchener Verlag, p. 23.
68 In Luke 3:4 it reads, "The voice of one crying out in the wilderness: "Prepare the way of the Lord, make his paths straight"". See section 2.2.
69 See also Luke 3:1–7, which quotes Isaiah 40:3–5; Luke 7:27.
70 Jeremiah 23:5; Zechariah 3:8; 6:12.
71 Fitzmyer, *The Gospel According to Luke (I–IX)*, pp. 387–388; Bovon, *Das Evangelium nach Lukas (Lk 1,1–9,50)*, pp. 109–110; Gathercole, *The Preexistent Son*, pp. 238–242.
72 See, e.g., Luke 1:6, 9, 11, 16, 17, 25, 28, 32, 38, 43, 45, 46, 58, 66, 68, 76; 2:9, 15, etc.
73 E.g., in Luke 7:13, 19; 10:1, 39, 41; 11:39; 12:42, etc.; see Fitzmyer, *The Gospel According to Luke (I–IX)*, pp. 200–204; C. Kavin Rowe (2006), *Early Narrative Christology: The Lord in the Gospel of Luke*. Berlin, New York: Walter de Gruyter.
74 Apart from the address 'Lord', which can also be understood as 'sir', the absolute use of 'the Lord' for Jesus in the other synoptic gospels might possibly occur in Mark 11:3 and Matthew 21:3; see also Matthew 24:42 and section 2.2.
75 Ehrman, *The Orthodox Corruption of Scripture*, pp. 62–67.

did contain the text from Psalm 2:7, this would emphasize the great importance the evangelist attached to this event, in which the Spirit of God descended upon Jesus. This does not alter the fact, that in this gospel God's involvement with Jesus as God's Son does not begin at his baptism, but at least at his conception in the Virgin Mary.

In a different way, the subsequent genealogy traces back Jesus' origin to God via seventy-seven forefathers. Joseph is named first, with the comment that Jesus was believed to be his son, and Adam is mentioned last as '(the son) of God' (3:23-38). This genealogy of Jesus stemming from God seems a confirmation of the previous stories, but actually does not tell anything extraordinary. In this way, it can after all be said of all of Jesus' forefathers that they stem from Adam and thus from God.

A statement of Jesus which only appears in the Gospel of Luke reads, 'I came to bring fire to the earth; and how I wish it were already kindled!' (12:49).[76] Apparently, it is suggested that this fire is thrown from heaven. This fire can point to punishment[77] or, which is more probable here, to Jesus' heavenly pre-existence.[78] This saying has been understood as pointing to Jesus' message and the Spirit.[79] but an objection to this explanation is that it does not say that Jesus came from heaven with this fire in his hand.[80] Yet, this statement does suggest that Jesus came to hurl this fire from a high position.

Finally, a remarkable aspect of the Gospel of Luke is the recurrent mentioning of God looking after his people or – translated differently – visiting his people.[81] Adelbert Denaux connects this theme with texts from the Hellenistic world and from the Old Testament in which a god or the LORD looks for people.[82] He points out that in the Gospel of Luke Jesus, on his journey to Jerusalem, visits this city and thus humanity. According to Denaux this suggests that in Jesus, God comes to mankind, and this gospel thus points to Jesus' divine origin.[83]

2.5 The Gospel of John

In the synoptic gospels we saw that Jesus is described in different ways as the Son of God and as the Lord. In a more or less concealed manner, they refer to his heavenly origin and therefore his pre-existence with God. This exalted view of Jesus' origin and identity comes to light much more emphatically in the Gospel of John.[84] This gospel is usually dated to the end of the first century (90–100 CE), but there are also scholars who believe that it was written in the 60s of the first century.[85]

The introduction (often called prologue) of this gospel begins like this:

> In the beginning was the Word, and the Word was with God, and the Word was God. He was in the beginning with God. All things came into being through him, and without him not one thing came into being. (1:1–3)

John 1:14 says that the Word became flesh, meaning that this divine Word became a mortal human being. The non-suspecting reader could possibly ask himself who is this Word (*Logos* in Greek). A bit later on it is disclosed that it concerns Jesus Christ in his pre-existence, for the evangelist continues,

> And the Word became flesh and lived among us, and we have seen his glory, the glory as of a father's only son, full of grace and truth. (John[86] testified to him and cried out, "This was he of whom I said, "He who comes after me ranks ahead of me because he was before me.'")) From

---

76 Other sayings in which Jesus discusses with what purpose he came can be found in Luke 5:32; 12:51; 19:10.
77 See, e.g., Genesis 19:24; 2 Kings 1:10-14; Luke 3:9, 17; 17:29; in Luke 9:54-55 Jesus rejects the suggestion of his disciples to command fire to come down from heaven and consume the inhospitable Samaritans.
78 Thus François Bovon (1996), *Das Evangelium nach Lukas (Lk 9,51–14,35)*. Zürich, Düsseldorf: Benzinger Verlag, Neukirchen-Vluyn: Neukirchener Verlag, pp. 346; 349–352; cf. Luke 3:16; Acts 2:3, 19.
79 Cf. Sevenster, *De Christologie van het Nieuwe Testament*, pp. 103–104; Gathercole, *The Preexistent Son*, pp. 161-163.
80 Thus correctly Theodor Zahn (1913), *Das Evangelium des Lucas*. Leipzig: Deichert, p. 514. According to him, the saying means that the fire would descend upon earth on Jesus' order or prayer, while he was on earth.
81 *Episkeptesthai* in Luke 1:68, 78 (where 'the dawn from on high' is the subject); 7:16; *episkopē* in Lucas 19:44.
82 In the Old Testament: Genesis 18–19; 21:1; 50:24–25; Exodus 4:31; 13:19; Psalm 8:5; 79:15 LXX/80:15 MT; Jeremiah 36:10 LXX/29:10 MT; Zephaniah 2:7; Zechariah 10:3.
83 Adelbert Denaux (1999), 'The Theme of Divine Visits and Human (In)hospitality in Luke-Acts. Its Old Testament and Graeco-Roman Antecendents', in J. Verheyden, ed., *The Unity of Luke-Acts*. Leuven: Peeters, pp. 255–279 (276–279). See also Rowe, *Early Narrative Christology*, pp. 159-166.
84 See for this section: Riemer Roukema (2006), 'Jesus and the Divine Name in the Gospel of John', in George H. van Kooten, ed., *The Revelation of the Name YHWH to Moses: Perspectives from Judaism, the Pagan Graeco-Roman World, and Early Christianity*. Leiden: Brill, pp. 207–223.
85 Klaus Berger (1997), *Im Anfang war Johannes: Datierung und Theologie des vierten Evangeliums*. Stuttgart: Quell; P.L. Hofrichter, ed. (2002), *Für und wider die Priorität des Johannesevangeliums*. Hildesheim: Olms.
86 John the Baptist is meant here.

his fullness we have all received, grace upon grace. The law indeed was given through Moses; grace and truth came through Jesus Christ. No one has ever seen God. It is God the only Son, who is close to the Father's heart, who has made him known. (John 1:14–18)[87]

It appears that, according to the evangelist, Jesus is the 'Word incarnate' and the Son of God, who since the beginning of creation is with God the Father and is himself also God. Just as Paul wrote earlier in 1 Corinthians 8:6, it is written here that everything originated by him (the Logos, Jesus Christ). The evangelist does not write that the Logos was already called Jesus during his pre-existence, but elsewhere in this gospel, Jesus alludes to his origin prior to his life on earth. So he says, 'before Abraham was, I am' (8:58). While according to the synoptic gospels, Jesus merely alludes to his pre-existence in a concealed manner, according to the Fourth Gospel, he refers to it without any reservation.

In this gospel, John the Baptist points right away to Jesus' heavenly origin when he says that the one whom he announces was before him (1:15, 30). The Fourth Gospel, as opposed to the synoptic gospels, does not relate explicitly that Jesus was baptized. Therefore, no voice sounds from heaven calling him 'my Son'. John the Baptist does testify, however, that he saw the Holy Spirit descend upon Jesus and that he then called him 'the Son of God' – at least, according to most manuscripts (1:34).[88] As opposed to the synoptic gospels, in the Fourth Gospel Jesus' disciples immediately acknowledge him as the Messiah and as the Son of God (1:41, 49). This acknowledgement is confirmed in various passages in this gospel.[89] Jesus also speaks here about himself as the Son of Man who descended from heaven.[90]

Like the synoptic gospels, the Gospel of John suggests that Jesus is the LORD of the Old Testament. John 1:14 says that the Word is full of grace and truth, and John 1:17 says that grace and truth came through Jesus Christ. In Exodus 34:6, the description 'full of grace and truth' (also translated as 'great in love and faithfulness') refers to the LORD when he appears to Moses on Mount Sinai. Anthony T. Hanson rightly deduces from this similarity in formulation that on occasions in Israel's history where God appears, in the view of the Gospel of John, not God (the Father) appears, but the Logos, i.e. the Word.[91] Further on we will see again that in the theology of this gospel the terms Logos and LORD refer to the same divine figure.

That the LORD has come in the person of Jesus is confirmed by a few Old Testament prophecies and images in which statements about the LORD are related to Jesus. Just as in the synoptic gospels, the prophecy from Isaiah 40:3 appears.[92] In John 1:23, John the Baptist quotes this text, 'I am the voice of one crying out in the wilderness', "Make straight the way of the Lord"'. In Isaiah 40:3, this text is about the way of God the LORD, but John the Baptist means that he wants to prepare the way for Jesus. 'The LORD' therefore refers to Jesus. Likewise, this gospel holds more allusions to Jesus' heavenly identity. In a similar way to Mark 1:8, John the Baptist says in John 1:33 that Jesus 'baptizes with the Holy Spirit'. We already saw that in the Old Testament it is the LORD who will pour out his Spirit.[93] In John 3:29, John the Baptist uses the image of the bride, the bridegroom and the friend of the bridegroom; he distinctly regards himself as the friend of the bridegroom. Thus he alludes to the Old Testament image of the LORD who as bridegroom marries his people, and he associates Jesus as bridegroom with the LORD.[94] Like the synoptic gospels, the Gospel of John tells of Jesus' entry into Jerusalem. According to the Fourth Gospel, the crowd greets him crying, 'Hosanna! Blessed is he who comes in the name of the Lord, the King of Israel' (12:13). To this quotation of Psalm 118:26, the title 'the King of Israel' has been added from Zephaniah 3:14–15. Andrew C. Brunson explains that in the person of Jesus, it is in fact Yahweh (the LORD) who visits his city.[95] A final example: in John 12:40, the evangelist quotes Isaiah 6:10

---

87 The reading 'God the only Son' (*monogenēs theos*; 1:18) appears in the oldest manuscripts and with a few early church fathers, but the variant reading 'the only Son' (*ho monogenēs huios*) is much stronger attested. Ehrman, *The Orthodox Corruption of Scripture*, pp. 78–82, argues that 'the only (or: unique) Son' is the original reading, which has been replaced by 'God the only Son' (or, as he translates it, 'the unique God') for dogmatic reasons. Probably he is right in this. – In older translations the term 'only' (*monogenēs*) was translated as 'only-begotten'. For this, see section 9.1, note 7.

88 There are, however, also manuscripts which read in John 1:34: 'that he is the elect of God', and Ehrman, *The Orthodox Corruption of Scripture*, pp. 69–70, might be right in his argument that this has been the original reading, which has been replaced in most manuscripts by 'the Son of God'.

89 E.g., John 3:18; 4:25–26; 5:25; 10:36; 11:27; 17:3; 20:31.

90 John 3:13; cf. 1:51 [52]; 3:14; 6:27, 53, 62; 8:28, 9:35; 12:23, 34; 13:31.

91 Anthony T. Hanson (1980), *New Testament Interpretation of Scripture*. London: SPCK, p. 103 = Hanson (1976), 'John i. 14–18 and Exodus xxxiv'. *New Testament Studies*, 23, 90–101 (p. 96); also in Hanson (1991) *The Prophetic Gospel: A Study of John and the Old Testament*. Edinburgh: T&T Clark, pp. 21–32; and Nils A. Dahl (1962), 'The Johannine Church and History', in W. Klassen, G. Snyder, eds, *Current Issues in New Testament Interpretation: Essays in Honor of Otto A. Piper*. New York: Harper, pp. 124–142 (132).

92 See sections 2.2 and 2.4; Mark 1:3; Matthew 3:3; Luke 1:17; 1:76; 3:4–6.

93 Isaiah 44:3; Ezekiel 36:25–27; Joel 2:28–29.

94 See Isaiah 54:4–8; 62:4–5; Jeremiah 2:2; 3:20; Ezekiel 16:8; 23:4; Hosea 2:19–20.

95 Andrew C. Brunson (2003), *Psalm 118 in the Gospel of John: An Intertextual Study on the New Exodus Pattern in the Theology of John*. Tübingen: J. C. B. Mohr, pp. 179;

which says that the people of Israel have a hardened heart and blinded eyes, so that they cannot turn and be healed. Isaiah heard these harsh words in the temple in Jerusalem, where he saw the LORD sitting upon his throne and he himself was called to be a prophet (Isaiah 6:1–7). The evangelist quotes these words because he believes they can be applied to those contemporaries of Jesus who did not believe in him. Furthermore, he declares in John 12:41 that Isaiah said these things 'because he saw his glory'. This means that Isaiah saw Jesus' glory in the temple, i.e., Jesus Christ in his pre-existence.[96] Thus, in the view of this gospel, the pre-existent Jesus Christ appeared as the LORD upon his throne to Isaiah in the temple of Jerusalem. What is important here is the expression 'his glory' (12:41). This term 'glory' (*doxa* in Greek) is also found in John 1:14, which says of the incarnate Word, 'we have beheld his glory, glory as of the only Son from the Father'. This text about the glory of the Word refers to the glory he had with God the Father and corresponds to the glory of the LORD which Isaiah witnessed in the temple. This correspondence again demonstrates that 'the Word' (the Logos) from the prologue to this gospel is identical to the LORD (Yahweh) of the Old Testament. In both cases it concerns the glory of Jesus Christ in his pre-existence. We can add that, according to John 17:5 and 17:24, Jesus himself also mentions the 'glory' that he possessed with his Father before the world existed.

Furthermore, the Gospel of John points out with yet another Old Testament motive that Jesus is the manifestation of the LORD. It contains a large number of sayings of Jesus stating or beginning with 'I am'. In our examination of the Gospel of Mark, we saw that Jesus said, 'It is I' (or 'I am') in Mark 6:50 and 14:62, and that in the Old Testament it is repeatedly the LORD who says this. In the Gospel of John, Jesus' 'I am' sayings can be divided in two categories. First, there are sayings in John 6:20, where Jesus (as in Mark 6:50) says, 'It is I, do not be afraid'.[97] In John 8:24, 8:28, 18:5–6 and 18:8, Jesus also says 'I am' in the absolute sense, which is a strong reminder of the words of the LORD in the book of Isaiah[98] and of the explication of his name as 'I am who I am' in Exodus 3:14. In the second category after 'I am' follows what Jesus then states to be: for example, 'I am the light of the world' (8:12). In this way Jesus identifies himself with the light of the Word which, according to John 1:4–9, shines in the darkness to enlighten everyone. In the Old Testament the LORD is often represented as light.[99] Another example: in John 10:11, Jesus states, 'I am the good shepherd.' This points, among other things, to the prophecy we examined in the discussion of the Gospel of Matthew, Ezekiel 34, where the LORD is the good shepherd who will look after his people.[100] So, these texts affirm what we saw in the use of other Old Testament texts and motives, that Jesus is presented as the LORD.

There is yet another aspect of the Gospel of John that deserves our attention. A few times, Jesus speaks of the name of his Father. In John 5:43, he says, 'I have come in my Father's name', and in John 10:25, 'The works that I do in my Father's name testify to me'. In John 12:28, Jesus prays, 'Father, glorify your name'. In John 17:6, he says, 'I have made your name known to those whom you gave me from the world', and in 17:26, 'I made your name known to them, and I will make it known.' C. H. Dodd connects this revelation and glorification of God's name with Jesus' 'I am' statements and with the previously mentioned prophecies from the book of Isaiah, where these words sound as utterances of the LORD.[101] Jesus' revelation and glorification of God's name mean, therefore, that in his teaching and deeds he has shown who his Father really is. His extremely close bond with the Father can also be read in Jesus' saying, 'I and the Father are one' (10:30).

Finally, at the end of the gospel an important statement comes from the mouth of Jesus' disciple Thomas, when he says to the risen Jesus, 'My Lord and my God' (20:28). In this gospel, Jesus is often addressed as 'Lord', and in John 13:13, Jesus says that his disciples rightly call

---

223–239; 277–279. He refers, e.g. (p. 237) to Numbers 23:21; Psalm 146:10; Isaiah 6:5; 24:23; 33:22; 43:15; 52:7; Jeremiah 8:19; Micah 2:13; 4:7. See also Psalm 89:19; Isaiah 41:21; 44:6.

96 Thus Rudolf Bultmann, *Das Evangelium des Johannes*. Göttingen: Vandenhoeck & Ruprecht 1953, p. 347; Rudolf Schnackenburg, *Johannesevangelium 2*, Freiburg: Herder, p. 520; also M. J. J. Menken (1996), *Old Testament Quotations in the Fourth Gospel: Studies in Textual Form*. Kampen: Kok Pharos, p. 119; G. Reim (2001), 'Wie der Evangelist Johannes gemäß Joh 12,37ff. Jesaja 6 gelesen hat'. *Zeitschrift für die neutestamentliche Wissenschaft*, 92, 33–46 (35–36).

97 Cf. Genesis 26:24 LXX; 46:3 LXX; Isaiah 41:10 LXX; Jeremiah 1:8 LXX; 1:17 LXX; 26:28 LXX/46:28 MT; 49:11 LXX/42:11 MT.

98 Isaiah 43:10, 25; 45:18–19; 46:4; 48:12, 17; also 41:10; 43:10; 45:22; 52:6. See D. M. Ball (1996), '*I Am*' *in John's Gospel: Literary Function, Background and Theological Implications*. Sheffield: Sheffield Academic Press, and C. H. Williams (2000), *I am He: The Interpretation of 'Anî Hû in Jewish and Early Christian Literature*. Tübingen: J. C. B. Mohr, who repeatedly refers to Deuteronomy 32:39.

99 Exodus 13:21–22; Psalm 27:1; Isaiah 60:1, 19.

100 Ezekiel 34:12–22, 31; in 34:23 only, it is David, who is the good shepherd. See also the Old Testament texts mentioned in note 58.

101 C. H. Dodd (1963), *The Interpretation of the Fourth Gospel*. Cambridge: University Press, pp. 93–96, 417; as also Raymond E. Brown (1970), *The Gospel According to John (xiii–xxi)*. Garden City NY: Doubleday, pp. 755–756; C. T. R. Hayward (1978), 'The Holy Name of the God of Moses and the Prologue of St John's Gospel'. *New Testament Studies*, 25, 16–32 (29: 'Jesus is God's name come in the flesh'); see also Jean Daniélou (1958), *Théologie du Judéo-Christianisme*. Paris: Desclée, pp. 199–216.

him 'Teacher and Lord'.[102] It is, however, indisputable that the phrase 'my Lord and my God' coming from the mouth of Thomas, has a much deeper meaning than the address 'Lord'. The title 'my God' refers to John 1:1, which reads, 'In the beginning was the Word, and the Word was with God, and the Word was God.' We saw that in this gospel the pre-existent Word, which is God, corresponds to the LORD of the Old Testament and that both names can be applied to Jesus. This correspondence is confirmed by Thomas calling Jesus 'my Lord and my God' in the same breath.

2.6 Evaluation of the New Testament data

Besides the 'undisputed' letters of Paul and the four gospels, the New Testament contains several other letters, a book of Acts and the Revelation of John, in which various authors have written about Jesus' origin and identity. Although these writings certainly have their own character, they barely offer new views on Jesus' origin and identity. Because we do not strive for completeness, we will pass over these New Testament writings.[103] Before examining various other early Christian writings and testimonies which are not included in the New Testament, we will first evaluate what Paul and the New Testament evangelists write about Jesus' origin and identity. We have seen that their writings share various views, even though not every element is presented to the same degree. In all of them, Jesus is regarded as the Son of God. With 'God', the God of the Old Testament is meant. It is of importance that Paul, as well as the four evangelists, regularly quote the Old Testament to support their views. It is remarkable that in the gospels Jesus is also described in terms of the LORD; this is the name of God originally read as Yahweh. Especially in the letters of Paul and in the Gospel of John, a subtle difference is made between God (the Father) and Jesus, who is the LORD in its Old Testament meaning. This points to a certain plurality in God. Furthermore, in the Gospel of John, it appears that the LORD of the Old Testament is equated to the Logos or Word. According to the letters of Paul (1 Corinthians 8:6) and according to the prologue of the Gospel of John (1:1–3), the Lord Jesus Christ or the Logos was involved in the creation of the world. From this, and from various other texts, it seems that Jesus was regarded as pre-existent; this

means that he was with God long before he was born as a human being. In the synoptic gospels an allusion is made to his pre-existence, when Jesus states the purpose of his coming and in his discussion about Psalm 110:1. Furthermore, it can be deduced from the description of Jesus as Son of Man and as the LORD, that he did not only have a human origin.

These elevated views on the man Jesus of Nazareth can be regarded as *theological* interpretations of his identity. This is different from our being able to *historically* determine that Jesus was the pre-existent Son of God and is to be regarded as the manifestation or incarnation of the LORD. On a historical level, we can determine that Paul and the authors of the gospels thought of Jesus in this way, but that does not imply that they were right in their theological views. We could, however, try to determine that Jesus as a historical person had a strong awareness of his high calling and heavenly identity. Then we would leave aside the question of whether Jesus correctly considered himself the pre-existent Son of God. Even though, in my view, it is very well possible that the historical Jesus had such a strong awareness of his high calling and heavenly identity, it remains impossible to prove this conclusively. As already remarked in section 1.2, practice proves after all that opposite New Testament scholars who trace Jesus' divine awareness and identity back to himself, there are those who rather tend to discredit the New Testament testimonies. But even if one believes that the testimonies of the New Testament about Jesus as the LORD and as the pre-existent Son of God go back to his own life, it remains impossible to determine by historical means that he truly was so. In historiography, after all, one cannot make theological statements about God, and therefore one cannot make them about the Son of God either. Everyone who reads the New Testament may decide for him- or herself whether to believe in this high description of Jesus or not.

Does this interim evaluation clear the way for unrestrained subjectivity? I would not agree with this, for it is possible to show historically that the terms in which Jesus was described in the oldest writings about him were known in contemporaneous Judaism. We will examine this in chapter 8. Along this line can be demonstrated that, historically speaking, it is possible that these terms were applied to Jesus early on and perhaps in part go back to Jesus himself. But first we will go on with the discussion of documents and testimonies outside the New Testament.

2.7 *The Gospel of Thomas*

The first work to be considered is the Gospel of Thomas. This collection does not contain stories about Jesus' birth, nor about his baptism by John the Baptist. The compiler of this gospel assumes, however, that

---

102 Jesus is addressed to as 'Lord' in, for example, John 4:11, 15, 19, 49, 5:7; 6:34, 68; 9:36, 38, etc.; 'Lord' can, however, sometimes be understood here as 'sir'. Texts in which Jesus is described as 'the Lord' are John 4:1 (according to important manuscripts); 6:23; 11:2; 20:2, 13, 18, 25; 21:7.
103 In section 9.4 (note 37) we will briefly refer to Acts 2:36 and 13:33, texts that have been interpreted in an adoptianistic sense.

1

John among the Gospels: The Problem and Its Earliest History

The problem of John among the gospels is chiefly the question of the relation of John to the Synoptic Gospels. For the obvious reason that John and three other gospels are now found in the New Testament, attention has centered on their relationship, and rightly so, for these gospels are historically and theologically most important, in the sense of being most widely used or read, in the early church. Yet perhaps even the first century and certainly the second saw the writing of other gospels or gospel-like documents, and this fact must not be lost from view. Hence we prefer to speak of John among the gospels rather than John and the Synoptics. At the same time, discussion, both ancient and modern, has naturally centered on the relationship of John and the Synoptic Gospels; so our attention also will be focused primarily there.

Accordingly, it will be helpful to ask, first of all, what the problem of John and the Synoptics is. At one level, it is quite analogous to the synoptic problem, that is, the problem of synoptic relationships. How does one explain John's differences from the Synoptics while taking account of its similarities to them? Thus it is a problem of literary and historical relationships. Behind it stands the question or concern of how these different Gospels relate to the history of Jesus that lies behind them and to the theology and proclamation of the church that lies, so to speak, in front of them. That is, how do they relate to the church's understanding of its mission and message as it seeks their authorization in the Gospels. These last questions are not the subject matter of this book, but they can never be far from view. The literary and historical problem has elements or aspects that modern criticism is well aware of but that should be noted briefly at the outset. Further, the problem of John's

1

differences from the Synoptics did not go unnoticed or unexplained in antiquity, a fact we modern critics should acknowledge. Therefore we shall describe briefly how the problem was perceived and explained then.

THE ELEMENTS OF THE PROBLEM

John is a gospel like the other gospels. It is arguable, of course, that only Mark and John are truly gospels, while Matthew is, for example, a manual of discipline and Luke is an ancient biography. We shall, however, stick with the churchly and commonsense definition of all four as gospels, that is, narratives of the ministry of Jesus.[1] John is as much such a narrative as the others. It begins the account of Jesus' ministry with the familiar story of his encounter with John the Baptist, continues through a public ministry and an extended narrative of his death, and ends with resurrection appearances of the crucified Lord to his disciples. The story of Jesus' passion is narrated in a way similar to that of the Synoptics, and at the center of his public ministry appear accounts of his feeding five thousand people, walking on the sea at night, and receiving the "messianic" confession of his disciple Peter. In all four Gospels it is taken for granted that Jesus was the expected Messiah of Judaism, the fulfillment of Israel's hopes. As such he taught, healed the sick, and finally was crucified and died. The general similarity of the Johannine and synoptic accounts is impressive.

Moreover, there are specific points of comparison where the similarities are real. In discussion of the synoptic problem, verbatim agreements in wording and the order of events or episodes play a significant role. Matthew and Luke frequently agree with Mark in both respects, and where they depart from Mark, they usually do so separately. So one finds threefold agreement of all the Synoptics, and agreement of Matthew or Luke with Mark but not, as a rule, agreement of Matthew and Luke against Mark. (Admittedly, there are some minor verbal agreements of Matthew and Luke against Mark that cause a problem for the Markan hypothesis of critical orthodoxy.) The synoptic narratives and the actual wording of the synoptic texts have such strong resemblances and points of agreement that it is meaningful to talk about the one narrative or text *departing* from the other in wording or order. Gospel parallels are published in which the closely related texts appear side by side, even if the fact that sometimes clearly parallel passages occur in different places, or in a different order, has to be indicated to the reader. When, however, John is introduced into such an arrangement, the Johannine column more often than not is blank, so different and diverse is this Gospel in sheer content.

Nevertheless, there are some verbatim agreements as well as striking agreements in the order of events. In *The Four Gospels: A Study of Origins*, B. H. Streeter singles out six striking verbatim agreements of John with Mark, which he thinks amply demonstrate the fourth evangelist's knowledge of the Second Gospel (Mark 6:37 = John 6:7; Mark 14:3, 5 = John 12:3, 5; John 14:31 = Mark 14:42; Mark 14:54 = John 18:18; Mark 15:9 = John 18:39; John 5:8–9 = Mark 2:11–12).[2] There are a number of others. What is more, despite the remarkable absence of most Markan material from John, particularly in the public ministry, wherever John has Markan episodes he usually presents them in the order in which they occur in Mark. As in the case of the synoptic problem where Matthew's or Luke's agreements seem to be through or with Mark, John's agreements in wording or order with the Synoptics seem to be principally agreements with Mark. This is a matter deserving closer scrutiny, and there may be some exceptions, but for the moment it suffices to observe that, with respect to order of events, where John agrees with the Synoptics he agrees with Mark. By the same token, the preponderance of John's verbatim agreements with the Synoptics are agreements with Mark. It is perhaps not surprising that the fact that Matthew's wording is very close to Mark is reflected in John's verbatim agreements with Matthew, as well as with Mark, being much more numerous than his agreements with Luke. The points of agreement with Luke often have to do with historical data or perspective. For example, in Luke as in John, and in these Gospels alone, Jesus is portrayed as feeding a multitude only once. In John and Luke only, there is no formal trial or conviction of Jesus before Jewish authorities. Only in John and Luke does Pilate three times declare Jesus innocent. Only in John and Luke is there no cry of dereliction from the cross. And only in these two Gospels does the risen Jesus appear to his disciples as they are gathered together on Sunday evening in Jerusalem. In fact, John and Luke alone depict the risen Jesus appearing to disciples in Jerusalem.

Despite the remarkable character of many of these agreements, it must be emphasized that they are scattered. It is not as if John were following one of

---

[1] On the use of the term "gospel" (*euangelion*) for written documents and the difficulty of establishing a single literary genre, see Helmut Koester, *Ancient Christian Gospels: Their History and Development* (Philadelphia: Trinity Press International, 1990), 1–48, esp. 24–31 ("Why Did Written Documents Come to Be Called 'Gospels'?").

[2] B. H. Streeter, *The Four Gospels: A Study of Origins* (London: Macmillan & Co., 1936; originally published 1924), 397–99.

the other accounts, as Matthew and even Luke so often seem to be following Mark. The striking verbatim agreements between John and even Mark represent only a very minor fraction of the text of either. Even where the two Gospel accounts are obviously narrating the same event (e.g., the feeding of the multitude or the arrest of Jesus), the amount of verbatim agreement is relatively small when compared with that among the Synoptic Gospels. (Strangely, this lack of agreement with the Synoptics seems to be paralleled in the so-called apocryphal gospels, insofar as we know them.)

Finally, the total presentation of Jesus and his ministry in John is vastly different from what one finds in the other, Synoptic Gospels. Each of the Synoptics has its own perspective and point of view; but when they are compared with John, their similarities to each other stand out. John's differences and distinctiveness can be summed up accurately, if somewhat simplistically, under three heads: ministry, miracles, and message.

The ministry of Jesus in John differs significantly from the synoptic version in its geographical locality and its temporal span. (There are also, of course, contradictory data, as when John dates the crucifixion on Nisan 14 rather than 15 as the Synoptics have it.) The traditional three-year ministry of Jesus assumes the distinctive Johannine chronology, in which there are three Passovers (John 2:13, 23; 6:4; 11:55) rather than the synoptic, according to which there is only one. In John, Jesus is much more frequently in Judea and Jerusalem than he is in the Synoptics, in which he goes there only once, at the very end. John creates the impression that Jesus worked mostly in Jerusalem or Judea. The model Beloved Disciple seems to join him there. Perhaps he was a Jerusalem disciple. For Luke too, Jerusalem was of very great importance, but his itinerary of Jesus' ministry is much closer to Mark's than to John's.

The presentation of miracles and Jesus' attitude toward them are again much different in John than in the Synoptics. The very terms used are suggestive. According to the Synoptic Gospels, Jesus accomplishes mighty works (*dynameis*), effecting healing and deliverance for those afflicted by sickness or demons. When accosted by any who are seeking a sign from heaven to test him (Mark 8:11; cf. Matt. 12:38–39), the Jesus of the Synoptics reacts quite negatively. (Admittedly, it is not certain that such a "sign from heaven" is a miracle, yet such an understanding of it fits Jesus' whole demeanor in the Synoptics, where he seems to retire in the face of public acclaim.) On the other hand, in the Fourth Gospel miracles are from the outset called signs (*semeia*), as it is simply assumed that their purpose is to point to Jesus and to signify who he is. Occasionally the other view of signs seems to break through (John 2:23–25; 4:48), but the difference from the Synoptics is nevertheless real and significant. In addition, the number and type of miracles are different. In John, Jesus exorcizes no demon and cleanses no leper—typical forms of Jesus' activity in the Synoptics. No Markan healing narrative is recounted, at least not in recognizable form. By way of contrast, most of the Matthean and Lukan healing narratives are clearly based on the Markan. In the light of this fact it is less surprising that the only miracle story recorded in all four Gospels is the feeding of the five thousand. Luke omits the walking on the water that occurs immediately following the feeding in the other Gospels. Luke and Matthew share with John the story of Jesus healing a centurion or ruler's servant or son at a considerable distance, but this episode is not found in Mark. Given the fact that all the Gospels present Jesus as a miracle worker, it is all the more astonishing that the divergences between John and the Synoptics are so great.

Jesus is a teacher and preacher in John as well as in the Synoptics, but the content of his message is quite different in the one and the other. (Although the verb "to preach" used of Jesus in the Synoptic Gospels is not found in John, Jesus is several times portrayed in John as "crying out.") Aside from the fact that the typically synoptic parables and epigrammatic sayings are largely missing in John, where Jesus engages in sharp debate and utters long discourses, the content of what Jesus has to say differs in ways quite familiar to readers of the New Testament. In the Synoptics, Jesus announces the imminence of the kingdom or rule of God and through parable or specific command calls for obedience to God's will as it can be known by common sense in the light of Scripture. In John, the kingdom of God fades into the background as Jesus speaks and debates about his own messianic status or, particularly, his relationship to God and the role he has been given to accomplish. In John, Jesus debates Christology with his opponents and teaches his disciples Christology as well as eschatology. Although he commands that his disciples should love one another, he speaks only in symbolic terms (for example, washing the disciples' feet) of what that love should consist.

Closely related to these differences in Jesus' message is a distinct difference in theological-ethical vocabulary often found on the lips of Jesus.[3] For example, the Greek words for love (*agapē*), truth (*alētheia*), knowing (*ginōskein*), and world (*kosmos*) are anywhere from twice to ten times as frequent in John as in the Synoptics. By the same token, typical synoptic terms for kingdom

---

[3] C. K. Barrett, *The Gospel According to St. John: An Introduction with Commentary and Notes on the Greek Text*, 2d ed. (Philadelphia: Westminster Press, 1978). 5–6, presents a convenient tabulation of significant differences in vocabulary.

(*basileia*), miracle (*dynamis*), parable (*parabolē*), and preaching (*kērussein*) among others, occur infrequently, if at all, in the Fourth Gospel. Not coincidentally, the vocabulary of the Gospel of John, and of the Johannine Jesus, is much closer to that of the Johannine Epistles than to the Synoptic Gospels. The difference of vocabulary is a good measure of their difference in theology.

The problem of John and the Synoptics is, then, how to account for John's extensive differences from the other Gospels within a generally similar overall framework. These differences embrace content and style and include major aspects of their respective portrayals of Jesus. In principle, the problem of John and the Synoptics may not be different from the synoptic problem, but in fact the problem is exacerbated by the extent of the divergences of John from the Synoptics. Their portrayals of Jesus are symptomatic. One can without great difficulty speak of the synoptic Jesus, based on Matthew, Mark, and Luke. Whether the synoptic Jesus and the Johannine Jesus present a common front or can be brought together only by main force and awkwardness or theological legerdemain remains a question.

THE EARLIEST PERCEPTION OF THE PROBLEM

In all probability the problem of John and the Synoptics lurks somewhere behind the emergence of the Fourth Gospel on the stage of church history. The evidence is less than explicit, but there was during the second century a kind of reticence or obscurity about the Fourth Gospel. We cannot be sure that this reticence was due to John's differences from the Synoptics. Certainly such differences were not the sole factor affecting the acceptance of the Fourth Gospel in the church. On the other hand, it is clear that serious questions about the relationship were raised, so that answers had to be given, and the problem of John and the Synoptics was perceived as such by the end of the second century.

Evidence of knowledge of the Fourth Gospel in the early church may be discernible as early as Ignatius of Antioch in the second decade of the second century, for at times he seems to reflect John's distinctive language (e.g., *Magnesians* 8.2). At mid-century Justin Martyr seems to know, and even quote, John (*1 Apology* 61), but he does not cite it by name as one of the memoirs of the apostles. In Irenaeus of Lyons in the final quarter of the second century we finally have an early church authority who knows and cites the Gospel of John, putting it on the same level as the others. From Irenaeus's own use of John, however, it is quite clear that he was not the first to draw upon or to cite it as authoritative. Earlier, gnostic exegetes had known and interpeted this Gospel, albeit erroneously, and therefore Irenaeus was at pains to set forth a proper exegesis of the prologue (*Against Heresies* 3.11.1–9). (Moreover, Origen's citation of his predecessor Heracleon, who wrote a commentary on John at mid-second century, suggests the widespread use of John among gnostic Christians.) Irenaeus's insistence upon the necessity of four gospels can be construed as an effort to gain support for a four-gospel canon, which was only then being disseminated in the church. The problem would have been the Fourth Gospel rather than the other three. Perhaps some conservative Christians were uneasy about John precisely because it was popular and widely used among gnostic Christians and others deemed heretical.

Just such a man, Gaius, an elder in the Roman church, and apparently by his own lights orthodox and conservative, opposed the use of the Gospel of John. Although he may have resisted the Gospel because it gave aid and comfort to heretics—in this case, Montanists, who claimed possession by the Paraclete promised in John—he apparently grounded his objections on the fact that John differed so obviously from the other, Synoptic Gospels, which were already being accepted as authoritative and, in effect, canonical.[4] Against him, Hippolytus, another elder of the Roman church, wrote a *Defense of the Gospel and Apocalypse of John* that is no longer extant. Quite possibly Irenaeus presents the usage that is establishing itself in the Roman church. Gaius protests against it in the name of an older conservatism, and Hippolytus attempts to deliver the coup de grace to this now obsolete position.

Residual reservations about the Gospel of John are perhaps reflected in the famous statement of Clement of Alexandria, perhaps a quarter of a century later than Irenaeus: "But that John, last of all, conscious that the outward facts had been set forth in the Gospels, was urged on by his disciples, and divinely moved by the Spirit, composed a spiritual Gospel" (*apud* Eusebius, *Ecclesiastical History* 6.14.7). This famous statement, which seems to capture so well the essence of the Fourth Gospel vis-à-vis the others, continues to be quoted as an apt characterization of the distinctiveness of that Gospel. Clement speaks in an entirely positive way, but it is not difficult to see in his statement a defense of the Gospel of John against the charge that it differs so markedly

---

[4] Recent research suggests that the case against the Gospel of John was based on its differences from the Synoptics, whatever the actual motivation may have been. See J. J. Gunther, "Early Identifications of Authorship of the Johannine Writings," *Journal of Ecclesiastical History* 31 (1980): 413–15, and especially Joseph Daniel Smith, Jr., "Gaius and the Controversy Over the Johannine Literature" (Ph.D. diss., Yale University, 1979), 289–92, 384–412. Smith argues that the Roman presbyter's opposition to the Fourth Gospel was motivated by its use among Montanists, whom he opposed (p. 426).

from the Synoptics: John wrote a spiritual gospel, intentionally and purposefully different from the other three. Clement also makes clear that John knew and approved of the others.

A century later Eusebius of Caesarea acknowledges the problem of John and the Synoptics but offers another version of why John wrote as he attempts to explain the existence of this rather different Gospel, which stood now in church usage alongside the other three:

> John, it is said, used all the time a message which was not written down, and at last took to writing for the following cause. The three Gospels which had been written down before they were distributed to all including himself; it is said that he welcomed them and testified to their truth but said that there was only lacking to the narrative the account of what was done by Christ at first and at the beginning of the preaching. The story is surely true. . . . Thus John . . . relates what Christ did before the Baptist had been thrown into prison [John 3:24], but the three other evangelists narrate the events after the imprisonment of the Baptist. If this be understood, the Gospels no longer appear to disagree.[5]

Interestingly enough, Eusebius states this not so much as his own view as a plausible opinion widely held. Perhaps he saw that the obvious overlap between John and other gospels renders it inadequate as a comprehensive explanation. Certainly Eusebius's statement indicates that the problem of John and the Synoptics, as we style it, had been the subject of continuing discussion, apparently even after John was being read as an authoritative book.

Just such prosaic, somewhat historicist, solutions as Eusebius describes were, however, strongly resisted by another exegete who nevertheless accepted the authority of John. Thus the great theologian and biblical scholar Origen, in his *Commentary on the Gospel of John*, espoused a totally different way of making sense of John and the Synoptics. Origen was well aware of major discrepancies between the Johannine and synoptic accounts of Jesus' ministry, and of early efforts to deal with them, but saw no point in trying to resolve them historically. Rather, he let them stand and interpreted John anagogically or mystically. Commenting on the problems created by John's chronology of the beginning of Jesus' ministry, which cannot be satisfactorily reconciled with that of the Synoptics, he writes:

> Those who accept the four Gospels, and who do not consider that their apparent discrepancy is to be solved anagogically [by mystical interpretation], will have

to clear up the difficulty, raised above, about the forty days of the temptation, a period for which no room can be found in any way in John's narrative.[6]

After enumerating additional problems, Origen concludes:

> There are many other points on which the careful student of the Gospels will find that their narratives do not agree; and these we shall place before the reader, according to our power, as they occur. The student, staggered at the consideration of these things, will either renounce the attempt to find all the Gospels true, and not venturing to conclude that all our information about our Lord is untrustworthy, will choose at random one of them to be his guide; or he will accept the four, and will consider that their truth is not to be sought in the outward and material letter.[7]

The latter alternative was, of course, consistently followed by Origen.

To give another example, in commenting on the cleansing of the temple, which occurs at the beginning of Jesus' ministry in the Gospel and toward the end in the others, Origen remarks: "I conceive it to be impossible for those who admit nothing more than the history in their interpretation to show that these discrepant statements are in harmony with each other" (*Commentary* 10.15). Accordingly, Origen argues for the necessity of his mode of interpretation by insisting on the impossibility of the alternative of historical harmonization. Again we may infer that he knowingly departs from an accepted, and probably dominant, mode of exegesis, by means of which the problem of John and the Synoptics was being dealt with. Doubtless Origen was swimming against the stream, but the acumen of his critical remarks was unmatched by his contemporaries. He saw clearly that the commonsense effort to harmonize John and the Synoptics made no critical sense at all. Nevertheless, the resolution of the problem of John and the Synoptics that Origen so vigorously rejected quickly became the accepted one in biblical exegesis in the church. An awareness of the seriousness of the discrepancies and the weight of the kinds of objections Origen raised had to await the rise of historical-critical exegesis. And even then efforts to see John's Gospel as somehow compatible with, or a supplement to, the Synoptic Gospels did not die out. Indeed, they continued down into the twentieth century and survive, if in qualified form, today. This century has, however, seen serious challenges to this traditional view, as it has to many positions long regarded as sure or settled.

---

[5] Eusebius, *The Ecclesiastical History* 3.24.7–13, eds. K. Lake, J. E. L. Oulton, and H. J. Lawlor, Loeb Classical Library (Cambridge: Harvard University Press, 1926–32).

[6] Origen, as cited in A. C. Coxe, ed., *The Ante-Nicene Fathers: Translations of the Writings of the Fathers down to* A.D. *325*, vol. 10. (Grand Rapids, Mich.: W. B. Erdmanns, 1986).

[7] Ibid. For this and the preceding quotation, see Origen's *Commentary* 10.2.

As John became part of a generally accepted fourfold Gospel canon, it was regarded as an apostolic writing, the work of John the disciple of the Lord, the son of Zebedee. That it had been composed in full cognizance and affirmation of the other three was scarcely doubted. Until about a century ago, the view that the Gospel was the work of the apostle still had strong and numerous defenders, and few thought to doubt its positive relation to the Synoptics. All that was to change. Rejection of its apostolic origin was already fairly common at the beginning of the twentieth century, and questioning of its relation to the Synoptics was not far behind.

The twentieth century has, in fact, more than once witnessed the dissolution of a consensus on the relationship of John to the Synoptic Gospels. At the beginning of the century John's knowledge and positive use of the Synoptic Gospels was widely, if not universally, granted. Even so self-consciously critical a scholar as Benjamin W. Bacon took this consensus as his beginning point. It remained for Hans Windisch to question whether the fourth evangelist's attitude toward the Synoptics was actually positive and for Percival Gardner-Smith to question his very knowledge and use of them. In the light of their proposals and the exegetical work of such prominent scholars as C. H. Dodd and Rudolf Bultmann, the earlier consensus that John knew and used the Synoptic Gospels crumbled and was replaced by a consensus that represented almost the opposite point of view. John did not know the Synoptic Gospels in their present form, or, if he did, they existed only at the periphery of his consciousness and purpose. Perhaps he became familiar with them only after his own work had basically been completed. Most commentaries on the Fourth Gospel written since World War II have followed this line. In the last quarter of this century, however, the ground seems to be shifting once again. Not that John's independence lacks proponents or defenders, but now the older view that John presupposed and used the Synoptics is being revived. Ockham's razor is invoked against the unnecessary multiplication of entities—in this case hypothetical sources—as one speaks of redaction-critical interpretation of the Fourth Gospel against the backdrop of the Synoptics. This significant problem affords an interesting example of the convolutions, as well as the evolution, of New Testament scholarship in this century.[8]

---

[8] The earlier history of the problem in modern research is treated by Hans Windisch, *Johannes und die Synoptiker: Wollte der vierte Evangelist die älteren Evangelien ergänzen oder ersetzen?* Untersuchungen zum Neuen Testament 12 (Leipzig: J. C. Hinrichs'sche Buchhandlung, 1926), 1–40. For the period up to the mid-1960s, see now also Josef Blinzler, *Johannes und die Synoptiker: Ein Forschungsbericht*. SBS 5 (Stuttgart: Verlag Katholisches Bibelwerk, 1965). For the last decade and a half, see Frans Neirynck, "John and the Synoptics: 1975–1990," in the proceedings of the 1990 Louvain Colloquium, *John and the Synoptics*, ed. A. Denaux, BETL 101 (Louvain: Louvain University Press, 1992), 3–62. Note also the *Forschungsbericht* of Jürgen Becker, "Aus de Literatur zum Johannesevangelium (1978–1980)," *ThR* 47 (1982): 279–301, 305–47, esp. 289–94, as well as Robert Kysar, *The Fourth Evangelist and His Gospel: An Examination of Contemporary Scholarship* (Minneapolis: Augsburg Publishing House, 1975), 54–66. Cf. also Kysar's "The Fourth Gospel: A Report on Recent Research," in *Aufstieg und Niedergang der römischen Welt*, ed. H. Temporini and W. Hasse (Berlin: Walter de Gruyter), II.25.3 (1985): 2389–2480, esp. 2407–11, and his "The Gospel of John in Current Research," *RSR* 9 (1983): 314–23, esp. 315–16. For the first half of this century there is the somewhat broader survey of W. F. Howard, *The Fourth Gospel in Recent Criticism and Interpretation*. rev. C. K. Barrett (London: Epworth Press, 1955), 128–43.

*Declaration on the Church's Relation
to Non-Christian Religions*
(Nostra Aetate)

The history of Vatican II's Declaration on the Church's Relation to Non-Christian Religions can be traced back to a half-hour conversation between Pope John XXIII and the Jewish scholar Jules Isaac. In June 1960, Isaac presented the pope with a lengthy memorandum summarizing the legacy of Catholic discrimination toward the Jewish people. He pressed the pope to use the council as an opportunity to move beyond this sad history. Isaac was a historian and an educator who had served as inspector general of public instruction in France until the Nazi occupation forced him out of office. He lost his wife and daughter at Auschwitz. Following the war, Isaac dedicated himself to promoting Jewish-Christian understanding. At age eighty-one, he spoke with great personal authority on a topic close to the heart of John XXIII.

After the audience, Pope John asked Cardinal Augustin Bea to meet with Isaac. By September the pope had commissioned Bea's Secretariat for Promoting Christian Unity to include "the Jewish question" in its preparations for the council.

For centuries, Catholic animosity toward the Jews was fueled by a theology of contempt that portrayed Judaism as a legalistic religion wholly superseded and rendered irrelevant by the New

153

Covenant in Christ. Christian theologians argued that God continues to punish the Jewish people for rejecting and killing Jesus. According to this view all Jews—past and present—bear the collective guilt of the crime of deicide ("God murder"). Their only hope is to accept Jesus as the true Messiah, leave behind their mistaken ways, and enter into the church.

As Bea would argue again and again, this antisemitic tradition was a deep distortion of Jesus' own teaching and of St. Paul's claim that God's covenant with Israel remains (Rm 11). In the months leading up to the council, the Secretariat for Christian Unity prepared a brief text that condemned antisemitism in all its forms, clearly stated that the Jewish people are not guilty of deicide, and stressed the intimate links between the Jewish and Christian faiths. The draft was scheduled for discussion by the Central Preparatory Commission in June 1962, its final meeting before the opening of the council. But at the last minute, the draft "On the Jews" was dropped from the agenda. The reason was not theological, but political. The Vatican Secretary of State, Cardinal Amleto Cicognani (who also chaired the Central Preparatory Commission), was feeling intense pressure from several Arab governments who perceived the statement on the Jews as an indirect endorsement for the State of Israel. They complained that the church was taking sides in a political dispute between the Israelis and the Palestinians. Bishops from Arab nations worried that Christians would suffer reprisals as a result. A recent announcement coming from the World Jewish Congress that an official in the Israeli Ministry of Religious Affairs, Dr. Chaim Wardi, had been named their "representative" to the Second Vatican Council only exacerbated the problem.

Though he insisted that the document "On the Jews" was a theological statement, not a political one, Bea agreed with Cicognani that it would be better to set it aside for the time being. Between the council's first and second sessions, however, Bea rescued the text by including it as chapter 4 in the Decree on Ecumenism. This chapter was submitted to the bishops for consideration, but not debated. Along with chapter 5 on religious freedom, it was separated from the ecumenism decree, and time ran out before it could be discussed. In his closing remarks at the end of the second session, Cardinal Bea assured the assembly that "what is put off is not put away."

When the text was finally brought before the bishops for debate at the start of the third session, it had been slightly expanded and significantly weakened—and Bea suggested as much in his introduction. The word "deicide"—so important to so many Jewish observers—had been dropped (although the text condemned the concept) and a sentence on Muslims had been added, presumably as an attempt to better balance the text. Although the draft was now titled "On Jews and Non-Christians," it dealt almost exclusively with Judaism. As debate began, objections came from all sides. Cardinal Ernesto Ruffini criticized the excessively laudatory tone of the document and insisted that the content did not match the traditional teaching of the church. We don't need to be told to love Jews, Ruffini argued. They need to be told to love us. The conversion of Jews to Christ ought to be the church's aim here. In a more delicate vein, the Syrian patriarch, Ignace Tappouni, repeated the concerns of many Eastern Catholic bishops from the Middle East, who worried about political reprisals against Arab Christians. He called the document "inopportune" and asked the council to remove it from the agenda. Bishops from Asia and Africa complained that, if the council was going to address Jews, it should also address the other great religions of the world. But the majority of the opposition to the draft text came from those who felt it had become too weak. They asked for the stronger and more positive statement about Judaism that had marked the earlier draft.

When debate ended three days later, the Secretariat for Promoting Christian Unity felt they had received the justification they needed to prepare a stronger text. When the Secretariat received sudden instructions to drop their revisions and fold the material on the Jews into the Dogmatic Constitution on the Church (Lumen Gentium), Bea worried that too much would be lost. His Secretariat decided to consider this request only after they had prepared their larger, revised draft. And within a few short weeks, the basic outline of what would become Nostra Aetate appeared. It consisted of five sections: (1) a statement on the unity of the human family and the innate spiritual impulse of all people; (2) a brief description of various religions, Hinduism, and Buddhism, concluding with the statement that the Catholic Church rejects nothing of what is true and holy in these religions; (3) a positive treatment of Islam; (4) a substantive section on Judaism, which recalls the validity of the covenant between God and the people Israel, calls for mutual understanding, and condemns antisemitism unequivocally; and, finally, (5) a rejection of discrimination in all its forms. The new text so impressed the pope and the Coordinating Commission that it was placed before the assembly for a vote as an independent document. It was formally approved at the fourth session of the council, on October 28, 1965, by a vote of 2,221 to 88.

In many ways, the story of the Declaration on the Church's Relation to Non-Christian Religions is a story of setbacks that opened up surprising ways forward. Reflecting later on the troubled history of this declaration, John Oesterreicher (one of the architects of the document) observed that the opposition to this text had a positive result: It forced the council to consider entirely new horizons. In presenting the expanded document to the assembly, Cardinal Bea pointed to a parable. What began as a small mustard seed—a brief statement on the right attitude of Christians to the Jewish people—had grown to become a tree in which all religions could build their nests.

Nostra Aetate
Declaration on the Church's Relation to Non-Christian Religions

TRANSLATED BY LEO ARNOLD, S J

1 In our age, when the human race is being daily brought closer together and contacts between the various nations are becoming more frequent, the church is giving closer attention to what is its relation to non-christian religions In its task of promoting unity and charity among people, indeed also among nations, it now turns its attention chiefly to what things human beings have in common and what things tend to bring them together.

All nations are one community and have one origin, because God caused the whole human race to dwell on the whole face of the earth.[1] They also have one final end, God, whose providence, manifestation of goodness and plans for salvation are extended to all,[2] until the elect be gathered together in the holy city which the bright light of God will illuminate and where the people will walk in his light.[3] Women and men expect from the different religions an answer to the obscure riddles of the human condition which today also, as in the past, profoundly disturb their hearts. What is a human being? What is the meaning and purpose of our life? What is good and what is sin? What origin and purpose do sufferings have? What is the way to attaining true happiness? What are death, judgment and retribution after death? Lastly, what is that final unutterable mystery which takes in our lives and from which we take our origin and towards which we tend?

2. From ancient until modern time there is found among various peoples a certain perception of that unseen force which is present in the course of things and in events in human life, and sometimes even an acknowledgement of a supreme deity or even of a Father. This perception and acknowledgement permeates their lives with a deep religious sense. The religions associated with the development of civilisation, however, strive to answer these questions with more refined ideas and more highly developed language. Thus in Hinduism the divine mystery is explored and propounded with an inexhaustible wealth of myths and penetrating philosophical investigations, and liberation is sought from the distresses of our state either through various forms of ascetical life or deep meditation or taking refuge in God with loving confidence. In Buddhism, according to its various forms, the radical inadequacy of this changeable world is acknowledged and a way is taught whereby those with a devout and trustful spirit may be able to reach either a state of perfect freedom or, relying on their own efforts or on help from a higher source, the highest illumination. In like manner, too, other religions which are to be found throughout the entire world strive in various ways to relieve the anxiety of the human heart by suggesting "ways," that is teachings and rules of life as well as sacred rites.

The catholic church rejects nothing of those things which are true and holy in these religions. It regards with respect those ways of acting and living and those precepts and teachings which, though often at variance with what it holds and expounds, frequently reflect a ray of that truth which enlightens everyone. Yet, without ceasing it preaches, and is bound to preach, Christ who is "the way, the truth and the life" (Jn 14, 6), in whom people find the fullness of religious life and in whom God has reconciled all things to himself.[4]

It therefore calls upon all its sons and daughters with prudence and charity, through dialogues and cooperation with the followers of other religions, bearing witness to the christian faith and way of life, to recognise, preserve and promote those spiritual and moral good things as well as the socio-cultural values which are to be found among them.

3. The church also looks upon Muslims with respect. They worship the one God living and subsistent, merciful and almighty, Creator of heaven and earth,[5] who has spoken to humanity and to whose decrees, even the hidden ones, they seek to submit themselves whole-heartedly, just as Abraham, to whom the Islamic faith readily relates itself, submitted to God. They venerate Jesus as a prophet, even though they do not acknowledge him as God, and they honour his virgin mother Mary and even sometimes devoutly call upon her. Furthermore they await the day of judgment when God will requite all people brought back to life. Hence they have regard for the moral life and worship God especially in prayer, almsgiving and fasting.

Although considerable dissensions and enmities between Christians and Muslims may have arisen in the course of the centuries, this synod urges all parties that, forgetting past things, they train themselves towards sincere mutual understanding and together maintain and promote social justice and moral values as well as peace and freedom for all people

4 Reflecting on the mystery of the church, this synod recalls the link whereby the people of the new covenant are spiritually united with the descendants of Abraham.

For the church of Christ recognises that the beginnings of its faith and election are to be found already among the patriarchs, Moses and the prophets. It states its belief that all believers in Christ, children of Abraham according to faith, [6] are included in the same patriarch's calling and that the salvation of the church is mystically prefigured in the exodus of the chosen people from the land of slavery. Hence the church cannot forget that through that people with whom God out of his ineffable mercy deigned to enter into an ancient covenant, it received the revelation of the old Testament and is nourished from the root of the good olive tree, onto which the branches of the wild olive tree of the gentiles have been grafted.[7] For the church believes that Christ our peace reconciled Jews and gentiles and made us both one in himself through the cross.[8]

The church also keeps constantly before its eyes the words of the apostle Paul concerning those of his own race: "and to them belong the adoption as children, the glory, the covenant, the giving of the law, the worship and the promises, to them belong the patriarchs, and of their race, according to the flesh, is Christ" (Rm 9, 4–5), son of the virgin Mary. It also recalls that the apostles, the foundations and pillars of the church, were born out of the Jewish people as were many of those first disciples who proclaimed the gospel of Christ to the world.

As holy scripture is witness, Jerusalem did not know the time of its visitation,[9] and for the most part the Jews did not accept the gospel, indeed many of them opposed its dissemination.[10] Nevertheless, according to the apostle, because of their ancestors the Jews still remain very dear to God, whose gift and call are without regret.[11] Together with the prophets and the same apostle, the church awaits the day known only to God on which all peoples will call upon the Lord with one voice and "will serve him with one arm" (Zp 3, 9).[12]

Since, therefore, the spiritual heritage common to Christians and Jews is so great, this synod wishes to promote and recommend that mutual knowledge and esteem which is acquired especially from biblical and theological studies and from friendly dialogues.

Although the Jewish authorities with their followers pressed for the death of Christ,[13] still those things which were perpetrated during his passion cannot be ascribed indiscriminately to all the Jews living at the time nor to the Jews of today. Although the church is the new people of God, the Jews should not be represented as rejected by God or accursed, as if that follows from holy scripture. All should therefore take care that in holding religious instruction and preaching the word of God, they teach nothing which is not in keeping with the truth of the gospel and the spirit of Christ.

Moreover, the church, which condemns all persecutions against any people, mindful of its common inheritance with the Jews and motivated not by political considerations but by the religious charity of the gospel, deplores feelings of hatred, persecutions and demonstrations of antisemitism directed against the Jews at whatever time and by whomsoever.

Moreover Christ, as the church has always maintained and maintains, went willingly and with immense love to his passion and death because of the sins of all people so that all may obtain salvation. It is the duty of the preaching church, then, to proclaim the cross of Christ as the sign of God's universal love and the source of all grace.

5 We cannot, however, call upon God the Father of all if we refuse to behave like sisters and brothers towards certain

328 | Vatican II

people created to the image of God. The relation of man and woman to God the Father, and their relation to their fellow human beings, are linked to such a degree that scripture says "Whoever does not love, does not know God" (1 Jn 4, 8)

Therefore the basis is taken away from any theory or practice which draws distinctions between people, between nation and nation, with reference to human dignity and the rights flowing therefrom.

The church therefore condemns as foreign to the mind of Christ any kind of discrimination whatsoever between people, or harassment of them, done by reason of race or colour, class or religion. Consequently, following in the steps of the holy apostles Peter and Paul, this synod earnestly begs the faithful that, "maintaining good conduct . . . among the gentiles" (1 Pt 2, 12), they do what they can to be at peace with all people,[14] so that they may really be children of the Father who is in heaven.[15]

—October 28, 1965